NERO

THE BELKNAP PRESS OF
HARVARD UNIVERSITY PRESS
Cambridge, Massachusetts
London, England
2003

NERO

EDWARD CHAMPLIN

Title page: Graffito portrait of Nero, from the Domus Tiberiana on the Palatine.

Library of Congress Cataloging-in-Publication Data

Champlin, Edward, 1948–

    Nero / Edward Champlin.

       p.   cm.

    Includes bibliographical references and index.

    ISBN 0-674-01192-9 (alk. paper)

      1. Nero, Emperor of Rome, 37–68.   2. Emperors—Rome—Biography.

  3. Rome—History—Nero, 54–68.   I. Title.

  DG285.C53   2003

  937′.07′092—dc21

  [B]   2003045268

For Kit and Alex

Contents

Illustrations

NERO

The Once and Future King

Can you remember, Acte . . . how much easier our belief in Nero made life for us in the old days? And can you remember the paralysis, the numbness that seized the whole world when Nero died? Didn't you feel as if the world had grown bare and colourless all of a sudden? Those people on the Palatine have tried to steal our Nero from us, from you and me. Isn't it splendid to think that we can show them they haven't succeeded? They have smashed his statues into splinters, erased his name from all the inscriptions; they even replaced his head on that huge statue in Rome with the peasant head of old Vespasian. Isn't it fine to teach them that all that hasn't been of the slightest use? Granted that they have been successful for a few years. For a few years they have actually managed to banish all imagination from the world, all enthusiasm, extravagance, everything that makes life worth living. But now, with our Nero, all these things are back again.

LION FEUCHTWANGER[1]

After lunch one afternoon in the latter half of March, AD 68, the emperor Nero learned while staying in Naples that Julius Vindex, the governor of Lugdunensis, one of his provinces in Gaul, had rebelled. He showed himself serenely undisturbed by the news, going on to visit and even to participate in a local athletic contest. An upsetting letter arrived at dinner, but this roused him merely to make threats against the rebels. For eight more days Nero ignored the problem, as Vindex bombarded him with insulting edicts. His one response was to send a letter to the senate in Rome, urging it to take vengeance in his name and in the name of the state, but excusing himself from attendance in person: he had a sore throat. Otherwise he largely ignored the charges which Vindex flung at him. Only two of the rebel's many taunts stung the emperor into reaction: when he accused him of playing the lyre badly, and when he called him Ahenobarbus rather than Nero. The latter gibe he deflected by declaring that he would indeed resume his old birth-name, Ahenobarbus, and give up the name Nero, which was his by adoption. But the calumny against his talent, he as-

serted, showed the falsity of all the other accusations, since he had labored
so hard to achieve perfection in his art. Nevertheless he offered a reward, a
very large reward, of 10 million sesterces for the head of Julius Vindex.[2]

Further urgent messages brought Nero back to Rome in some trepidation, but his spirits rose in the outskirts of the city, when he passed a tomb
which depicted a Gallic warrior being run down by a Roman cavalryman
and dragged by the hair; he thanked heaven for the good omen. (Vindex,
"the Avenger," was both a native of Gaul and governor of a Gallic province.) In Rome he carried on as before, splendidly dedicating a temple
to his late wife, Poppaea Sabina, who had died in the summer of 65 and
was now a goddess, Diva Poppaea Augusta. Still he treated the revolt as
a minor matter, refusing to address the senate or the people. Once he
hurriedly summoned leading senators and knights for consultation, but
he astonished them by introducing the main item of business with these
words: "I have discovered how to make the water-organ produce a larger
and more tuneful sound." In the long lecture that followed, Nero introduced to his advisers new kinds of water-organs, pointed out the nature
and difficulty of each, and promised that he would exhibit them all in the
theater, if (as he added sarcastically) Vindex would allow him.

This show of unconcern came to an abrupt end, probably in early
April, with word that his Spanish provinces had also rebelled, led by the
governor of Tarraconensis, Servius Sulpicius Galba. Indifference was replaced with a show of extravagant concern. On hearing the news, the emperor collapsed in a dead faint—Galba was a patrician, with blood as blue
as his own. When he came to himself he tore his clothing, beat his brow,
and declared that he was finished. His old nurse tried to console him by
recalling the similar woes of other princes; somewhat annoyed, he replied
that his were in fact unprecedented in their magnitude. Nevertheless he
rallied remarkably, celebrating any good news from the provinces with
elaborate feasts, and ridiculing the leaders of the revolt in obscene and humorous verse, which he accompanied with appropriate gestures. He was
too busy to attend the theater openly, but on one supposedly incognito
visit the actor-emperor sent a message to a successful performer that he
was taking advantage of Nero's other preoccupations.

In fact he was very active in a peculiarly Neronian way, combining
pointed, often extravagant, gestures with effective measures. The mixture
is best embodied in his removing the two consuls from office and taking
over the old supreme magistracy of the Republic himself alone, alleging

that it was fated that the Gaulish provinces could be subdued only by a consul. After assuming the consulship he announced his plan of campaign while leaving the dining room after a banquet, leaning on the shoulders of close friends. As soon as he reached Gaul he would appear before the army unarmed and do nothing but weep. Having thus won the rebels to penitence for their deeds, on the following day he would sing songs of victory among his rejoicing subjects, songs which he ought to be composing that very moment. To that end, he took care to choose wagons that could transport theatrical props and organs for his great performance, and the concubines who were to accompany him were given masculine haircuts and armed with the axes and shields of Amazons.

Behind the histrionics lay vigorous preparation. Nero summoned the citizen residents of Rome to enlist, and when there was no response he enrolled many slaves. A large number of marines were conscripted as legionaries; elements of several legions which had been sent to the East in preparation for an expedition to the Caspian Gates were recalled; and a defensive command was established in the Po valley under a consular general, Petronius Turpilianus.[3] To pay for all this activity, the emperor levied a special income tax and ordered all tenants of private landlords to pay the equivalent of one year's rent into his fisc.

Public feeling reportedly ran high against him. Rumors flew that he was consumed with wild plans for massacring all governors, all exiles, all Gauls living in Rome, the whole senate. In a time of scarcity and high prices a ship was said to have arrived from Alexandria laden not with grain for the people but with sand for the use of court wrestlers. Anonymous placards attacking the emperor appeared in public places; omens and portents abounded; Nero was said to be afflicted with terrible dreams. As usual, chance words were considered particularly foreboding when taken in another context. When a speech of the emperor attacking Vindex was read to the senate, at a passage promising that the wicked would be punished and would soon make a fitting end *(brevi dignum exitum facturos)*, all the senators cried out, "You will do it *(facies)*, emperor!" meaning "you will make it so," but taken to suggest that he too would make such an end. And someone observed that the last line of his last public performance, a tragedy on Oedipus in Exile, was especially relevant to the incestuous Nero: in Greek, "My father and co-husband drives me cruelly to death."[4]

In early June he received crushing news. More armies had defected, including his own forces in Northern Italy.[5] In a rage he tore the letter announcing this to pieces, overturned a table, and dashed to the ground two prized crystal goblets, cups which he used to call "Homeric" because they were carved with scenes from the poems of Homer.[6] He then took some poison from his favorite poisoner, Lucusta, placed it in a golden casket, and moved from the palace to a suburban property, his Servilian Gardens. There he dispatched his most trusted freedmen to the port of Ostia to prepare a fleet, while he tried to persuade the tribunes and centurions of his Praetorian Guard to accompany him in his flight. Some evaded answering directly; some refused outright; one even taunted him with a tag from the *Aeneid:* "Is it such a wretched thing to die?" One of his praetorian prefects, Nymphidius Sabinus, had offered them large sums of money to abandon their emperor.[7]

In desperation he considered various courses of action. Should he seek the help of the Parthians as a suppliant? Should he throw himself on Galba's mercy? Or should he appear in public dressed in black, the color of mourning? Should he then mount the speakers' platform in the Forum and beg as pathetically as possible for pardon for his past deeds? And if he did not succeed in that, should he plead to be given the prefecture of Egypt? A speech to this effect was later found in his letter-case, but he was too terrified to deliver it. Egypt and the great city of Alexandria were the obvious refuge for a man so in love with Hellenistic culture: "Even if I am driven from empire, this talent of mine [playing the lyre] will support me there." He would decide the next day what to do.

It was too late. He awoke around midnight to find that his military escort had disappeared. He leapt from bed and sent for his friends. When no one responded he went to their rooms himself, accompanied by a few attendants. Their doors were closed; no one answered; he returned to his own bedroom. There he discovered that his private bodyguards had fled, taking with them even his bedclothes and the box of poison. Immediately he sent word for his favorite gladiator, Spiculus, or any professional killer. No one could be found. "So, do I have neither friend nor enemy?" he cried, and he ran out as though to throw himself into the Tiber.

Checking himself, he decided to seek some out-of-the-way place where he might collect his thoughts. His freedman Phaon offered him a suburban villa which lay between the Via Nomentana and the Via Salaria, near the fourth milestone to the north of the city. This was in the opposite direction from the port of Ostia: the Alexandrian plan had been abandoned.

Barefoot and clad in a tunic and a faded cloak, with his head covered and holding a handkerchief to his face, he mounted a horse and rode into the night, accompanied by just four companions, all freedmen: Phaon, Epaphroditus, Neophytus, and the eunuch Sporus.[8] It was a nerve-shattering journey. The earth quaked, lightning flashed. As he passed the praetorian camp, which lay near the Via Salaria outside the city, he heard the shouts of the soldiers predicting disaster for himself and success for Galba. A messenger cried out, "These men are pursuing Nero"; another asked, "Is there any news of Nero in the city?" His horse shied at the smell of a corpse which had been thrown into the road, his face was uncovered, and a passing veteran of the Praetorian Guard recognized and saluted him. The party reached the turn-off for the villa and let their horses loose.

Their path now lay through thickets and bramble-bushes and reeds. Only with difficulty—sometimes he was obliged to spread a robe beneath his bare feet—was Nero able to reach the back wall of the villa. Here Phaon urged him to hide for a while in a sandpit, but he refused, saying that he would not go underground while still alive. Forced to wait as his companions dug a makeshift entrance into the villa, he passed the time by drinking water from a nearby pond—"This is Nero's boiled water!"—and plucking the twigs from his torn cloak. Morning had come, the morning of 11 June 68.[9] He crawled through the narrow tunnel they had dug, entered the first room he came to, and threw himself onto a bed with a thin mattress and an old coverlet. Hungry and again thirsty, he nevertheless refused a piece of filthy bread and drank only some lukewarm water. His companions then urged him to escape by suicide from the outrages that were awaiting him. He ordered them to dig a trench that would fit his body and to look out for any fragments of marble for a monument; also to bring water to wash his corpse and wood to burn it. While they carried out these tasks for him, he wept and declared repeatedly (or so we are often told, mistakenly), "What an artist dies in me!"[10]

In the meantime Phaon received a note by messenger. Nero tore it from him, to read that the senate had declared him a public enemy and that he was being sought out to be punished in the ancestral manner. He asked what that punishment might be and they told him: he would be led naked through the streets with his neck in a yoke, he would be beaten with rods until he died, and his body would be thrown from the Tarpeian Rock.[11] Terrified, he snatched up two daggers which he had carried away with him and tested the point of each, but he replaced them in their sheaths, pleading that the fated hour had not yet come. He urged Sporus to begin weeping and lamentation; he begged that someone should help by giving him an example of how to kill oneself; and all the while he rebuked his own sluggishness: "I am living badly, disgracefully"; (then, in Greek) "This does not become Nero, does not become him," and "One should be resolute at such times—come, rouse yourself!"

Hoofbeats could be heard. He gasped out a line from the *Iliad,* "The thunder is beating against my ears of fast-running horses," and drove a sword into his throat with the help of his secretary Epaphroditus. A centurion rushed in and pressed his traveling-cloak to the wound as if to aid the dying man. Nero responded only with the words "Too late" and "This is loyalty." He died with his eyes so bulging from his head that all around him were struck with horror.

The first person of consequence to arrive at the scene was Icelus, a freedman of Galba who had been put into chains at the time of his master's revolt. Not believing the news of Nero's death, he had come out to view the corpse himself. He then gave permission for the emperor's household to cremate and bury him properly, and immediately set off to Galba in Spain with the news.

The funeral was expensive and elaborate, the corpse covered by white cloth laced with gold. Members of the household, including Sporus, attended the cremation, and the ashes were buried by his old nurses, Egloge and Alexandria, and his former concubine, Acte, in the tomb of the Domitii which stood on the Pincian Hill (the ancient Mons Pincius, or the Hill of Gardens), in full view of the Campus Martius below. Nero's last resting place within the family tomb was a sarcophagus of porphyry over which stood an altar of white Carrara marble, both surrounded by a low wall of white marble from Thasos.[12]

The vividly circumstantial details of Nero's last days, based certainly on eyewitness accounts, the close involvement of friends and foes, male and female servants, soldiers, even the cautious agent of the rebel Galba, make it as certain as anything can be in ancient history: at the age of 30 years and almost six months, the emperor Nero was, apparently, dead and buried.

POPULAR reaction to Nero's fall and death was, in part, euphoric: people ran about the streets of Rome wearing caps of freedom, such as were given to slaves at their manumission. Tacitus claims that the senators and leading men of the equestrian order rejoiced in their newfound liberty, a liberty made even sweeter to them by the fact that the new emperor was far away (that is, Galba, who was in Spain), while the respectable part of the common people and those attached to the great senatorial families, the clients and freedmen of aristocrats who had been condemned and exiled, were buoyed with hope.[13] The city itself for the time being was under the control of the praetorian prefect Nymphidius Sabinus. This man who had betrayed his master even nursed hopes of succeeding him as emperor, spreading the rumor that he himself was the bastard son of Caligula. To that end he courted the senate and suborned the Guard, while to curry favor with the mob he allowed it to rampage unchecked against the memory and the minions of Nero. Some of the emperor's statues in the Forum were knocked down and dragged about, and the gladiator Spiculus was thrown to his death under them; another favorite, an informer named Aponius, was crushed under wagons filled with stones. Others, the innocent as well as the guilty, were crucified or torn to pieces. A young senator named Junius Mauricus told his colleagues that he was afraid they would soon be wanting Nero back.[14]

His words were prophetic, for the reaction to Nero's death was by no means unanimous. The *plebs* were overjoyed, writes Suetonius, and ran about the city in their caps of liberty. And yet, there were some who for a long time afterwards would adorn Nero's tomb with the fresh flowers of spring and summer. Sometimes they would bring into the Forum statues of him dressed in the *toga praetexta,* the purple-bordered toga of the Roman magistrate. And they would even produce edicts of his, written as if he were alive and would soon return to the dismay of his enemies. Tacitus too admits that there was another opinion. After describing the joy of the senators, the knights, and the better part of the common people, he admits that others were upset by Nero's death: the *plebs sordida,* the dregs of the common people who were addicted to the circus and the theaters, along with the meanest of the slaves and the wastrels who were supported by Nero's depravity—all these were despondent at his loss and eager to believe every rumor.[15] Despite the historian's moralizing dismissal, the number of those who regretted their emperor must have been significant, probably a majority.

In fact, for more than a year after his death, Nero's reputation hung in the balance. The elderly Galba wanted to project an image of ancient Ro-

man virtue, to contrast with the excessive luxury of the man he had replaced. Accordingly, he revoked Nero's extravagant public largesses and
put to death several of his more obnoxious followers.[16] But Galba fell
in mid-January of 69 to the plots of Marcus Salvius Otho, a supporter
who was disappointed at the 71-year-old emperor's choice of someone
else to succeed him. A very different character, only half as old as Galba,
Otho had been one of Nero's closest cronies, wild, extravagant, corrupt,
influential at court and deeply involved in his plots against his mother,
Agrippina. Disgrace had overtaken him when Nero fell in love with his
wife, Poppaea Sabina. He had been sent off into honorable exile as governor of the province of Lusitania, on the Atlantic coast, which he had ruled
well for a decade. Then in 68 his chance had come, when Galba, the governor of the neighboring province, had rebelled, and Otho became the
first of his colleagues to declare his support for him. But failing to achieve
what he felt to be his just reward, he had seduced the Praetorian Guard
and now, with their murder of Galba on 15 January 69, he was emperor,
although not recognized by the legions on the Rhine, who were preparing
to march on Italy. Otho's position was precarious. Restoring exiles, woo-
ing the senate, the guard, and the people, extending citizenship rights in
the provinces, punishing malefactors and overlooking private offenses, in
short acting as a good emperor should—all this was no substitute for true
legitimacy. His singular achievement was that he had removed the man
who had overthrown the last of the Caesars. He began accordingly to exploit an identification of himself in the public eye with Nero, "in the hope
of winning the common people to his side."

By a decree of the senate he had the statues of Poppaea, the wife who
had infatuated both him and Nero, restored, and when busts and statues
of Nero were brought forth by private citizens he did nothing to restrain
them. Some days, in the theater, the people and the soldiers would hail
him as "Nero Otho." He took the hint: dispatches and letters to provincial governors were sent in the name of Nero Otho. Those of Nero's procurators and freedmen who had lost their offices under Galba were now restored, and one of the new emperor's first official acts was to devote 50
million sesterces to the completion of Nero's Golden House. In the end,
nothing came of it all; the three-month reign was too brief for Nero Otho
to develop. Significantly, while the people had pressed the identification
on him, the leading men of the state disapproved, and Otho hesitated to
pursue it.[17] To the ancient authors, this flirtation with the memory of

Nero is a minor matter, and they emphasize the division of opinion between vulgar mob and responsible aristocracy. Here as elsewhere, they mislead.

Otho's forces were defeated in the north of Italy by the armies of the Rhine and he committed suicide in mid-April of 69, but imperial flirtation with the memory of Nero continued. The new emperor was the legate of Lower Germany, Aulus Vitellius, a middle-aged voluptuary who had rebelled against Galba and refused to change his course for Otho. Vitellius had been a prominent courtier whose love of chariot-racing and dicing, as well as his subservience, had endeared him to Nero, and in the words of Suetonius, he left no one in doubt as to what model he had chosen for ruling Rome. In the center of the Campus Martius, perhaps in sight of the tomb, he performed funeral sacrifices for Nero on altars built for the purpose; the fires to burn the victims were set alight by the Augustales, a college of state priests founded by the emperor Tiberius for the task of honoring the house of the Caesars, and including in its number some of the leading men of the state. In the solemn public banquet that followed, a citharode (lyre-player) performed remarkably well. Pleased, Vitellius urged him to name something from the imperial property: *admonuit, ut aliquid de dominico diceret,* that is, to choose a reward. The nimble-witted artist deliberately misunderstood the emperor as commanding him to sing something of the master's (the Latin will bear both meanings), and started into one of Nero's own compositions. Delighted, Vitellius leapt up to lead the applause.[18]

But any rehabilitation of Nero was lost with the defeat of the armies of Vitellius by those of Vespasian in the autumn of 69, the capture of Rome, and the murder of Vitellius in December. The parsimonious Vespasian, who honored the memory of Galba, revoked the liberty granted to Greece by Nero, opened the Golden House to the public, and dedicated the Colossus of Nero to the Sun. With the entrenchment of his new dynasty, the Flavians, and the ascendancy of a stricter morality, together with the publication of such inimical works as the play *Octavia* and the history of Pliny the Elder,[19] Nero's reputation as a monster was fixed for eternity.

But THE STANDARD view of Nero is not the only view, or necessarily even the "right" view, as the conflict of opinion in 68 and 69 might suggest. Monster or not, Nero had an afterlife that was unique in antiquity.[20]

There were some men, Alexander the Great above all, whose reputation survived their deaths to set a standard of conduct which would be sedulously imitated by the great men of Greece and Rome who followed, and remolded to the mythic needs of each succeeding generation. There were also some men who were thought not to have died at all, but who were confidently expected to reappear sometime after their disappearance, who would return to overthrow established authority; and some of these actually did reappear, only to be killed in battle, to be executed, or to vanish a second time, inevitably to be branded by posterity as frauds: the False Antiochus, the False Drusus, the False Nero.[21] These two figures—the man who has not died but will return, and the man who died but whose reputation is a powerful living force—sound an echo of collective thoughts, emotions, and memories, which are not always those shared and circulated by the dominant political and intellectual elite, but which may be no less valid. At first glance the two figures, dead and living, might appear to be mutually exclusive, but they need not be: rather, as we shall see, they may largely overlap and can be difficult to disentangle, as in the case of Nero. For the sake of convenience we can separate them initially. The goal is the same, however—the recovery of another, a different image of the "monster": a man who was very much missed.

Many believed that Nero did not kill himself in June of 68. From the beginning, his disappearance was not unexpected. Astrologers had once predicted that he would be forsaken, just as he was at the end. But there were those among them who had promised him dominion over the East when he was overthrown; some even specified the Kingdom of Jerusalem; several predicted the restoration of all his former fortune.[22] For a remarkably long time, these prophecies struggled to fulfill themselves. As Tacitus admits, various rumors circulated about Nero's death and, because of them, many believed or pretended to believe that he was still alive. The contemporary Greek orator, Dio of Prusa, writing at an unknown date in the four or five decades after Nero's death, adds startling if rhetorical confirmation. Even now, he claims, it is not actually clear what happened at the time of his alleged suicide. Even now everybody wants Nero to be alive, and most people think that he is.[23] Everybody? Most people?

Over the next two decades at least three men tried to give the public what it wanted.[24] Their brief careers are significant. Around March of 69 the first of the "False Neros" appeared in Greece, taking advantage of the rumors about Nero's death to spread turmoil in the provinces of Achaia and Asia. His true name was never known, and it was later disputed whether he was originally a slave from Pontus or a freedman from Italy (he could have been both). His skill at singing and at playing the lyre, a facial similarity to the late emperor, and promises of grand rewards were enough to attract the support of some impoverished deserters from the army. Setting sail for Syria, he was forced by bad weather to put into the Cycladic island of Cythnus, off the coast of Greece. There he fell in with a deputation of soldiers on their way from the armies of Syria to proclaim their solidarity with the Praetorian Guard in Rome. He managed to persuade some of them to declare for him, executed others, robbed merchants, and armed slaves. A centurion who escaped spread word of his advent, and "many," *multi,* were excited by the prospect. A senator named L. Nonius Calpurnius Asprenas, whom Galba had appointed governor of the provinces of Galatia and Pamphylia, was given two triremes from the fleet at Misenum to pursue the pretender. When these arrived at Cythnus, the new Nero summoned the captains of the vessels to him, sorrowfully appealed to their loyalty to him as old soldiers, and begged them to set him down in Syria or Egypt. The captains temporized, asking for time to consult their soldiers, and, as they did, their commander, Asprenas, had the pretender's ship boarded and the man summarily executed. His corpse was sent first to Asia and then to Rome, presumably for public display.

The story as told by Tacitus is obscure in many parts, the chronology is unclear, the motivations of the actors are mysterious, the witness is hostile and elliptical.[25] Why the governor of Galatia, a province in central Asia Minor, and why ships from the Misenine fleet, based on the west-central coast of Italy, were involved in the Aegean is not revealed. Nevertheless, the sequence was probably as follows: Galba appointed Calpurnius Asprenas to the governorship of a newly created complex of Asian provinces in the summer or early autumn of 68, with military power, *imperium,* and he assigned to him the task of running the pretender to earth while en route to his command. That is, although Tacitus assigns the denouement of the affair to the spring of 69, the False Nero must have appeared in Greece in the summer months of 68, not long after reports of Nero's death were received there, and less than a year after his triumphant tour of the province in 67.[26]

The second False Nero appeared in Asia, a native of that province named Terentius Maximus, in the reign of the emperor Titus, that is, in 79/81.[27] He too resembled Nero physically and could sing like him while

playing the lyre. The surviving account based on Dio adds some plausible
if unsurprising claims which the pretender may have made: that he had
escaped the soldiers sent to find him in 68, that he had lived in hiding
since then, that the Parthians should welcome him for returning Armenia
to them. With a few Asian followers he moved to the East, toward the
Euphrates, gathering many more adherents as he went and eventually
crossing over the border to Artabanus, a short-lived Parthian usurper.
Artabanus, for reasons of his own, was contemplating an attack on the
Roman empire, and intended to restore his Nero to the throne, but somehow the true identity of Terentius Maximus was exposed and the imposter died.

The third False Nero is an even shadowier figure. In the last sentence of
Suetonius' *Life of Nero,* the biographer remembers that when a man of unknown origin arose to claim that he was Nero, so honored was the emperor's name among the Parthians that they supported him strongly and
could hardly be brought to surrender him. This occurred twenty years after Nero's death, when Suetonius was himself, as he says, a youth. That
would place the appearance around the year 88 or 89, and it may be connected with other political upsets in that period of Domitian's reign.[28]

To make a success of being Nero you clearly needed to look like him
and to play the lyre reasonably well, as he had done. But, less predictably
perhaps, your chances of support improved as you moved east, while for
restoration you ought to look beyond the border of the empire, to Parthia.
The third False Nero was the last actually to appear, but the emperor was
now entering an apocalyptic phase denied to most historical figures, and
the apocalypse is set firmly in the East.[29]

His story is taken up there by a heterogeneous group of poems known
as the *Sibylline Oracles.* Written in Greek hexameters, based on the inspired prophecies of the Greek Sibyls, traditionally fourteen in number, in
fact they are together and individually a hodgepodge—pagan, Jewish,
Christian, with layers, accretions, interpolations, and pastings together of
Near Eastern materials culled from the second century BC to the seventh
century AD. More important politically than theologically, their penchant
for long and enthusiastic prediction of imminent disasters lends them a
particular value as they echo, often, the voices of the oppressed in the eastern half of the Roman empire and its predecessors. Their view of Nero in
particular helps to explain the successes of the False Neros.

Incorporating earlier elements, the Fourth Sibylline Oracle is agreed to have received its final form soon after the momentous eruption of Mount Vesuvius in 79, which the oracle sees as punishment for the Roman sack of Jerusalem and the destruction of the Great Temple there in 70. The oracle's Jewish compiler looked forward with zest to the end of the Roman empire. The tone of coming retribution is set after the sack of the Temple and its accompanying atrocities:

> Then a great king will flee from Italy like a runaway slave
> unseen and unheard over the channel of the Euphrates,
> when he dares to incur a maternal curse for repulsive murder
> and many other things, confidently, with wicked hand.
> While he runs away, beyond the Parthian land,
> many will bloody the ground for the throne of Rome.

And later:

> Then the strife of war being aroused will come to the west,
> and the fugitive from Rome will also come, brandishing a great spear,
> having crossed the Euphrates with many myriads.[30]

Then the eastern empire of Rome will suffer, as the narrator describes it lovingly: Antioch destroyed, Cyprus ravaged, and so forth. Nero has become, if not quite the champion of the oppressed, their instrument of retribution.

The Fifth Sibylline consists of six or more different oracles composed in (roughly) the late first and early second centuries, and is essentially Jewish in outlook. The Nero figure appears in three of them,[31] of which the first is exceptionally circumstantial:

> The poets will bewail thrice-wretched Greece
> when a great king of great Rome, a godlike man
> from Italy, will cut the ridge of the isthmus.
> Him, they say, Zeus himself begot and lady Hera.
> Playing at theatricals with honey-sweet songs rendered
> with melodious voice, he will destroy many men, and his wretched
>   mother.
> He will flee from Babylon, a terrible and shameless prince
> whom all mortals and noble men despise.

For he destroyed many men and laid hands on the womb.
He sinned against spouses, and was sprung from abominable people.
He will come to the Medes and to the kings of the Persians,
those whom he first desired and to whom he gave glory,
lurking with these evil ones against a true people.
He seized the divinely built Temple and burned the citizens
and peoples who went into it, men whom I rightly praised.
For on his appearance the whole creation was shaken
and kings perished, and those in whom the sovereignty remained
destroyed a great city and righteous people. (5. 137–154)

This striking alternation between history and prophecy presents a Nero who has at least some good qualities, and whose great sin is his ultimate responsibility for the destruction of the Temple (which occurred more than two years after his death). It assumes as fact that he has fled from Rome to Parthia, but the identification of Rome and Parthia with ancient enemies of the Jews (Babylon and the Persians, respectively) seals the hostile verdict, and in the succeeding verses the prophet moves on to predict the punishment of Rome.

Similar elements emerge in the next appearance of Nero in the Fifth Oracle:

You too, Corinth, bewail the mournful destruction within you.
For when the three sister Fates, spinning with twisted threads,
lead the one who is (now) fleeing deceitfully
beyond the bank of the isthmus on high so that all may see him,
who formerly cut out the rock with ductile bronze,
he will destroy and ravage your land also, as is decreed.
For to him God gave strength to perform
things like no previous one of all the kings.
For, first of all, cutting off the roots from three heads
mightily with a blow, he will give them to others to eat,
so that they will eat the flesh of the parents of the impious king.
For murder and terror are in store for all men
because of the great city and righteous people which is
preserved throughout everything, which Providence held in special
   place. (5. 214–227)

Again, the elements of Nero's attempt to cut the isthmus of Corinth, the woes of Greece, Greek myth, and the emperor's flight are tied to the coming catastrophe, with Nero acting as God's instrument of retribution for the attack on Jerusalem.

The third appearance of Nero in the Fifth Sibylline is the most striking of all:

> There will come to pass in the last time about the waning of the moon
> a war which will throw the world into confusion and be deceptive in
>   guile.
> A man who is a matricide will come from the ends of the earth
> in flight and devising penetrating schemes in his mind.
> He will destroy every land and conquer all
> and will consider all things more wisely than all men.
> He will immediately seize the one because of whom he himself
>   perished.
> He will destroy many men and great rulers,
> and he will set fire to all men as no one else ever did.
> Through zeal he will raise up those who were crouched in fear.
> There will come upon men a great war from the West.
> Blood will flow up to the bank of deep-eddying rivers,
> wrath will drip in the plains of Macedonia,
> an alliance to the people from the West, but destruction for the king.
> Then a wintry blast will blow throughout the land,
> and the plain will be filled again with evil war. (5. 361–376)

In that terrible war which follows the death of the king, all kings and nobles will be destroyed; then war will end, and the people will have peace. Here, at last, is the good Nero undiluted by hostile Jewish propaganda. He is a wise and clever conqueror returning from the ends of the earth to overthrow his successor, to destroy great tyrants *(turannous),* and to raise up the downtrodden. He is the champion of the East who will fall in battle against the forces of the West (Rome), but that battle will signal the war to end all war. He is, in short, the very ideal of those who were led astray by the False Neros.

The first half of the Eighth Sibylline Oracle is a virulently anti-Roman tract, primarily Jewish in origin, with pagan and Christian insertions; it can be dated to the reign of Marcus Aurelius (161–180). The Nero here is recognizably descended from the figures of the earlier oracles:

> One, an old man [Marcus], will control dominions far and wide,
> a most piteous king, who will shut up and guard all the wealth
> of the world in his home, so that when the blazing
> matricidal exile returns from the ends of the earth
> he will give these things to all and award great wealth to Asia.
>   (8. 68–72)

And two further predictions (lines 139–150 and 151–159) foresee his destruction of the Jews and the Romans, "when he comes from Asia, conquering with Ares" (146). The latter ends:

> Celebrate, if you wish, the man of secret birth,
> riding a Trojan chariot from the land of Asia
> with the spirit of fire. But when he cuts through the isthmus
> glancing about, going against everyone, having crossed the sea,
> then dark blood will pursue the great beast. (8. 153–157)

Matricide, cutter of the isthmus, champion of the East, apocalyptic destroyer of Rome—even a century after his death, Nero's return could still be prophesied.

That is the end of Nero's return as far as the Sibyls are concerned. In the Twelfth Oracle, a mainly Jewish work from Egypt which reviews the emperors of Rome from the death of Augustus to the death of Severus Alexander in 235, Nero is a wicked man whose reign ends with his flight and miserable death (12. 78–94). Yet even here, in the mid-third century, there is an echo of the False Neros: "even unseen he will be destructive to the Italians" (85). In the Thirteenth Oracle, however, compiled in Syria during the 260s, he has become a literary conceit, when lines from the Fourth are quoted to be applied to a contemporary usurper (13. 119–130).

We must disentangle two interwoven strands in the complex image of Nero's return. The first and earlier appeared in the immediate aftermath of the emperor's sudden fall and obscure death, and even before. According to this account, as the astrologers had predicted and many believed, he had not died but had fled to the East and even into Parthia, whence he would return to overthrow the usurpers and retake his throne. Integral to this strand is the faith, however confused, that, for reasons yet to be determined, Nero championed a cause, be it of the East against the Roman West, or of the oppressed against the oppressors. Closely intertwined with this is a second, ambiguous, and specifically Jewish strand, which has its origin in events soon after the emperor's death, with the sack of Jerusalem and the destruction of the Temple in AD 70. (The ambiguity springs from Nero himself, who began the Roman war against the Jews but did not survive to see its bloody end.) The instigator of the destruction of the Temple has now become God's instrument in the punishment of the Romans, as the returning champion of the oppressed is transformed for some Jews into the beast of murder and terror who will shake creation. The two strands are interwoven confusingly. Neither overwhelms the other in the century after Nero's death, but it is essential to realize that they precede in time and explain the third, longest-lasting, and most notorious strand in the myth of his return: Nero the Antichrist.

Nero's promotion to demonic status by the Christians first appears in two works from the second generation after Nero's death. The first, embedded in a larger composite text known as the *Martyrdom and Ascension of Isaiah,* which contains elements stretching from the second century BC to the fourth century AD, is a Christian fragment which can be dated with rough certainty to the very late first century AD.[32] At the end of the world, so Isaiah prophesies,

> Beliar will descend, the great angel, the king of this world, which he has ruled ever since it existed. He will descend from his firmament in the form of a man, a king of iniquity, a murderer of his mother—this is the king of this world—and will persecute the plant which the twelve apostles of the Beloved will have planted; some of the twelve will be given into his hand. This angel, Beliar, will come in the form of that king, and with him will come all the powers of this world, and they will obey him in every wish. (4. 2–4)

The identification with Nero the matricide, under whom were martyred Saints Peter and Paul, is clear. The prophet next describes the reign of Beliar, his imitation of Christ, his working of miracles, his seduction of most of the followers of Christ, and the flight of the rest, the true believers. Then, "after one thousand three hundred and forty-two days the Lord will come with his angels and with the hosts of the saints from the seventh heaven . . . and will drag Beliar, and his hosts also, into Gehenna." This Second Coming leads to Judgment Day.

The *Martyrdom of Isaiah* is by far the clearer of the two earliest manifestations of Nero as Antichrist, but it is overwhelmed in significance by the prophecies recorded by St. John in the Book of Revelation, which conventionally concludes the Christian New Testament. Its subject is the end of this world. To simplify vastly a rich and endlessly explored allegorical prophecy, and to concentrate on one figure which may support a host of interpretations simultaneously: the earth will be oppressed by a great red dragon (Satan) and his assistants, two beasts, one from the sea and one from the earth. The first beast is a composite of different wild animals with ten horns and seven heads—"One of its heads seemed to have received a death-blow, but its mortal wound had been healed"—and to it the dragon gives authority over every tribe and people on earth. All the inhabitants of the earth worship it; it blasphemes against God and makes war on the saints (13. 1–8): it is, in short, Rome. The second beast, from the earth, has horns like a lamb and speaks like a dragon. It controls the earth on behalf of the first beast, performs miracles, and by a mixture of force and persuasion induces the people of the earth to worship the image of the first beast. Most important, the second beast marks everyone, from the highest to the lowest, with its own mark, and no one without the mark can buy or sell (13. 11–17). "This calls for wisdom: let anyone with understanding calculate the number of the beast, for it is the number of a person. Its number is six hundred sixty-six" (13. 18). 666, it has long been recognized, is (among many other things) the sum of the numerical equivalents for the Hebrew letters which spell the words "Neron Caesar." By this reckoning, Nero is the second beast of Revelation.[33]

Later an angel reveals to John the great whore of Babylon, seated on a scarlet beast. "I will tell you the mystery of the woman, and of the beast with seven heads and ten horns that carries her. The beast that you saw was, and is not, and is about to ascend from the bottomless pit and go to destruction. And the inhabitants of the earth, whose names have not been written in the book of life from the foundation of the world, will be amazed when they see the beast, because it was and is not and is to come" (17. 7–8). In the war to come the Lord will defeat the beast and his followers, and the whore that is Rome will be destroyed.

Nero has returned from the bottomless pit only to fall into bad company here. By the time of the living Nero, two separate Hellenistic Jewish beliefs had coalesced, one concerning the Anti-God (or Antichrist), a human being or human power who opposes God, and the other concerning Beliar, or Satan, a demonic power who likewise opposes God: together, they allow the myth to take shape that Satan had assumed human form.[34] To the early Christians, who were familiar with this belief, Nero was the manifest incarnation, the man who had first persecuted the Christians and who had executed both Peter and Paul, the figure who would return from hiding to harry the Roman world. To them, he becomes the Antichrist, or the precursor of the Antichrist, at the beginning of the end of the world.

The vagaries in the development of Nero as Antichrist, or rather forerunner of Antichrist, from the third century onward add up to a long story which can be reduced to two essential variants: that of those Christians who believed it, and that of those who did not. Of the former, the best and earliest representative is the poet Commodian, writing in Latin around the year 260, probably a Syrian and a clear prophetic descendant of the *Sibylline Oracles* and the Book of Revelation.[35] In one passage, "on the time of the Antichrist," Nero straightforwardly returns from hell at the end of the world. In another, longer piece, the man who first punished Peter and Paul will return at the end of time from hidden places, defeat a Gothic horde, be welcomed by Romans and Jews, persecute Christians, and in his turn be destroyed by the true Antichrist from the East.[36] A near-contemporary, the martyr-bishop Victorinus of Poetovio, in Pannonia, asserted flatly that Nero was the beast of Revelation. He did indeed kill himself as he was pursued by cavalry sent by the senate, but God resuscitated him and sent him as king to the Jews and the persecutors of Christians, who deserved him.[37] A hundred years later, at the beginning of the fifth century, the Gallic historian Sulpicius Severus ends his account of Nero's reign and his cruelty to the Christians with the emperor's disappearance. His body was never found, and even if he did kill himself it was believed that he recovered from his mortal wound, as Revelation foretold, in order to return in evil at the end of the world. Better, Severus' master, St. Martin of Tours, had told him that at the end of the world Nero and Antichrist would come at the same time, Nero to reign in the West, Antichrist in the East (in Jerusalem), and they would persecute the Christians. Then Antichrist would overthrow Nero and Christ would return to overthrow Antichrist; even now the Antichrist had been born, and he was growing up . . .[38]

It is nevertheless clear that this belief in Nero and the Antichrist was a popular one with which the Christian intellectual elite was not happy. In the second decade of the fourth century the rhetor Lactantius, who was tutor to one of the sons of the first Christian emperor, Constantine, published his *On the Deaths of the Persecutors,* a work devoted to the evil lives and grisly ends of those tyrants who had persecuted Christians. It must have been frustrating to report that the first persecutor, Nero, had simply disappeared—that nowhere on earth could the beast's grave be found. For that reason, Lactantius continues, some misguided people believe that he is somewhere in hiding, as the Sibylline Oracle had predicted: "The matricide is to come, an exile from the ends of the earth." The first persecutor of the church will return to persecute it at the end, before the Antichrist appears. But "it is not right to believe this," Lactantius concludes, although he must admit that even some Christian writers continue to do so.[39] St. Jerome, writing at length about the Antichrist later in the century, merely comments in passing that "many of our people [*multi nostrorum*] believe that because of his cruelty and the magnitude of his infamy, Domitius Nero will be the Antichrist."[40] It is left to St. Augustine, in his great *City of God,* written in North Africa between 413 and 426, to explain. A discussion of Antichrist in Paul's second letter to the Thessalonians leads naturally to Nero. Some think, Augustine writes, that Paul is covertly discussing the Roman empire of his day. On this assumption, "the secret power of wickedness already at work" would be intended as a reference to Nero, whose actions already seemed like those of Antichrist.

> Hence there are people who suggest that Nero is to rise again and become Antichrist, while others suppose that he was not killed, but withdrawn instead so that he might be supposed killed and that he is still alive and in concealment in the vigour of the age he had reached at the time of his supposed death, until "he will be revealed at the right time for him" and restored to his throne. For myself I am much astonished at the great presumption of those who venture such guesses.[41]

Nero the monstrous enemy of Christ would have a long life in the Middle Ages, but two aspects of his early career need emphasis. The first is that Nero as Antichrist first took shape in the cloud of rumors and beliefs that swirled about the emperor's reappearance. It was not an original idea with the Christians, but a negative image of the return of a champion, a hope turned into a fear. The second is that when it was revived, from the later third century onward, it remained a popular belief and one that made leaders of the church uncomfortable. In fact, Augustine's description of the alternate conviction, the man hidden in suspended animation until the time is ripe for his restoration, has nothing noticeably Christian about it. It is remarkable that it was written three and a half centuries after Nero's death.

The persistent expectation that Nero would return from hiding (or from the dead, in the negative formulation of the Antichrist) puts him into the select company of historical figures whom people wanted to return, figures like King Arthur, Charlemagne, Saint Olaf, Frederick Barbarossa, Frederick II, Constantine XI, Tsar Alexander I, Elvis Presley. They all fit into two related motifs found in folklore around the world: the motif of the culture hero or divinity who has not died but is still alive, sometimes asleep in a hollow hill or hidden on a mysterious island (or at "the ends of the earth"); and the motif of the culture hero or divinity who is expected to return at the proper time ("revealed at the right time for him") to rescue his people from misfortune.[42] That is to say, whatever mutations the story may have undergone at the hands of Jews, Christians, and hostile pagans, Nero was, by definition, a hero.

The evolution of a historical person into a folkloric hero says little about the actual person but much about what some people, the "folk," believe. Character is simplified to a handful of vivid and often contradictory traits.[43] The hero is recalled as a benefactor and protector; his misdeeds are forgotten or favorably interpreted (as in robbing the rich to give to the poor). Places and objects serve as conspicuous mnemonic devices for the events of his career.[44] Subsequent lapse of time means little to those who remember him. Common to folk heroes is their undiminished contemporary relevance: a great man like Julius Caesar, for all his attractions, is not a hero to folklore, he is a dead great man. But the immortal hero of folklore embodies a longing for the past, an explanation for the present, and, most powerfully, a justification for the future. Folk beliefs are thus generally important for movements of regeneration during periods of social upheaval. Particularly relevant to the figure of Nero are the large-scale millenarian movements of the Middle Ages based on expectations of the imminent appearance of the Messiah, movements which reflected deep social change, disorientation, religious dissent, and a need to escape from present afflictions into the bliss of the impending golden age. Kingdoms were shaken and thousands died or saw their lives ruined when they turned to follow their false saviors.

Two examples from Norman Cohn's *The Pursuit of the Millennium* put Nero's legend into context. One is that of Baldwin IX, Count of Flanders, who in 1204 became Emperor of Constantinople after the diversion of the Fourth Crusade from the Holy Land. In 1205 he died at the hands of the Bulgarians, and his daughter Joanna succeeded him as countess. She was unable to resist the pressure from her aggressive neighbor, Philip Augustus of France, under whose dominion her country fell. Flemish resentment of the French then found an outlet in longing for the late Baldwin. He became a figure of superhuman vice and virtue, one who had sinned greatly and was now carrying out a penance for the pope. But his time as a wandering beggar was nearing its end. In 1224 a hermit living in the woods near Tournai was identified as Baldwin come back. A court grew up about him; Baldwin's nephew recognized him, as did leaders of the Flemish resistance and subsequently most of the nobility and bourgeoisie of Flanders and Hainault. The countess, who refused to acknowledge him, was deposed by force and fled; civil war broke out; pillage and murder followed; and the hermit was regarded as a holy man, whose hair, clothing, and even bathwater were fought over by the faithful. He was crowned in May 1225 as Count and Emperor and distributed knighthoods, fiefs, benefices, largesse. Surrounded by pomp, adored by his people, courted by foreign powers, he eventually moved to treat with the new king of France, Louis VIII—fatally, for Louis exposed the man's ignorance of the life of the real Baldwin and identified him as a serf from Burgundy and former minstrel in the service of the dead count-emperor. The imposter fled and won much popular support, but he was captured and hanged in October 1225. Even though he confessed before his death, the people still believed in him: "Although the Countess Joanna ruled her dominions with prudence and courage, for many generations after her death she continued to be execrated as a parricide, while the figure of Baldwin, the Latin Emperor of the East who for a few weeks had appeared among the Flemish masses as their messiah, took his place . . . amongst the sleeping monarchs who must one day return."[45] The episode gives some hint of the popular fury that might be unleashed by a false hero.

Even more striking, if that is possible, is the fate of the Holy Roman Emperor Frederick II, Stupor Mundi, who died in 1250, "a most brilliant figure, whose versatility and intelligence, licentiousness and cruelty combined to fascinate his contemporaries." His quarrels with the church led to his branding by some as the beast of the Apocalypse, his empire as its Babylon. But in and around 1284 not one nor two but three men in Germany claimed to be Frederick. Two disappeared quickly but the third, who seems actually to have believed that he was the emperor, set up court at Neuss near Cologne, claiming at one time that he had wandered for years as a penitent pilgrim, at another that he had lain hidden in the earth. Italian towns sent him ambassadors; opponents thought he was indeed Frederick come back as the Antichrist. He was captured and executed by the German king Rudolph, but his place was taken by another person who promptly claimed that he had returned from the dead three days after being burnt. That man too was executed, but ever wilder legends grew up around the now immortal Frederick, well into the fourteenth century and beyond.[46] The similarities with the returning Nero are striking: the flamboyantly paradoxical character of the original historical figure; the diversity of possible reactions, from those who want him and believe in him after his death, to those who don't believe in him, to those who believe in but decidedly do not want him; and the effect that an exposed imposter has on his successors, fanning rather than stifling belief in the return of the hero.

Such histories are rooted in the needs—social, political, spiritual, material—of subsequent generations. They tell nothing certain about the real person whom they exalt: generally speaking, folklore cannot be used to recover facts about actors in history. But they do cast a strong oblique light. They *may* reveal something about how the actors were perceived by their contemporaries. The historian Martin Charlesworth suggested that there were three conditions necessary for belief to grow that a historical figure will return: "(1) that the person should be regarded with affection and with hope by a large section of a people as its well-wisher and benefactor or defender; (2) that he should have died with his work incomplete, and (3) that his death should have been sudden and mysterious."[47] Many men and women have met the last two criteria, but most fall short of the first: very few come back as folk heroes. It should be clear, then, that while later social conditions are crucially necessary to the hero's return, they are not sufficient to account for it. Simply put, the person must also have been extraordinarily popular during his lifetime. Just how popular, and among whom?

THE HERO living somewhere hidden in suspended animation and, even more strongly, the Antichrist risen from the dead bridge the gap between the hero who does not die and the hero who dies but who lives in vivid memory. *He has died, but he returns anyway.* Among those who honored the dead Nero, there were surely some who yet harbored hopes that he would return. The belief in the return of a hero flourishes, not in a vacuum, but in a matrix of favorable memories; movements to follow the returning hero grow in fertile soil. However unanimous the surviving written sources may be in their hostility and misapprehension, these apocalyptic movements must imply considerable posthumous popularity. The evidence for the cultivation of the memory of the dead Nero is far more diffuse than that for his return, and difficult to weave into a coherent account. It is best taken as representing the visible outcroppings of a large submerged mass. Were it not for passing mention in church writers and documents, and in the triumphant inscription of a Persian shah, we would have no idea that a city in eastern Cilicia continued to call itself "Neronias," or "the city of Nero," up to the mid-fourth century. Were it not for the chance discovery of an epitaph from the city of Amaseia in Pontus, we would have no idea that in the mid-third century the local calendar still retained the month "Neroneios." And were it not for the survival of fragile glass flasks depicting the topography of Nero's beloved Bay of Naples, we would not know that the lake which he had constructed at Baiae, the *stagnum Neronis,* still went by that name in the fourth century.[48]

Before we consider such echoes of a positive memory of the dead Nero, we should realize that this nostalgia was nourished not only by the popular belief that he would return, but also by the recognition even among the educated that the "bad" Nero might have some good in him.

That opinions could be mixed is clear. The Jewish historian Josephus, who had visited Nero's court and benefited from the patronage of Poppaea Sabina, asserts that Nero's record had been both whitewashed and blackened by historians accordingly as they had flourished or suffered under him: the former were careless with the truth, but the latter lied monstrously.[49] The poet Martial, who had lived in Nero's Rome, varied the standard attack on his character with some grudging praise for his building program ("What is worse than Nero? What is better than Nero's baths?") and particularly for the learning displayed in his poetry ("the poems of learned Nero")—learned, *doctus,* being a term of the highest praise in literary circles.[50] Most tantalizing of all is a remark attributed to the emperor Trajan (98–117) by two historical epitomators of the later fourth century, to the effect that Trajan, apparently when the matter of public buildings came up, would often remark that all the emperors were outstripped by *Neronis quinquennium,* five years of Nero. Despite intense scholarly dispute, it is quite unknown whether Trajan actually made the remark and what he might have meant by it if he did.[51] Its real value lies in the knowledge that historical writers of the fourth century thought that the best of emperors, *optimus princeps,* could find something to praise in one of the worst.[52]

In the light of Nero's posthumous popularity in the East, the attitude of Greek intellectuals is strikingly ambivalent. First among these is the biographer, philosopher, and essayist Plutarch of Chaeronea, who had lived through the reign and who as a young man may even have seen the emperor during his visit to Greece. He had no doubt that Nero was a disaster, both for his personal tyranny and for the license to misgovern which he had allowed to his procurators and freedmen. He "became emperor in my lifetime, murdered his mother, and through his folly and madness brought the Roman empire to the verge of destruction."[53] But Plutarch could find mitigation: it was flattery by others which set the emperor to acting; a word from Seneca did once teach him to moderate his anger; just before executing his enemy Thrasea Paetus, he was said to have wished that Thrasea were as good a friend to himself as he was an excellent judge.[54] Plutarch presents a Nero who is not fundamentally evil, but whose weak good nature is deeply suppressed. Why he does so becomes clear in an astonishing passage to be found in his essay on "God's Slowness to Punish." The narrator of this piece has a vision of souls being prepared for reincarnation, their metal twisted, hammered, and torn apart by infernal workers before their transmigratory return to earth. Among them he sees the soul of Nero, "pierced with incandescent rivets." The suffering emperor is scheduled to return to earth as a viper, appropriate to Nero as the snake which reputedly ate its way out of its mother's womb,

> When suddenly (he said) a great light shot through and a voice came out of the light commanding them to transfer it to a milder kind of brute and frame instead a vocal creature, frequenter of marshes and lakes, as he had paid the penalty for his crimes, and a piece of kindness too was owing him from the gods, since to the nation which among his subjects was noblest and most beloved of Heaven he had granted freedom.[55]

The frog is just as proper an embodiment for the soul of an emperor whose singing voice was naturally thin and hoarse, and the change from viper to frog transforms him from an object of hatred to one of mild ridicule.[56] All of his crimes are expunged by his great act of philhellenic generosity—the liberation of the province of Achaia from taxes. The sentiment lies closer to the Eastern world of the false Neros than it does to the Rome of Tacitus.

This curious Hellenic ambivalence continues in later generations. The traveler Pausanias, writing in the third quarter of the second century, mentions both Nero's robberies from the sanctuaries of Greece and his dedications to them.[57] For him the attempt to cut the Isthmus of Corinth was against nature, and Nero's treatment of his mother and his wives was loathsome, but the liberation of Greece from taxes was a noble deed, leading Pausanias to a reflection which comes very close to Plutarch's view: "When I consider this action of Nero's I think that Plato was telling the purest truth when he said that the greatest and most daring crimes are not the product of ordinary men, but of a noble spirit corrupted by a perverted education."[58]

From around the same time as Pausanias comes a brief dialogue entitled *Nero, or Digging through the Isthmus of Corinth,* which is found among the works of the satirist Lucian but which is generally agreed to have been written by a sophist named Philostratus. In it the emperor, whose death is announced at the end, is portrayed as one who has acted foolishly and even criminally, but whose singing voice is no worse than mediocre, and whose plan to dig the canal is praised for saving travelers the long voyage around the Peloponnese, and as benefiting both trade and those cities along the way which depended on it.[59]

And from the early third century comes a long romantic novel purporting to be a biography of the first-century sage and miracle worker, Apollonius of Tyana, written by another Philostratus, probably the son of the first and a courtier of Julia Domna, the mother of the emperor Caracalla. Nothing in the book can be taken as history, but it does offer precious insight into the opinions of its intended audience. Apollonius never actually meets Nero face to face in the course of the narrative, but he does condemn him for his antipathy to philosophers, his murder of his mother, his love of singing, acting, and gladiators.[60] This is standard calumny, but the two standard themes for praise are also sounded: that his scheme for the Isthmus canal was an excellent one, and that "Nero, by a decision of uncharacteristic wisdom, had given Greece its liberty, and the cities went back to their Doric and Attic customs, and there was prosperity everywhere as well as concord in the cities, which there had not been even in ancient Greece."[61] The idyll is soon broken by Vespasian, to the disgust of Apollonius, but this is an exceptional glimpse of a legend in the making: a man who did, however briefly, bring back a Golden Age.

In the second and early third centuries, an age marked by a literary movement known as the Second Sophistic, Nero was still a live issue for Greek intellectuals. Like other members of the ruling classes, they had to despise the monster, but they also felt obliged to make excuses for the man who had tried to dig the Corinth canal and who had liberated Greece: his was a good or a weak nature overthrown; perhaps these uncharacteristic acts even pardoned a life of crime. This is particularly suggestive. If some members of the elite which had most hated Nero could still feel ambivalent about him, might not other natural enemies also display hesitation?

One of the most curious of all the stories about Nero is to be found in the tractate *Gittin,* part of the Babylonian Talmud compiled in the fifth century but embracing material from much earlier eras. Several tales from the time of the great Jewish Revolt of 66–70 are used to illustrate the complex discussion of a legal point arising in connection with divorce in Jewish law. In one of them, God sends "Nero Caesar" against the Jews in Jerusalem. Prophecy reveals to him that he is fated to destroy the Temple. "He said: The Holy One, blessed be He, desires to lay waste his House and to lay the blame on me. So he ran away and became a proselyte, and Rabbi Meir was descended from him."[62] That is, Nero, who is elsewhere God's scourge against the Jews, absconds, converts to Judaism, marries, and becomes the ancestor of a great figure of second-century Judaism, Rabbi Meir, one of the leaders who would arise after the revolt of Bar Kochba (135–138) and counsel moderation in the Jews' relations with the Roman government. This sequence interweaves two Jewish traditions— that of the pious gentile who converts, and that of the persecuting gentile who becomes the ancestor of pious and learned Jews—and it appears to reflect the widespread belief in Nero's posthumous escape to the East.[63] When the story was born, where it came from, what convictions it reproduces—all these are a mystery.

Less mysterious perhaps is another story which seems even more paradoxical: a favorable Christian view of Nero. "He was tall, slender, handsome, with a good nose, a florid complexion, large eyes, straight completely grey hair, and a bushy beard; he was well-disciplined. As soon as he began to reign, he made a thorough investigation of Jesus. Being unaware that he had been crucified, he asked that he be brought to Rome, since he was a great philosopher and wonder-worker." So wrote John Malalas in the late sixth century. Nero, an Epicurean, is outraged when he finds that Jesus is dead, and ends by executing not just St. Peter but Pontius Pilate as well ("Why did he hand the Lord Christ over to the Jews, for he was an innocent man and worked miracles?"). Greek priests poison him, and Galba, on pretext of visiting the sick emperor, stabs him to death in the palace. "So Nero died at the age of 69."[64] Malalas, the author of this farrago, was one of the supreme fantasists of antiquity, but this particular vision is found repeated solemnly in the great tenth-century Byzantine lexicon, the *Suda*.[65] Whether it was invented by Malalas or merely handed on is unknown.

In short, even among those who had most reason to loathe him, the memory of the monster could yet be honored in some part. Along with the belief in his return, this provides a context for what follows.

However ferocious the initial reaction of some may have been to the news of Nero's death, more positive feelings soon asserted themselves. In 69, Otho and Vitellius clearly demonstrated not only their own inclinations but their sensitivity to popular opinion, and some wished to portray Otho as the new Nero. Ordinary citizens continued to model their private portraits on Nero's likeness after his death, and to carry on the widespread practice of inserting his coin-portrait on their personal mirror boxes.[66]

The beginnings of a cult can be traced in the flowers that decorated Nero's tomb "for a long time after," and the reappearance of his statues in the Forum. In the case of the statues, this was literally a cult, for they were dressed in the toga of a magistrate, not carved as such but dressed in real clothes. This was nothing less than an act of emperor-worship, the dressing of an emperor's image being part of the elaborate ceremonial of the imperial cult.[67] Cultic too in the looser sense is the epitaph of the emperor's old nurse, Egloge or Ecloge, one of the women who had helped to conduct his funeral and to bury his ashes in the tomb of the Domitii in Rome. The plain marble slab was discovered in the suburb to the north of the city, bearing the dramatically simple inscription *Claudiae Ecloge piissim[ae]*, "to Claudia Ecloge, most pious." The nature of her piety would be immediately apparent to an observer, for she was buried almost certainly on the spot where Nero had killed himself.[68]

It is repeated endlessly in modern literature that Nero underwent something called *damnatio memoriae*, damnation of memory. He did not, and the term is incorrect and misleading in various ways. Indeed it is found in no ancient work, being a modern coinage crafted from the quite unrelated legal concept of *memoria damnata*, which referred precisely to the posthumous condemnation in court of a person accused of *perduellio*, high treason.[69] Nevertheless, the phrase has come to be applied indiscriminately to various posthumous attacks on emperors, members of their families, aristocrats, and high officials who fell from power. It originates in specific punishments in law which were meant to dishonor condemned criminals by attacking their memory, by harming their reputation not only in life but in death as well: thus portraits of a criminal might be destroyed, his or her name might be expunged from records and monuments and others might be forbidden to bear it, burial and mourning might be refused. Nero had been declared a public enemy in his last days, but none of these penalties had been applied to him; indeed the funeral had been splendid and normal, his statues reappeared in the Forum, and his acts as emperor were not abolished by the senate or his successors. His name might be, and sometimes was, erased from monuments, but, as with the destruction of his statues in the chaotic days after his death, such acts were outbursts of private zeal, not responses to public mandates.[70] Nero's memory was *not* condemned, and how openly or secretly it was celebrated was more a gauge of the state of popular opinion and imperial policy.

The expression *damnatio memoriae* has also been taken over by art historians and applied to the widespread practice of recarving the portrait of an earlier emperor, or a member of his immediate family, into the features of one of his successors.[71] This use of an already unfortunate term is misleading. The prime motive for such reuse was admittedly economic: sculptors presumably had busts sitting in their storeyards, and they would not want to destroy valuable stock because of changes in the regime. That is, no moral or political statement need be involved in the supposed "condemnation." The term *damnatio memoriae* must also exclude those admired emperors, blameless princes, and indeed ordinary citizens whose portraits were reworked after their deaths. But since no suspicion of condemnation hangs over *their* reputations, why should it be presumed that recarving a conventionally "bad" emperor into a better, or at least a living, Caesar reflects *damnatio*? Reputation, memory good or bad, is not so simple a matter.

The problem is important in the case of Nero. Careful investigation has recovered an extraordinary number of images of Nero which were recarved into those of later figures. The standard study by Bergmann and Zanker identifies four or five portrait busts of Nero reworked into the features of Vespasian (70–79), to which Pollini would add two more; some eleven to thirteen reworked into Domitian (81–96); one into Nerva (96–98); one possibly into Trajan (98–117); two into third- or fourth-century portraits; and one into a fourth-century or even later portrait, to which Maggi would add another fourth-century reworking. Similarly, Megow's monograph on imperial cameos shows examples of Nero's image being altered into those of Galba, Domitian, Trajan, Hadrian's favorite Antinous (who died in 130), and probably Caracalla (211–217), to which he subsequently added an image of Titus.[72] The quality of these busts and cameos varies greatly, from fine to crude; the results of their reworking range from radical transformations of Nero's portrait to images which still clearly show his features even to the untrained eye; and the provenance of most of the works is unfortunately unknown. What do they tell us of Nero's memory, when we know that it was not officially condemned and that many people unofficially honored it? One possibility is that the reworking is neither condemnatory nor neutrally economical, but rather an intentional confusion of images: that is, especially where the features remain obviously Neronian, might it not be that the artist intended to identify his subject with Nero? Even more striking is the longevity of the original

Neronian images. It strains belief that all or even most of these busts and cameos lay around in workshops not only for years but for decades and even centuries. The arresting aspect of such works is not that changes were made, but that somebody, somewhere, preserved portraits of Nero for a long time. By the same token, finely worked souvenir mirrors with Nero's coins in them turn up in graves as late as the mid-second century.[73]

That they should do so is not surprising, for Nero was certainly accorded the rare honor of posthumous portraits. The evidence is scattered but impressive. First is an unprepossessing statue of Nero in an elaborate military cuirass, found in the city of Tralles in Asia Minor—despite its lack of a head there is no doubt that it means to portray Nero, for an inscription at the base names the dedicatee as (in Greek) Nero Claudius, son of the god Claudius Caesar. But the formulation of the inscription is idiosyncratic, and expert analysis of the elements of the breastplate assigns the whole piece without a doubt to the age of the Antonines (mid-second century).[74] That is to say, someone erected an over-life-size statue of Nero in Asia a century after his death. Similarly, there is the striking bronze portrait bust of Nero now in the Vatican Library, which has recently been identified as a Renaissance casting of an ancient original; there is a marble version of the same portrait in the Louvre. It represents a full-bearded variant of Nero's last known portrait type, from the final years of his reign, but on the basis of style there can be no doubt that it was commissioned two centuries after his death, during the reign of the philhellenic emperor Gallienus (253–268).[75] These are not random *objets d'art:* at the least they show an active concern with the emperor's memory.

That concern flourished even later. Hundreds of medallions known as contorniates have survived from the later fourth and early fifth centuries.[76] What they were used for is unsure—memorabilia perhaps to celebrate the New Year or public games. Their obverses offer portraits of great Romans of the past, emperors, and philosophers, for reasons which are still unknown. Since all the men depicted were pagans, it has been argued that they served to convey anti-Christian propaganda in the struggle between paganism and Christianity in the later fourth century, though that seems unlikely. At any rate, Nero was one of the three most popular figures on these medallions, and between about 395 and 410 he was the most popular of all. Certainly his memory was despised by Christians, as the first persecutor and perhaps as the beast of the Apocalypse, so the pieces may bear an anti-Christian message; but more positively, he may simply have been remembered with pleasure as a great giver of games and builder of buildings.[77]

This connection with the games is favored by one of the Nero contorniates which bears on its reverse a picture of Sol Invictus, the Unconquered Sun, riding in his four-horse chariot *(quadriga)*. Very similar to this image is that found on a cameo of the fifth century which depicts not the Sun in his *quadriga* but the emperor Nero in his, wearing the military cloak *(paludamentum)* and on his head a radiate crown, with rays like those of the sun. That it is Nero is left in no doubt, for over his head are the words (in Greek letters) *Neron Agouste* [*sic*], Nero Augustus. In his left hand he holds the eagle-headed scepter of imperial power, while his raised right hand bears a napkin *(mappa)*. The significance of the latter is explained by an anecdote found only in a letter written in the early sixth century on behalf of Theodoric, Visigothic King of Italy, by the senator and royal servant Cassiodorus: "Now the napkin [*mappa*], which is seen to give the signal for the races, came into use by this chance. When Nero was prolonging his dinner, and the people, greedy for the spectacle, was making its customary demand for haste, he ordered that the napkin he was using to wipe his hands should be thrown from the window, to give permission for the requested contest."[78] Thus, some four centuries after Nero's death at least one racing enthusiast, the owner of the cameo, held his memory in honor.

The most astonishing of all posthumous portraits of Nero is a cameo now in the public library at Nancy, in southern France. There has been no sure dating for it—it seems to represent his portrait type of AD 59–64—but there is no doubt that it means to represent a Nero who is no longer alive.[79] Dominating the lower half of the piece is an eagle standing with its wings outspread, its body facing the viewer, its head in profile, turned to the right. In the upper half of the piece and right of center sits Nero on the eagle's back, his body also facing the viewer, his head in profile, turned to the left. He is lightly bearded and wears a laurel wreath in his hair. Around his shoulders is the aegis with the gorgoneion, that is, the emblem of Jupiter with the head of Medusa on it, its end fluttering in the breeze. A mantle covers his lower body, the folds of which are visible behind the eagle's head. The emperor's feet are sandaled, his right arm is outstretched. A small Victory, or possibly a statue of the goddess, wearing a girdled chiton seems to fly up from his hand; both her hands are raised high, holding out what may be a laurel crown to Nero. In the bend of his left

Apotheosis of Nero, based on Nero's portrait of 59–64, but surely posthumous.

arm he carries a cornucopia with tendrils of fruit overflowing. The eagle bearing him holds thunderbolts and gazes back up at Nero-Jupiter, the bearer of victory and of abundance. There is no doubt, iconographically, what is going on here. It is an apotheosis. Surrounded by divine attributes, Nero is being carried up to the gods after his death: traditionally, it was the eagle of Jupiter which carried dead emperors up to join the gods. Here the emperor is not just Nero the Hero; he is Divus Nero, Nero the God.[80]

Nero's posthumous popularity, whether alive and waiting to return, or well and truly dead, will astonish anyone familiar with the standard accounts, pagan and Christian, of his life and crimes. Whether these authors ignored it, attacked it, or belittled it, his memory remained a live force for centuries. Why? Different influences can be seen to converge and shape the legend. Nero's strong philhellenism, the sincere admiration felt for him in Parthia (and Parthia's self-interest), eastern resentments against Rome's domination, Jewish hopes and Christian fears, the predictions that Nero would flee to the East and establish his rule there: all contribute to a strong Asian and hellenic flavor in the story. His passion for charioteering, his great building program, the revered and later haunted site of his burial, all helped to support his continuing reputation in Rome. But we still come up against the central problem: even with these and other factors weighed in the scale, how could people look back so fondly on a monster?

To be a hero it is not at all necessary to be a good man. Arthur, Charlemagne, Barbarossa, Elvis, and their peers are not noted for their mild restraint; all were capable of acts of savagery. More germane to Nero is that one can even be judged a bad man by history and still be a hero. Thus, legends grew up around Emico, Count of Leiningen, both before and after his death in 1117. "A feudal baron notorious for his ferocity," who claimed to be the Emperor of the Last Days, Emico and his followers were responsible for massacring Jews in the cities of the Rhine.[81] But perhaps the best perspective on Nero is offered through the spectacular character of Ivan the Terrible. In the Russian folklore of subsequent centuries Ivan is a *popular* figure, the good Tsar who protects his people against the boyars, one given to the company of bandits and cossacks and to mingling incognito with the poor. Ivan cuts a very human figure—impatient, hotheaded, prone to overhasty and sometimes fatal misjudgments which he later deeply regrets. His cruelty, the terror he inflicts, are the just deserts of traitors; when the innocent do suffer at his hand, he has been misled by false witnesses or by his own zeal. As his modern biographer puts it, "Because the terror is directed against enemies and traitors, real and imaginary, it is not seen as an expression of Ivan's personal viciousness and savagery, but as an indication of his strength and his resolution to pursue the interests of the state, and to avenge injustice against the people."[82] That, in a nutshell, is why an Ivan the Terrible or a Stalin can exercise such power even after their deaths: "tyranny and terror can have a certain popular appeal."[83]

The pages of Tacitus, Dio, and Suetonius drip with the blood of Nero's victims. Horror mounts on horror. But what if we were to accept the writers' facts and reject their explanations—what if we were to adopt Nero's version of events? That is, the executions, the forced suicides, the matricide, were necessary for the safety of the emperor and the good of the state? Much of Nero's monstrosity would fall away. But there would be more. Nero was an infinitely more sophisticated man than Ivan, his crimes far more varied. What if we also accepted his own explanations for his other villainies or, where such explanations are lacking, what if we tried to set them against the expectations of his contemporaries, rather than the condemnations of posterity? We might then create a new vision of the man, a vision shared with those who followed the False Neros into oblivion.

Awareness of Nero's afterlife may not help to paint any new historical picture of the last of the Julio-Claudians, but it should change our perspective. The issue is one of image. For centuries, an unknown number of people in usually unspecified places paid honor to Nero for a variety of reasons. Whatever their numbers and rank and locations and motives, that honor must be significant for the duration and diversity of its manifestations, and for the conspicuous lack of rival analogues: there is simply nothing like it among the conventional Bad Men of antiquity. These witnesses had no superior knowledge of the facts, but they did pay allegiance to an image of the emperor quite different from that etched by our mainstream sources, an image which is at bottom favorable to him. Awareness of his vibrant afterlife should direct our attention not so much to what Nero's real intentions may have been or what his actions really were—though these will come into play—as to how he might have wished them to be perceived, and how they might indeed have been perceived by a receptive audience. The question raised by his afterlife is not whether Nero was a good man or a good emperor, but how he might be seen as such.

2

Stories and Histories

Many historians have written the story of Nero, of whom some, because they were well treated by him, have out of gratitude been careless of the truth, while others from hatred and enmity towards him have so shamelessly and recklessly revelled in falsehoods as to merit censure. Nor can I be surprised at those who have lied about Nero, since even in writing about his predecessors they have not kept to the facts of history . . . Nevertheless, we must let those who have no regard for the truth write as they choose, for that is what they seem to delight in.

JOSEPHUS

Tell me, Muse, what my Canius Rufus is doing: is he putting on paper the acts of Claudian times for posterity to read, or the deeds which a mendacious writer ascribed to Nero? Or does he emulate the fables of rascal Phaedrus?

MARTIAL[1]

We all know about Nero. Nero was emperor of Rome from AD 54 to 68. Nero murdered his mother, and Nero fiddled while Rome burned. Nero also slept with his mother. Nero married and executed one stepsister, executed his other stepsister, raped and murdered his stepbrother. In fact, he executed or murdered most of his close relatives. He kicked his pregnant wife to death. He castrated and then married a freedman. He married another freedman, this time himself playing the bride. He raped a Vestal Virgin. He melted down the household gods of Rome for their cash value. After incinerating the city in 64, he built over much of downtown Rome with his own vast Xanadu, the Golden House. He fixed the blame for the Great Fire on the Christians, some of whom he hung up as human torches to light his gardens at night. He competed as a poet, a singer, an actor, a herald, and a charioteer, and he won every contest, even when he fell out of his chariot at the Olympic Games. He alienated and persecuted much of the elite, neglected the army, and drained the treasury. And he committed suicide at the age of 30, one step ahead of the executioner. His last words were, "What an artist dies in me!"

How do we know all of this? About twenty-five ancient, non-Christian writers have something of value to say about the emperor Nero, but our main picture comes from just three of them: the historians Tacitus and Cassius Dio, and the biographer Suetonius.

Publius(?) Cornelius Tacitus (c. AD 56 – after c. 120) was a senior senator, consul in 97, proconsul of the province of Asia in 112/113, and one of Rome's great historians. His last work was the *Annals (Annales),* a history of Rome year by year from the death of Augustus (AD 14) to Nero's death and the accession of Galba in 68, at least. (He had already covered the period from 69 to 96 in his *Histories.*) His grim and powerful picture of the early principate and the tragic corruption of the Julio-Claudian dynasty has set the tone for all subsequent understanding of the era, no matter how hard we try to escape his sharp pessimism. The precise terminal date of the *Annals* is unknown. Nero's reign from AD 54 to 66 is covered in Books 13 through 16, where the manuscript breaks off in the middle. Tacitus appears to have composed his work in the teens of the second century, and perhaps into the 120s. Whether he survived to complete it is unknown.

Gaius Suetonius Tranquillus (c. AD 70 – c. 130) was an equestrian man of letters and senior imperial official in the later years of the emperor Trajan and the early years of Hadrian. Most of his many works survive only in sparse fragments, with the exception of his *Lives of the Twelve Caesars,* as it is popularly known (*De Vita Caesarum,* or *Caesares*). This work, covering Julius Caesar (100–44 BC) to Domitian (AD 51–96), is substantially complete. Arranged topically rather than chronologically, each life is a remarkable trove of facts and human details which has indelibly stamped our understanding of the personalities of the Julio-Claudian family and their immediate successors—a mix of sharp detail, naiveté, and insight. The *Life of Nero,* sixth in the series, was probably written in the 120s, though precisely when is much debated.

L. Cassius Dio (c. 164 – after 229) was another very senior senator, consul c. 204 and for a second time in 229 with the emperor Severus Alexander as his colleague, proconsul of Africa, and governor of the military provinces of Dalmatia and Upper Pannonia. His huge *Roman History,* written in Greek in the first three decades of the third century, covered the entire history of Rome from Romulus the founder up to his own lifetime. Lacking the vividness of Tacitus and Suetonius, long on imaginary speeches, short on critical independence, Dio suffers by comparison with his predecessors, but he preserves much material not found in either. Of the original eighty books of his history, three (Books 61–63) were devoted to the reign of Nero. Unfortunately, only about a third of the original work is still available, mostly covering the years from 69 BC to AD 46. We do have substantial fragments for other periods in Byzantine excerpts, but our only real sources for Dio on the years of Nero are found in epitomes of his work compiled by two Byzantine monks, Zonaras in the twelfth century and Xiphilinus in the eleventh. These works offer a complex problem for the student of Dio in that both use other sources as well, neither gives anything like a complete summary of their readings in Dio, and neither is very careful. Thus, when we refer to Dio, who is already a secondary, non-contemporary source, we should in principle think of him as "Dio," a tertiary source and a rather elusive shadow.

The point to be made here is not so much the obvious one—that each of these three writers has his own character, prejudices, agenda, strengths, and weaknesses, of which readers must constantly be aware. It is rather the simple observation that none of them was an eyewitness to the events they record. Tacitus was twelve or thirteen years old when Nero died; Suetonius was probably not yet born; Dio would not appear for another century, and "Dio" for a millennium. It becomes then a matter of fundamental importance to know who *their* sources were, what the characters, agendas, and so forth of those sources might be, and how our surviving authors used them.

First, it is generally agreed, after intense scholarly scrutiny, that our three major sources are essentially independent of one another. That is, Suetonius did not use Tacitus, Tacitus did not use Suetonius, and Dio did not use either to any significant extent, if at all.[2] Suetonius and Tacitus were contemporaries, men of eminence in both politics and literature. They must have been acquainted, each must have known the other's earlier writings, and both certainly knew the Younger Pliny well, but careful study can find no clear sign of dependence, one on the other. The autonomy of the three authors helps to clarify matters substantially. That is, where their treatments are markedly similar to each other, even down to vocabulary and expression, they are probably following the same earlier, now lost, authority.

We know of several kinds of sources available to our three authors, about which we can say very little. Most important and least measurable was hearsay: both Tacitus and Suetonius grew up in the generation after Nero; they knew, listened to, and remembered the opinions of survivors.[3] Moreover, there were public records available, now lost: particularly the record of the proceedings of the senate, *acta senatus,* and the daily register of events in the city, the *acta diurna urbis.*[4] And beyond these there were all kinds of archives, private and public, to be consulted: Suetonius and Tacitus both refer to private letters, imperial edicts, court transcripts, inscriptions in stone and bronze, and so forth. All of these were useful to our three authorities, but relatively unimportant in shaping their portraits of Nero: what really matters were their literary sources.

The ghosts of several lost authors beckon to us.[5] First, two important but minor types of writing stand out. One is the memoir written by members of the imperial family or of the aristocracy, all with a highly personal agenda—a record to put straight for posterity. Preeminent among these were the *Memoirs* of Agrippina, presumably written during her enforced retirement between 55 and 59. Earlier in his *Annals* Tacitus cites them for a detail about her mother which he says he could not find in any other history.[6] Retailing her version of the family history and her own life, Agrippina's memoirs are assumed to have been both lurid and self-justifying, laying out what she had done for her son and his stupendous ingratitude. The other important memoir was that of the general Domitius Corbulo, in the form of *Commentaries* on his campaigns in the East, where he spent the entire reign, from 54 until his enforced suicide in 67.[7] Presumably Nero came in for nothing but praise in them.

The other minor literary form is best described as martyrology, the accounts of the defiant lives and glorious deaths of illustrious men under the tyrant, written later in the century. For example, there was the outspoken critic of Nero, Thrasea Paetus, consul in 56, whose grandstanding punctuates the narratives of Tacitus and Dio; his life was written much later by a friend, Arulenus Rusticus, consul in 92, who had been tribune in the year of Thrasea's death, 66. One of the letters of the Younger Pliny, written around 105, contains the obituary of a recently deceased friend, Gaius Fannius, who had died while compiling *The Deaths of Those Slain or Exiled by Nero, Exitus occisorum aut relegatorum a Nerone.* Fannius had dreamed that Nero had sat at the end of his bed, read through three volumes of his "crimes," and gone away. Fannius was horrified to think this meant that his writing would stop where Nero had left off reading, and he was right. Such biographies must have been highly tendentious, not merely because Nero was automatically assumed to be a tyrant, but because they had a point to make in the ideological struggles of their own era, under Domitian and Trajan.[8]

That said, we know of three, and only three, histories, all lost, which dealt with Nero's reign and were written by his contemporaries. Understanding them is crucial to understanding the era.

It is not common for ancient historians to name their sources or to reflect on their use of them, but, in Book 13 of his *Annals,* Tacitus for once does both. The question arises for him whether the emperor could trust his Praetorian Prefect Afranius Burrus, in 55:

> According to Fabius Rusticus, Nero sent a message to Caecina Tuscus, placing him in charge of the praetorian cohorts, but Burrus kept his office through the influence of Seneca. But Plinius and Cluvius show no doubt about the prefect's loyalty; and after all Fabius does incline to praise Seneca, through whose friendship he flourished. I intend to follow the consensus of my sources, and whatever divergent accounts they may give I shall note under their own names.[9]

Thus he names the three authorities whom he and his colleagues follow. Others existed, but their names are unknown and their traces are lost.

First of the three is Pliny the Elder, Gaius Plinius Secundus, who was born in 23 or 24 and who died gallantly in the eruption of Mount Vesuvius on 24 August 79. He was certainly in Rome by AD 35, and eyewitness reports of events in the city appear throughout his huge surviving work, *Naturalis Historia,* the *Natural History.* His nephew, Pliny the Younger, has preserved a list of his many writings, one of which was a *Historia a fine Aufidi Bassi,* a *History from the End of Aufidius Bassus.* Unfortunately, it is quite unknown just when the (to us) obscure historian Aufidius Bassus concluded *his* work: guesses as to his terminal date range from AD 37, through 47, to 54. Pliny's own history certainly covered all of Nero's reign—Tacitus cites him under the years 55, 65, and 68—and extended into that of Vespasian.[10]

Certain characteristics of Pliny's lost work might be deduced from the tone and contents of his extant *Natural History,* which is an encyclopedic compilation wrapped in a polemic against mankind's abuse of nature, and from remarks made about him by Tacitus and by Pliny the Younger. Most important, he loathed Nero: throughout the *Natural History* Nero's follies and extravagances are exposed, as he is repeatedly castigated for his crimes and his madness, and portrayed as the enemy of mankind.[11] Less certain is the modern assumption that Pliny was the major source for surviving antiquarian details about statues, portraits, buildings, oddities, prodigies, and that Tacitus therefore had a low opinion of him.[12] In fact, when read neutrally, Tacitus neither praises nor denigrates him. At one point he follows Pliny's version (as related above) simply because he, Pliny, is in agreement with another source. Elsewhere, Tacitus relates a story passed on by Pliny, only to dismiss it because "handed down from whatever source I had no intention of suppressing it, however absurd it may seem"—hardly a damning indictment of Pliny.[13]

More suggestive is the development of Pliny's career in the imperial service.[14] Of his background and early life, we know only that he came from a distinguished local family from Comum in the lake district of Northern Italy and that he spent parts at least of his childhood and youth in Rome, for in his *Natural History* he offers vivid eyewitness accounts of occurrences in the capital under Tiberius, Caligula, and Claudius (14–54). Between the years 46 and 58, he performed his military service as an officer in three different auxiliary units in Germany, between the ages of about 23 and 35. As an ambitious knight who had proved his competence as a soldier and who was beginning to make a name for himself as a man of letters, he would normally be expected to rise into the service of the emperor as a *procurator Augusti.* In fact, he stayed in retirement until about the year 70, when, in his late forties, he took up the first of three or perhaps four provincial governorships as procurator. Thereafter he was appointed prefect of the imperial fleet, *praefectus classis,* at Misenum on the Bay of Naples, where he met his death in 79. That is to say, throughout most of Nero's reign, from 59 to 68, Pliny was in retirement. He was certainly in Rome for at least part of the time, but nothing in his *Natural History* suggests that he witnessed events at court, or that he had any personal contact with Nero or his cronies. Thus we could speculate just *why* Pliny passed most of the reign in private life—righteous outrage and withdrawal? or resentment at being passed over? However that may be, while the nature of his work remains unknown, its tone can be recovered with certainty, as virulently anti-Neronian. The remarks in his encyclopedia are condemnatory virtually without exception, either explicitly or implicitly.

The picture of Nero to be derived from our second lost source, Fabius Rusticus, was at least as negative as that painted by Pliny and perhaps even more so. This animosity, and therefore questionable reliability, recurs in two passages of Tacitus. In discussing the shocking allegation of incest between Nero and his mother, Tacitus reports that Cluvius made Agrippina the instigator of the act, alleging as a motive her desperation to retain power, while Fabius made Nero the culprit, but gave no reason. It is clear where Tacitus' sympathies lie, for he says that all other authorities supported Cluvius (including Pliny?), and so did popular rumor. Interestingly, in his life of Nero, Suetonius follows Fabius' version without naming him and without betraying a hint of any dissension among his sources.[15] Equally revealing is the divergent treatment of the loyalty of the prefect Burrus, in the passage of Tacitus mentioned earlier—a loyalty unquestioned by Pliny and Cluvius, but questioned by Fabius if only to show off the influence of Seneca, "through whose friendship he [Fabius] flourished."

Seneca's patronage is the central element. Fabius was his protégé and, as Tacitus puts it, he "does incline to praise him." Not surprisingly, Tacitus quotes Fabius in his account of the death of Seneca: presumably Fabius was an eyewitness and a major source. In fact, there is no hint among the fragments that Fabius wrote a history of the period at all, for the concentration on Seneca would better fit a biography or martyrology of the philosopher.[16] However that may be, Fabius was a friend and follower of Nero's most important victim, and certainly not in imperial favor from the time of Seneca's fall, in 62, until Nero's death. The tone of the fragments is decidedly anti-Neronian.

Pliny and Fabius were no friends of Nero, either before or after his death. That was not the case with the third and by far the most interesting of the lost historians, Cluvius Rufus, who is cited by Tacitus and Dio, by the second-century biographer Plutarch, and almost certainly by Josephus, the contemporary historian of the Jews. Where Pliny was a knight and Fabius no more than a knight (if that), Cluvius was a prominent senior senator, the scion of an old senatorial family, the intimate of emperors, and a respected orator. If, as it appears, he had already held the consulship by the time of Caligula's death in 41, he must have been born by about AD 8; that is, he was a man of mature years throughout Nero's reign. And, unlike Pliny and Fabius, he spent much of the reign near the center of power, for he was a friend of Nero and acted as his herald at the

Neronian games in 65 and during the tour of Greek games in 66 and 67. A striking anecdote in the letters of the younger Pliny records an exchange between two of the grand old survivors of Nero's reign, Cluvius Rufus and Pliny's guardian Verginius Rufus, the general who was a key player in the tumultuous events of 68:

> This was the occasion when Cluvius said, "You know how a historian must be faithful to facts, Verginius, so, if you find anything in my histories which is not as you like it, please forgive me." To this he [Verginius] replied, "Don't you realize, Cluvius, that I did what I did so that the rest of you should be at liberty to write as you please?"

Pliny's point in relating the story is irrelevant (he was, after all, the ward of Verginius and the nephew of Cluvius' rival as a historian). What is clear is that Cluvius respected, or professed to respect, accuracy, when he spoke of the *fides* owed to history.[17]

What was the nature of Cluvius' history? In a pathbreaking series of articles in the 1960s, G. B. Townend provided a startling answer. Noting the extraordinary number of quotations in Greek provided by Suetonius in his (Latin) biographies of the emperors from Caligula to Vitellius (AD 37–69), and noting that Josephus seems to tell us that Cluvius also wrote in Latin but likewise quoted in Greek, Townend thought he could use this as the clue to untangling the sources of Suetonius, Tacitus, and Cassius Dio, and this insight led to a series of close, complex, and fascinating readings of our three extant sources. His investigation into the authority behind the Suetonius passages quoting Greek for this period—Cluvius Rufus—is generally accepted, but his opinion about the nature of Cluvius' history has met determined resistance. After considering the passages, Townend concluded that it was a "scabrous, unchronological *chronique scandaleuse.*" This reconstruction was effectively dismantled by D. Wardle, primarily by demonstrating that the Greek does not appear in especially scabrous parts of Suetonius, and he has resuscitated the older view that Cluvius was a "man of acute insight and eloquence," writing under the Flavians. His work was probably annalistic—that is, arranged more or less by year by year, like Tacitus' *Annals* and *Histories*—and he himself was a major historian of the first century. More particularly, there is no sign that his work betrayed any notable animus against Nero.[18] Moreover, we might add that, when recriminations broke out after Nero's death and old scores were settled against his cronies, a senator prosecuting one of those cronies contrasted his despicable victim with Cluvius Rufus who, though as rich a man and as formidable an orator, had never harmed anyone (with a prosecution) under Nero.[19]

The score is thus as follows. Two major lost narratives written by contemporaries are assured, those of Pliny and of Cluvius Rufus. Both were, in all likelihood, exceptionally accurate by contemporary standards—one was written by a relatively dispassionate insider, the other was composed by an angry outsider. Along with them, a work by Fabius Rusticus was available to later authors as well; whether historical or biographical, it was hostile to Nero. And beyond these three there lay a host of lesser sources, all now forgotten, all more or less negative. Together, they form the basis of our three surviving narratives, all of them in their turn highly negative toward Nero. Of the other historians who wrote favorably of the emperor because they had been well treated by him (in the words of Josephus) and were thus, out of gratitude, "careless of the truth," not even a name survives.

When we have some notion of the faults and virtues of our sources, both lost and extant, primary and secondary, how does that affect our understanding of history? Four notorious episodes from different periods of Nero's life will show that matters are never so simple as they first appear: how his stepfather Claudius died; how he wooed his second wife, Poppaea Sabina; how he fiddled while Rome burned; and how he spoke his Famous Last Words.

I.   On 13 October, AD 54, the emperor Claudius died, poisoned with a doctored mushroom (or so we are told) by his wife Agrippina, so that her son Nero might become emperor. In his narrative of the new reign, Tacitus has Agrippina reproach Nero with the death, having her almost but not quite say that she poisoned Claudius for his sake. Soon after Nero's death, Pliny the Elder would assert bluntly that Agrippina had poisoned Claudius with a mushroom, and the anonymous play the *Octavia* would assume that she poisoned him. A spate of mushroom jokes followed the death, perhaps set off by Nero's jest that mushrooms must be the food of the gods since Claudius died from eating one. That need not be taken to imply intentional poisoning, no more than does Martial's remark to the greedy host eating a good mushroom before his guest, "May you eat such a mushroom as Claudius ate," but the satirist Juvenal made the point explicit in *his* dismissal of a similarly greedy host: "to the master, a mushroom just like those which Claudius ate, before the one prepared by his wife put an end to his eating." However, there was no mention of a mushroom in Seneca's vicious satire on the death of Claudius, the *Apocolocyntosis,* written within months of Claudius' death, nor of course in the official proclamation.[20] What do our three major sources—Suetonius, Tacitus, Dio—tell us?

As Suetonius puts it in his *Life of Claudius,*

> That Claudius was poisoned is the general belief, but when it was done and by whom is disputed. Some say that it was his taster Halotus, as he was banqueting on the Capitol with the priests. Others say that at a family dinner Agrippina served the drug to him with her own hand in mushrooms, a dish of which he was extravagantly fond.

Tacitus reports essentially the same story as Suetonius' first alternative: to forestall Claudius from making Britannicus his heir, Agrippina chose a rare poison, which was prepared by a convicted poisoner, Locusta; it was to be given to Claudius by his taster, the eunuch Halotus; and everything was so well known about the plot that writers of the time, *temporum illorum scriptores,* relate that the poison was served in a tasty mushroom. Dio relates the same tale: Agrippina determined to poison Claudius to forestall his plan to make Britannicus his heir; she sent for the convicted poisoner Locusta; the poison was served in a dish of mushrooms. Neither Dio nor Tacitus says where the murder took place, and neither betrays any knowledge of Suetonius' different versions or disputes among their common sources. Suetonius, for his part, says nothing of Locusta.[21]

He continues:

> Reports also differ *(varia fama)* as to what followed. Many *(multi)* say that as soon as he swallowed the poison he became speechless, and after suffering excruciating pain all night, died just before dawn. Some *(nonnulli)* say that he first fell into a stupor, then vomited up the whole contents of his stomach, and was given a second dose, it is unclear *(incertum)* whether in a gruel, under pretense that he must be refreshed with food after his exhaustion, or *(an)* administered in an enema, as if he were suffering from a surfeit and required relief by that form of evacuation as well.

Here Tacitus and Dio diverge, again without a hint that there might be differing stories. Dio tells us that Claudius was carried off drunk; he could neither hear nor speak; and he died during the night from the poison. This is essentially Suetonius' first version, retailed by "many." Tacitus, however, tells us that the drunken emperor had a bowel movement which may have saved him; that Agrippina was terrified and directed his doctor, Xenophon, to induce vomiting, as if to relieve the emperor further; but that he did it with a feather dipped in a swift-acting poison, "so it is believed," *creditur*. This is closer to Suetonius' second story, in that it shares the basic assumption that Claudius survived the initial attack only to be poisoned again, but differs from it in essential details as to the manner of his escape from the first poison—bowel movement vs. vomiting—and the manner in which the second and fatal dose was administered—feather vs. gruel vs. enema!

All three of our authors agree without a doubt, even the suspicious Tacitus, that Agrippina was behind the murder of her husband, alarmed as she was at recent hints that Claudius aimed to promote Britannicus. But the variations in their accounts of the deed are not petty details: they betray the simple fact that no one *really* knew what happened, who did it, where it was done, or how it was done. The point here is not to recover the "true" version of what happened. It may very well be that Agrippina did indeed poison Claudius in one of the versions presented to us. On the other hand, Claudius was a notorious glutton and drunkard, and was prone to stomach-aches so violent that he considered suicide; it may well be that he died from over-indulgence, even that he ate a poisonous (as distinct from poisoned) mushroom, or one that had gone bad. Agrippina may even have claimed credit for a murder she did not commit—we shall see an instance of similar audacity later—or her enemies may have pinned the "crime" on an innocent empress. The point is that, despite the apparent unanimity of these three sources and the smooth modern narratives derived from them, we know that *their* sources disagreed in all significant details, and yet two of the three authors (Tacitus and Dio) give no hint of this. And despite the seeming unanimity of our three sources, despite even the likelihood that a crime was involved, we simply do not know whether Claudius was murdered by his wife.[22]

II.   In the year 58, Nero was enslaved by passion for the woman who would become his second wife: the proud whore, *superba paelex,* Poppaea

Sabina. Tacitus had claimed that when his sources agreed he would follow them, but where they diverged he would name names without comment. He does not seem to have done so in the matter of Claudius' death, but the case of Poppaea tells us even more.

In his first foray into the writing of history, the *Historiae,* Tacitus had the following to say about the short-lived emperor Otho:

> For Otho's had been a neglected boyhood and a riotous youth, and he had made himself agreeable to Nero by emulating his profligacy. For this reason the emperor had entrusted to him, being the confidant of his amours, Poppaea Sabina, the imperial favourite, until he could rid himself of his wife Octavia. Soon suspecting him with regard to this same Poppaea, he sent him out of the way to the province of Lusitania, ostensibly to be its governor.

Essentially the same story appears in Suetonius' *Life of Otho.* Otho wormed his way into Nero's favor, even helped in the murder of Agrippina. Nero took Poppaea from her then-husband and consigned her temporarily to Otho in a pretense of a marriage, *nuptiarum specie.* Otho fell so violently in love with his new wife that he turned away Nero's emissaries and once even refused to allow in the emperor himself, who was reduced to threats and pleas. Nero then had the marriage end and sent Otho to Lusitania on the excuse of governing the province.

Plutarch's account is similar, in his *Life of Galba.* Otho came of good family but was corrupted by luxury from his youth onward. Nero fell in love with Poppaea while she was still married to Crispinus. Out of respect for Octavia and fear of Agrippina, he set Otho to woo Poppaea. Otho seduced her and persuaded her to leave her husband and marry himself. He was then unhappy at the prospect of sharing his new wife with Nero, and, "so they say," Poppaea enjoyed the two men's rivalry, to the point where she would shut Nero out even when Otho was away from home. Otho was rescued from his peril by Seneca, who persuaded Nero to send him to govern Lusitania.

And finally, Dio's version: Nero removed Poppaea from her husband, gave her to Otho, and shared her with him. So far, then, there is general agreement among our sources, with some variety of details.[23]

The surprise comes in Tacitus' second version of the story of Poppaea Sabina, written for his *Annals,* some years after the *Histories.* The love of

Nero's life is introduced with a brilliant portrait sketch. This was a woman who had it all—beauty, wealth, high birth, intelligence, wit—everything except a good character. While still the wife of Rufrius Crispinus she had had an affair with the young Otho, whom she subsequently married. Otho praised her so frequently and so fervently to Nero that he inflamed the emperor's passion. Poppaea worked to charm Nero, pretending to be overcome with love, but refusing to spend more than a night or two with him, since she was a married woman; at the same time she praised Otho and denigrated Nero's passion for the freedwoman Acte. Nero gradually froze Otho out of court, and eventually removed his rival to Lusitania.

This version of the affair, as has long been noticed, goes beyond mere divergence in details: it directly contradicts all the other versions, including Tacitus' own earlier account. In one rendering, Nero loves Poppaea and arranges the sham marriage with Otho, who then falls in love with his own wife. In the other, Otho marries his former lover, praises her, and Nero falls in love with her. One conclusion has been that "the odds are that one or other of the three main authorities for the reign of Nero [is] responsible for the vulgate version, which Tacitus adopted in the *Historiae* but on better knowledge rejected—hardly Cluvius Rufus the consular (he was intimate with the court), but Pliny and Fabius (either or both) might have been misled, innocent or avid for scandal." This may well be, but that Tacitus' second version is in any way the superior explanation is not obvious. Neither account is particularly convincing: both bear signs of embroidery, and the truth of the affair is beyond recall.[24]

We should keep three points in mind. First, no less a historian than Tacitus is shown to have suppressed a variant version, one which we know that he knew, and he did so a few pages after explicitly claiming that he would indicate wherever his sources differed among themselves. Second, if Tacitus had not survived to write his *Annals,* we would have no idea that there even was a second version of the tale. Third, when the divergent tales of the courtship of Poppaea are set beside the divergent tales of the incest with Agrippina, traces of two conflicting lost portraits of Nero seem to emerge: in one, he is the calculating villain; in the other, the weak victim of his passions.

III.   Everyone knows that Nero fiddled while Rome burned in 64.[25] The mixture of artistic obsession with callous indifference to human suffering is stunning: the man must have been a monster. Again, modern narratives tend to smooth over uncomfortable details, but again, the accounts of what he actually did vary disconcertingly.

Dio assures us that Nero ascended to "the roof of the palace" (or, to "the highest point of the Palatine") to get the best view of the fire; he put on the costume of a citharode; and he sang (or sang of) the Capture of Ilium. Suetonius reports that while watching the fire from the Tower of Maecenas—which stood, it is presumed, in the Gardens of Maecenas on the Esquiline, and certainly not on the Palatine—Nero was so delighted, as he said, "by the beauty of the flame" that he put on his theatrical costume (*scaenico habitu:* not, perhaps, the uniform dress of a citharode) and recited, *decantavit,* the Capture of Ilium. Tacitus offers yet a third account, with a strong dose of disbelief: all of Nero's prompt actions in relieving public misery were set at naught by the rumor which spread everywhere, that while the city was in flames the emperor had appeared on his private stage (that is, not gloating on high in his tower, or on his roof) and had sung of the destruction of Troy, comparing current evils with ancient disasters. In brief, we can see the very origins of a legend: no one knows where the incident occurred, no one actually saw it, details vary significantly as to where it happened, but two of our three sources are sure that it did happen.

What did *their* sources tell them? Tacitus offers the crucial observation: for him it is not a fact but a contemporary rumor. That is, Suetonius and Dio chose to ignore what at least one authority reported, an authority serious enough to convince Tacitus. Presumably for them the story was so true to Nero's real character that its authenticity did not matter.

IV.   Nero committed suicide on 11 June, AD 68. His death presents a quite different source problem, above all in his famous cry, *Qualis artifex pereo!*, which is usually translated something like, "What an artist dies in me!"

The story of Nero's flight from Rome in his last days is a stunning, hour-by-hour drama of mounting desperation, as recounted in the previous chapter. The accounts in Suetonius and Dio are so similar in sequence and detail that they must derive from a single source, and there are strong reasons to believe that Cluvius Rufus was that source. Cluvius was not with Nero at the end—he was in Spain—but he must have interviewed eyewitnesses among Nero's final companions, and he was also almost certainly responsible for the equally brilliant account of the death of Caligula which is preserved in Josephus' *Antiquities of the Jews*.[26]

Cluvius Rufus has been recognized more and more as "a literary artist of some stature," and it has been observed that his description of Nero's transition from life to death is richly colored by other accounts of journeys to the underworld, notably by the myth of Er in Plato's *Republic*. And the matter is considerably complicated by the astonishingly rich folkloric content of these final hours: the barefoot entry into a weird realm; the hero's escape in humble disguise; the soldier's recognition of the hero in disguise; the earthquake and lightning, sure signs of the impending death of an important person; the fairy-tale thickets and bramble bushes and reedy marshes impeding the hero's entry; the robe spread on the ground to protect the ruler's feet (in this case, his bare feet).[27] In short, the seemingly circumstantial narrative is a work of considerable artifice.

The matter is even more complicated when we recall that there is a source for Nero's last days behind Suetonius, beyond Cluvius Rufus, and beyond the surviving companions, and that source is Nero himself. His biography and his life are punctuated with self-conscious, self-dramatizing epigrams, and nowhere more so in the highly self-conscious, even theatrical, staging of his own flight and death. Of his plan to flee to Egypt and set up there as a citharode, he said: "This little talent shall support us there." When he can find no one to kill him in the palace: "Have I neither friend nor foe?" When he drinks from his hand some water scooped from a pond: "This is Nero's boiled water!" (referring to his luxurious habit of boiling water and then cooling the glass in snow). He talks to himself in the first, second, and third person: "I am living badly, disgracefully"; then, in Greek, "this does not become Nero, does not become him—one should be resolute at such times—come, rouse yourself!" When he hears the horses of his pursuers, a Homeric quote: "The thunder is beating against my ears of fast-running horses." And, after stabbing himself, to a centurion who tries to staunch the blood: "Too late" and "This is loyalty."[28] Two observations are easily made: that all of these remarks are closely tied to the context in which they are made; and that several of them are self-consciously bathetic. As such, they are typically Neronian—or just what a narrator might think Nero *should* have said.

But let us for a moment set aside the considerable doubt that Nero actually did and said what is alleged of him. What of the most famous words of all, *Qualis artifex pereo?* Dio postpones them dramatically to the very end: "and so he killed himself, after uttering that oft-quoted remark, 'Jupiter, what an artist perishes in me!'" But Suetonius places it earlier in the narrative, just after Nero has arrived at his freedman's suburban villa, hungry and thirsty, his cloak torn, and has lain down on a couch with a small pillow and an old cloak:

> At last, while his companions one and all urged him to save himself as soon as possible from the indignities that threatened him, he bade them dig a trench in his presence, proportioned to the size of his own person, collect any bits of marble that could be found, and at the same time bring water and wood for presently disposing of his body. As each of these things was done, he wept and said again and again: "What an artist the world is losing!"[29]

Nero's meaning is consistently misunderstood by modern readers, and the translations given here are representative.[30] *Artifex,* in Dio's Greek *technites,* can mean "artist" in the sense of performer, but surely the primary meaning here is "craftsman." Again, context is essential: Nero is directing the construction of his last resting-place, a mere trench in the ground decorated with odd fragments of marble; and he is therefore an artisan. And again, the remark is bathetic, of a piece with his boiled water: this is no grand tomb, but a pathetic hole in the ground, and Nero is drawing attention to the contrast between the great artist he once was and the pitiful artisan he has become, "as each of these [artisanal] things was done." In other words, he is *not* saying "what an artist dies in me," but virtually the opposite, so low has he fallen: "what an artisan I am in my dying!"

The lesson is a simple one, but worth emphasizing. Our picture of Nero the egomaniac, the monster, is so strong that we are in danger of falling into the same trap as Tacitus, Suetonius, and Cassius Dio, that is, of fitting pieces of evidence into our preconceived picture of the tyrant. "What an artist dies in me!" seems so right for Nero; but it is not what he said, not even what he is alleged to have said.

In BRIEF, our three main sources for the life of Nero, all of them deeply censorious of their subject, derive much of their narrative from three now lost sources, two of which were decidedly negative, while the third was appreciably more even-handed. Tacitus, Suetonius, and Dio can each be shown to have suppressed information that might have placed the emperor in a more favorable light, and to have presented as fact what was by no means certain. In the previous chapter we surveyed the extensive traces of a long tradition that saw him as a good man and a good ruler. Where does that leave us? There is no need to whitewash Nero: he was a bad man and a bad ruler. But there is strong evidence to suggest that our dominant sources have misrepresented him badly, creating the image of the unbalanced, egomaniacal monster, vividly enhanced by Christian writers, that has so dominated the shocked imagination of the Western tradition for two millennia. The reality was more complex.

When reading Tacitus and his colleagues, two principles of healthy skepticism should be kept in mind. In considering the "facts" they present to us we should not only weigh them for accuracy and probability, we should also be alert to the authors' constant, often implicit, interpretation of those facts: we should never accept without questioning their interpretations of the facts. And we should never, ever, accept without questioning their explanations of Nero's motives.

Portrait of the Artist

3

The people . . . once watched and applauded an actor-emperor *(scaenici imperatoris)*.

PLINY

No wonder a nobleman acts in a farce, when the emperor plays the lyre *(citharoedo principe)*.

JUVENAL

Above all, he was carried away by a craze for popularity . . . It was the general belief that after his victories on the stage he would at the next lustrum have competed with the athletes at Olympia . . . Since he was acclaimed as the equal of Apollo in music and of the Sun in driving a chariot, he had planned to emulate the exploits of Hercules as well.

SUETONIUS[1]

According to tradition, the Olympic Games were first celebrated in the year 776 BC, in honor of Zeus of Olympia, in central Greece. As the centuries passed, several competitions were added to the original foot races and wrestling contests—horse races and chariot races, discus and javelin throwing, boxing and long jump, and more—and the program expanded from one day to five. Many other international contests grew up to honor other gods, in Greece and abroad, but for more than a thousand years the Olympics remained the pinnacle of achievement, as victorious athletes won eternal glory, olive wreaths from Olympian Zeus, and prizes and pensions from their ecstatic home towns. Regardless of war and natural disaster, the Games went on at Olympia, every four years in high summer, each celebration marking the start of a new "Olympiad." From the third century BC onward, all Greek chronology was based on or synchronized with these four-year Olympiads. Only once was this fundamental cycle of historical time disrupted.

Nero arrived with a large and colorful entourage in Greece in the early autumn of the year AD 66, ready to participate in all of the major Greek contests. To do this, even though the different games were normally celebrated in different years, he ordered that they all be held within the year of his visit. Some of them then had to be given twice, but the Olympics, whose celebration had been due in the year 65, were actually postponed, for the first time in more than eight centuries, until his arrival in the following year.

Nero, who desperately wanted the glory to be won in these most traditional of competitions, was nevertheless determined to recreate the tradition on his own terms. Not only were the games of the 211th Olympiad delayed for a year, they were also pushed back from summer to autumn. To the athletic contests were added for the first time artistic competitions, which included singing and acting, for Nero's sake. In the area near the gymnasium where visitors to the games had pitched their tents for centuries, Nero erected an elaborate pavilion, tent-like but permanent, while near the great sanctuary of Zeus he built a luxurious palaestra in which to train. In one dangerous race he fell out of his chariot, but the Hellenic Judges in charge of the games nevertheless granted him the wreath of victory; he rewarded these traditionally unpaid officials with one million sesterces. Without a doubt, the emperor won every contest in which he competed. After his death the Games reverted to their normal cycle, with the 212th Olympiad beginning on schedule in 69, but Nero's bold experiment left a permanent blemish: for chronographical reasons the 211th Olympiad could not be omitted, but the official Olympian records at Elis passed over its games and their winners in silence.[2]

Nero did not go to Greece to see the sights: he went to be seen.[3] In practice, his vaunted "philhellenism" was sharply limited. The first ruling emperor to visit old Greece since Augustus did not act as Roman tourists normally acted. With certain particular exceptions, he ignored the great religious sanctuaries, and he was not initiated into any religious mystery. He did not go to Athens to study with the philosophers and rhetors of his age, and no learned conferences with any guardians of Hellenic culture are on record. Astonishingly, although he spent a year in the province of Achaia, the great philhellene never set foot in Athens or, for that matter, in Sparta. Why? Nero's presence is well attested in five cities, and in them as a group lies the answer. His sole purpose was to compete in the six great athletic and artistic contests of the time: the Actian

Games at Nicopolis; the Olympian Games at Olympia; the Nemean and the Heraean Games at Argos; the Isthmian Games at Corinth; and the Pythian Games at Delphi. Before he left Rome, he announced that he wished to become *periodonikes,* victor on the circuit of great festival games, and as he progressed through Greece accumulating prizes he was hailed by soldiers and civilians alike as *periodonikes pantonikes,* all-conquering circuit-victor.[4] The chronology of his visit in 66 and 67; his itinerary around the province; what contests he entered in which games—very little is certain.[5] But we do know in what *kinds* of contests Nero competed. They were four: the emperor of Rome sang on stage, accompanying himself on the lyre; he acted in tragedies, wearing mask and costume and supported by one or more other actors; he raced chariots in several places; and he participated in the contests of heralds, so that he could announce his own victories.[6] The Greek expedition, *peregrinatio Achaica,* was the acme, or the nadir, of Nero's career as a performer.

His conduct in Greece aroused a mixture of emotion in later writers: outrage, contempt, even baffled admiration. Central to these reactions, central to the very choice of material to report, is a paradox. There could have been no serious question as to the outcome of the "competitions." Nero had won any contest he had entered in Italy; he had even been awarded prizes for which he did not compete; and long before his arrival in Greece, the cities that held artistic competitions there were accustomed to send him their victory crowns for playing the lyre.[7] The descent of the emperor onto the stage or into the hippodrome, the confusion of patron with player, effectively stifled true competition, yet Nero seems to have been oblivious of reality. In many of his words and deeds in other contexts we can glimpse hints—through or despite our sources—of humor, however bizarre, often of ironic self-dramatization, but when we watch his actual performances from 65 onward we sense real obsession. Toward the end of his reign at least, the aspect of life which Nero took most seriously was role-playing. That fixation is the underlying theme of his Grecian adventure, as he carefully watched and tried to regulate not only his own conduct but that of his competitors, his judges, and his audience. Even discounting the intense hostility of our sources, Nero's stay in Greece looks disconcertingly like a grand fantasy.

His own role there he played in deadly earnest. He suffered dreadfully from stage-fright before competitions, and while singing he sedulously obeyed the rules, never daring to spit, and wiping the sweat from his brow

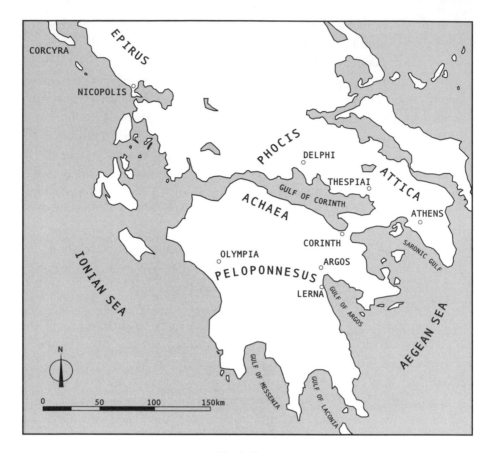

Nero's Greece

with his arm (handkerchiefs were forbidden). When performing in tragedies he wore the full costume with high boots and mask, the mask sometimes showing the likeness of the character, sometimes his own portrait,
but in the case of women's roles it was always the visage of his late wife,
Poppaea Sabina. Once, while acting in a tragedy, he dropped and quickly
recovered his scepter. He was terrified that he might be disqualified for the
lapse, but his fellow actor assured him that the audience, in its joy, had
not even noticed. Later tradition embroidered this stage-fright, having
him worry about making the wrong entrance, wearing the wrong costume, even choosing the wrong scepter, and Dio in fact confirms that he
spoke and acted and suffered on stage just as ordinary actors did—with
the single exception that when the plot required him to be bound, the
chains were to be not of iron but of gold, as befitted an emperor.[8]

This elaborate attention to the rules of competition appears in Nero's first public performance in Rome, at the Second Neronia in 65: in Tacitus' account, "he entered the theatre, and conformed to all the laws of harp-playing, not sitting down when tired, nor wiping off the perspiration with anything but the garment he wore, or letting himself be seen to spit or clear his nostrils. Last of all, on bended knee he saluted the assembly with a motion of the hand, and awaited the verdict of the judges with pretended anxiety." *Ficto pavore,* "pretended anxiety": the pretense is surely Tacitean comment, for Suetonius notes, of Nero's tour of Greece, "The trepidation and anxiety with which he took part in contests, his keen rivalry of his opponents and his awe of the judges, can hardly be credited," and proceeds to illustrate his behavior.[9]

That he was perfectly serious in performance is confirmed by his utter seriousness in training. From the beginning of his reign, a decade before he competed on the lyre in public, he had thrown himself into the discipline:

> As soon as he became emperor he sent for Terpnus, the greatest master of the lyre in those days, and after listening to him sing after dinner for many successive days until late at night, he little by little began to practice himself, neglecting none of the exercises which artists of that kind are in the habit of following, to preserve or strengthen their voices. For he used to lie upon his back and hold a leaden plate on his chest, purge himself by the syringe and by vomiting, and deny himself fruits and all foods injurious to the voice.

Pliny adds that he would sing while lying under the leaden plate, and even went so far as to eat nothing but chives in oil on certain days each month. Nero would carefully maintain this kind of training and discipline throughout his reign, up until his very last days, with fatal results.[10]

No ancient estimate of Nero's skill as a charioteer survives, but there were clearly two opinions about his talent as a singer and actor. The main tradition has it that his voice was "husky and feeble," or "slight and indistinct," and the legend that saw him reincarnated brought him back as a frog. On the other hand, an anonymous critic wrote of his "honey-sweet songs in melodious voice"; another author mentions a poor voice much improved by training; a contemporary critic admitted that he sang well; and for a False Nero to succeed, he needed to show his skill with lyre and song.[11]

That is to say, he had some talent, but talented or not, Nero's punctili-
ousness about training and the etiquette of competition suggests that he
believed in his abilities. When Vindex insulted him in edicts circulated toward the end, nothing stung like the taunt that he was a bad performer,
malum citharoedum. The charge refuted itself, Nero said: how could he
possibly be accused of lacking skill in an art in which he had so labored to
perfect himself? Nevertheless, he would frequently ask people if they knew
anyone who was his superior.[12] It is this very insecurity that is so telling:
he knew that he was good, but he was not sure how good. It may be that
when he performed everyone else pretended to be impressed, but he was
in deadly earnest. He knew that the stakes were high for a man in his position. According to Dio, all his victories were proclaimed thus: "Nero
Caesar wins this contest and crowns the Roman people and the civilized
world."[13]

He was, accordingly, highly competitive. If his rivals on the Grecian
tour were as talented as he, he would treat them respectfully and try to
win their favor, but he would slander them in private. Sometimes he
would glower at them as he strolled about with his attendants, sometimes
actually hurl abuse at them. If they were very talented, he would try instead to bribe them. How these rivals reacted, we do not know, but in
citharody they included the greatest virtuosi of the day—Terpnus, his
own teacher, and Diodorus, who was happy at least to ride in Nero's chariot when the emperor held a triumph back in Rome for his artistic victories in Greece.[14]

Suetonius further claims that Nero attacked even the memory of earlier
victors in the sacred games, ordering that their statues and busts be overturned and dragged off to the latrines. This is surely exaggerated, but the
charge that he did abuse at least some competitors persists in the tradition: it is alleged that he not only defeated the superannuated citharode
Pammenes, whom he had forced to come out of retirement, but vandalized his statues as well. A source of dubious reliability goes even further, to
claim that Nero had a rival tragic actor grotesquely murdered at the Isthmian Games, his throat smashed in by the writing tablets of other actors.[15]
True or not, again the accusation that his artistic rivalries turned lethal
stuck to him. While he was still in Greece, his agent in Rome allegedly
had a nobleman and his son murdered because they would not surrender
the family surname Pythicus, "Pythian Victor," a title which now belonged to Nero after his triumphs in the games at Delphi. And after he re-

turned to Rome, the emperor had Paris the pantomime killed, according to one version of the story because he wished to learn the art of dancing from him but had no talent for it, according to another version simply because he was a serious rival; the two stories may actually be one.[16]

That his aggressive competitiveness might lead (or be thought to have led) to murder is not difficult to understand. One story is particularly telling. In a notorious incident at the Olympic Games, Nero tried to race a ten-horse team. He was thrown from the chariot, climbed back in (or rather, was replaced, *repositus*), but could not finish the course. The judges awarded him the crown anyway. It is easy to react to this episode with contempt: Nero fell out of his chariot, and *still* the servile Greeks gave him the prize. But the proper response should be one of astonishment. Racing a chariot drawn by the normal two- or four-horse team was difficult and dangerous at the best of times, demanding extraordinary skill: "bumps crashes and head-on collisions were the rule rather than the exception." Trying to control, let alone direct, a team of ten horses around twelve laps of a course with hairpin turns was an act of hubris which Nero himself had criticized in a friend, Mithridates, King of the Bosporus. Yet he had felt impelled to try, perhaps precisely because his friend had done it. When he fell from the chariot, we are told, he came very close to being run over. Yet despite this fright and despite the pain, he had insisted on returning to the race. In any other man but Nero this might be have been taken for courage, however foolhardy. But what should be remarked upon is both the grandness of the folly and the extraordinary determination in pursuit of it. This was no pretense: it was obsession.[17]

Not surprisingly, Nero lived in fear of the judges, particularly those at the Olympic Games, who wielded whips, and (so Dio reports) he tried to bribe them. Before he began to perform he would address the judges with the greatest respect: "I have done everything that I should, but the outcome is in the hand of Fortune; you, being wise and experienced men, ought to discount anything due to mere chance." When they reassured him he went away somewhat calmer, but even then he worried and openly declared his suspicion that what appeared to be silent modesty among the judges was in fact sullen malice. Yet not only did he richly remunerate the Olympian judges who awarded him the crown for chariot-racing, despite his not completing the course, he also bestowed on the Isthmian judges a large sum of money and Roman citizenship as well.[18]

All great performers had their own claques (*fautores histrionum*) to cheer them on and to whip up the audience with elaborate rhythmic chants and hand-clapping. It was at his private Juvenile Games, celebrated in 59, that Nero first introduced his Augustiani, Roman knights in their prime who made both day and night ring with applause and praise of Nero's godlike beauty and voice: "Beautiful Caesar, Apollo, Augustus, another Pythian! By yourself (we swear), Caesar, no one conquers you." By the time Nero first appeared in public in Naples, in 64, these Roman knights were backed by some 5,000 hardy plebeian youths. They were divided into groups, *factiones,* to learn the different elaborate forms of clapping (imported from Alexandria)—"the buzzings," "the tiles," "the bricks"—by which Nero had been captivated and which they performed vigorously when he sang. For they too were performers, remarkable for a sort of uniform, with thick hair, dandified dress, and their left hands bare of rings.[19] They accompanied the emperor to Greece and returned with him to celebrate his "triumph" in Rome in 68, where they followed his chariot, shouting out that they were the Augustiani and the soldiers of his triumph, and surely leading the acclaim:

> Hail, Olympian victor! Hail, Pythian victor! Augustus! Augustus! To Nero Hercules! To Nero Apollo! The only victor of the grand tour, the only one from the beginning of time! Augustus! Augustus! Divine voice: blessed are those who hear you!

It is also alleged that the audience was strictly controlled during the emperor's performances, in Greece certainly, and perhaps at the Neronia in 65, but whether this was by Nero's order is not clear. Gates were shut and no one could leave the theater. We are told that women even gave birth there, while many desperate people either jumped down from the walls or pretended to be dead in order to be carried out. Tacitus says that soldiers beat those who did not applaud with sufficient enthusiasm, and that several knights died either in the crush of bodies or from staying in the same seats day and night. According to Dio, those who showed any emotion less than rapture were denied admission to the emperor. Suetonius echoes this in one passage, alleging that the emperor's friendship was given or withdrawn according to the enthusiasm with which one praised him. Elsewhere he gives an actual instance: when Nero was singing, one of his companions, the future emperor Vespasian, either left the theater frequently or fell asleep, with the result that the deeply offended Nero removed him from his entourage and refused to admit him into his presence. Again, later tradition embellished this portrait of a tyrant, to the point of imagining the spectators being prosecuted: "you didn't come to hear Nero," "you came but you were distracted," "you laughed," "you didn't clap," "you didn't sacrifice on behalf of his voice, with a prayer that he would have even more success with it at Delphi."[20] Most important, however, is that we are told reliably that the crowds in general and the soldiers in particular approved his performances and chanted their praises of him. A cynic might say that Nero bought their favor as he had that of the judges: the people he won with his announcement of the liberation of Greece; the soldiers (we are told) had been bribed.[21]

Thus we have a picture of an emperor who believed in his own talent, an emperor who thought that when he performed he represented Rome as surely as a general on campaign, an emperor who competed strenuously on stage or in the circus, before thousands of his subjects. Rivals, judges, and audiences were cajoled or bullied into playing along. How had the principate reached such a pass, and what did it mean?

SPECTACULA, the Roman games, long regarded as peripheral to the study of Roman life, crude relaxations at best, have assumed a centrality in modern understanding of it.[22] By Nero's day there was a broad range of public entertainments available for Romans rich and poor, and they would find it in three places above all. If size is an indication of popularity, then the most popular amusement was to be found in the circus, the long ellipse devoted to competitive racing of chariots; the largest site for this (though by no means the only one) in Rome was the Circus Maximus, which lay in the valley between the Palatine and the Aventine Hills, covering an area some 650 by 125 meters, and which may have seated as many as 150,000 people. Next came the amphitheater, a towering open cylinder, roughly circular, in which spectators surrounded and looked down on the arena where gladiators fought each other, hunters pursued wild beasts, criminals were executed, and (when flooded) naval battles might be reenacted. The largest of these, begun soon after Nero's death, was the Flavian Amphitheater, the famous Colosseum, which could hold 70,000 to 80,000 people; before that, the main arena had been that of the Amphitheater of Statilius Taurus, which was located somewhere in the Campus Martius and was destroyed in the Great Fire of 64. The third venue, much smaller again, was the semicircular theater where several thousand spectators might watch and listen to all manner of drama, music, and dance on stage and in the orchestra. Of these the most important, often called simply the Theater, was the Theater of Pompey, which may have held about 12,000 spectators and which again lay in the Campus Martius, as did the other two great theaters, that of Marcellus (perhaps 13,000 spectators) and that of Balbus (c. 8,000).[23]

In fact the three sites—theater, amphitheater, circus—overlap functionally. Actual games, *ludi,* might include any or all of the different performances, and with the exception of chariot-racing each might be held anywhere. The confusion of categories is well illustrated by the inauguration of Pompey's Theater in 55 BC, when both musical and athletic contests were held there, while in the Circus some 500 lions were slaughtered over five days, and 18 elephants fought with men in heavy armor.[24] The vocabulary of spectacle likewise blurs easy distinctions: *histrio,* actor, can also mean dancer (in pantomime); theater can signify amphitheater as well; *cantare,* to sing, can also mean to act in a tragedy. This looseness of boundaries is significant: gladiatorial combat is highly theatrical, for instance, while real sex and violence can invade the stage. All public entertainments were subsumed under the single word "spectacle," as in the late Republic and early Empire (it has been claimed) *civis Romanus* became *homo spectator.*

As Ludwig Friedlaender demonstrated over a century ago, and as has been confirmed repeatedly, Roman games, far from being peripheral entertainments, constituted a central act of empire. The satirist Juvenal put a famously gloomy face on it: the Roman people "set aside their cares when they stopped selling their votes. For they who once bestowed command, rods of office, legions, everything, now have restricted themselves to praying anxiously for only two things: *panem et circenses,* bread and circuses." But Juvenal's younger contemporary, the orator and teacher of emperors Cornelius Fronto, put the same matter much more positively. Speaking of the warrior emperor Trajan's success in the arts of peace, and his consequent vast popularity, Fronto wrote, "They seem to be based on the loftiest principles of political wisdom, that the Emperor did not neglect even actors and the other performers of the stage, the circus, or the amphitheatre, knowing as he did that the Roman People are held fast by two things above all, *annona et spectaculis,* the grain-dole and the shows, that the success of a government depends on amusements as much as more serious things; neglect of serious matters entails the greater loss, ne-

glect of amusements the greater discontent; . . . by largesses of food only
the proletariat on the grain-register are conciliated singly and individually,
whereas by the shows the whole populace is kept in a good humour."[25]

Cicero, speaking in the 50s BC, claimed that "there are three locations
especially in which the Roman people can give expression to their judgment and sentiment: the public meetings, the polls, and the games and
gladiator shows."[26] Beginning in the last decades of the Republic, the
games at Rome—particularly theatrical plays, gladiatorial combats, and
chariot races—took on an ever more overtly political aspect. There the
"Roman people," often prompted by paid claques, but more often it
seems spontaneously, took advantage of large numbers and individual an-
onymity to proclaim their views about current public issues, loudly and
directly, to their leaders. It was generally understood that things could be
said within the special confines of a theater, circus, or arena which could
not be said elsewhere: Tacitus has a phrase for it, *theatralis licentia,* theatrical license.[27] Such expressions of popular sentiment could be aroused by
any issue—a tax, a law, a grain shortage, or the popularity or unpopularity
of prominent men and women, whose public bearing and private lives
would be scrutinized remorselessly, often in their presence. This outlet
provided by the games became even more important under the principate,
as one-man rule stifled republican politics, and the institutions of debate
(the public meetings) and voting (the assemblies) faded away. At the
games it soon became the custom for the people to make requests directly
to the emperor, often to determine the fate of an individual, from freeing
a successful gladiator to removing a hated courtier, often to win public
concessions such as a reduction in taxes or in the price of grain. The conventionally "good" emperor, the *civilis princeps,* always granted such requests or offered reasons for not doing so, and he did it if possible in person, in his own words and gestures. He in turn could assure himself of his
people's loyalty; he could assure his people of their mutual interests; and
he could diminish public tension. In short, theatrical license continued an
important element in public life at imperial Rome.

The games themselves, it has been observed, became a sort of political
theater, and there is certainly a strong theatrical element to all of them.
Like a play, they were held at a special time and in a special place, they followed elaborate rules, and the spectators themselves acted out a particular
role. What that role was is not hard to define. Rules varied according to
location (theater or amphitheater—the circus was much less regulated),

they shifted over time, and their observation fluctuated considerably, but by convention and by law from the last century BC onward, spectators at the public games were required to wear costumes as well: ordinary citizens were to put on their togas, with senators and knights having special marks of rank; soldiers were to wear decorations; priests and priestesses were to don their ceremonial robes. To underscore the formality of the occasion, the spectators were to sit in sections assigned not according to ticket price or ease of watching, but according to their place in society—senators and knights in the front rows, soldiers and civilians separated, married and single, free and slave, and so forth.[28] Dressed in the appropriate costume, then, assigned to the appropriate social grouping, the members of the audience were not mere spectators, but actors as well, playing themselves, the Roman people. Thus, behind the cynicism of Juvenal and the earnest precepts of Fronto about *"annona et spectacula,"* there lay a positive truth: the games lent themselves to a ritualized dialogue between the emperor and his people.

The ambiguities of the Roman games, the blurring of distinction between spectacle and spectator, extends to the role of performers. At first glance, there was a tremendous gulf between audience and performers. The physical boundary, augmented by an open space or a barrier, and defined vertically (spectators looking down), was strongly reinforced by a social divide: performers were by definition different and inferior. Actors, dancers, gladiators, charioteers were overwhelmingly foreign in origin, often from the Greek East, and more often than not ex-slaves or the descendants of slaves. They also tended, in the eyes of some, to be immoral, artificial, sexually ambiguous, and—equally contemptible to old-fashioned Romans—they were paid for their services. Yet, at the same time, they could be sex symbols who might be powerfully attractive by birth and by training; they could even be larger-than-life culture heroes, their images circulated everywhere in every imaginable kind of souvenir; some were wealthy beyond the dreams of avarice, idolized by the people and lionized by the aristocracy. Seneca observed: "I could show you youths of the bluest blood who are enslaved by dancers: there is no servitude more disgraceful than that which is voluntary."[29]

The deepest ambivalence toward performers and performance was to be discovered within the educated upper classes, who might both despise performers and fear their disruptive effect on society. Their objections had two aspects: critics found the spectacles politically suspect in that (in the succinct formulation of a modern scholar, referring to the theater alone) they "brought people together for no legitimate purpose, excited them, cost money, and won popularity for the giver"; and critics found the games morally corrupt, in that (in the formulation ascribed to a conservative senator in Tacitus' *Dialogue on Orators*) the Roman passion for actors, gladiators, and horses, inculcated almost in the womb, drove out all virtue.[30] At the same time, others in the aristocracy not only shared the common passion for performers and the games but even felt an irresistible desire to cross over the gap into the spectacle, just as players and performance crossed into real life. In each generation from the days of Julius Caesar, numbers of senators and knights repeatedly succumbed to the urge to perform in public at the games, acting on stage or fighting in the arena (but seldom racing chariots in the circus)—not because of poverty or coercion, but because they wanted to. This desire ran quite contrary to the maintenance of aristocratic dignity, and a series of legal measures reiterated complex (and often flouted) prohibitions on members of the two upper orders of society and their immediate families performing in public on stage or fighting in the arena.[31] (Professional chariot-racing was apparently far less seductive a pastime for the aristocracy: their amateur status was more clearly observed, the professionals were less stigmatized by law and society, and there is no record of legal strictures.)[32]

Thus, Nero did what many of his peers had done for generations. When he came to present himself to the public in 59 as a charioteer and an actor, he was able to appeal to antiquity. He reminded his subjects that horse-racing was the pastime of kings and that it was indulged in by the leaders of the (Roman) state, as indeed abundant evidence makes clear for the days of the kings and the early Republic.[33] He also claimed, again correctly, that it honored the gods: the races were religious in origin at Rome, and a religious procession, bringing the gods down from the Capitol to the Circus, marked the beginning of each circus games, *ludi circenses*. Turning to the art of the citharode, he noted that songs were sacred to Apollo, and that the great and prescient god was portrayed in the dress of a singer not only in the cities of Greece but in Roman temples.

Our major ancient sources (Tacitus, Suetonius, Dio) are somewhat misleading when it comes to Nero's performances: according to them, not only was he disgracing his dignity, but the elite of Rome had to fall in with his plans, impelled by fear, flattery, or bribery. In fact the evidence for coercion is sparse and unreliable, yet Tacitus' picture of Nero's praetorian prefect Burrus, weeping as he led the applause, is indelible. As we have seen, Nero was far from alone in his urge to perform, and Tacitus admits that some men actually indulged his tastes because they wanted to. The ex-consul and future emperor Vitellius made no secret of the fact, well after Nero's death, that he had admired him and truly enjoyed his singing, while Fabius Valens (consul in 69) had as a young man played in mimes at Nero's games, at first "as if" by necessity, then of his own free will. To Tacitus these men were examples of depravity; but what did he make of the serious historian Cluvius Rufus, whom he trusted as an authority and who as an ex-consul had acted as Nero's herald when he sang at Rome in 65 and in Greece in 66? We do not know, but Tacitus mentions without comment a curious incident involving Nero's conservative critic, Thrasea Paetus. Thrasea was notably cool to Nero's Juvenile Games of 59, in which Nero performed as a citharode, and this particularly annoyed the emperor because Thrasea himself had not long before dressed up in the costume of a tragedian to sing in ancient games at his home-town of Patavium. Dio makes it clear that this action was rightly brought up as a criticism of Thrasea at the time, when he ostentatiously refused to listen to Nero's performances, to sacrifice to his divine voice, or to give recitals himself. Neither author records why Thrasea had acted on stage, or how his actions differed from Nero's performances at his own private festival. Similarly, Tacitus does not comment on the noble conspirator Calpurnius Piso, who enjoyed acting in tragic costume.[34] In short, the aristocrat's attitude to performance, despite the condemnation of our sources, is by no means one of simple repulsion. Nero could count on considerable sympathy among the leaders of society.

At the same time, the common people egged Nero on, early and late. Soon after the murder of Agrippina in 59, he invited the people of Rome to watch him race chariots in the Vatican Gardens, and "they extolled him in their praises, like a mob which craves amusements and rejoices when a prince draws them the same way." At the second Neronian Games in 65, when he was too modest to appear, the crowd called for his "divine voice," *caelestis vox,* and demanded that he share the fruits of his artistic endeavors. Nero hesitated; the soldiers added their pleas to those of the people; and Vitellius persuaded him to return to the theater. He then performed to the lyre, assiduously following all the rules, and in return the people treated him as they did all professionals. Tacitus records the scene with astonishment: "And then the city-populace *(plebs urbis),* who were wont to encourage every gesture even of actors, made the place ring with measured

Nero's Italy

strains of elaborate applause. One would have thought they were rejoicing, and perhaps they did rejoice, in their indifference to the public disgrace."[35] Just as the whole population had welcomed Nero's return from
Naples after the death of Agrippina, so it turned out in 67 to cheer the return of their emperor from his artistic and athletic victories in Greece.[36]
Explain it as they may, no ancient writer denies that the common people
of Rome loved what Nero was doing. The younger Pliny, in his panegyric
of the later emperor Trajan, flatly asserts that the people were different in
Nero's day: "And so the same populace which once watched and applauded the performances of an actor-emperor *(scaenici imperatoris)* has
now [AD 100] even turned against the professional mimes and damns their
perverted art as a taste unworthy of our age. This shows that even the vulgar crowd can take a lesson from its rulers."[37]

Despite the moral strictures of the authors who report Nero's actions, the social context must be seen as an ambiguous one, and public attitudes as deeply ambivalent. Many of his people surely disapproved of their emperor's games and the damage done to his imperial dignity, but many more just as surely applauded him. His actions sprang from patterns of behavior familiar in contemporary noblemen and approved by ancient precedent, and his people encouraged him. Killing relatives and rivals, real or imaginary, was cold political reality; performing in public may have been a fantasy, but it was one shared by a large part of Roman society. Whether it could be seen as part of the supreme imperial virtue, *civilitas,* is a matter for debate.[38]

Nero the performer is inseparable from Nero the patron, the giver of the games. To trace and evaluate his career as an artist it is necessary to look at the games of his reign, to identify as closely as possible the nature of each spectacle and of Nero's involvement, and to emphasize certain themes which are easy to overlook when the games are viewed piecemeal.

AD 55.   In 55, some time after the break with his mother, Nero presented a spectacle with men hunting bulls from horseback, while the cavalry of his bodyguard slew 400 bears and 300 lions with javelins, and some 30 knights fought as gladiators (there is no hint of coercion).[39] These are presumably the same games which were being prepared in that year by Nero under the direction, the *cura ludorum,* of Arruntius Stella, an ally of Agrippina.[40]

AD 57.   In 57, Tacitus remarks sarcastically, little worthy of note happened, unless one wished to praise the foundations and the wooden beams of the huge amphitheater *(molem amphitheatri)* which "Caesar" constructed in the Campus Martius.[41] This wooden amphitheater, which was erected in less than a year, was the site of a *gladiatorium munus* in which the emperor had no one killed, not even criminals.[42] It was apparently at the same *munus* that Nero exhibited 400 senators and 600 knights (the numbers are impossibly high) as gladiators, beast-fighters, and various functionaries of the arena; a sea battle, *naumachia,* was fought in sea water among sea creatures; and various pyrrhic dances were performed—dances that were originally Greek war dances, but seem now to have been realistic reenactments of Greek myth, including Pasiphae and the bull, and the fall of Icarus, whose blood splashed the emperor.[43] Dio elaborates: Nero flooded a "theater" with sea water and sea creatures, and exhibited a naval battle between "Persians" and "Athenians"; he then had the area drained and dried, and reverted to gladiatorial fights between both individuals and groups.[44]

Although Nero was the president of the games, the 19-year-old emperor rarely presided, preferring to watch them from a private box.[45] There is again no suggestion that aristocratic performers were coerced.

AD 59.   Sometime after the murder of his mother in late March of 59 Nero presented two great games, both novelties in the history of Roman spectacle. Together they marked a turning point in his career as emperor.

The first of these were the Ludi Maximi, "the games which he wished to call 'the greatest' because they were undertaken for the eternity of the empire."[46] Men and women of both the senatorial and the equestrian order took part (again, no mention of coercion), among them a distinguished knight who rode an elephant down a tightrope. A comedy, "The Fire," by the second century BC playwright Afranius was revived with such a degree of realism that the actors were allowed to keep whatever furnishings they could save from the burning house on stage. Every day gifts or tickets for gifts were showered down on the crowds: birds, food, grain, clothes, gold, silver, jewels, pearls, paintings, slaves, draft animals, trained wild animals—even ships, apartment buildings, and estates. All of this extravagance Nero watched from the proscenium of the stage, that is, (presumably) from a balcony on the set.[47]

Suetonius gives no indication of the date of the Ludi Maximi in his account of Nero's spectacles. It is only when we turn to Dio, as represented in epitome, that we can appreciate the enormity of Nero's actions. The chronological sequence in Dio-Xiphilinus is important. In the stunned aftermath of the murder of Agrippina, Nero was reassured by envoys expressing their joy at her death and his salvation. The senate and the people of Rome rejoiced, and their emperor entered the city to public applause.[48] Covert protest also surfaced in the form of pasquinades, but Nero would allow no charges to be lodged against the alleged authors.[49] There were bad omens: while sacrifices were being offered "because of Agrippina," by decree of the senate, there was a total eclipse of the sun; when elephants drawing the chariot of Augustus entered the Circus and had advanced to the seats of the senators, they stopped short and would not go further; and Nero's own banqueting table in his villa at Subicao was struck by lightning.[50] The emperor allegedly arranged the demise of his aunt Domitia.[51] Then, "because of his mother he celebrated the lavish Ludi Maximi for several days in five or six theaters together." That was when the elephant walked down the tightrope from the highest vault in the theater; the men and women of both the senatorial and the equestrian orders performed in theater, amphitheater, and circus; and the valuable presents (horses, slaves, draft animals, gold, silver, clothes) were given away in the form of tokens thrown by Nero into the crowd.[52] At the same time he celebrated many sacrifices "for his preservation *(soteria),* as he put it," and dedicated a large public marketplace.

Three points emerge when Dio's narrative is placed next to that of Suetonius (both of them reflecting a common source). First, the Ludi Maximi were staged to celebrate Nero's salvation from the plots of his mother, the "eternity of the empire" being equated with the preservation of the emperor.[53] His letter to the senate from Naples soon after the deed had so magnified her crimes as to make her death a public blessing, and emphasized his own amazement that he was now actually "safe." The senate decreed thanksgivings to the gods, and various other forms of commemoration, while the Arval Brothers, a priestly college composed of senators, sacrificed on 5 April for the "safety" of Nero Claudius Caesar and on 23 June for his safety and his return, on the latter occasion (significantly) in the Forum of Augustus to Mars the Avenger.[54]

Second, although Nero presided over the games and threw out *missilia,* tokens to be redeemed for presents, he did not himself perform in the games.

Third, there was no overt coercion of the upper classes to participate: Suetonius registers their actions neutrally, and while Dio asserts vaguely that some of them performed willingly, some unwillingly, that assertion is deeply embedded in a long passage of outraged opinion and rhetorical embellishment.[55] Tacitus, while not mentioning the Ludi Maximi by name, refers to them in his condemnation of Nero's yearning to play the cithara and to race chariots in public, at the time of the rejoicing at his mother's death.[56] Thus, he brought on stage members of the nobility, who were driven by their poverty, and whom he rewarded well; and he "forced" prominent knights to appear as gladiators "with huge gifts, since payment from one who can command carries the force of compulsion." That is to say, despite his insinuations, Tacitus had no evidence that anyone was compelled to participate.[57]

The other new games celebrated in 59 were the Ludi Iuvenalium, the Juvenile Games, or Juvenalia for short.[58] Tacitus and Dio both give roughly the same narrative of the event, under the year 59, and after the Ludi Maximi, although only Dio notes the reason for the games—that they celebrated the first shaving of the 21-year-old Nero's beard, which he placed in a golden ball and offered to Jupiter Capitolinus.[59]

There are three essential elements in the pertinent narratives of Dio and Tacitus. First, as in the Ludi Maximi, men and women of high rank and every age took part in theatrical performances: they acted in both Greek and Latin, with most unmasculine gestures and noblewomen playing unseemly roles (Tacitus);[60] a lady in her eighties, Aelia Catella, danced in a pantomime; others too old or too ill to perform alone sang in chorus; people of both sexes and all ages took classes in the performing arts; and Nero forbade anyone to wear a mask on stage, saying that it was the people's will (Dio). Elderly ex-consuls and aged matrons took part (Suetonius).[61]

Second, the entertainment included elaborate refreshments as well. In the grove surrounding the Naumachia of Augustus, across the Tiber, Nero erected booths to sell food, drink, and other luxuries, and he gave spending money to people of all ranks (according to Tacitus, who waxes eloquent but vague on the opportunities thus afforded for indulgence in vice). After his own performance, the emperor feasted his people on boats in the Naumachia, and sailed from there at midnight down a canal into the Tiber (Dio).

Third, the climax of the occasion was the emperor's own appearance on stage. He sang to the lyre, with his voice coaches standing by; soldiers and officers of the Praetorian Guard, including the prefect Burrus, were in attendance; and his claque of Roman knights, the "Augustiani," made their first appearance to applaud the emperor's beauty and talent and to shower him with divine epithets (Tacitus). On another view, he appeared in the theater dressed as a citharode and announced by Gallio (an ex-consul); he sang in the presence of soldiers and a large civilian audience a piece called "Attis, or the Bacchantes"; Seneca and Burrus acted as prompters; and 5,000 Augustiani led the audience in cheers, comparing their emperor to Apollo (Dio).

Again the story is plausible and consistent. The Juvenalia involved the

people of Rome as spectators and the nobility, including Nero, as performers. Again, there is no sure testimony that anyone was coerced to participate. But the Ludi Iuvenalium are sharply distinct from the Ludi
Maximi. The Ludi Maximi had been public games, celebrating the preservation of emperor and empire; they had included spectacles in theater,
amphitheater, and circus; and the emperor had presided over them. The
Juvenalia, on the other hand, were private games, instituted by Nero (in
Tacitus' opinion) "so that he might not yet be disgraced in the public theater." They celebrated the private ceremony of shaving and dedicating a
young man's beard; they seem to have involved only theatricals in the
strict sense; and it was perfectly legitimate for citizens to participate in
what were (ostensibly) purely private performances.[62]

AD 60.   The following year saw another sensational innovation, not in
the identity of the performers, but in the nature of the spectacles themselves. Nero introduced Greek games to Rome. As described by Suetonius,
"He was also the first person to found at Rome quinquennial games, in
three parts, in the Greek fashion, musical, gymnastic, and equestrian,
which he called the Neronia."[63] While in many ways similar to Roman
spectacula, these were very much modeled on the great games of old
Greece—the Olympic Games, the Delphic Games, and the like. Just as at
those games, which were sacred to the gods, so here, pantomimes were explicitly excluded: this meant no wild factional scuffling, and no octoge-
narian noblewomen dancing. Nero dedicated his new baths and the ad-
joining gymnasium in the Greek style, the first in Rome, and as a good
Greek patron he distributed oil to the senators and the knights, while the
people of Rome played along by wearing Greek dress.[64]

Curiously, there is no record of the equestrian contest, while of the
gymnastic contests we know only that he invited the Vestal Virgins to
watch, just as the priestesses of Ceres were allowed to observe the Olympic Games.[65] But the story of the musical contests is remarkable. Nero
placed ex-consuls, chosen by lot, in charge of the games. He himself sat in
the orchestra of the theater with the other senators. The crown for Latin
oratory and poetry (apparently a single prize), which had been contended
for by men of the highest distinction, was nevertheless conceded by them
to Nero. In the words of Tacitus, no one took the first prize, but Caesar
was declared the victor.[66] (According to his biography, the young Lucan

first came to public attention for his *Laudes Neronis,* or Praise of Nero, at these games, and he even won a crown for it in the Theater of Pompey.)[67] In another version, the judges offered Nero the crown for playing the lyre without even holding a contest, but this he refused, paying honor to the crown and ordering it to be carried to the statue of Augustus.[68] He nevertheless proceeded in the dress of a citharode to the gymnasium to be enrolled as the victor.

Beyond the momentous innovation of bringing Greek games to Rome, one that was accepted by the public and imitated by Nero's successors, there are two aspects of the First Neronia to be emphasized. One is that for all his talent, Nero was still not a competitor—indeed seems not to have performed at all. An unfortunate corollary of this non-involvement was the novel practice of awarding him prizes regardless. From now on all of the crowns won for playing the lyre in all contests were sent to him as the only one worthy of victory.[69] These he received gratefully, granting to the envoys who brought them priority in admission to his presence and even inviting them to his private banquets; when some of them begged him to sing during dinner and praised him lavishly, he exclaimed, "Only the Greeks know how to listen and only they are worthy of my efforts!" (Suetonius). The other image to be noted is that of Nero, dressed as a citharode, not only accepting the prize but being inscribed formally as the victor—a large step on the road to professionalism, for all his amateur status.

AD 63.　This year witnessed gladiatorial *spectacula* as magnificent as any in the past, but several senators and noblewomen disgraced themselves by appearing in the arena, according to Tacitus.[70] Again, there is no mention of coercion.

AD 64.　In 64, Nero for the first time raced chariots in public.[71] According to Dio, he also produced a wild-beast hunt; then flooded the "theater" to stage a sea-battle; then drained it and presented gladiators; and then flooded it again to hold a public banquet, the notorious banquet of Tigellinus. This banquet was also recorded by Tacitus without any reference to the preceding marvels of engineering, and it is assigned by him not to a theater but to the Lake of Agrippa in the Campus Martius.[72]

After the Great Fire, Nero held a private *spectaculum* in his gardens at which the Christians convicted of burning the city were executed in various dramatic ways, and at the accompanying circus games he himself mixed with the people dressed as a charioteer or standing in a chariot.[73]

AD 65.   In 65 the Neronia were celebrated for the second time. A chronological problem in our sources should be mentioned here, although it is not too important.

Directly after his account of the public debut in Naples, which occurred in 64, Suetonius continues that Nero was so eager to sing in Rome that he brought back the Neronia before it was due.[74] Everyone demanded to hear the "divine voice," so he promised that he would give the opportunity to do so to anyone who wanted it in his gardens. But when the soldiers of his guard added their prayers to those of the people, he happily agreed to perform immediately, and without delay he ordered that his name be added to the list of citharodes who were competing. He cast his own lot into the urn with the others, and when it was his turn he entered with the praetorian prefects bearing his lyre and followed by the tribunes of the guard and his intimate friends. He stood there, made his introduction, announced through the ex-consul Cluvius Rufus that he would sing "Niobe," and kept at it until late in the day. But he then announced that he was postponing both the awarding of the crown and the other events of the games until the following year, in order that there might be more occasions for him to sing.[75]

Tacitus fills out the story of the Second Neronia, but he assigns it to the year 65, after the Pisonian conspiracy, with no mention of the postponement from 64. This second celebration of the games took place amid rumors that the treasure of Queen Dido had been discovered in North Africa, and this gave orators excellent material for praising the emperor and the dawn of a new Golden Age.[76] As the games approached, the senate (in order to avoid disgrace, in Tacitus' opinion) again offered him the crowns for both oratory and singing. This time, however, Nero refused, confident that pure talent would win him the prizes. He recited a poem onstage. Then, when the crowd demanded that he make public all of his talents, *ut omnia studia sua publicaret* (Tacitus quotes their exact words), he returned to the theater to sing, following all the rules of the contest and then anxiously awaiting on one knee the verdict of the judges, while the crowd went wild with elaborate applause.[77] The same incident is recounted from a different angle by Suetonius, in his *Life of Vitellius* (4). Vitellius presided over the *certamen Neroneum.* Nero wished to compete in the citharodic contest but did not dare to, even though "everyone" was calling for him. He had left the theater when Vitellius called him back as if undertaking an embassy from the persistent populace and thus offering him a chance to be persuaded. This story, Suetonius' version in his *Life of Nero,* and Tacitus' account all fit together neatly, depicting a Nero eager but hesitant to compete as citharode, an adoring public demanding that he do so, his acquiescence, and his artistic triumph. The Second Neronia of 65 thus marked the last step in Nero's evolution as an artist: he was now a competitor in public.[78]

AD 66.   In 66 Nero competed as a citharode. After his teacher Menecrates held a victory celebration in the circus, Nero also raced his chariot.[79]

In late May of that year Rome witnessed the fabulous reception of the Armenian king Tiridates, and his elaborate coronation by Nero in the Forum and in the Theater of Pompey. Suetonius was so impressed by the ceremony as to comment, "I might also rightly include among the *spectacula* produced by him the entrance of Tiridates into the city."[80] After performing the ceremony in the Forum, Nero led the king into the theater, where he knelt a second time before his benefactor, who raised him to sit at his right hand. This sort of "instant replay" before a theater audience of an already highly theatrical public ceremony brilliantly captures Nero's merging of life and art, and Suetonius was right to include it among his "games." Afterwards the emperor again performed on the lyre in public and drove a chariot while wearing the costume of the Green racing faction which he favored.[81]

In the late summer of 66 Nero departed on his long-postponed visit to Greece, where he threw himself enthusiastically into the festival circuit as a full-fledged competitor in playing the lyre, acting in tragedies, racing chariots, and announcing the results. He trained hard, played by the rules, feuded with rivals, bribed judges, and the rest, as recounted earlier.

AD 67.   In 67 Nero continued to compete in the Greek games. He did not return to Rome until the autumn of that year. After his notorious "triumph" there, he continued to race, sing, and act competitively until the end.[82]

The participation of the upper classes in the games, senatorial and equestrian men and women, needs further definition. It is clear from their insinuations that our sources had little hard evidence of coercion, and there are signs of voluntary participation which should be taken at face value, but the extent of coercion is probably not worth debating: it could be argued away as an anti-tyrannical topos; or it could be agreed, as Tacitus put it, that "rewards" offered by an emperor are tantamount to compulsion. More significant is the pattern of aristocratic participation. Despite a century of legal disapproval, senators and knights appeared in Nero's three gladiatorial *munera* of 55, 57, and 63. This draws little comment from our sources. What does spark their indignation is the large-scale and officially encouraged involvement of the upper classes in the two games of 59, the Ludi Maximi and the Juvenalia. By contrast, there is not a hint of their engagement afterwards in either Neronia, beyond the mention of Lucan, or on the tour of the Greek games, and of course no disapproval. The year 59 was a watershed. Was the sensational participation of senators and knights in the games of 59 meant to serve as a backdrop for the leader of Roman society likewise to engage as a performer?

Nero's progression from private to public performance, and from amateur to professional, develops in three distinct stages. Music and chariots had been his passions from boyhood. Immediately after his accession as emperor in 54 (stage one), he summoned the leading citharode of the age, studied with him intensely, and began a rigorous program of training. In 59 (two) he first sang before the people on stage at his private Juvenalia. And in 64 (three), after repeating the Greek proverb that "hidden music wins no respect," he first appeared on a public stage at Naples and sang in Greek, only later to compete in the Neronia in Rome.[83] His career as a charioteer is precisely parallel to this musical progression. As a schoolboy he had been obsessed with the Circus, and as soon as he became emperor in 54 (stage one) he played a circus board game every day, attended all races big and small, and increased the prizes and the number of races. In 59 again (two) he invited the people of Rome to watch him race in a circus built for the purpose in his gardens in the Vatican on the right bank of the Tiber, gardens actually inherited from his mother; this was not a public spectacle (as Tacitus explains), but like the theatrical Juvenalia a private event by invitation only. And again, only in 64 (three) did he first race chariots in public.[84] In short: up to the time of his mother's death, Nero had practiced and performed in private; the year 59 marked the important intermediate stage, public in all but name, where he first presented himself to the people as his invited guests in a private setting; and it was to be another five years before he would progress from this "hidden music" to actual competition in public, in 64. Tacitus comments adversely on Nero's ancient desire to race chariots and his equally repellent zeal for singing to the lyre "after the fashion of the stage." However, the real problem would lie not so much in this shift from private to public (Nero had long since displayed his talents to the people) as in the accompanying progress from amateur to professional, and to formal competition on stage and in the circus.[85]

WHAT DID NERO actually do when he performed privately and publicly, as amateur and as professional competitor? Popular entertainment ran across a broad spectrum of forms, but his active participation was confined to a few. The list of his public performances is a convenient point of departure.

As a lyre-player he is attested as singing "Attis, or the Bacchantes" at his Juvenalia in 59 and "Niobe" at the Second Neronia in 64. During the Great Fire of July 64, rumor had it that Nero sang in stage costume, *scaenico habitu,* about the sack of Troy; Dio asserts precisely that he was wearing the costume of a lyre-player.[86]

Of Nero's roles in tragedy, Dio reports that his favorites were Oedipus, Thyestes, Heracles, Alcmaeon, and Orestes, and elsewhere he adds Canace in Childbirth, all six in the context of the tour of Greece. Suetonius lists Canace Giving Birth, Orestes the Matricide, Oedipus Blinded, and Hercules Insane, and adds an anecdote about the Hercules performance which Dio likewise assigns to the Greek sojourn.[87] In his *Life of Apollonius of Tyana* (a dubious source), Philostratus speaks of Nero acting Creon and Oedipus in Greece, while Juvenal writes of him wearing the tragic robe of Thyestes and the mask of Antigone or Melanippe (on what authority, and with what concern for historical precision, we do not know).[88]

As a pantomime, in his final days Nero planned to crown the games celebrating his victory over Vindex by dancing the role of Vergil's Turnus.[89]

He is also on record as simply reciting poetry. In the early days of his reign, Suetonius tells us, he performed both at home and in the theater, to such universal joy that a supplication to the gods was decreed to celebrate the recitation, and some of the poems were written in golden letters and dedicated to Jupiter Capitolinus. During the Second Neronia he also recited onstage some of his own poetry on the Trojan War before he reappeared to sing to the lyre.[90] There is no hint on either occasion that he wore a costume of any kind while reciting.

It appears at first glance that Nero's twin artistic passions were *tragoedia,* tragic acting, and *citharoedia.*[91] Citharody, playing the lyre as one sang a tale, is by far the most commonly recorded of Nero's pastimes, and the one most identified with him. The citharode, or lyre-player, was instantly recognizable by his standardized costume, for he was always dressed in the long flowing chiton of his patron Apollo, he wore elevated boots (the *cothurni*), and he carried the lyre of Apollo. After his victories in Greece, Nero had statues of himself in the garb of a lyre-player set up in his private chambers and (Suetonius believed) depicted on his coinage.[92] The tragic actor, by contrast, wore a costume appropriate to the character he played, be it a beggar in rags or a king in royal robes; his face was obscured by a mask (in Nero's case showing either his own face or that of Poppaea Sabina); he used props (in Nero's case a scepter and chains are attested); and he might be assisted by another actor in the supporting roles, the *hypocrita.*[93]

To complicate matters for modern observers, very late in his reign Nero took up a third and related art, that of the pantomime, one of the most popular entertainments under the principate. This art has nothing to do with the English stage tradition of the same name, but is distinctly reminiscent of modern mime, in that the silent performer "speaks" through imitative movement. This dramatic dance was introduced to Rome from the Greek East in the reign of Augustus, taking both tragic and comic forms, although the tragic eventually dominated. It was in essence a solo ballet, sometimes a *pas de deux,* backed by a chorus and orchestra, although song and music were clearly subordinated to the performer's movements, posture, and gestures. Like the citharode, the pantomime wore a flowing robe, but one that allowed easy movement; like the tragic actor, he wore a mask, but one with closed lips; and unlike either he wore low shoes.[94] Nero certainly included pantomime contests in games that he produced, although he excluded them from his Greek-style Neronia. He did not attempt to practice the art himself until the last six months of his life, when he took up training seriously.[95]

To define the precise nature of these three arts—lyre-playing, tragic acting, pantomime—and the relationship among them is to raise serious and often insoluble problems, both generally and with regard to Nero. Very similar pursuits, they can be hard to disentangle in our sources, since all dealt with the same Greek myths, all were performed in the same theaters, and all shared some technical vocabulary.[96] Nevertheless, some basic observations can be made.

First, what distinguishes these particular three arts is that, whether the performer had assistants or not, the performances were very much the solos of a master, be he actor, citharode, or dancer. We should thus expect a unity in the telling. That is, either a single protagonist dominated the action (Thyestes, Orestes); or the subject was a single tale such as the adulterous affair of Mars and Venus (which the second-century satirist Lucian describes in detail) or the sack of Troy; or a single character dominated a single story (Hercules Insane, Oedipus in Exile, Canace in Childbirth, Niobe, Turnus).

By the same token, in no case should we imagine performances of great length: they must have been much shorter than a staged play, for instance. The citharodic *nomos,* words and music, has been compared to a modern operatic aria, while the tragedies enacted were neither the full dramas of the Greek tragedians nor the versions of Seneca (whether they were staged or not), but rather what have been called "concert tragedies," essentially monologues.[97] There is no reason to assume anything different of pantomime. To further underline their brevity, it must be remembered that all three performance types had to be of a length tailored to delivery by a single competitor in a competition among many. Thus the spotlight remains on the single artist, Nero.

The survey of his stage career from 59 to 68 immediately yields one arresting observation: there is no sign that Nero ever acted in a tragedy before his departure for Greece in 66. That is to say, without exception all of the considerable evidence shows him performing as a citharode until then, and the tragic actor appears only in the context of the Grecian tour. This is confirmed by a remark made early in 65 by the Pisonian conspirator Subrius Flavus. He was popularly rumored to have planned to murder Piso after Nero's overthrow and to replace him in his turn with Seneca, because, he believed, "it made no difference as far as disgrace is concerned if a *citharoedus* [Nero] is removed and a *tragoedus* [Piso] succeeds."[98]

Perhaps the most remarkable aspect of Nero's life as a performer is the development of his interests over his brief but energetic reign, not only in their progression from private and amateur to public and professional, but also in their expansion into new areas. The step from citharody to tragedy was a natural one, particularly where the same texts were performed in each. Likewise natural was the advance from *tragoedia cantata* (sung tragedy) to *tragoedia saltata* (danced tragedy), for again the very same subjects were enacted, and actors or a chorus recited or sang libretti to accompany and explain the dancer's movements.[99] So the progression from citharody to tragedy in 66, and thence to pantomime in 68, is neither impossible nor even unlikely in a tyrant of artistic bent. By the same token, Nero took up another new competitive art, the practice of acting as a herald *(praeco)* only when he went to Greece.[100] Similarly, his claim that if spared he would celebrate his victory over Vindex in 68 with public performances on the water organ, the reed pipe, and a sort of bagpipe was no idle boast—he had certainly learned enough about water organs in his last days to lecture on them to a group of very anxious senators and knights, while his reputation on both the reed pipe and the bagpipe was known to Dio of Prusa in the East.[101]

As with his artistic performances, so too with athletics: there are indications that Nero intended to expand his range of activities, not just from racing four-horse to racing ten-horse chariots, but to two other endeavors. One is actual gladiatorial combat, although here the tradition is weak. He certainly enjoyed watching gladiators and presented them himself in games in 55, 57, 63, and 64. He also patronized and presumably owned troupes of gladiators, his *neroniani,* in Rome, Pompeii, Corduba, and Arausio, and his favorite gladiator, Spiculus, was both lavishly rewarded and promoted to be commander of his bodyguard.[102] A late and novelistic source even claims that Nero lived and fought with gladiators, but the best evidence for his intention actually to fight in the arena comes in Suetonius: when Nero came to develop his own image as Hercules, "they say" that a lion was prepared for him to kill in the amphitheater before the public.[103]

Be that as it may, his interest in pursuing a somewhat less dangerous career in wrestling is well attested. He certainly built gymnasiums at Rome, Baiae, and Naples; wrestlers competed at his Neronia; he enjoyed watching them in Naples; and he actually employed court wrestlers, *luctatores auli.* Contemporary rumor had it that he intended himself to compete in the next Olympic Games among the athletes, for he wrestled constantly and watched gymnastic contests throughout Greece, even acting as a judge would act, sitting on the ground in the stadium and personally thrusting back any pairs of wrestlers who strayed too far—this glimpse in Suetonius of amateur passion working up into competitive zeal has the authentic Neronian air to it, and Dio of Prusa confirms that the emperor was interested in both wrestling and the pankration.[104]

The survey of Nero's career as an artist and an athlete produces a complex result. The negative is all too clear, and the charges are irrefutable. Beyond the indulgence in trivialities and the disturbing acts of arbitrary cruelty, there are two great and all too obvious crimes rooted in his growing professionalism. One is the stifling effect on competition that we have seen already, to which Nero himself seems to have been blind. A patron with twenty-eight legions at his command cannot compete as a performer, and the fantasy tour of Greece clearly shows him corrupting performers, judges, and audience alike. The other problem is that emperors simply should not be professional performers. Amateur indulgence in an art or a sport might be pardonable; obsessive dedication was not. The indignity of it appalled his ancient critics, and the concomitant abdication of imperial responsibilities would prove fatal.

Thus we are left with the nightmare vision of the last days of Nero's reign, when his devotion to artistic discipline overwhelmed his sense of duty, indeed of reality. It is reported that after returning from Greece he never addressed his soldiers in person, but always by letter or through an intermediary, in order to conserve his voice. When Vindex rebelled in Gaul he did not go up to Rome to address the senate in person, alleging a weakness in the throat, and even when he did come back he still avoided speaking to the senate or the people. He did nothing without a voice coach, a *phonascus,* at his side, who would warn him to spare his throat and to cover his mouth with a handkerchief—indeed, whenever he was upset by events and began to shout, he could be calmed quickly by the reminder he was going to perform.[105] By not addressing the soldiers or the senate or the people in person, by reserving his voice for artistic performance, Nero was neglecting one of the prime duties of an emperor. Indeed in his last days, he conceived his appearances before his subjects as performance rather than address:

> He declared as he was leaving the dining-room after a banquet, leaning on the shoulders of his comrades, that immediately on setting foot in the province [Gaul] he would go before the soldiers and do

nothing but weep; and having thus led the rebels to change their purpose, he would next day rejoice among his rejoicing subjects and sing paeans of victory, which he ought at that very moment to be composing.

In short, tragedy and citharody up to the end. His last fantasy, in the chaos of the final days, was to sail away from his troubles to Alexandria and take up life there as a professional citharode.[106]

Yet, even so, there is a more positive side to this portrait of the artist that should not be overlooked. Nero was, undoubtedly, very serious about his art. Ignore for the moment the appalling impropriety of an emperor as performer; ignore the criticism of his talent (which is irrelevant anyway). Concentrate rather on his ferocious energy, his passionate determination, and behind them his fecund imagination. Like it or not, Nero had a vision and, astonishingly, a real strength of character. He worked in deadly earnest to improve himself in his chosen fields, training hard, studying the discipline, carrying on despite setbacks. Egomaniacal perhaps, he did submit himself repeatedly to judgment at center stage and, servile perhaps, the people of Rome responded repeatedly with great enthusiasm. What is particularly striking is the restless expansion of his interests, following the careful shift of activities from private to public, as lyre-playing is joined by tragic acting, then pantomime, then public announcing and musical instruments, chariot-racing by sword-fighting and wrestling: old passions joined, not replaced, by newer ones.

And a creative imagination informed it all. Nero wrote poetry easily and without effort, as Suetonius testified after examining the versions of his best-known poems, *notissimis versibus ipsius,* as preserved in his own handwriting, with erasures and corrections. Indeed, the poems of *doctus Nero,* the learned Nero, were read and applauded in the months after his death, and for generations and even centuries afterwards.[107] His range was certainly wide and expanding, running from mordant satire to hymns to a proposed epic on Roman history, and almost certainly included the appropriate monologues, arias, and libretti for his performances on stage.[108] His *Troica,* either an epic poem or a series of poems, included a fascinating passage about Paris, elsewhere a figure of ambiguous virtue, here the bravest of the Trojans. Paris, the Trojan prince handed over to shepherds at birth, goes to Troy clad in his rustic garb, to take part in the games there. He wins both races and boxing matches, defeating even Hector himself, and when Hector grows angry and draws his sword, Paris produces evidence that he is in fact his long-lost brother. The story of his prowess in the games was to be found in the ancient tragedians, but the defeat of the great Hector seems, along with other curious details, to be Nero's own invention. Paris the hero: the fascinating suggestion has been made that he was chosen to reflect the paradoxes of Nero's own character, with its combination of sensual living and careful training.[109] The role would appeal to Nero.

Thus we have a creative artist who was both a determined performer and the emperor of Rome. We should expect from his reign if not the triumph of art over life, then at least an assault on the boundary between the two, and some rather surprising roles.

4

The Power of Myth

In putting on the mask [he] threw off the dignity of his sovereignty to beg in the guise of a runaway slave, to be led about as a blind man, to be heavy with child, to be in labour, to be a madman, or to wander as an outcast, his favourite rôles being those of Oedipus, Thyestes, Heracles, Alcmeon, and Orestes[.] The masks he wore were sometimes made to resemble the characters he was portraying and sometimes bore his own likeness; but the women's masks were all fashioned after the features of Sabina, in order that, though dead, she might still take part in the spectacle. All the situations that ordinary actors simulate in their acting he, too, would portray in speech or action or submitting to the action of others—save only that golden chains were used to bind him; for apparently it was not thought proper for a Roman emperor to be bound in iron shackles. All this behaviour, nevertheless, was witnessed, endured, and approved, not only by the crowd in general, but also by the soldiers.

CASSIUS DIO

He also put on the mask and sang tragedies representing Gods and heroes and even heroines and Goddesses, having the masks fashioned in the likeness of his own features or of those women of whom he chanced to be enamored. Among other themes he sang "Canace in Labor," "Orestes the Matricide," "The Blinding of Oedipus," and the "Frenzy of Hercules."

SUETONIUS[1]

While Nero was still a child, his mother, Agrippina, consulted astrologers about his destiny. When they told her that he would become emperor and would kill his mother, she replied with passion, "Let him kill me, so long as he rules." The first defining act of Nero's reign was to be the murder of his mother in 59, when he was 21 years old and she was 42 or 43.

Their relationship deteriorated rapidly after his accession in 54.[2] After the death of Claudius, Agrippina took charge. Her special position was immediately recognized by the coinage, where her profile appeared with that of her son, by the watchword given by Nero to the guard, "best of mothers," *optima mater*, and by the decree of the senate that she be granted two lictors (public servants who normally attended only high magistrates) and that she be appointed priestess of the new god Claudius.[3] But she wanted more than the trappings of power. Senators were summoned to the palace so that she might listen to their debate out of sight, and once, when Nero was receiving ambassadors from Armenia, she moved to join her son on the tribunal. Seneca forestalled the scandal by having his young pupil rise to meet his mother.

Within a year the two had split irrevocably. In 55, at the age of 17, Nero fell deeply in love with a freedwoman, Acte, while a pair of young men-about-town, Otho and Senecio, guided him into a life of luxurious excess. Agrippina was furious. By one account she beat some of his servants and dismissed others, but when she violently scolded Nero himself, "he cast off all respect for his mother and committed himself to Seneca." She then shifted abruptly from attack to complaisance: she apologized for her thoughtless severity, she handed over to Nero her vast private fortune, she even offered her own bedroom for his experiments in vice (so says Tacitus). But this pliancy was short-lived. When her son magnanimously sent her a robe and some jewels which had belonged to earlier imperial princesses, she complained that he was simply keeping her out of the rest of the treasure, dividing with her what had once been all hers. Nero, enraged, retaliated by removing from office the powerful freedman Pallas, his mother's lover and ally, the secretary in charge of imperial accounts (*a rationibus*) since the early days of Claudius. Agrippina now lost all semblance of rationality. She would tell anyone, including her son, that her stepson Britannicus was now both old enough and worthy to hold power, and that Nero was an intruder who abused his ill-gotten power by attacking his mother. Once set on this track she followed it to the logical end, exposing her whole supposedly criminal career, from her marriage with Claudius to his murder, the career which had had the single goal of winning power for her ungrateful son. She threatened to appeal with Britannicus to the praetorian guard. But she then discovered that Nero was her own true son when, to her shock, he moved quickly to have Britannicus poisoned.

Agrippina countered by cultivating relations with her stepdaughter Octavia, Britannicus' sister and Nero's wife. She intrigued with Octavia's friends; she received the officers of the guards; she wooed possible supporters among the nobility. Nero responded by stripping her of her bodyguard and removing her from the palace. Thereafter, whenever he visited his mother, he did so briefly and surrounded by centurions—an effective charade. Agrippina's friends now deserted her, while enemies at court charged that she was plotting to marry a cousin, Rubellius Plautus, a descendant of the emperor Tiberius, and to make him emperor. This accusation was presented to Nero late one night by the skilled pantomime actor Paris, who so terrified the emperor that he then first decided (so we are told) to kill his mother. Burrus, the commander of the guard, agreed reluctantly that she might be put to death, but only after a proper trial and conviction. Agrippina vigorously denied all of the charges outright and furiously denounced her accusers. After a personal interview, Nero backed down. The accusers were punished with exile or death.

Then, in all the accounts, there is a silence for three or four years, as Nero governs with the help of Seneca and Burrus—a silence which suggests that the alleged intention to murder his mother was retrojected to these early days by later writers. A few years later, in 58, the now 20-year-old emperor fell in love again, this time with Poppaea Sabina, the ambitious wife of his friend Otho. It was she who badgered him into at last removing Agrippina, for she realized that she could never replace Octavia as Nero's wife until his strong-willed mother was dead.

In response (it is said) to this new onslaught, Agrippina's lust for power moved her to an act of desperation.[4] What actually happened is not clear, as the different accounts both vary and conflict. Cluvius Rufus, the historian whom Tacitus chose to follow here, wrote that frequently, in the middle of the day, when her son was heated with food and tipsy with wine, Agrippina would offer herself to him beautifully made up and (so we are told) ready for incest. Their passionate kisses and suggestive terms of affection so shocked the courtiers that Seneca decided to fight fire with fire: he sent in the concubine Acte to deflect the emperor's lust by warning him of the clear political dangers of the situation. Against Cluvius, the very hostile Fabius Rusticus claimed that it was not his mother but Nero himself who had started the affair, but Tacitus rejects this version even as he reports it, since it was inconsistent with Agrippina's known character and contrary both to every other source and to popular belief. Tacitus never actually claims that the liaison was consummated, while Cassius Dio is unsure whether it happened at all, wondering if it might have been invented to suit the characters involved. But one fact, Dio asserts, was agreed upon by everyone: there was a courtesan whom Nero particularly

Copy of Nero's official portrait, AD 55–59.

favored because of her resemblance to Agrippina, so that when he was relaxing with her himself or displaying her to others, he would say that he
was having intercourse with his mother.

Finally, Suetonius credits the version (unique to Fabius Rusticus) that
made Nero the seducer, adding explicitly what seems to be implied by
Tacitus, that Agrippina's enemies prevented consummation in their fear
that it would increase her power over her son. Suetonius also mentions the

courtesan, who he says was recruited among Nero's concubines because of her resemblance to his mother. Yet he adds something found nowhere else—that "they say" that earlier, whenever Nero had been borne about in the litter with his mother, their stained clothing would betray the fulfillment of their incestuous lust. This contradictory last charge, which must refer to a much earlier period—for Nero and Agrippina shared a litter only during the first months of their joint power—looks purely gratuitous.[5] In short, whatever the truth, the common version appears to have been that Agrippina offered herself to Nero in 58 or 59 but was circumvented by her enemies; and that he himself did nothing either to prevent her or to suppress the rumor. Nero stopped seeing his mother in private, she withdrew to her estates, and he came to resolve that she must be removed permanently.

How to do it? Poison and the dagger were considered, only to be rejected as too obvious, although one story charges that he did try to poison his mother several times. Then the freedman Anicetus, an old teacher of Nero and now prefect of the fleet at Misenum, offered a brilliantly theatrical scheme: a collapsible ship would make her death seem like an accident, and Nero could afterwards mourn her extravagantly. The young emperor loved the idea—some even said that it was his own, inspired by seeing just such a ship at the theater—since he would soon be celebrating the festival of Minerva at Baiae on the Bay of Naples, in late March of 59. So with offers of reconciliation he lured Agrippina to his villa there, greeted her fondly on the shore, and led her into a banquet where she was treated with honor. They talked deep into the night, Nero growing more withdrawn and serious. At last, kissing her eyes, clinging to her bosom, professing eternal gratitude, he escorted her down to the shore. There the lavishly equipped vessel, in which Nero had himself sailed from Rome, waited to bear her home. As Tacitus describes it, a bright starlit night and a calm sea witnessed the crime: the ship foundered as planned, some of Agrippina's companions were killed, and the wounded empress swam to some nearby boats, which deposited her on shore near her own villa. Fully aware of her son's plot, she decided that the best course would be to ignore it. She sent a freedman to announce that by the grace of the gods and Nero's own good fortune she had escaped grave danger, but she begged him, despite his concern for his mother's safety, to leave her to rest for the moment.

Nero, nervously awaiting good news, was devastated, terrified that his vengeful mother would stir up the slaves or the soldiers or the senate and people at Rome. He summoned Seneca and Burrus for advice. They doubted whether the guard could be trusted to slay the daughter of Germanicus, the soldiers' hero: Anicetus would have to finish the deed. To the emperor's delight, Anicetus promptly agreed, and Nero exclaimed, characteristically, that this was the day on which he truly received the empire, and to think that an ex-slave was the giver of so great a gift. After Anicetus had departed on his mission Nero added his own dramatic flourish. When the messenger from Agrippina was admitted, he cast down a sword at the man's feet and ordered him to be thrown into chains immediately, as an assassin caught in the act. Thus he would be able to put the story about that his mother had plotted his murder and had then committed suicide when discovered.

In the meantime Anicetus with a party of sailors and marines had surrounded Agrippina's villa, broken in, and rushed to her chamber. There she confronted them boldly: if they had come to get news of her, they were to tell the emperor that she was recovering; if they had come to commit a crime, she would never believe that it was her son's wish, he could not have ordered parricide. The murderers surrounded her couch, and a naval captain clubbed her on the head. When a centurion drew his sword, she thrust forward her womb and cried out, "Strike my belly." She was killed, brutally, and the corpse was cremated that same night.[6]

The news was greeted with public delight, real or feigned. The officers of his praetorian guard (which received a bonus) congratulated the emperor on his escape. His friends gave thanks to the gods at the temples, and their example was soon followed by the neighboring towns of Campania, who sacrificed on Nero's behalf and sent embassies to compliment him. Seneca now composed in his name a careful letter to the senate. It recounted the story of the shipwreck and of the freedman and the sword, and it claimed that in her guilt Agrippina had killed herself when discovered. One rhetorical line of the letter survives, a breathless exclamation: "I cannot yet believe or rejoice that I am safe."[7] Seneca, writing in Nero's name, also raked up, or invented, all the old accusations: that Agrippina's original purpose had been to share the power of the emperor; that when frustrated in this she had turned against the soldiers and the senate and people, refusing them their accustomed largesse; that she had endangered the leading men of the state; that she had had the temerity to enter the senate house and to receive foreign embassies; and that she had been responsible for all the crimes of the reign of Claudius. Her death, Nero asserted, had been brought about by the good fortune of the state.

At Rome the senate responded with enthusiasm, decreeing that thanksgivings be offered at every shrine. The festival of Minerva was to be celebrated henceforth with annual games, to commemorate the day on which the plot was discovered, and a golden statue of the goddess was to be set up in the senate house next to a statue of Nero. The day of Agrippina's birth, 6 November, was to be entered in the list of unhallowed days, days on which no public business might be conducted. For his part, Nero recalled from exile prominent enemies and victims of his mother. Finally, after a delay of three months, the emperor returned from Campania to a rapturous public welcome in Rome.[8]

This was the publicly staged display of shock and relief shared by the emperor and his people: a great crime against the state had been uncovered and suppressed, to universal joy. Nero was saved, the empire was secure. But there was at the same time another dialogue between Nero and his subjects whose tone is more difficult to catch. It concerns guilt.

On his side, Nero's initial reaction to the death of his mother was presented as one of sorrow, not joy: he was saddened, he seemed almost to be angry at his own preservation, and he wept over the death of his parent. But again the sources diverge on the reality behind the image.[9] Without hesitation, Dio gives the most luridly detailed account of what happened next. In a moment of Grand Guignol, the emperor views his mother's corpse, strips it, examines it and its wounds with care, and then utters the chilling line, "I did not know that I had so beautiful a mother." Suetonius' version concurs, but with a notable difference. Nero hurries off to see the corpse; he handles the limbs, denigrating some and praising others, and he becomes so thirsty at this work that he calls for something to drink. These actions Suetonius presents as atrocities vouched for by "trustworthy writers"—which is to suggest that there was some dispute, and indeed Tacitus notes curtly, "Whether Nero looked on his dead mother and praised the beauty of her body, there are those who say so and those who deny it." Where Tacitus is doubtful, we should be skeptical. The important point is not whether Nero toyed with his mother's corpse, but that some believed he could and did.

Unable to face the scene of his crime, according to Tacitus, Nero withdrew to Naples; from there he sent to the senate the letter which accused his mother. In Dio's version of events he lived in a state of terror, unable to sleep at night or to stay long in any one place because of his conscience and the sounds of trumpets near Agrippina's grave. Tacitus, more restrained, mentions that some believed a trumpet was heard nearby and sounds of lament issued from the grave, but he does not say that Nero heard or was upset by any of this. Neither author adds anything further about the emperor's conscience, but Suetonius reports that Nero would often admit that he was tormented by the ghost of his mother and by the scourges and burning torches of the Furies, a theme which was quickly taken up by writers after his death.[10] He even tried with the help of Persian wise men to call forth and placate her shade, and during his tour of Greece in 67 he did not dare take part in the mystery rites of Eleusis, since they started with the solemn removal of impious and criminal observers, by order of a herald.

There was another, popular view of Nero's guilt, expressed particularly in the pasquinades (visual or verbal satires posted anonymously in public places) dear to the hearts of the Romans.[11] One night after his return to Rome, a leather sack was hung around one of Nero's statues, to suggest that he should be put in one—the standard penalty for parricide was to be drowned in a sack along with a snake, a dog, and a cock—while in the last weeks of his life, another sack was hung around the neck of one of his statues with the inscription "What could I do? But you have deserved the sack."[12] Again, after Nero's entry into the city in 59, in one of those casual incidents that draws a modern observer up short, a baby was thrown into the Forum with a placard which read: "I will not raise you and you will not kill your mother." And a statue of Agrippina which had not been removed in time was covered in rags, giving her the appearance of being veiled; an inscription duly appeared, proclaiming, "I am ashamed and you are not." A Latin couplet circulated: "Who can deny that Nero springs from the great family of Aeneas? The one carried off his mother, the other his father." And in Greek, probably scrawled on the base of a statue of the emperor: "Nero Orestes Alcmaeon, mother-slayer. Or put it another way: Nero killed his own mother."[13]

There was also criticism more direct than these anonymous barbs. A Cynic philosopher rebuked the emperor in the street one day with an oblique reference to his deed, while a popular comedy actor turned lines in a farce against the emperor: to accompany the words "Farewell father, farewell mother" in a Greek song, he made motions of drinking and swimming, to recall the deaths of Claudius and Agrippina. With the last line of his piece, "Orcus [god of the underworld] guides your feet," he gestured toward members of the senate, who would have been sitting in the front rows of seats reserved for them by law.[14]

Nero's reaction to such attacks on his crime is remarkable. He was exceptionally lenient *(leniorem)* to those who attacked him in speech or verse. The actor and the philosopher he simply banished from Italy, and he took no action against the senator Thrasea Paetus, who ostentatiously walked out of the senate when it was voting its thanks for the death of Agrippina. Most significantly, when eager informers lodged charges against people who dared to say that Nero had killed his mother—the accusation would be one of treason—the emperor simply refused to allow such cases to be brought to court. This restraint baffles Dio and Suetonius, who speculate about it: perhaps he didn't wish to fan the flames of discontent, perhaps he didn't really care. But the reason is a simpler one: Nero agreed that he was guilty.

N ERO'S STRATEGY is best understood in the context of two related phenomena in Roman public life of the late Republic and early Empire. The first may be called the power of myth.

In the middle and late Republic a fashion developed among the Roman upper classes for linking themselves genealogically with the gods and heroes (the latter themselves being children or descendants of the former) of myth, typically by claiming descent from a Greek or Trojan hero who had wandered to Italy, often to found not just a family but a town or city. Thus, Julius Caesar and his adoptive son Augustus could present themselves as representatives of the Trojan prince Aeneas, the founder of Rome and son of Venus (hence the claim of their heir Nero to "spring from the great family of Aeneas"); indeed, almost every contemporary politician could lay claim to a similarly grand origin.[15] This genealogical fashion is itself but one aspect of the massive hellenization of every aspect of Roman and Italian culture—or the domestication of classical and hellenistic Greek culture—over the third, second, and first centuries BC, as Rome established herself, by conquest, by imitation, and by attraction, as the epicenter of a Graeco-Roman world. That such genealogies were not strictly verifiable is irrelevant. They were a single facet of the reconciliation between Greek and Roman cultures, part of a much larger bilateral accommodation to the realities of power: Greek orators and poets could address their new masters in terms of praise already forged for other, Hellenic rulers; while Roman statesmen could present themselves as legitimate participants in a culture that was older than their own. But heroic pedigrees also had a more immediate purpose, as weapons deployed in politics at Rome.

Legendary genealogies form a single strand, the most literal-minded, in the general weaving of myth into contemporary Roman political life. By appropriating the gods and heroes of myth and legendary history, if not as ancestors, then at least as exemplars, politicians could present images laden with meanings which were quickly recognizable to a broad public.[16] Hence everywhere, from the coins in their purses to the decorative programs of their greatest public buildings, citizens could decipher with relative ease the claims of their leaders when they were couched artistically in mythical and legendary terms, messages which the literate could also read in contemporary writings. Thus world conquerors and benefactors, like Alexander or Pompey the Great, or a would-be conqueror-benefactor like Mark Antony, would turn naturally to the global exploits of Dionysus or Hercules to represent their own deeds. Antony's rival, the future emperor Augustus, early on in his career adopted the symbols or persona of Apollo, the god of peace and the arts, the bringer of the new Golden Age. He took, for instance, the sphinx (a symbol of Apollo) for his signet ring, wore Apollo's laurel wreath in public, attributed the final victory at Actium over Antony and Cleopatra to the god's protection (as the poets would proclaim at length), and built the great Temple of Apollo on the Palatine, beside and connected to his own house.[17]

The clearest example of the use of myth (and legend), in a city overflowing with similar architectural complexes, is the Forum of Augustus in the center of Rome, an open rectangle about 125 by 90 meters. In the center of the square stood a large statue of the *princeps* Augustus, riding in a triumphal chariot with inscriptions added to its base which described his victories and called him by the title given him at the time of the dedication of the Forum in 2 BC, *Pater Patriae,* father of his country. Running the whole length of both sides of the square were two-story colonnades, with niche after niche holding over-life-size statues of all the great Romans of the past. On one side, near the top end, stood Romulus, the founder of Rome, larger than all the rest, shown with the spear and military spoils, the *spolia opima,* which were awarded to the rare Roman commander who killed the enemy leader in personal combat. On the other

side, facing Romulus, stood father Aeneas, the founder of the Roman
race, in the classic pose of piety, carrying his father and leading his son
by the hand, away from the flames of Troy. Aeneas was flanked by statues
of his descendants, including the family of Julius Caesar, the mythical
and historical ancestors of Augustus. Thus the two founders of Rome
and all her great men gazed down on Augustus in the center. The top
end of the Forum was dominated by the great Temple of Mars Ultor,
Mars the Avenger, the avenger of Augustus' father, Julius Caesar, against
his assassins, and the avenger of Rome against the Parthians. The god
Mars was shown fully armed at the center of the temple's pediment,
flanked by his wife Venus on one side, the ancestor of the Julian family,
and on the other by the goddess Fortuna, the Fortune pointedly brought
back to Rome by Augustus in 19 BC: a nice family affair, then, Mars the
father of Romulus, his wife Venus, the mother of Aeneas, both looking down on their descendant Augustus in the middle of the square. A
brief and selective description does scant justice to the elements of the
complex, but their programmatic nature is clear. Augustus the conqueror
was presented as the culmination of Roman history—the new Aeneas,
the new Romulus, the third founder of Rome and guardian of its military glory.[18]

These were but a few of the images which were displayed in every
public corner of the city of Augustus, replicated in private works of art,
and elaborated by the poets, orators, and historians of the day. Indeed,
there was no need to portray the emperor exclusively in terms of a single
god or hero. Augustus, for example, was also linked to portrayals of the
Athenian hero Theseus, western conqueror of the Amazons of the East
(just as Octavian/Augustus would overcome Antony), or of Diomedes, or
of Orestes, each figure of myth bearing with him an often simplified message that would be significant to contemporary observers.[19] The point
here is that daily life was permeated by such examples from the past, all
dedicated to comment on the present. It was customary to present Rome's
leaders wrapped in the deeds and virtues of figures from myth and legend,
and the Roman people were thoroughly accustomed to read and appreciate the messages they bore.

We have already seen the second phenomenon to be considered here,
theatralis licentia, theatrical license. Where the power of myth can be
taken to convey the manipulation of a symbolic vocabulary by the leaders
of the state, theatrical license suggests the other side of the coin, the vigorous expression of popular sentiment on public issues within a privileged

public space. One striking aspect of this license is particularly important: the prominence of the double entendre in plays, if we can stretch the phrase to include both speech and action. Again from the late Republic onward, an abundance of evidence shows that Roman theatrical audiences were extraordinarily quick to hear the words spoken and to see the actions presented on stage as offering pointed commentary on contemporary public life.[20]

How such messages were transmitted varied. The playwright himself might be the source, as when Julius Caesar forced the elderly Laberius to perform in one of his own mimes; Laberius got his own back by appearing as a slave who had just been whipped and crying out the line, "Henceforth citizens we have lost our liberty," at which the whole audience turned to look at Caesar. Such outspokenness might be dangerous under the empire: Caligula had a writer burned alive in the arena for writing a humorous double entendre, *ob ambigui ioci versiculum.* But more often it was the actors themselves who would speak lines, even changing words, so as to produce an appropriate effect, a proclivity that made performers very dangerous indeed. Cicero describes at some length (and probably with some exaggeration) how the great actor Aesop wound up his audience to a fever-pitch of sympathy for the orator when he was in exile, emphasizing appropriate lines such as those dealing with a father driven away and his house demolished (as Cicero's had been), encouraging requests for encores of pointed remarks, adding his own lines, and gesturing to different parts of the audience as they seemed relevant. The play, a tragedy, takes on a new life. Under the empire such behavior was riskier: a good emperor like Marcus Aurelius might sit unmoved through an exaggerated pun on the name of his wife's alleged lover, but less philosophical rulers like Nero and Commodus sent foolhardy performers into exile.[21]

Not only the author and the actors but the producer of the play himself might also make a statement through the drama he chose or the manner in which it was presented. The best example is that of the general Pompey who, for his great Eastern conquests, celebrated a triumph of unprecedented magnificence in 61 BC, at the same time dedicating a temple to Venus Victrix, victorious Venus, where his military trophies would be on permanent display. Attached to this temple, and likewise built from spoils, was to be a theater, and at the dedication of the complex in 55 Pompey presented plays whose production gave new meaning to the word "theatricality": in *Clytemnestra* there appeared 600 mules bearing Agamemnon's plunder from Troy, while *The Trojan Horse* saw hundreds of extras carrying 3,000 bowls heaped with booty. The props were real, the identification of the Greek king Agamemnon, first among equals, on stage with the Roman *triumphator* behind it irresistible.[22]

What gives a special flavor to the transmission and reception of these double entendres is their occasional spontaneity. That is, "the audience sometimes saw an allusion where none was intended."[23] Augustus for instance was embarrassed once when a crowd leapt to its feet and applauded the line "O just and good lord." But in 68, when actors in a performance at Rome took up the comic song "Onesimus is coming from his villa" (otherwise unknown), their audience finished the words and repeated them several times, apparently in mockery of the new emperor Galba, then on his way from Spain.[24] This remarkable sensitivity on the part of the audience underscores the heightening of awareness within a Roman theater: audiences *expected* to find contemporary relevance in the productions; performers *expected* to have their pointed remarks and actions caught, interpreted, and appreciated.

Theatrical license meets and merges with the power of myth in the conveyance of messages between rulers and ruled: almost all tragic drama and some comic drama portrayed the already familiar adventures of Greek gods and heroes. In short, the Roman people were accustomed to seeing their rulers everywhere presented as figures of well-known myths, and they were accustomed to performances on stage that commented directly on their own contemporary concerns. We must remember the expectations of the Roman audience when we read the hostile or dismissive accounts of Nero's performances: every person there would expect that when their emperor himself entered the theater to perform, he would be identifying himself in some way with the character he played: he could not have avoided it, he could not have done it unthinkingly. On occasion, in his most extravagantly theatrical gesture—one that seriously undermines the nature of ancient drama—Nero would wear a mask showing his own features. That could not possibly leave anyone in doubt: Nero *was* Orestes the matricide, Orestes was Nero; Nero *was* Oedipus, the man who had killed his father and married his own mother.

Even though he did not appear on the tragic stage until 66, it was the death of Agrippina in 59 that prompted Nero's interest in acting. Orestes and Oedipus were two of his favorite roles.[25]

The tale of Orestes was one of the best known (and most complex) in antiquity. His father, Agamemnon, King of Mycenae, had been commander-in-chief of the Greek army at Troy. Returning home after the Trojan War, Agamemnon had been slaughtered in his bath by his wife, Clytemnestra, and her lover, Aegisthus. His son, Orestes, was spirited away, and when he had grown to manhood he inquired of Apollo's oracle at Delphi whether he should avenge his father by killing his murderers. The god replied that he must. In disguise he went to Mycenae to inform the murderous adulterers that he, Orestes, was dead. They were completely taken in, and Orestes slew Aegisthus. Recognizing her son, Clytemnestra tried to appeal to his filial feelings by baring the bosom which had nourished him, but he struck her down as well. That same night the terrible Erinyes, the Furies, appeared with their scourges to harry the matricide, and he fled for protection to Delphi. There the god told him that after a year of exile he must make his way to Athens, where Athena would end the curse. He wandered through many lands, often in a state of madness, and he was ritually purified many times, but with no success: always the Furies pursued him, spurred on by the ghost of Clytemnestra. At last, in a great murder trial at Athens, with Apollo defending and the eldest Fury prosecuting him, Orestes was acquitted by one vote, the vote of Athena.[26]

For Nero, the golden key to the story of Orestes was not that he was a matricide, but that he was a *justified* matricide.[27] Indeed, there were two justifications which might palliate the horror of the deed. One was vengeance for the murdered father, vengeance which was not only proper but demanded. Nero at 16 had played no role in the death of Claudius, his father by adoption, but Agrippina, in her passionate resentment of her son's rejection of her, did apparently claim responsibility for murder, portraying herself as the mother who had sacrificed everything so that her son might rule. Yet there seems to be no hint that the image of Nero as avenger of his father Claudius was ever developed, or even that anyone at the time took seriously the notion that Claudius had been murdered.

But Nero did offer the other reasonable defense against the charge of matricide. Orestes had killed his mother not just because his father's death and the command of Apollo clamored for vengeance, but because Clytemnestra had stolen his inheritance from him and the people of Mycenae were suffering under the tyranny of a woman. In the words given him by Aeschylus:

> Here numerous desires converge to drive me on:
> the god's urgency and my father's passion, and
> with these the loss of my estates wears hard on me;
> the thought that these my citizens, most high renowned
> of men, who toppled Troy in show of courage, must
> go subject to this brace of women . . .[28]

This was the essence of the posthumous campaign against Agrippina, especially as recounted in Seneca's letter to the senate, that she had gone beyond her womanly role to aim at supreme power, undermining loyalties and even planning to murder her son, as indeed Clytemnestra was said to have threatened the infant Orestes: Nero's preservation, as we have seen, was closely tied to the preservation of the empire, *aeternitas imperii*. A skillful performance might even draw a parallel between Agrippina pointing to her womb and Clytemnestra baring the breast which had nourished Orestes: the public good had overcome filial piety.[29] Just as Orestes' heroic act had liberated Mycenae, so Nero's great sacrifice saved Rome.

Of course Nero carried the performance as Orestes beyond the limits of the stage, in his complaint for the rest of his days that he was harried by his mother's ghost and by the Furies with their scourges and their flaming torches. Again his interest first appears seven years after her death, in 66, when he came into contact with the *magi,* Persian wise men. Through them he tried to summon and appease his mother's ghost, but he soon found that they were frauds and gave up magic when the implacable spirit of his mother proved to be uncharacteristically shy.[30] The following year, during his tour of Greece, as Suetonius records, he avoided the mystery rites at Eleusis as one who was impure. Dio, perhaps misreporting this same refusal, adds that he kept away from Athens "because of the story about the Furies," and from Sparta because of the restrictive laws of Lycurgus.[31] But there is a far more plausible explanation for his avoidance of these places: he had no interest in them. He was there for the games.[32] The story about the Furies was a dramatic excuse, possibly by then even a joke, but he was quite willing up to his last days to identify himself with the archetypal matricide.

The identification with Orestes was further emphasized when Nero added to his repertoire another favorite character, Alcmaeon—a virtual double, the other matricide of myth. His tale is far less familiar today.[33] Alcmaeon was the son of the seer Amphiaraus, who was one of the Seven against Thebes, the heroes from Argos who took the part of Polyneices against his brother Eteocles when those two sons of Oedipus fell out over the rule of their father's kingdom. Amphiaraus, who foresaw his own death, refused to march against Thebes, but Polyneices bribed his wife, Eriphyle, with an antique necklace to persuade her husband to go. He went to Thebes and died there, along with most of the Argive heroes, or at least he disappeared forever. His son Alcmaeon was likewise reluctant to march against Thebes, when he was asked to lead an expedition of the sons of the Seven seeking vengeance. Thersander, the son of Polyneices, then bribed Alcmaeon's mother, the same Eriphyle, with an ancient robe to persuade her son to go to war. Under Alcmaeon's leadership Thebes was captured, and it was only then that he learned by chance that his mother's greed had brought death to his father and danger to himself. An ambiguous oracle from Apollo, that Eriphyle deserved to die, led to his murdering his mother. The Furies pursued him and he wandered, sometimes mad, until the river god Achelous purified him and gave him his daughter in marriage; but the necklace and the robe led eventually, through a separate sequence of events in which the Furies played a role, to Alcmaeon's own murder by another father-in-law outraged at his bigamy.[34]

The parallels between the tale of Alcmaeon and the tale of Orestes make it clear why the role of Alcmaeon appealed to Nero: the perfidious mother who caused the death of the father and threatened the safety of her son, the ambiguous oracle from Delphi, the matricide, the pursuit by the Furies and the madness. The divergences between the two also suggest why Alcmaeon might be less attractive to Nero, and why less is heard of the role: no kingdom was at stake, reports differed as to whether the father had died or disappeared, the hero himself was responsible for his own death.

The central point is that it was Nero and not his enemies who chose to mythologize the murder of his mother. By presenting Orestes as one of his favorite roles, by underscoring this predilection with Alcmaeon, by dramatizing the torments of conscience in his life offstage, by performing the matricide on stage in a mask that bore his own features, Nero framed the terms of the debate over his own guilt.

Unquestionably, he succeeded. The clue lies in this: his ancient critics were compelled to react by seeking to demonstrate that he was *not* comparable with Orestes. Juvenal objected that Orestes had acted on the authority of the gods, and he never killed his sister or his wife, poisoned his relatives—or sang the part of Orestes on stage, or wrote a *Troica!* Philostratus, in his *Life of Apollonius of Tyana,* noted that Orestes' father had been murdered by his mother, but that Nero owed his adoption and the empire to his mother. The elder Philostratus pointed out that while Orestes had been avenging his father, Nero had no such excuse. The contemporary graffito recorded by Suetonius runs in the same vein: the first part seems to represent the heroic posturing of the official version, "Nero Orestes Alcmaeon, mother-slayer," parodying his official name, Nero Claudius Caesar; but the second half refocuses attention on its simple horror: "Or put it another way: Nero killed his own mother."[35]

The clearest glimpse into the public debate over guilt comes in an obscure anecdote. One day, as Nero was passing by, the Cynic philosopher Isidorus loudly reproached him in public, crying out "that he sang the ills of Nauplius well, but disposed of his own goods badly." Around the clever puns on good and evil *(mala bene / bona male)* was built a pointed contrast between Nero's success on stage and his failure as emperor, a criticism that sent Isidorus into exile. The ills of Nauplius, *Naupli mala,* need explanation. Nauplius was the father of the wise Palamedes, a great inventor and one of the leaders of the Greek army at Troy. Odysseus, to settle a personal grudge, and with the connivance or acquiescence of the other kings, accused Palamedes of betraying the Greek army to the Trojans for gold. He was convicted on the strength of fabricated evidence, and stoned to death. In revenge, his father Nauplius later lured the Greek fleet to its destruction by false signals, as it was sailing home from the war. The evils of Nauplius have been taken to refer in some way to the death of his son Palamedes, and it has been assumed that Nero must have written a poem on the theme.[36] But it is simpler to understand *mala* not as the woes suffered by Nauplius, but as the evils he caused. For when he had failed to win any recompense for his son's death from the Greek leaders, Nauplius sailed back from Troy and visited many of their wives in turn, telling each one that she would be replaced by a Trojan concubine. Several of the queens then fell into adultery, chief among them being Clytemnestra, the wife of Agamemnon. Thus, with the *Naupli mala,* Isidorus was alluding to the tragic events which culminated in the story of Orestes, and which were performed in public by Nero—rather well performed, as he had to admit, if only to keep the epigram pointed. On that reading, Isidorus tried to rebuild the barrier between theatrical myth and real life; he tried as well to sever the specious bond between the tale of Orestes and the fortunes of Nero's empire.

THE STORY of Oedipus must be examined next to that of Orestes. If anything even more familiar, and as a folktale even more widespread, it was a story whose retelling had a similar goal.

Laius, King of Thebes, was warned by the Delphic oracle that a son born to him and his wife Jocasta would kill him. In time a baby was born, exposed by the king on Mount Cithaeron, and by a series of coincidences saved and reared as their own son by the king and queen of Sicyon. Later the youth Oedipus was told by Delphi that he would kill his father and marry his mother. Horrified at the thought, he fled, only to fall in with Laius, his true father, and kill him in a roadside brawl. He then came to Thebes, which he freed from the shadow of the murderous Sphinx by correctly answering her riddle. The thankful Thebans made him their king and he married the now-widowed queen, Jocasta, by whom he had two sons and two daughters. When his city was ravaged by plague, Oedipus consulted Delphi, which ordered him to expel the murderer of Laius. Obediently he cursed the unknown killer and sentenced him to exile. Soon thereafter it was dramatically and irrefutably proven that he, Oedipus, had killed his father, Laius, and married his mother, Jocasta. Jocasta hanged herself and Oedipus stabbed out his eyes with her brooch. He was then driven from the city by her brother Creon and wandered the world, guided by his daughter Antigone and hounded by the Furies until he finally died at Colonus near Athens.

It is clear that Nero portrayed Oedipus as he was after the gods had stricken him with the knowledge of murder and incest. Suetonius writes of Nero's Oedipus Blinded, *Oedipus Excaecatus,* Dio of his being led about as a blind man.[37] He probably played the role in his victory at the Olympic Games in the summer of 67. Suetonius, in his account of Nero's punctilious attention to the rules of competition at Olympia, recalls his fear that he might be disqualified when he dropped his *baculus,* a staff or scepter, during a performance, a fear that was relieved when the actor appearing with him (his *hypocrita*) assured him that no one had noticed the accident amid the uproar of acclaim. What may be a distorted version of this anecdote appears in the third-century novelistic *Life of Apollonius of Tyana* by Philostratus, when the hero criticizes the emperor's excesses at the Olympics: "What do you think of his being so perfect in the role of Creon and Oedipus that he is worried he may accidentally get his entrance or his costume or his sceptre wrong?"[38] And in Nero's last public performance in Rome the following year, he sang Oedipus the Exile, presumably the same as or a sequel to Oedipus Blinded; with Roman alertness for the double significance, someone noticed that the last line he sang in public was "My father and co-husband drives me to my death."[39]

The unconscious but intentional murder of the father is less important in the story and for Nero than is its central element, the unconscious and unintended incest with the mother, whereby the father is supplanted. Incest between mother and son, though relatively rare in life and legend, had a clear symbolic significance, and stories about it share one characteristic, that the hero was or wished to be the conqueror of a homeland from which he was at the time in some way excluded.[40] Great men could be assured by consulting dreambooks that their mothers symbolized their country, so that when they dreamed of lying with their mothers they would either win power over their land, or at least die and be buried in it. Nero had to look no further than his own family for precedent: the night before Julius Caesar crossed the river Rubicon to begin his domination of the Roman world, he was said to have dreamed that he slept with his mother. To conquer one's mother was to conquer the earth, mother of all.[41]

Again, it was Nero and not his enemies who made the comparison with Oedipus. After all, it was he who chose to flaunt a concubine who looked like Agrippina and to say when he was with her that he was having intercourse with his mother, and it was he who chose to play the role of Oedipus before a public which was notoriously quick to pounce upon any contemporary parallel, real or imagined. Oedipus conveyed a lesson which Orestes could not: he was indeed guilty of incest, but it was not his fault—he had acted out of ignorance.[42]

The myth of Oedipus intersects with the myth of Orestes (and its doublet, Alcmaeon) in Neronian ideology: both traced the close relationship between royal mother and royal son which led to or was revealed as a crime; both crimes required the death of the mother; both crimes were intimately linked with the seizure of power by the legitimate heir. Sleeping with and killing one's mother are taboo for ordinary men, but both myths might be harnessed to show how the breaking of a private taboo by a prince could be tantamount to, even excused as, the legitimate seizing of public power. A great deal of the process is lost to us. We can never know Nero's state of mind or the opinions of his counselors before and after the murder of his mother; we may never know for certain the truth behind the rumors of incest; we will never know (the worst loss of all) the texts which Nero performed, the words he sang, the gestures he acted out. But we can see the boldness and the skill with which he acted to mitigate the horror of his act. Rome by Nero's day was a city thoroughly accustomed to the widespread, programmatic representation of myth in public life, and to the deep implication of the audience in theatrical performance. As emperor he deliberately invited comparison with the most familiar of Greek heroes, and as a competent performer he acted out the parallels in his life and on the stage. By mythologizing himself and his crime, he both distanced the crime and clothed himself in the aura of a hero. The goal was not to prove his innocence, but to accept guilt and to justify it.

A LITTLE over six years after the death of his mother, in the early summer of 65, the 27-year-old Nero inadvertently killed his second wife, Poppaea Sabina, who was then in her early thirties. All the sources agree that he had been madly in love with her since the year 58. In their significance for Nero, the life and death of Poppaea rivaled those of Agrippina.

The real Poppaea is all but lost to history, permanently obscured by the ferocious caricature of her in the fourteenth book of the *Annals* of Tacitus as the implacable mistress who drives Nero into removing her rivals, first his mother Agrippina in 59, then his wife Octavia in 62. Tacitus asserts (without evidence) that behind a veil of modesty she was sexually voracious, and he charges her with using sex as a means to power. But she rarely appeared in public, and it is remarkable how little the historian says about her, introducing her only five times into his narrative: at her original seduction of Nero, at the two dramas of 59 (the Death of Agrippina) and 62 (the Death of Octavia), at the birth of her child in 63, and at her own death. Tacitus offers much about her motives, much about her speeches exhorting Nero to crime, but not a word about her four years as mistress and three years as empress.[43] Dio paints the same picture, but without the nagging. Suetonius does no more than report without any criticism Nero's infatuation with her, their marriage, and her death. Her only crime may have been to supplant Octavia, who was canonized by some as the rightful empress. Soon after Nero's death the anonymous play *Octavia* would label Poppaea as the proud mistress, *superbam paelicem,* and the word "mistress" seems to have stuck.[44]

The woman Nero chose to marry—Octavia was not his choice—would have to be extraordinary. Tacitus, for all that he detested her morality, admitted that Poppaea was indeed that: "Her mother, who had surpassed all the women of her day in beauty, had given her both fame and good looks, and her wealth matched the splendor of her family. She was pleasant to converse with and her nature was by no means dull: she made a show of modesty."[45] She took great pains with her beauty, keeping wrinkles at bay by daily baths in the milk from 500 she-asses, and she prayed that she might die before she began to lose her looks. Her hair was the color of amber, and when Nero praised it in a poem other women copied what had previously been thought an unattractive shade.[46] Yet she was as intelligent as she was beautiful. The poet Leonides of Alexandria gave to Poppaea Augusta a globe of the heavens as a birthday present because, as he says in the accompanying epigram, she enjoyed gifts worthy of her marriage-bed (as the "wife of Zeus") and of her learning *(sophie).* She also took a fashionable interest in Judaism, twice interceding compassionately with her husband on the Jews' behalf, and subsidizing the future historian Josephus.[47] Nero's third wife and widow, Statilia Messalina, was similarly remarkable for her wealth, her beauty, and her character, and was such a devotee of oratory that she even practiced the art of declamation: would he have settled for anything less in her predecessor?[48]

On 21 January 63 Poppaea bore Nero his first child, a daughter, Claudia, at Nero's own birthplace, Antium, an event which Nero greeted "with more than mortal joy." Mother and daughter were both given the imperial title of Augusta, the gods were elaborately thanked, a temple was proposed for the goddess Fecundity, public games were decreed, golden statues of Fortune (the two Fortunes, goddesses of Antium) were added to the throne of Capitoline Jupiter in Rome, and a chariot race was established at Antium in honor of the Claudian and the Domitian families. Within four months the baby died, and Nero's grief was as unrestrained as his former joy: the baby girl became the Goddess Claudia, *diva Claudia,* with a temple and a priest.[49]

Within two years, Poppaea was again pregnant with a potential heir. The alleged manner of her death in the summer of 65 was to become as notorious to later ages as that of Agrippina. According to Tacitus, it was after the celebration of the second Neronian games that Nero chanced to kick his pregnant wife, and she died. Some writers, he adds, swayed more by hatred than by love of truth, had suggested poison, but Tacitus (rightly) refused to believe them, because Nero wanted children and was deeply in love with his wife. Suetonius embellishes the tale somewhat: Poppaea, pregnant and ill, reproached him for returning home late from chariot-racing (nothing about the Neronia), and Nero killed her with a blow of his heel (*ictu calcis,* the same phrase used by Tacitus). Cassius Dio says simply that he kicked her to death, either intentionally or unintentionally.[50] Again, while the stories generally cohere, there is that hint of doubt—was it really an accident, did he mean to poison her?—but the standard version was that Nero had lashed out in blind ferocity. It was a tragically domestic incident: a wife in discomfort nags her husband, perhaps he has had a bad day at the races, a flash of temper, an eternity of sorrow.

Nero's mourning was worthy of Nero. Rather than the normal cremation, Poppaea's body was embalmed with spices in the Egyptian fashion and placed in the mausoleum of Augustus. At a great public funeral, a fortune in perfume was burned and Nero himself delivered her eulogy from the Rostra in the Forum, praising Poppaea's beauty and counting it among her virtues that she had been the mother of a divine child. She was deified as a matter of course, appearing as the goddess Poppaea, *diva Poppaea Augusta,* on coins and inscriptions, and just before his own death three years later Nero completed and dedicated a temple to the goddess Sabina Venus, with an inscription proclaiming that the women of Rome had built it.[51] But the extravagance of his mourning went far beyond anything ever seen at Rome. Embalming the corpse was not enough. Eerily recalling his treatment of Agrippina, Nero sent for a woman who reportedly looked like Poppaea and kept her, presumably as a concubine. But the next year he discovered an ex-slave boy who so resembled his late wife that he castrated him, called him Sabina, married him in a solemn ceremony, and dressed and treated him in all ways as his empress. And whenever he played a woman's part on stage, he wore a mask with the features of Poppaea.[52] Again, as after the death of Agrippina, Nero chose his parts with care.

His most unusual role was Canace in Childbirth, *Canace Parturiens,* noted by Suetonius as one he undertook after the second Neronia, that is, after the death of his wife. The joke went around, apparently during the Grecian tour in 67, that a soldier who asked, "What is the emperor doing?" received the reply, "He is in labor."[53] Canace was the daughter of Aeolus, the king of the winds and friend of the gods, who lived with his wife and their six sons and six daughters in isolation on the Aeolian Islands in the Tyrrhenian Sea. Versions of the story differ substantially in details, but the essential elements are that Canace bore a child to her brother Macareus and that when their father discovered the affair he sent a sword to Canace, with which she killed herself. Macareus persuaded his father to change his mind, but it was too late and he too killed himself.

This minor tale would be familiar to the educated from the now lost play *Aeolus* by Euripides, but even more from the *Heroides* of Ovid, the collection of letters in verse from heroines of myth to their husbands or lovers, published less than eighty years before Nero's performance. Ovid subscribed to the version that portrayed Canace as her brother's eager lover. Through her he describes in detail the shame and pain of the childbirth. Aeolus hears the cries of the newborn and flies into a rage, threatening his daughter even as she lies on her bed. He orders the baby to be cast out to the wild animals, and almost immediately after he leaves her room, a messenger brings in the sword. After recounting these events, Canace bids her brother farewell, asking him to place her own and their child's remains in one urn and to mourn them both.[54]

The version performed by Nero was surely close to this in its pathos. The parallels between life and myth need not be exact—the emotional resonance would be enough—and events succeed each other in Ovid's poem so rapidly that the tale could easily be encompassed within a piece entitled Canace in Childbirth. Out of the whole repertoire Nero deliberately chose a rather obscure myth in which he played on stage a mother giving birth who was soon after killed at the same time as her baby and bitterly mourned by the child's father and grandfather. He did so as he wore the mask of his late wife Poppaea Sabina, struck down in her pregnancy. Bizarre though the whole affair might appear to us, no Roman audience could miss the personal relevance of the tale; some might even be touched.

Another favorite role taken up by the emperor after his wife's death was that of *Hercules Furens,* Hercules Gone Mad, best known from Euripides' play *Heracles* and from Seneca's *Hercules Furens.* Briefly stated, the great hero is driven mad by the goddess Hera and slays his sons and their mother, his wife Megara, the daughter of Creon, King of Thebes. The oracle at Delphi then orders him to serve King Eurystheus, for whom he will perform the Twelve Labors. In Euripides' play the height of pathos is reached when the hero comes to his senses to discover that he is bound to a column, surrounded by the corpses of his family and by his bow and arrows, and learns to his mounting horror that he was the murderer. This scene was certainly replicated by Nero in his performance, for rumor asserted that once a young soldier, who was posted to guard the entrance, rushed to the emperor's assistance when he saw him in his finery and bound with chains, as the role required. The chains were, of course, of gold.[55]

The story of Hercules is key—the father who kills his wife and his sons and heirs but who is not responsible for the deed, driven mad as he is by the anger of a god.[56] As with the death of Agrippina, so with that of Poppaea: Nero consciously presented his own versions of myths on stage before an audience eager to discover the slightest nuance of contemporary relevance. The desired response is likewise clear, though not explicit. Like Hercules, whom he wished to imitate in other ways, Nero had destroyed the woman he loved, and the child who was to succeed him, not because he was a murderer, but in a fit of divine madness. In short, the story was true: he had killed Poppaea Sabina as rumor had it, and he had slaughtered their unborn child, but like Hercules (and like Aeolus in his own way), he was innocent.

BUT WAS the story true? Probably not. It was certainly not original. Despite the absolute silence of our sources, it looks as if Nero tried to reinvent publicly a significant part of his private life in the image of one specific model: the notorious Periander, tyrant of Corinth in the first half of the sixth century BC.[57] The distinctive reminiscences are stunning.

First, Periander was the only other important figure of Graeco-Roman antiquity who was accused of sleeping with his mother, and, as with Nero, the event was the turning point in his life. The story is best known as presented in chapter 17 of the *Unhappy Love Stories, Erotika Pathemata,* written by the Greek poet Parthenius in the first century BC. As he grew to be a gentle and handsome youth, Periander's mother fell ever more passionately in love with him. Unable to restrain herself, she finally persuaded her reluctant son to meet secretly with a beautiful married woman who was hopelessly enamored of him. Conditions of modesty were set: they were to meet in a room without a light, and he was not to make the woman speak to him. They met, and Periander was delighted with his unseen mistress. Naturally his curiosity grew without being satisfied as his mother continued to protect the woman's identity. At last, when she came to the room one night he lit a lamp; then, struck with horror to discover that his lover was his own mother, he tried to slay her. The gods intervened to prevent him, his mother killed herself, and Periander, his mind unbalanced, sank into ferocious tyranny. His biographer, Diogenes Laertius, quotes a much-truncated version of this folktale, to the effect that the tyrant committed incest with his mother and when the truth was revealed turned brutal. The mother's name, we are told, was *Crateia,* Power.[58]

Next, as Diogenes relates the matter in his brief Life of Periander, "in a fit of anger, he killed his wife by throwing a footstool at her, or by a kick, when she was pregnant."[59] He had been egged on by the lies of his concubines, whom he later burned alive, and in a (fictitious) letter to his father-in-law he protests that he had not meant to do it. In destroying the unborn baby he also ensured that he would leave no child as the heir to his power: one son was feeble-minded, the other was killed later, and Periander was succeeded by his nephew.

Herodotus adds a strange story.[60] Happening to lose an object of value one day, Periander sent an embassy to an oracle of the dead. The ghost of his wife Melissa appeared but would not help: "She was chill," she said, "having no clothes; the garments buried with her were of no manner of use, since they had not been burnt. And this should be her token to Periander, that what she said was true—the oven was cold when he baked his loaves in it." Periander understood the sign at once, for he had made love to her dead body. He therefore summoned the women of Corinth to the temple of Hera. When they arrived in their finery, as for a festival, he stripped them all naked, slave and free alike, and burned their clothes for Melissa. She then told a second inquiry to the oracle where to find the lost valuable. Thus, even though incest with a mother and unintentionally kicking to death a pregnant wife in a fit of fury might be enough to draw the parallel, Nero went further. The embalming of Poppaea, the union with her double, the marriage with Sporus, might all be taken to echo Periander's obsession with his dead wife; certainly the temple dedicated to the divine Sabina Venus by the women of Rome was built with money extorted from them, just as Periander had forced the women of Corinth to dedicate their finest clothes to his dead Melissa.[61]

Finally, Periander was the first to think of cutting a canal through the Isthmus of Corinth. Others after him were said to have considered the attempt—Demetrius Poliorcetes, Julius Caesar, Caligula—but only Nero, a lover of grand engineering projects, tried seriously to put the plan into action. The cutting of the Isthmus, although of undoubted benefit to mankind, came to be regarded as an act of hubris, an overbearing trespass into the affairs of the gods, and the mark of a tyrant.[62] The next man after Nero who was said to have weighed the possibility was the wealthy and imperious Athenian orator and sophist Herodes Atticus, a Roman senator and consul in the year 143. Not a tyrant himself, he nevertheless had several run-ins with the democratic elements in Athens, and his grandfather had actually been condemned on a charge of aiming at tyranny. More peculiarly, Herodes was charged by his brother-in-law with beating his wife so as to cause her death in the eighth month of her pregnancy, in the year 157. We are told, moreover, in addition to his accuser's inability to bring any proof, that Herodes' defense was helped by the fact that he had not intended to kill her, and that his grief for her was uncommonly extravagant.[63] Just the man to dream of a Corinthian canal.

The Periander of legend provided for Nero a veritable mirror for princes. On the surface, as we see it, the image is horrific: the savage sexuality of a man who violated his mother, who violated the mother of his child, who violated Mother Earth; the violent conquest and exertion of unrestrained power; the proverbial cruelty. Periander had learned well from his teacher, the older tyrant Thrasybulus of Miletus. In a celebrated tale which attaches itself to other similar figures, Periander sent to Thrasybulus to ask what was the best way to govern. Thrasybulus replied by taking the messenger for a walk, during which he lopped off all the tallest heads of grain. The messenger was mystified that Thrasybulus said nothing, but Periander understood, and the lesson was not lost on Nero.[64]

Yet the mirror reflects simultaneously a quite different image. Periander had made Corinth great. He built up its navy and dominated the seas, he conquered, he colonized widely, he promoted trade from Illyria to Egypt. He legislated against luxury, forced his subjects to work hard, abolished taxes. His court attracted artists and poets, chief among them the singer Arion. He beautified the city with great buildings. He won the chariot race at the Olympic Games. At the heart of it all lay his own tremendous personality, and a practical and gnomic wisdom that gained him a place on lists of the Seven Sages of Greece. Many Greeks had trouble accepting Periander as one of the wise men. Plato omitted him; Aristotle included him; several others in their discomfort concluded that there must have been two Perianders, the despot and the sage.[65] Nero would be quite happy with the paradox of the man whose superior virtues and abilities absolved him from the moral constraints of society.

For nero, it was not a matter of art for art's sake. He used the stage—he could not have avoided using the stage—as a platform for his views, presented in mythological dress. From that assumption several conclusions follow.

First, we can see at least three messages in transmission. One is the image of the matricide, driven by the gods, tormented by the Furies, but ultimately absolved for his crime—in the case of Orestes, seizing power from the female usurper. The second is that of the incestuous son who sleeps unawares with his mother; and the third is that of the man who unintentionally causes the death of wife and child. No myth was, or was expected to be, an exact fit with real life; an allusion was enough for the audience to create its own story.[66] The common thread of the tales enacted by Nero on stage, sometimes in a mask displaying his own features, was one of justification for acts that were essentially unjustifiable. At some deeper level, he was saying, he was innocent.

Moreover, since Nero chose to act out the tales on stage, he himself must either have created or soon appropriated them. This is best seen in the identification with Orestes, which was asserted by him and rejected by his critics, but it casts light on the other notorious stories as well. In folklore, mother-son incest normally occurs between two unwitting parties, or else the mother seduces the son; seldom is the son at fault.[67] Nero brilliantly combined elements of the Oedipus tale with elements of Orestes to double the horror of Agrippina's lust for power. He also succeeded in getting his message across. The serious doubt that incest actually occurred, and the certainty shared by all but his most virulent detractors that, if it did occur, Agrippina must have been the aggressor—not having one's cake, but eating it anyway—surely both can only have started with

Nero. Whatever later generations made of the affair, popular rumor, *fama,* blamed Agrippina.

Similarly with the treatment of the death of Poppaea, Nero got his message across, whatever later generations made of it. Despite grumbling, most agreed that it was an accident. No one really questioned whether Nero had kicked her, or even whether Poppaea was pregnant at all. The claim that he was innocent of the crime by reason of temporary insanity brilliantly diverts attention from the fact of the crime itself. That Nero seems to have studied the life of Periander with extraordinary care strongly suggests that there may have been no crime at all—that Poppaea's fortuitous death was made into something more interesting and the excuse for even more immoderate mourning. Sleeping with his mother and kicking his pregnant wife to death are stories too good to be true.

Finally, behind the masks lies a daring new conception of Roman power. By presenting himself as the heroes and heroines of myth, Nero of course raised himself above the level of ordinary action and responsibility. That fits in well with the model of Periander drawn from legend. There were other models which he could imitate, the most obvious being Augustus and Alexander. Augustus followed by his successors was the civil prince, *civilis princeps,* the first among equals, but poised between Republican nobleman and Hellenistic monarch. Alexander followed by his successors was something different: world-conqueror, patron of arts and letters, close to divinity on earth. But Periander was something quite different again, an older and much more elemental creature, not a god or godlike but a great tyrant, superhuman in his emotions and his wisdom, writer and Olympic victor, conqueror and patron of the arts—in short, a Greek rather than a Hellenistic or Roman monarch, and one much closer to the heroes of myth than of history.[68]

5

Shining Apollo

Apollo is in the full vigor of youth, the time of life at which men seem their most handsome. For the sun is most beautiful and youthful to see. Next, he is called Phoebus [radiant] because he is clean and shimmering. They apply other epithets to him, calling him "golden-tressed" and "unshorn youth," for he is golden-faced and stands outside of grief because of his purity. They call him "Delian" and "Light-bringing" because things are revealed through him, and the cosmos is enlightened.

CORNUTUS

"Take nothing away, Fates," Phoebus said, "let the duration of human life be surpassed by him who is my like in looks and grace, and my equal in voice and song. He will guarantee an era of prosperity to the weary and break the silence of the laws. Like the Morning Star, as he rises scattering the stars in flight, or like the Evening Star, as he rises when the stars return (at dusk), like the gleaming Sun, as soon as rosy Dawn has dispelled the shadows and led in the day, as he gazes on the world and begins to whip up his chariot from the starting-barrier: such a Caesar is at hand, such a Nero shall Rome now gaze upon. His radiant face blazes with gentle brilliance and his shapely neck with flowing hair."

SENECA[1]

The murder of Agrippina in March of 59 released the ferocious creativity of her 21-year-old son. Singing and acting led him into the realm of the heroes of myth. Singing and racing chariots would raise him to the gods.

As Tacitus tells it, with intense disapproval, Nero had long wanted to race four-horse chariots, and (no less shameful) to sing to his own accompaniment on the lyre, as a contestant. Now, when he had returned to Rome three months after the death of Agrippina, he could at last indulge his desire. The historian reports the young prince's own rationalizations for such unusual conduct by an emperor. Nero appealed to precedent, as we have seen. Kings and great men of old had raced horses; poets had celebrated their deeds and the gods were honored by them. And singing was sacred to Apollo, the great prophetic deity whose statues in the dress of a lyre-player stood not just in the cities of Greece but in Roman temples as well. From this Tacitus passes immediately to the disgraceful spectacle of a Roman prince racing chariots in his private gardens in the valley of the Vatican, before an appreciative mob of spectators, and then to Nero's Juvenile Games, which he closed with a careful recital on the lyre, to the delirious praise of his Augustiani. Day and night resounded with the applause of his claque as they showered the epithets of divinity on both his appearance and his voice. Tacitus is vague here, but Dio records their precise words: "Beautiful Caesar, Apollo, Augustus, another Pythian. By yourself (we swear), Caesar: no one can defeat you."[2] Rome had a new Apollo.

As in the selection of characters to play on the stage, the choice of role was his own. There is a great deal of evidence to suggest that Nero did not emerge in the image of Apollo until the latter half of 59, after his return from Campania, released at last from maternal restraint: all references to Apollo in Tacitus, Suetonius, and Dio postdate the return; many Neronian coins, imperial and provincial, depict the god, but none appeared before 60 at the earliest; and the epigraphical evidence likewise either postdates that year or is undatable. Against this, there seems to be some literary evidence that a new Golden Age of Apollo was trumpeted earlier, in 54. This discrepancy with the rest of the historical record is especially clear in two works: in the seven Eclogues of a minor poet named Calpurnius Siculus, who sought the patronage of a new emperor, a Phoebus Palatinus; and in the savage satire on the death of the emperor Claudius known as the *Apocolocyntosis,* which is generally agreed to have been written by Nero's teacher, Seneca. But the new Golden Age supposedly proclaimed in 54 is an anachronism. It can be shown that Calpurnius Siculus wrote considerably after the reign of Nero; and the prophecy of the Golden Age sung by Apollo in Seneca's satire (quoted above in the epigraph) is a later addition to the work, written with knowledge of the events of 59.[3] This is not to deny that the idea of a Golden Age of Apollo was in the air. It is rather to insist that it was Nero himself in 59—not his teacher or a hopeful poet in 54—who put it into circulation.

He chose an image which by his day would call to mind a web of familiar attributes. Apollo was both the god of healing, father of Aesculapius, and god of the plague, the far-shooter, *hekatebolos,* whose merciless arrows struck down both the innocent and the guilty. He was the god of music and poetry, leader of the Muses, *mousagetes,* singer and player of the lyre, *kitharoidos,* and also the god of prophecy, which was so close to the art of the poet—several oracles transmitted his visions, the greatest being that of Delphi at the center of Greece and the world. Representations of the god would be recognizable immediately by his attributes: his bow, or his lyre, or the wreath or branch of Delphic laurel which he wore or carried, and his long, often unkempt, golden hair. By Homer's day he was felt to be the most Greek of gods, the acme of the physical and spiritual development of man.

Yet there is one very special aspect of Apollo that first appeared later, in the early Classical Age of Greece. For all his benefits to mankind, Apollo's character also emanates a sense of distance from human affairs, and so by the early fifth century he had begun to be identified with the Sun—Helios to the Greeks, the Roman Sol—the distant giver of light and life, the impartial judge who sees all, both bad deeds and good. Thus by the time of the early Empire Apollo was commonly confused with the god of the Sun, the driver of the chariot of the sun, Phoebus Apollo, the gloriously beautiful Shining Apollo—most notably by Ovid in the second book of his *Metamorphoses.*

Intellectuals responded with enthusiasm to Nero's fresh assumption of the role. The first certain appearance of the Apolline theme, after the carefully prepared applause of the Augustiani in 59, comes in the very next year, in words recited by Rome's brilliant 20-year-old poet, Lucan, at the Neronian Games of 60. Lucan's verses were part of the introduction to the *Pharsalia,* his epic-in-progress about the Civil War between Caesar and Pompey which was to bring down the old Roman Republic. An invocation customarily starts such works, and Lucan is at no loss in the poem for a patron deity. When Nero rises to heaven after his death he will naturally become chief of the gods, taking either the scepter from Jupiter or the reins from Phoebus—Phoebus as an alternative to Jupiter himself is noteworthy—to guide his flaming chariot, and the joyful earth will no longer fear the vagaries of the changing sun. Even better, Lucan does not have to wait for this inevitable apotheosis. To him Nero is already a god, and the poet has no need to appeal to Apollo or to Bacchus for inspiration, for Nero himself will give him the strength to sing a Roman song.[4] Thus, by the year 60, the two main notes in the theme are neatly sounded: Nero as the driver of the chariot of the sun and hence benefactor of the whole

Copy of Nero's official portrait, AD 59–64.

earth; and Nero as the god of song and hence patron of the poet. In both cases, he assumes the role of Apollo.

Another would-be poet went even farther. In the last months of Nero's life the Greek doctor Andromachus sent the emperor a sovereign remedy against snakebite. He shrewdly wrote it out in 174 elaborate hexameter verses which end with an invocation to Apollo, here addressed as Paean, that is, both physician and savior, but also the appropriate recipient of a song of thanksgiving. Andromachus asks the god to transmit his panacea to Nero—a striking picture of Apollo as intermediary between subject and emperor.[5]

Sometime in the 60s a passage was inserted into the *Apocolocyntosis* of Seneca, by him or by someone else, which neatly picks up the themes of 59.[6] Here Phoebus Apollo appears, urging the Fates to extend the life of the young emperor beyond the normal span, for Nero is similar to Apollo himself in his beauty of face and carriage and his equal in song and voice. And he is also like the Sun, gazing down on the earth as he whips up his chariot at the starting gate. Naturally, such a prince will restore prosperity and justice to a weary world. Genius in song and racing, brilliant personal beauty, good rule: these are the central elements of Nero's particularly solar Apollinism.

These images of Nero as—or with—Apollo and the Sun were not merely the conceits of a court circle; the prince broadcast widely, and his people responded. On the one side, at his professional debut as a citharode before the public in 64, he chose to sing the story of Niobe, the presumptuous queen who had boasted that she was greater than Leto because where Leto had borne only Apollo and Artemis she had borne fourteen handsome sons and daughters. Grievously insulted, the divine brother and sister took a horrific revenge, shooting down all of Niobe's children before her eyes. The choice of this particular myth for the emperor's first appearance before his people as a citharode was not mere chance: to sing the woes of Niobe was to sing the fearsome power of Apollo. On the other side, in 62, a graffito encapsulated the dialogue between ruler and ruled neatly if negatively, reacting to the defeat of Caesennius Paetus by the Parthians by recalling two aspects of Apollo: "While ours strums his lyre, the Parthians' draws his bow; ours shall be Paean, theirs the Far-Shooter."[7]

The best projection of official intentions is offered by the imperial coinage minted at Rome and Lyons. Nero's head is shown "radiate," that is, wearing a diadem with sharp rays rising from it; this clear reference to the sun appears commonly on the obverse of his bronze coins in Rome from 64 onward. Two particularly interesting images of Nero crowned with rays appear on the reverses of both gold and bronze coins of 64–65: one, with the inscription "Augustus Augusta," shows the emperor in his toga with the radiate crown, holding a patera (for sacrifice) and a scepter (signifying rule), and the empress veiled with patera and a cornucopia (signifying plenty); its companion piece, with the inscription "Augustus Germanicus," shows the emperor seated, holding a branch in one hand and a figure of Victory on a globe in the other (referring to Corbulo's successes in Armenia). And between 62 and 65, Apollo Citharoedus is frequently found depicted on coin reverses, advancing in flowing robes, his right hand plucking the lyre which he holds in his left. Suetonius knew these coins and assumed, understandably, that they represented the statues of Nero in the dress of a citharode which the victorious emperor set up after his triumph of 67.[8]

Local response to such images can be seen in the coinage of provincial cities and districts, much of it prompted by the liberation of Greece in 66. Corinth has a coin with a laureate Nero (that is, he is shown wearing a laurel wreath) on the obverse, with a reverse of Helios in his *quadriga*. The proud "Neronian Colony of Patras" depicts Nero as he arrives by ship in 66, with "Apollo Augustus" on the reverse, playing the lyre. Nicopolis honored "Nero Apollo the Founder," showing him playing his lyre. These were places which the emperor actually visited, but Apollo the citharode likewise appears on the reverse of Neronian coins of the Thessalian League (with a radiate "Nero of the Thessalians" on the obverse), of Thessalonica in Macedonia, and of Perinthus in Thrace; while in Asia Minor a radiate Nero was shown on their coins by Nicaea in Bithynia and by Thyatira in Asia.[9]

Particularly interesting as the official manifestation of local sentiment is the inscription from Acraephia in central Greece, which records Nero's speech granting freedom to the Greeks in 66. The official decree of thanks from the town offers him various honors and calls him "the New Helios lighting the Hellenes."[10] Scores of other towns must have done the same. Three inscriptions in Athens identified statues of Nero (now lost) as the "Emperor Nero Caesar Augustus, New Apollo," and the "Emperor Caesar, son of a God [namely, Claudius], Augustus Nero, New Apollo"; whether they were public or private is not clear. But in another inscription from Sagalassus in Pisidia, in Asia Minor, a private citizen hails Nero as the New Sun, while a soldier from Prostanna (also in Pisidia) calls him the New Sun God.[11]

The diffusion of the twin images—of Apollo the lyre-player and of Sol/Helios the charioteer—is well attested, and Nero clearly conceived of them as a special pair. Thus, in 66, according to Dio, after he had contended among the citharodes, his teacher Menecrates celebrated a triumph for him in the circus, after which the emperor drove as a charioteer: that is, when he appeared in one guise he appeared in the companion role as well. Similarly, after he had crowned Tiridates as king of Armenia later in the same year, Nero sang and played his lyre before the people; then he drove a chariot dressed in the uniform of the Green faction and wearing a charioteer's helmet.[12] But the most revealing instance of this special pairing is his behavior at the end of his artistic triumph in late 67. He had of course entered and won the full range of competitions in the six great Greek games which he had attended, but when he returned it was the singing and the racing which he emphasized in his triumph, in a very personal way. Since the time of Romulus, military triumphs had traditionally ended on the Capitoline Hill with a sacrifice to Jupiter Optimus Maximus. But for Nero, Jupiter was just the first stop. Next he went over to the Temple of Palatine Apollo, presumably to sacrifice to the god there represented as the Citharode, and he set up his victory crowns and statues of himself as citharode in the bedrooms of the adjacent palace. He then proceeded to the Circus Maximus, where he placed all of his racing crowns around the Egyptian obelisk which stood on the central *spina* of the track, after which he raced around the course.[13] The obelisk had been raised some twelve centuries earlier by Ramses II at Heliopolis, the City of the Sun, and was brought to Rome by Augustus, who set it up in the circus in 10 BC, adding to it the very visible inscription which proclaimed that, having subjugated Egypt to the power of the Roman people, he dedicated the obelisk as a gift to Sol.[14] Thus, in 67 Nero offered his victory crowns to Apollo, the god of song, and to Sol, the god of racing.

Nonetheless, there is at the same time good reason to separate Apollo and Sol, or rather to concentrate on Sol—the solar aspect of Apollo—and in so doing to follow Nero's lead. The contrasting dedications of 67, to Apollo in the private bedchambers of the palace and to Sol in one of the most public places in Rome, could be read metaphorically: Apollo the citharode was an artist, but Sol was the benefactor of mankind, and certainly offered an image more appropriate to a ruler of the world. Likewise, whereas on the coins Nero may be *associated* with Apollo the Lyre-Player, he himself is *shown* wearing the radiate crown of the Sun. The scattered surviving remnants and reflections of his official portraiture bear this preference out: all are solar, none are otherwise Apolline.[15]

The emperor's solar personality could be amply indicated by the crown of rays alone, as can be seen on the radiate heads on the coins. A splendid example of just such a portrait is the great black basalt head of Nero in his final portrait type, now in Florence, which wears a radiate crown carved in high relief.[16] But there was another portrayal of the emperor as the Sun in circulation, symbolically richer and even more appropriate to Nero—that is, the one depicting him dressed as a charioteer and driving the solar chariot. The headless statue of a Julio-Claudian prince from the theater of Caere in Etruria wears a breast-plate showing the griffins of Apollo, above which rises the chariot of the Sun seen face-on, with the horses turning outward to the right and left. The curly-haired charioteer wears a crown with seven long rays, but his face, far from being the abstract idealization of solar beauty, is instead round and fleshy. Surely this is Nero himself, superimposed on the image of Sol in precisely the same way as that seen in the fifth-century cameo of Nero in the solar chariot, and the stylized reflection is one of an official image.[17] The image is alluded to by Cassius Dio in his account of "the Golden Day" in 66, when Tiridates of Armenia received his crown from Nero. On that day, in the Theater of Pompey where part of the celebration occurred, "the curtains stretched overhead to keep off the sun were purple and in the center of them was an embroidered figure of Nero driving a chariot, with golden stars gleaming all about him."[18] That is, when the audience looked up to the sun, they would see Nero himself instead—in fact the emperor's image very neatly protected his people from the sun's burning rays, and the stars around him indicated that his chariot was indeed a heavenly one. Although Dio is silent about it, we can assume that by 66 Nero was shown wearing a radiate crown.[19]

Presenting himself as the solar charioteer was a brilliant stroke, for not only was Sol the charioteer of the heavens, but his earthly home was the Circus Maximus (and by extension all circuses). In the words of Tertullian, "The Circus is consecrated mainly to the Sun, whose temple stands in the middle of it and whose image shines forth from its summit."[20] The ancient association of sun and circus eventually gave rise to an elaborate astrological interpretation of the circus as the world in miniature: the arena was the earth, the channel of its euripus was the sea; the obelisk in the center represented the sun; the 24 races, 24 hours; the seven laps, the days of the week; the 12 gates of the *carceres*, the months or the signs of the zodiac; the four main racing factions, the seasons (Green/ spring, Red/summer, Blue/autumn, White/winter); and so forth. In rac-

ing around the circus, Nero followed the course of—imitated—the sun.[21]
It was only appropriate that he should dedicate his racing trophies there,
and the divine relationship between emperor and circus was cemented
by the crushing of the Pisonian conspiracy in 65: "Then offerings and
thanksgivings to the gods were decreed [by the senate], with special honours to the Sun, who has an ancient temple in the circus where the
crime was planned, as having revealed by his power the secrets of the conspiracy."[22]

According to legend, from the moment of his birth Nero was destined
for solar greatness. Very dramatically, he was born on the morning of 15
December just as the sun rose, so that he was touched by its rays almost
before he was touched by the earth (that is, before he was laid on the
ground to be picked up and acknowledged by his father). Or, in another
and even more thrilling version of the story, he was born before sunrise
and surrounded by rays from an invisible source.[23] Despite this prophecy,
the real creation and development of the radiant Nero which it celebrates
after the fact can be traced only much later in his life, as the image of
Nero as the Sun was developed in full and spectacular fashion in his last
four years.

The first stage of the evolution starts in 59, with his decision to sing and
to race. As Tacitus reports Nero's words, he called on Apollo to justify his
singing, but for chariot racing, he simply appealed to the pastimes of ancient kings and great men (that is, with no mention of Sol). Similarly, his
supporters, the Augustiani who sang his praises as Apollo and another
Pythian, were strictly music lovers: they have no word for his prowess as a
charioteer. That is to say, racing was at first a quite separate activity, with
no connection made to Apollo the singer. Likewise, in his proem to the
Pharsalia in 60, Lucan has Nero replacing Apollo as the patron of poets
immediately, but for Lucan his apotheosis as Phoebus lies in the future.
This suggests that the two roles of divine citharode and solar charioteer
were still separate, and that Nero was not yet playing the second one; indeed, Lucan may have held out the tantalizing possibility of a new role for
the aspiring charioteer. And while Apollo Citharoedus appears on the
coins around 62, the radiate Nero does not turn up until 64.

In 64, Dio complains, Nero reached new heights of excess by driving
chariots in public, and the year is significant. No evidence associating him
with the Sun is known to predate 64, and whatever evidence can be dated
comes from that year or later: the radiate coins, the Acraephia decree

("new Helios lighting the Hellenes"), the unmasking of Piso's conspiracy, the awning on the Golden Day, the dedication of the Greek trophies to Sol in the Circus.[24] It seems, in fact, that the New Helios arose from the flames of the Great Fire of July 64.

THE DEVASTATION of his city by fire in the summer of 64 was certainly as great a stimulus to Nero's imagination as the murder of his mother had been in the spring of 59, and the new role as the Sun of Rome was by no means the least of his creations.[25] When the fire began he had acted with decision and compassion, rushing back from Antium to Rome to direct the fire-fighting and relief efforts. When it was at last contained, much of the city lay in ruins. He began rebuilding immediately, taking extensive measures to prevent or impede future fires. As a matter of course for a *princeps,* he took equal care to appease the gods, who must have been deeply offended. The Sibylline books were consulted in the Temple of Apollo Palatinus—the emperor was a member of the priestly college entrusted with the task—and supplications prescribed in ancient times by the Sibyl were made to various concerned deities. But, Tacitus claims, neither these nor the urban planning measures were enough to allay popular suspicions that the emperor himself had ordered the fire. To quash the rumor, Nero identified as the culprits a group loathed by the mob: the Christians. Many of them were arrested, and they were convicted less for the crime of arson than for their "hatred of the human race." Tacitus continues:

> Mockeries were added to their dying, so that they perished wrapped in the skins of wild beasts and torn by dogs, or nailed to crosses, or in flames, and when day departed they were burned to light up the night [*in usum nocturni luminis*]. Nero had opened up his gardens for the spectacle and he put on a circus game, himself mixing with the people dressed as a charioteer or standing in a chariot. Wherefore, although it was for people who were guilty and deserving of the utmost punishment, pity was aroused, as if they were being consumed not for the public good but for the savagery of one man.[26]

These festivities probably took place in the Vatican across the river, on Nero's estate with a private racecourse, untouched by the fire.

Punishment at Rome was always a very public act. The Romans of the late Republic and early Empire distinguished themselves by transforming it into a public spectacle. In fact, the deaths of the Christians correspond to the three common forms of execution at one time: being thrown to the beasts, being crucified, and being burned alive (the ancient penalty for arson). But often a theatrical element might be added. Executions could be presented as "fatal charades," tableaux or scenes from the more bloodthirsty myths being reenacted for the enjoyment of the spectators, with lethal consequences for the actor-criminals.[27] The mass execution of the Christians was turned into just such a show (Tacitus calls it a *spectaculum*), and the mockeries, *ludibria,* added by Nero are central to understanding it. Thus "condemnation to the beasts," *damnatio ad bestias,* normally meant that the criminals, men and women, often naked, sometimes bound or sometimes with inadequate weapons, would be exposed to ferocious wild animals. But on this occasion they have themselves become the beasts, and are attacked by hunting dogs. How the act of crucifixion was modified Tacitus neglects to say, but the transformation of burning criminals into lights for the night is extraordinary. The emperor strolling among the crowd in the costume of a charioteer is equally astonishing. Indeed, the whole affair was irregular. It does not appear to have been a normal *spectaculum,* arranged in advance by the emperor or a magistrate and presented in one of the great public spaces set aside for it (theater, amphitheater, circus) before an audience of holiday-makers dressed in their best clothes and arranged by social order. It was rather part of a public expiation for a great crime against the gods, held on the emperor's private grounds, hastily presented to a crowd of frightened, angry, exhausted citizens. The first, Neronian persecution of the Christians is so familiar now that we forget how unusual it was at the time.

The punishments fit the crime. Tacitus, our main source for the Great Fire, says that he could not begin to count the number of mansions and apartment buildings and temples destroyed, so he would mention and dwell on only the most ancient temples of the Roman people, to symbolize the terrible loss. First in his account is the temple of Luna, the moon, erected by King Servius Tullius in the sixth century BC. This has generally been taken to be the temple of Luna on the Aventine Hill, but that cannot be true.[28] In the 80s, the emperor Domitian set up inscribed altars to mark the boundaries of the Fire of 64. One of them was found on the slope of the Aventine overlooking the Circus Maximus where the fire began—that is, the Aventine hill must have escaped unscathed. Moreover, the temple of Luna on the Aventine is not mentioned before 182 BC, and it has surely been confused by Tacitus or his source with the famous Servian temple of Diana (who was also goddess of the moon) on the Aventine. If the temple mentioned by Tacitus cannot be the one on the Aventine, only one other temple to Luna is known to have existed in Rome, the shrine attested in a single passage in the late Republican antiquarian writer, Varro: Luna Noctiluca on the Palatine, Luna Light of the Night, which was probably lit up at night. The Palatine was severely damaged by the Great Fire, which started at night. Presumably the light of Luna Noctiluca was extinguished by it, and that is why the Christian martyrs were burned, to light up the night again.[29]

By the same token, presenting the Christians as beasts to be torn by the dogs must have reminded spectators of Actaeon transformed into a stag and torn to pieces by hunting dogs. His sacrilegious crime had been to gaze upon the goddess Diana while she bathed. Diana was not only goddess of the hunt, she was also goddess of the moon, and it would be appropriate to propitiate her with the lives of the criminals who had supposedly attacked her temple.[30]

Thus far can Tacitus be explained, but he chose not to tell the whole story of the destruction of the city. Unfortunately, Dio seems to say nothing of the Christians in his report of the Great Fire, while Suetonius in his brief account of the Christians says nothing about the Fire. There is, however, a Christian source which does appear to transmit some genuine information: the letter to the Corinthians from Clement, Bishop of Rome, which is traditionally dated to around AD 96. In the fifth and sixth sections of that letter Clement, who is warning against jealousy, talks of the heroes of recent times, his own generation, who suffered by it, meaning in this case martyrs. He writes of Peter and Paul (who had died under Nero) and many others whom he does not name. Even women had suffered persecution because of jealousy, bearing witness to their faith in the guise of Danaids and Dirce. This is a precious glimpse into the "fatal charades" of the spectacle—its context is certainly Neronian, and the only concerted persecution of the Christians which involved large-scale, not to mention theatrical, suffering in the first century was that of Nero after the Fire.[31] That is, Nero must be the anonymous dramaturge here. Why did he choose the Danaids and Dirce?

The fifty daughters of Danaus were the subject of one of the most familiar of myths. Danaus, having fallen out with his brother Aegyptus, fled from Egypt to Greece where, with Apollo's help, he seized the city of Argos. The fifty sons of Aegyptus, who had been betrothed to his daughters, the *Danaides,* pursued them to Argos and demanded them in marriage. On the wedding night all but one of the fifty daughters, following the command of their father, slew their bridegrooms. In Hades the forty-nine murderesses were punished terribly for their crime, condemned to carry water in leaking jars throughout eternity. How could this be translated into the setting of a Roman amphitheater? It might be a tedious spectacle for a crowd looking for rivers of blood, but Roman audiences were satisfied with the sketchiest of symbols: give each woman a jar, then let loose the beasts. The point of the entertainment lies not in the manner of punishment but in the persons of the criminals or victims.

There was one site in Rome associated with the Danaids: the Temple of Apollo on the Palatine, which had been dedicated in 28 BC. Closely attached by a ramp to the house of Augustus himself, in a complex reminiscent of the Hellenistic royal capital at Pergamum, it was the great monument to Augustus' patron, the god who had helped him defeat the forces of Egypt (that is, of Antony and Cleopatra) at the Battle of Actium in 31 BC. In the last three decades the complex has become much better understood, thanks to excavation in the house of Augustus, investigation of old excavation reports, and careful evaluation of the extensive literary descriptions of the temple (especially that by the poet Propertius) and of the considerable archaeological fragments and copies.[32] Although much about the temple remains obscure, it is now known that the portico surrounding the sacred area before it contained statues of all fifty Danaids, with certainly some, perhaps all, bearing water jugs, each standing between columns of Numidian marble. This was confirmed recently when three stunning life-size herms (that is, the top half of a human figure, set on a squared column), found on the site of the temple over a century ago, were convincingly identified as three of the original Danaids.[33] Archaizing in style, executed with great virtuosity out of black marble, they stood in their long and uncanny lines around the portico before the Temple of Apollo, an ambiguous reminder of Octavian's great victory over a Roman general and the Queen of Egypt. What precise message they were meant to convey is still unclear—perhaps, in some way, not only victory but the horror of civil war.[34]

Tacitus and Dio both write of the devastation caused by the Great Fire to the Palatine, and excavation has shown that buildings on the hill were heavily hit, particularly Nero's new palace.[35] The temple of Apollo Palatinus must have been damaged, for it stood in a position of great danger, overlooking the Circus Maximus, where the Fire had started. At the very least the temple and its precinct were threatened, and those who threatened it must be punished. The choice of the Danaids would be quickly understood by a Roman audience.[36]

Dirce too can be fitted into Nero's *spectaculum,* and she was much closer to what the audience normally enjoyed. Dirce, wife of the King of Thebes, was an ingeniously wicked stepmother who (in one version of the story) tried to trick her stepsons into attacking their long-suffering mother. The angry youths turned instead on Dirce the violence intended for their mother: they tied their stepmother by her hair to the horns of a bull, which then trampled and gored her to death. The death of Dirce was a common enough theme in art, and death by tying to bulls is a well-attested hazard of the Roman arena, but again it was a particularly pointed punishment for the condemned arsonists of 64. Of all the destruction caused by the Great Fire, Cassius Dio picks out by name only the devastation of the Palatine and the burning of the first and—until then—the only permanent amphitheater in Rome, the one built somewhere in the Campus Martius in 26 BC by Augustus' successful general, Statilius Taurus.[37] This major monument was known, as Dio tells it, as the *(amphi)theatrum Tauri,* the Amphitheater of Taurus or, literally, the Amphitheater of the Bull. To Roman connoisseurs of execution, death by raging bull for those who had destroyed the amphitheater of the bull would be the height of verbal wit.

Presiding over this grand spectacle, and participating in it, was Nero himself.[38] Whether he actually raced is unclear, but he took care to impersonate a charioteer as he wandered among the crowd. Given his artistic propensity for playing significant roles on and off stage, and if we accept that the condemned Christians were indeed reluctant actors in significant charades conceived by him and fatal to them, then we should presume that he had again a more creative reason for appearing as a charioteer than merely to win popularity and annoy his critics. The punishments meted out to the Christians particularly recalled their alleged attacks on the shrines of Apollo/Sol and his sister Diana/Luna. Nero, dressed as a charioteer, restored light to the night. It would not require too much imagination to see that he was bringing a new dawn to Rome after some of its darkest days. It was now, in 64, that Apollo the singer was joined in Nero's program by his alter ego, Sol the charioteer. It was the dawn of a new era.

THE NEW ERA that dawned in 64 was a Golden Age. In 65, Nero was for a time the willing dupe of a deranged North African knight named Caesellius Bassus, who claimed that the hidden treasure of Queen Dido of Carthage had been revealed to him in a dream: a mass of gold bullion lying in a great cave under his estates. Without checking either the source or the story itself, Nero dispatched an army of treasure-seekers. After a long and frenzied search nothing was found, and Bassus killed himself. But during the weeks and months of waiting, gold fever consumed the capital, rumors flew, and the emperor was alleged to have spent vast sums recklessly, in the anticipation that his treasury would soon be replenished.[39] This period of happy suspense coincided with the second celebration of the Neronian Games, and the competing orators seized the occasion to heap praise on the emperor: the earth, they claimed, teemed with new fertility and the gods were bringing forth unexpected wealth—pure gold, not gold alloyed with other metals as before. Gold indeed glitters everywhere in Nero's reign, from the emperor's poems written in letters of gold to the gold casket containing his first beard; from his golden fishing net to the gold chains he wore on stage as Hercules to his golden box of poisons; from Poppaea's gold-shod mules to Nero's golden chamber pot.[40] But there is more here than just imperial luxury. Gold was the symbol of the sun, Apollo was the god with the golden hair and the gilded face, and the Sun was the source of life.[41] From 64 on Nero tried to make the Golden Age of the Sun a reality, in the most flamboyant way.

In late May of 66, Rome witnessed the extraordinary Golden Day.[42] This was the day on which the emperor crowned Tiridates King of Armenia at fabulous expense. It received its name from the people because of a stunning embellishment of the Theater of Pompey, where the stage, the walls, everything portable, were all in some way gilded. Pliny the Elder, who must have seen it, says simply that Nero covered the theater with gold for that one day. It would have been blinding were the crowd not protected from the sun by the awning, at the center of which was Nero driving the chariot of the Sun.

Earlier on the Golden Day the emperor had received the homage of Tiridates in the Forum and crowned him before a vast crowd.⁴³ The ceremony was timed to begin at sunrise, and Dio's source remarked on the white clothes of the civilians who crowded everywhere, even on the rooftops, and the shining armor of the soldiers in their ranks, with their weapons flashing like lightning. The theatrical effect when the rising sun first hit the Forum must have been dazzling. It was indeed an effect, one that was deliberately planned: an earlier day for the ceremony had been set by edict, but it had been postponed *because of clouds*. In the Forum as in the gilded theater, where Nero repeated the coronation under his solar awning, the Golden Day was also the Day of the Sun.⁴⁴

Pliny remarked that the gilded Theater of Pompey was but a fraction of the size of the *aurea domus*, Nero's famed Golden House, which (he claimed) surrounded the city.⁴⁵ The name of the house, it must be understood, was Nero's own, and he coined it after the Great Fire of 64. Construction had been undertaken of a palace which connected the complex on the Palatine Hill with the imperial gardens on the Esquiline, and to which Nero had given the simple name of *Domus Transitoria*, the Connecting House. This had been destroyed by the Fire and was afterwards redesigned and rebuilt at lavish expense. The new palace, which was going up even as the Golden Day dawned, he called simply the Golden House, *Domus Aurea*. He planned to erect a 120-foot statue of Sol in its enormous vestibule: no one could doubt that this was the house of the Sun.

Petronius, in his contemporary novel, the *Satyricon*, would mock Roman youths who wasted their hard-conquered spoils in raising buildings of gold, but Nero's old tutor, Seneca, knew that there was more to the Golden House than the luxury, which he too condemned. Writing in the late summer or autumn of 64—that is, after the Golden House had begun to rise from the ruins of the Domus Transitoria—he offered a clear and precise denunciation of the new solar ideology:

People seem to think that the immortal gods cannot give any better gift than wealth—or even possess anything better [here he quotes Ovid's *Metamorphoses* 2. 1]:

The sun-god's palace, set with pillars tall
And flashing bright with gold

Or look at the chariot of the Sun:

Gold was the axle, golden too the pole
And gold the tires that bound the circling wheels
And silver all the spokes within the wheels

And finally, when they would praise an epoch as the best, they call
it the "Golden Age" (saeculum aureum).[46]

This passage shows startlingly open contempt for the new Golden Age, as
Seneca attacks the very equation of gold with the Sun which underlay
Nero's project, drawing on the tale of Phaethon in Ovid for some all-too-
apt quotations. The vulgarity, the superficiality of people who define the
gods in terms of gold are mercilessly etched in Neronian terms—the palace of the Sun, the chariot of the Sun—and the concept of a new Golden
Age is turned upside down, not sublime but ignoble.

Seneca goes on to dissect lines from the Greek tragedians which seemed
to praise wealth. In one, from a play by Euripides about Bellerophon,
money is deemed superior to love. When, at its first performance, the entire audience rose as one to eject from the theater the actor who had spoken these words, Euripides himself (writes Seneca) jumped up and urged
them to wait and see quem admirator auri exitum faceret, how one who
adored gold would die.[47] Not perhaps the most politic anecdote for Seneca to repeat when his gold-obsessed former pupil was raising his Golden
House: Nero was overjoyed at his old teacher's enforced suicide the following year.[48]

Earlier in the same letter, Seneca dwells on being dazzled by light, in
a remarkable discussion of moral chiaroscuro. The philosopher distinguishes between misleading superficial beauty and the true inner radiance
of the virtuous soul. The problem is a matter of vision: we cannot see inner beauty because we have been blinded by too much exterior splendor,
or by too much darkness. If we could but purify our vision we would see
internal beauty, however buried it might be beneath outward poverty, or
lowliness, or disgrace. "Conversely," he continues, "we shall get a view of
evil and the deadening influences of a sorrow-laden soul, in spite of the
hindrance that results from the widespread gleam of riches that flash
round about, divitiarum radiantium splendor, and in spite of the false
light, falsa lux, . . . of great power which beats pitilessly upon the be-

holder."[49] The evil, unhappy soul, masked by the splendor of radiant riches, the false light of great power—all this just before Seneca turns to describe the Sun god's palace.

Seneca wrote, in Ovid's words, of the Sun god's palace flashing bright with gold, *regia Solis . . . clara micante auro.* Safely after Nero's death, Martial would sing of new works rising where the hateful hall of a savage king once shone, *invidiosa feri radiabant atria regis.* Why did it shine? In his precious account of the Golden House, Suetonius describes in order the vestibule, the lake, its buildings, and the open countryside; then he says, "in other parts everything was covered with gold and studded with gems and pearls"—after which his tour proceeds to the dining-rooms and baths. Presumably the gilt and jewel adornment covered not just the interiors but also the exteriors of the Golden House, just as the Theater of Pompey was gilded throughout for one day. Nero, as we have seen from the Golden Day, was interested in dazzling light effects. Curiously, Pliny tells of a Temple of the Fortune of Sejanus which the emperor set up somewhere in the grounds of the Golden House to house an ancient statue of the goddess Fortuna, rescued from a shrine supposed originally to have been built by King Servius Tullius in the sixth century BC and probably damaged or destroyed in the Great Fire. What made Nero's temple memorable was that it was built of a marble-hard stone recently discovered in Cappadocia—*phengites,* the shining stone, white, streaked with yellow veins. Pliny was deeply impressed by its translucence, which made the temple as light as day even when the doors were shut, uncannily striking the viewer as lit from within.[50]

Imagine a visitor toiling up the straightened and splendidly redeveloped Via Sacra from the Forum, to approach the doors of the Domus Aurea. There, in the enormous vestibule, dominating the vista, indeed visible throughout much of the city, Nero intended to install the dazzling bronze colossal statue of the Sun which he had commissioned. It would view the stars close-up (in Martial's words), and would mark the transition from the old center of Republican Rome to the new imperial palace.[51] It is standardly and authoritatively asserted, and almost universally accepted, that the notorious Colossus was erected in Nero's lifetime, and that the Sun was depicted with the emperor's own features.[52] However, R. R. R. Smith has argued with great force that neither assumption is warranted: Pliny the Elder, who had watched in awe as the sculptor Zenodorus built his model, erected the scaffolding, and molded the great

work out of bronze, does *not* say that it was a remarkable likeness of the
emperor, only that it was remarkably lifelike; Suetonius does *not* say that
it stood in the vestibule, but rather that the vestibule was one in which the
120-foot Colossus might stand, *staret* (that is, the vestibule was also very
large; others have pointed this out, as Smith notes).[53] Both observations
are correct.

Of the two questions—did the statue originally represent Nero? and
was it erected during his lifetime?—the second is the easier to answer. As
Smith remarks, "When Pliny saw it, it was still in the workshop, and
Tacitus, always keen-eyed for any new signs of Nero's *audacia,* does not
even mention it." Since, moreover, Suetonius cannot be taken to say that
the statue stood in the vestibule in Nero's day, and since Dio tells us
straightforwardly that in 75, under Vespasian, the Colossus was erected in
the Sacred Way, there is absolutely no reason to believe that Nero saw the
statue standing in the Domus Aurea before his death in 68.[54]

Less clear is the answer to the first question. That the Colossus which
survived into the fourth century represented the sun, there is no doubt:
"the mass of the marvelous Colossus, crowned with rays, delights in over-
coming the work of Rhodes."[55] The scholarly consensus has been that after his death the emperor's image was reworked into the more standard
features of the sun, although no ancient author says so.[56] This view rests
mainly on Pliny's assertion that the statue was intended, *destinatum,* to
represent Nero, but was dedicated to the sun after the emperor's crimes
were condemned; and on Suetonius' observation in passing that Vespasian
richly rewarded the restorer, *refector,* of the Venus of Cos and the Colossus
(generally taken to signal the reworking of the statue from Nero into Sol,
although Smith observes that it can mean merely that the statue was finished under Vespasian). There is no evidence that the statue was reworked
into the sun—Pliny certainly does not say so—and Smith argues that
Nero's alleged "intention" to portray himself as the sun was the invention
of posthumous rhetoric, designed as an index of a "bad" emperor's mega-
lomania. Thus Suetonius' observation that the vestibule was large enough
to contain a 120-foot colossus "with his own features" is simply misleading, and it should be noted that, according to Dio's source, some said the
statue erected in 75 bore Nero's features, others those of Titus.[57] Smith
concludes, "There are many other paper monuments and untestable rhetorical charges attached to these figures [that is, "bad" or failed emperors]
. . . which are often accepted as unproblematic evidence on a kind of *ad
hominem* basis simply because no ground rules have been established for

engaging with this genre of literary representation." That Nero intended to erect a huge statue of himself looming over the city certainly fits in with other unfounded posthumous allegations against him, and it does not correspond either with his other, real intentions or with the program of the Golden House.

Whether he lived to see the Colossus in place or not, let us pursue Nero's intentions. Past the overwhelming vestibule his amazed visitor would find not the expected "house," but a bowl of open countryside dotted with woods, pastures, fields, animals, and different buildings, all scattered around an artificial lake: the "Golden House" was not a house at all, but a large suburban villa set down in the heart of the city, *rus in urbe*.[58] Its grounds covered the valley where the lake lay (the site today of the Colosseum) and the slopes of the surrounding hills—the Esquiline to the north, the Caelian to the south, the Palatine to the west.

Looking from the vestibule to the left across the valley, the visitor's eye would be drawn immediately to the tremendous façade of the main residential complex, set carefully on, out from, into, the side of the Oppian Hill, which was part of the Esquiline. Carefully indeed, for terraces were imposed on the landscape, as part of the hill was removed behind and strong substructures were added in front.[59] This must have been intended to facilitate one of the most remarkable features of the building, its alignment, which was imposed on, not by, the topography. The Oppian complex (along with the later, dependent Baths of Titus) is unique among the public buildings of Rome in its strict orientation, lying precisely on an east-west axis. The significance of this is still not known,[60] but undoubtedly a building that faced due south would be washed with sunshine throughout the day. The effect of sunlight hitting a gilded and bejeweled façade, over 360 meters long, from dawn till dusk, would be blinding: "the sun-god's palace, set with pillars tall and flashing bright with gold."

This Golden House looked down from the periphery of the area onto a world in miniature.[61] Tacitus curtly dismisses the artificiality of the landscaping imposed on downtown Rome by Nero's engineers, as "fields and lakes and, to give the impression of wilderness, woods here and open spaces and prospects there." But Suetonius is more precise as he moves methodically in his description from the vestibule where the Colossus might stand over to the actual villa itself:

There was also a lake like the sea, encircled by buildings meant to look like cities. There was moreover countryside of various kinds, fields, vineyards, pastures, and woods, along with a great number of every kind of tame and wild animals.⁶²

What the visitor standing by the Colossus would realize immediately was that this artificial landscape was a microcosm of the world. More precisely, the "sea" surrounded by "cities," farms and wild countryside, humans and animals, may have represented the Roman Empire in miniature, with the Mediterranean at its center. Overlooking this world from the Oppian Hill was the glittering façade of the Palace of the Sun, while high above its entrance would stand the shining statue of the Sun, its master, holding the world in his hand.

N OTORIOUSLY, when his house was ready, Nero declared that at last he had begun to be housed like a human being.⁶³ However such grandiloquence is to be interpreted, it has rightly been taken to show one thing: his interest in Apollo and the Sun was a matter of ideology, not of theology.⁶⁴ He did not actually identify himself with gods; he did not think himself divine; nor did he wish others to deify him. That is made clear in his decisive rejection of the divine honors which were offered to him not only at the beginning of his reign, but even a decade later. Indeed, while Nero participated conscientiously in all the many ceremonies in which he had to take part as a priest of the state, and while he was naturally curious and tended to superstition, Suetonius was probably not wrong in claiming that he held all cults, *religiones,* in contempt.⁶⁵

An exceptional key to Nero's thinking is provided by the *Epidrome,* a short, allegorical interpretation of Greek myth from a strongly Stoic perspective, written by a contemporary philosopher and grammarian whom the emperor would eventually banish, the learned L. Annaeus Cornutus.⁶⁶ Intended for classroom use, the *Epidrome,* or "Introduction to the Traditions of Greek Theology," sought to explain the gods of myth in terms of natural principles. Hercules, for example, represented the cosmic principle behind the power of Nature, "strong, in control, and indomitable . . . the distributor of strength and stalwart resistance." Apollo was, inevitably, the solar principle (as in the passage quoted at the head of this chapter). Above all, Apollo was master of the equilibrium of the cosmos: he assured a universal balance which was reflected on earth in the regular succession of the seasons, in musical harmony, in the just distribution of his gifts to humanity; and he was the embodiment of light, hence beautiful, brilliant, pure. This solar Apollo, Phoebus Apollo, was the perfect symbol, in short, for a man who was young, artistic, and the emperor of the world.

With that intellectual justification for his theatrical experiments, there is no need to think that Nero actually believed in Apollo. Indeed, his attitude toward regular cults is well demonstrated in his visit in the year 67 to Delphi, Apollo's major shrine. Without a doubt his reason for going there was not to pay homage to his patron deity, but to compete in the Pythian Games, one of the contests in his Greek tour. Nero's conduct toward the great shrine was decidedly ambiguous. On the one hand, his interest in Delphi set an encouraging precedent for later emperors. His visit revived for centuries afterwards an oracle which had languished in poverty and obscurity for several generations, and he may have completed in some way the building of the temple.[67] According to one story, he consulted the god about his own future and received the reply that he should beware the seventy-third year. Thrilled by these words, he persuaded himself not only that he would live to an old age but that he would also always enjoy exceptional prosperity. Indeed, when he later lost some extremely valuable goods in a shipwreck he blithely assured his friends that the fish would return them. The priestess of Apollo, the Pythia who had uttered the prophecy, received a huge reward, 400,000 sesterces.[68]

Yet even as he revived the shrine, he treated it abominably. His posthumous reputation at Delphi was appalling, even for Nero. Legends abound, ranging from the impossible to the unverifiable. In one story, Apollo's oracle has somehow learned of the pasquinade posted up in Rome, about his being Nero Orestes Alcmaeon the matricide, and it misquotes a shortened version to the infuriated emperor.[69] In another, along the same lines, the oracle simply refuses to reply to his inquiry: "I do not respond to parricides" (which was observably not true). And in a third, a floating story that is attached to other historical figures as well, Nero is enraged when the Pythia prefers the sacrifice of a poor man to his own.[70] He reacts to this rebuff with the fury of a tyrant: he takes away the shrine's territory and gives it to his soldiers; he tears down the rebuilt temple; he stops up with corpses the mouth of the cave from which the vapors were popularly thought to arise to inspire the prophetess. However much of this is to be believed, in sober truth Nero did loot the shrine (as he did other temples) of its artistic treasures, including some 500 bronze statues, to adorn his Golden House at Rome.[71] Moreover, beyond this casual contempt, there is no good evidence that he in any way paid particular honor to Apollo of Delphi, as he did to Apollo of the Palatine. His relations with the god were very much on his own terms.

Indeed, there are strong hints of a subversive element in these relations. The intriguing hypothesis has been advanced that some contemporaries wanted to portray the emperor Nero as Phaethon, and not to his discredit. Phaethon was the child of the Sun, who yearned to take over the reins of his father's chariot. When Helios reluctantly agreed, disaster ensued: the horses ran wild, the earth was badly scorched, and Zeus was forced to strike the youth out of the chariot with his thunderbolt. Not at first glance the most appropriate myth for Nero, but any tale can be reinterpreted. In his work *Natural Questions,* written some time after his retirement in 62, Seneca quotes with approval a ringing phrase from "that excellent poem," *in illo inclito carmine,* of Vagellius (the author's name is uncertain, his date unknown): "If I must fall, I would like to fall from heaven." Earlier in the same work Seneca had recalled more hexameter verse of "the excellent poet," *poetae incliti* (unnamed, but surely the same): "Let us bear stout hearts and do the greatest deeds in a brief time." It has been argued that these fragments represent an epic poem in which Phaethon was praised for his daring to perform great deeds—and Seneca had indeed approved elsewhere of the greatness of trying to scale heaven, even if the attempt ended in failure.[72] Thus, a standard myth about the transfer of power between generations is turned on its head: the foolish youth punished for his premature audacity becomes a great-souled symbol of change. If he failed, he failed greatly. The attraction of this daring but dangerous new image to the young Nero would be obvious.[73]

In the passage about Nero at the beginning of the *Pharsalia* (lines 45–58), Seneca's nephew Lucan showed in masterly fashion just how to handle Phaethon properly. There he suggested that Nero will replace Phoebus in guiding the chariot and that the earth will then *not* fear the change in driver of the sun—that is, the new Phaethon who takes over from Sol will be a success. Thus for Nero to present himself to the world as a successful Phaethon would be merely to act as what others called him, the *New* Sun.

If Nero in his solar capacity did toy with the role of Phaethon, it would give resonance to another of his gestures. One of the curious features of his reign was a fashionable obsession with amber. At an unknown date a Roman knight journeyed to the Baltic region to procure amber, *succinum,* for a gladiatorial show to be presented by the emperor. So much did he acquire that the very nets used to keep the beasts off the parapets were knot-ted with amber, and on a single day all the arms and equipment used in the show, even that for removing the corpses, were adorned with am-ber trimmings. Moreover, when Nero described his wife Poppaea's hair in a poem as *succinos,* amber-colored, he started a fashion for that shade among women in society.[74] For an emperor trying to portray himself as the New Sun of the world and a successful Phaethon, an amphitheater shining with amber—reminiscent of the shining Theater of Pompey on the Golden Day—and an empress with shining amber hair would be sat-isfyingly appropriate: amber was first formed by the tears of the daughters of the Sun, as they wept over the fall of their brother Phaethon.[75]

The role of Phaethon would, moreover, explain a remark which was to be turned against the emperor after his death. Someone quoted in conver-sation a line, perhaps from a Greek tragedy: "After I am dead, let the earth be consumed by fire." Nero replied, "Rather, while I am alive." On which Suetonius comments, "And he was as good as his word," leading into an account of the Great Fire which the biographer believes Nero started.[76] If, as we shall see, Nero did cause the fire, he was indeed the new Phaethon, with a purpose.

The value of Phaethon is to confirm that the emperor's preoccupation with Phoebus Apollo was purely aesthetic. He had no interest in the stan-dard cults of the gods except the one he chose to honor, Apollo the lyre-player, and he felt free to experiment with his elaborate conception and presentation of himself as the Sun—even to the point of suggesting not that he was assimilated to the Sun, but that he was replacing him.

Aesthetic experimentation is the key, for it is clear that the divine im-age was continually developing. The comparison with Apollo is first sung in 59; the Sun bursts forth in 64. The third stage would occupy the last months of the emperor's life, perhaps from late 66 onward, when Nero as-sumed the role of Hercules. As Suetonius tells it:

> For he had decided, since he was considered the equal of Apollo in singing and of Sol in driving chariots, that he would also imitate the deeds of Hercules. And they say that a lion was got ready, which he would slay naked in the amphitheater while the people watched, ei-ther with a club or by strangling it.[77]

When he returned from Greece for his artistic triumph in late 67 the whole population of Rome, senators included, greeted Nero with a new chant:

> Hail, Olympian victor! Hail, Pythian victor! Augustus! Augustus! To Nero Hercules! To Nero Apollo! The only victor of the grand tour, the only one from the beginning of time! Augustus! Augustus! Divine voice: blessed are those who hear you![78]

Again, Dio claims to give the exact phrasing of the cheer just as he had done for that of the Augustiani in 59. Apollo of course reappears, and the Olympic, the Pythian, and the other victories of the recent *periodos* are properly acclaimed, but Hercules is a novelty. Indeed, Nero's interest in the hero seems first to have appeared during the tour of Greece. Suetonius mentions his desire to imitate Hercules directly after discussing his newfound passion for watching the wrestling contests there, and in fact calling the victor in such contests "Hercules" was standard practice.[79] Hercules Augustus with his club and his lion skin turns up on the contemporary coinage of the Neronian colony of Patrai, as do other gods of special interest to Nero (Apollo, Diana, and Jupiter Liberator); at the same time, the authorities at Delphi seem to have erected an elaborate frieze depicting the Labors of Hercules on the front face of the stage there, the stage on which Nero was to perform at the Pythian Games; and the emperor himself dedicated a purple robe and a golden crown on an altar at the Temple of Hera at Argos which depicted the marriage of Hebe and Hercules, after the hero's reception among the gods.[80] And back in Rome, Nero planned in his last days (so we are told) to include in his campaign against Vindex his concubines with their hair shorn, and armed with the axes and shields of Amazons; as will become clear, this may be a reference to Hercules' own expedition against, and conquest of, the Amazons.[81]

Hercules was, like the Sun, the great benefactor of mankind, but where the Sun brought life he brought security. It was Hercules who had struggled to rid the earth of monsters, and in reward for his labors and for his sufferings on mankind's behalf, he had been raised to the gods. Again, as with Phoebus Apollo, there was more at stake than a passion for wrestling or singing or racing. Nero would be praised by the Greeks for two of his deeds, even after his death. One was the liberation of the province of

Achaia from taxes, and the emperor is accordingly associated with Jupiter Liberator / Zeus Eleutherios on coins and inscriptions, an association not seen since the days of Julius Caesar and not to be revived until the age of Diocletian.[82] His other great philhellenic benefaction was the commencement of work on the canal cutting through the Isthmus of Corinth, and there are strong hints that for this feat he intended to portray himself as Hercules / Herakles.

Cutting the Isthmus was a Herculean task which did not happen to be one of the labors of Hercules, yet two sources seem to invoke the hero's name at the Isthmus in a Neronian context. One allusion appears in the brief second-century work entitled *Nero, or the Digging of the Isthmus,* attributed to the satirist Lucian but in fact by a Philostratus. This very interesting piece takes the form of a dialogue between a certain Menecrates and the exiled Stoic philosopher Musonius Rufus, who is imagined to have been one of the prisoners working on the project (and who had certainly been banished to a nearby island, Gyara). Curiously, it seems to preserve, independent of any other source, details about Nero's stay in Greece which are worth taking seriously. At one point Musonius describes the ceremonial commencement of work on the canal: the emperor emerges from his tent to sing hymns to the gods of the sea; the governor of the province hands him a golden pitchfork; he digs briefly to the sound of applause and acclaim; he exhorts the workers (soldiers and prisoners); and then he returns to Corinth, "believing he had surpassed all the feats of Heracles."[83]

With this should be juxtaposed a striking passage in the play *Hercules on Oeta,* which clumsily and at interminable length treats its hero's suffering, death, and apotheosis. Attributed to Seneca, it is generally agreed that the piece was written by an inferior imitator of the master, in the late first or early second century.[84] At the beginning of the drama, Hercules appears alone, reproaching his father Jupiter for not making him a god when lesser men than he have been taken up into heaven. He has pacified the entire earth, rid it of its monsters: what more must he do? If he must join lands together, he will attach Sicily to Italy; or if Jupiter orders him to join the seas, he will commit the Isthmus to the waves, making a new road for the ships of Attica.[85] This cutting of the canal fits in very well with the new image of himself as Hercules which Nero began to develop in Greece. Presenting the superhuman task as Herculean was just what Nero would do. And lest there be any doubt as to his intentions, a relief sculpture of Hercules with his club survives on the south face of the present canal, "rather rudely carved and now badly weathered."[86]

As when he played the heroes and heroines of myth, the emperor moved beyond representation to action. Not only did he wish to be portrayed as characters from myth, and to act them on stage, he wanted to act like them in life, whether as Orestes the matricide or as Phoebus Apollo the charioteer. His alleged conduct at Delphi then becomes significant. Stories were told of his looting the shrine of its treasures (which he certainly did), and of his putting an end to its oracle in a rage. As with his alleged incest with his mother, the truth is unclear, but as with the incest, so with the stopping of the oracle: there must be a strong suspicion that the story originated with Nero himself. That is to say, he was again acting out a myth, imitating the one other man, mortal but superhuman, who had both looted the shrine at Delphi and stopped its oracle.

One day Hercules himself had come for help to the oracle of Apollo at Delphi. In one version of the tale, he suffered from a persistent illness which afflicted him after he had murdered a guest in a rage; in another, he sought purification for the murder of his wife and children (in the fit of madness portrayed by Nero on stage in Greece). Because of his pollution the Pythia, and through her Apollo, refused to give the hero an oracle (just as, in one story, they would refuse the polluted Nero). In a fury Hercules proceeded to shut down the oracle, plunder its votive offerings, and remove the tripod on which the Pythia sat to transmit the prophecies of the god. Apollo appeared, an epic battle between god and hero began, and the two combatants could be separated only by a thunderbolt hurled by Zeus. They then swore friendship, Hercules restored the tripod, and Apollo prescribed the proper penance for the hero's original crime.[87] The struggle and reconciliation of the two great benefactors of humankind, the god and the hero, must have appealed powerfully to Nero's imagination. If he did indeed somehow stop the oracle, its closure would have been at most symbolic and temporary. The role of Hercules is thus intimately connected with the role of Apollo: "Nero Hercules, Nero Apollo."[88]

As WE HAVE SEEN, Nero's divine image developed in stages, from Apollo in 59 to Sol in 64 to Hercules in 66. Each aspect corresponded to one of his interests—to singing, to charioteering, and (perhaps with less enthusiasm) to athletics and fighting wild beasts—and each represented divine attributes which were beneficial to humanity and therefore appropriate to an emperor. But, as with the mythical heroes whom he played both onstage and off, another purpose guided Nero's steps, that is, the imitation of a historical model. He had been fascinated and inspired by Periander, the epitome of the Greek tyrant, great of soul and beyond judgment. By that standard, any other model he chose to follow should be unusual—and it is, by its very unexpectedness. For later Greeks and Romans, the paragon for rulership was Alexander the Great, and much has been written about Nero's imitation of Alexander.[89] But the evidence is thin and tends to be confused with a general interest on his part in Hellenistic Alexandria, and when Nero does follow the great Macedonian his actions seem to be neither significant nor obsessive, as were, say, those of a later emperor like Caracalla.[90] The very fact that every other great man might indulge in *imitatio Alexandri* would be enough to ensure Nero's lack of interest. On his one trip outside of Italy he chose to go to Old Greece, the land of Periander, not to the marvelous center of the Hellenistic world, the city of Alexander himself, Alexandria. But there was another great historical figure whom Nero did imitate throughout his reign, closely and creatively, not to say surprisingly: his own great-great-grandfather, the first *princeps* Augustus. He proclaimed clearly at the beginning of his reign that he would rule according to the example of Augustus, *ex Augusti praescripto imperaturum se professus,* and he meant it.[91]

To Nero in 54, the imitation of Augustus brought with it a degree of legitimation: his connection with his predecessor, Claudius, had been questionable (great-nephew, stepson, son by adoption), but unlike Claudius he could claim that the blood of the first *princeps* ran in his veins. Thus, a cameo shows a bust of the young Nero flanked by facing busts of Augustus and his wife Livia; and Agrippina, so we are told, emulated the magnificence of her great-grandmother Livia when divine honors and a great state funeral were decreed for Claudius on the lines of those granted to Augustus. In 57, Nero dramatically drew attention to the dynastic connection by staging a naval battle of Athenians against Persians on the naumachia built for such naval displays by Augustus. In so doing, he paid tribute not only to the great battle of Salamis of 480 BC, marking the victory of West over East, but particularly to Augustus' own reenactment of it, a spectacle produced to celebrate the dedication of his new Temple of

Mars Ultor in 2 BC and with it the diplomatic subjugation of Persia's successor, Parthia, by Rome, the heir of Greece. Moreover, in 64, to celebrate the tenth year of his reign and the fiftieth year since the consecration of Augustus, Nero issued a series of significant coins.[92] One particularly stands out, depicting the Temple of Janus with its door shut and bearing the legend *Pace P.R. Terra Marique Parta Ianum Clusit S.C.,* "when the peace of the Roman People had been imposed on land and sea, he closed the Temple of Janus, by decree of the Senate." The door of the temple was shut only when the Roman state was at peace, and that happened rarely. The coin of 64 celebrated the submission of Tiridates and the peace with Parthia which would result in the Golden Day two years later. The last closing of the doors had been in the reign of Augustus, also precisely to celebrate peace with Parthia, a peace which Augustus had adorned with the same solemn phrase, *pace P.R. terra marique parta.*[93] The claim to comparison is unmistakable. Moreover, after ensuring that peace, Nero did something which no emperor had done since Augustus, and which Tiberius and Claudius had expressly refused to do. As the future Augustus had done in or before 38 BC, Nero took as his first name, or *praenomen,* the title granted to a victorious general: *Imperator.* It was a special link between the two men, and the name would thereafter be assumed automatically by the Flavians and all their successors as *Imperatores,* Emperors.[94]

Any *princeps* could proclaim that he was following the path laid down by Augustus, but Nero's *imitatio Augusti* was something special: it was bathed in the shining light of their patron Apollo. When Nero developed the image of Apollo that was so important to him, he did it not as the shocking departure from Roman decorum which our sources would lead us to believe, but precisely as an appeal to the traditions which meant so much to the Romans—to *mos maiorum,* the customs of our ancestors. For by imitating Apollo he was imitating Augustus.

In late 64 or early 63 BC a Roman matron named Atia attended a midnight ceremony at the Temple of Apollo in the Circus Flaminius at Rome, one that necessitated an overnight stay in the temple. While she and the other matrons slept, a snake entered suddenly and soon departed. Atia then arose and purified herself as if she had slept with her husband, whereupon the indelible image of a snake appeared on her skin. As Suetonius tells it, "Augustus was born nine months later and because of this he was thought to be the son of Apollo." Before she bore him, Atia dreamed that her entrails had been carried up to the stars and spread over heaven and earth, while her husband Octavius dreamed that the Sun had risen from her womb.[95] The future Augustus was duly born, just as Nero would be, shortly before the rising of the sun. And once, when he was an infant, he could not be found where his nurse had laid him down to sleep; they searched for a long time before they found him at the top of a tower, lying to face the rising sun.[96] Clearly he was born to rule.

Augustus, as he would be called after 27 BC, lost no opportunity to proclaim that Apollo was his special patron. To Apollo he attributed his two crucial naval successes, the victory of Naulochus over Sextus Pompey in 36, and the victory of Actium over Antony and Cleopatra in 31, and Apollo was duly rewarded with two great temples. One was the rebuilding of the Temple of Apollo Medicus in the Circus Flaminius by an old enemy and new ally, Gaius Sosius. It was now known as the Temple of Apollo Sosianus. Like other great monuments in the Campus Martius named after their builders, it was down to its smallest detail a paean to Augustus, and with good reason: it was in this very temple that he had been conceived as the son of Apollo.[97] The great frieze on its pediment showed the battle of Theseus and Hercules against the Amazons. Lifted bodily from a fifth-century temple in Greece, the frieze now dramatized the struggle of West against East which had just been fought again by Augustus, and it reflected the battle against the Amazons on the base of the victory monument raised by him at Actium. Inside, carved trophies with cuirasses and palm branches, carved tripods, and carved snakes all recalled Apollo; a frieze showed the procession of Augustus' triple triumph of 29 which would have formed up near this very temple. Similarly programmatic was the great temple of Apollo on the Palatine, next to the House of Augustus, celebrating the same victories, the same divine patronage, the same virtues in all of its elements, down to the smallest detail.[98]

At the same time, Apollo was also the prophet of a glorious future—the Golden Age, *aurea aetas,* the kingdom of Apollo, *regnum Apollinis*—all proclaimed by Rome's greatest poets and officially inaugurated by the Secular Games of 17 BC. Traditionally held to mark the passing of an age, or *saeculum*—100 or 110 years—and dedicated to the old gods, the Secular Games were taken by Augustus to mark the beginning of the new age; he timed them to celebrate a new program of social renewal and inserted Apollo (and himself) into the heart of their solemn ceremonies. The idea of renewal under the patronage of Apollo had grown during the darkest days of the late Republic. Augustus now transformed hope into bright reality. The symbols of Apollo accordingly became hugely fashionable in contemporary art—the Delphic tripod, the Sibyl, the cithara, the griffins found on the cuirass of the great "Prima Porta" statue of Augustus, the sphinx taken by him as his signet.[99]

Along with this association by patronage went a more intimate relationship, as was only fitting for the son of Apollo. Augustus' guardian spirit, his Genius, was closely associated in cult acts with Apollo.[100] On widely distributed earthenware from Arretium, known as *terra sigillata,* Apollo appears with the features of Augustus, and the most frequent representations on earthenware are Apollo, his sister Artemis (Octavia), their mother Leto (Atia), and Nike, Victory. An elegant carved carnelian shows a nude Augustus as Sol, driving the chariot of the Sun at just the time when poets were proclaiming the close alliance of Sun and Apollo, and the Sun in his chariot rose above the pediment of the Temple of Apollo Palatinus.[101] This identification of Augustus with his patron deity was his own idea, and it went back to early days. While a member of the triumvirate, probably in 40 BC when he was only 23 years old, he took part in a scandalous banquet, the dinner of the twelve gods, at which the diners dressed up as gods and goddesses: he of course appeared as Apollo.[102] His enemies mocked him, but it was an age of serious amateur dramatics, when other statesmen not only appealed to their guardian deities but on occasion acted as them. In the library attached to the temple of Palatine Apollo there stood a statue of Augustus himself, in the dress and with the attributes of Apollo.[103] That is, he was shown dressed as Apollo the Citharode.

Thus, for the public identification of himself with Apollo, Nero had the best of all possible precedents—the first *princeps,* Augustus, as both he and his people well knew. In AD 60, at the age of 22, he held the first Neronian Games, the Neronia. Although not a competitor, he did appear to perform in his new gymnasium complex, and he was awarded a special crown by common acclaim in oratory and in Latin poetry. But it was the judges themselves who granted him the crown for playing the lyre, a crown which he ordered to be gilded and then carried to the statue of Augustus.[104] He was surely paying the tribute of one citharode to another, honoring the statue of his ancestor which portrayed Augustus dressed as Apollo Citharoedus.

Four years later Nero celebrated his tenth anniversary in power, and a coinage reform of that year was accompanied and followed by a large issue of coins commemorating in one way or another the fiftieth anniversary of the death and deification of Augustus.[105] One coin, as described earlier, showed a male and a female figure labeled Augustus and Augusta—that is, either Augustus and Livia, or Nero and Poppaea meant to recall Augustus and Livia. The male figure is depicted with a radiate crown, a common attribute of Nero for the next four years. But this solar crown was also the attribute of a deified emperor, and since the year 14 it had been a standard element in the posthumous iconography of the deified Augustus. Now the emergence of Nero as the Sun takes on another significance. Just as he had imitated Augustus Caesar in choosing Apollo as his symbol, so now in assuming the role of Sol he was fashioning himself after *Divus Augustus.* And by the same token, the role of Hercules undertaken by Nero in 66 also has Augustan roots. The two great temples to Apollo—one restored and the other erected under the first emperor, and devoted to his deeds—both emphasized the relationship between hero and god: the frieze of Apollo Sosianus showed Hercules fighting the wild Amazons of the East, while exquisite, archaizing terracotta plaques from Apollo Palatinus depict the god and the hero equally balanced in their struggle for control of the Delphic tripod, signaling, it has been suggested, their eventual reconciliation.[106]

Nero's special affinity for his ancestor was likewise displayed in his penchant for celebrating triumphs, for Augustus had transformed the ancient military spectacle into a simultaneous victory celebration of the new kingdom of Apollo.[107] Although laurel had earlier been associated with the triumph, it was Augustus who began the custom of having the triumphant general wear a laurel wreath and carry a laurel branch, for the laurel was the tree of Apollo and as such appears widely as a decoration in Augustan art.[108] This Apolline aspect casts Nero's artistic triumph of 67 in a new light. Riding in the chariot which Augustus had used in his own triumphs, cheered by his "Augustiani" as they hailed him repeatedly as "Augustus," he directed his course in the end to Apollo, as Suetonius puts it. Suetonius was fascinated by the novelty of the spectacle; Dio was offended.[109] Passing beyond Jupiter the Best and Greatest on the Capitol, the normal guarantor of victory and recipient of thanks, Nero went on to thank Apollo the Citharode on the Palatine and Sol the Charioteer in the Circus Maximus. They were his special deities, of course, but they were something more. It was Augustus who had fixed them in Rome, for it was Augustus who had created the temple for Apollo on the Palatine, and had set up the obelisk of the Sun in the Circus which he had also repaired. In paying tribute to Apollo and Sol, Nero was also paying tribute to his ancestor, the first *princeps*.

The most arresting image in all of this is the tableaux of Nero dressed as a citharode, paying honor to the prize for lyre-playing awarded to him by the judges at the Neronia of 60, and then ordering the crown to be carried to the statue of Augustus, likewise dressed as a citharode, which stood in the library of Apollo Palatinus. The link with the first prince was palpable. No one could fault Nero for attempting to imitate Augustus, and no one could fault Augustus for claiming a special relationship with the god Apollo, for appealing to his special protection, and for proclaiming the advent of the god's new Golden Age. Nero, born at sunrise, pacifier of the Parthians, lyre-player, *triumphator*, knew that legitimation as the New Apollo could be supported through a very traditional appeal to Roman custom, in his case through the *imitatio Augusti* which was already so useful a political ploy.

There was a fitting end to all of his Apolline efforts. The laurel of Apollo and of the Roman triumph was closely bound up with the family of the first Augustus, for two laurel trees stood outside the door of his house on the Palatine, an honor voted by the senate, and a marvelous laurel grove grew on the suburban estate of his wife, Livia. There, right after their marriage in 38 BC, an eagle had dropped a hen into her lap. The hen bore in its beak a branch of laurel. Livia nursed the hen, which produced offspring, and she planted the branch, which grew. The custom arose that all *triumphatores* from the family of the Caesars would pluck their laurels from the tree, while they also each planted a new tree in the grove. In the last year of Nero's life and reign, and the last year of the dynasty, it was said that both the laurel grove and all the hens died.[110] The favor of Apollo, granted to Augustus Caesar, was in the end withdrawn from radiant Nero.

6

Saturnalia

He castrated the boy Sporus and actually tried to make a woman of him. He married him with all the usual ceremonies, including a dowry and a bridal veil, took him to his house attended by a great throng, and treated him as his wife . . . This Sporus, decked out with the finery of the empresses, and riding in a litter, he took with him to the fairs of Greece, and later at Rome through the Sigillaria, fondly kissing him from time to time.

SUETONIUS

As for [Nero] himself, to obtain additional credit that nothing anywhere was as delightful for him [as Rome], he set up parties in public places and used the whole city as if it were his own house; and especially celebrated for its luxury and notoriety was the banquet organized by Tigellinus, which I shall recount as an example, to avoid too frequent a narrative of the same prodigality.

TACITUS[1]

Nero's second wife, Poppaea Sabina, died in Rome and was deified in the summer of AD 65. In the first half of 66, he then took as his third wife the much-married Statilia Messalina (who would survive him), and late in that year or in 67 he formally married the young freedman Sporus. It was Sporus, not Messalina, who stayed at Nero's side until the end, one of the four companions on the emperor's harrowing last journey in June of 68; and it was Sporus to whom Nero turned to begin the ritual lamentation before he took his own life. Messalina Augusta was well-born, rich, beautiful, and talented; what she thought of her co-empress is not known.

The making or unmaking of Sporus was Nero's undying passion for his late wife, now the goddess Sabina. Suetonius ignores this, inserting his brief account of the affair into his report of Nero's sexual aberrations, between his rape of a Vestal Virgin and his incest with his mother. For once, Dio's narrative is superior. After his wife died, he asserts, Nero so pined

for her that when he heard of a woman who looked like Poppaea he sent
for her and kept her with him. But he then learned of a young freedman
whom he went so far as to castrate because of his resemblance to Sabina.
He called the boy Sporus, treating him in every way as a woman, and
eventually—although already married to another freedman, Pythagoras—
he wed Sporus properly, with contract and dowry, and with public celebration. Dio appends this notice to his account of the death of Poppaea,
but he elaborates in the context of the voyage to Greece. In Nero's company there was a rapacious noblewoman named Calvia Crispinilla (whom
Tacitus labeled his instructor in lust, *magistra libidinum*). He made her
guardian of Sporus/Sabina, and mistress of his/her wardrobe, *epitropeia
ten peri estheta.*

> Now Nero called Sporus "Sabina" not merely because, owing to his
> resemblance to her, he had been made a eunuch, but because the
> boy, like her, had been married to him, in Greece, by contract,
> Tigellinus giving the bride away, as the law ordained. All the Greeks
> held a celebration in honour of their marriage, uttering all the cus-
> tomary good wishes, even to the extent of praying that legitimate
> children might be born to them. After that Nero had two bedfellows
> at once, Pythagoras to play the role of husband to him, and Sporus
> that of wife. The latter, in addition to other forms of address, was
> termed "lady," "empress," and "mistress."[2]

The orator Dio of Prusa, a younger contemporary of Nero, confirms
the story and elaborates yet further. The emperor castrated his lover and
gave him the female name of his old mistress and wife (that is, Sabina).
Dio indignantly refuses to give the name of this lover, "but he actually
wore his hair parted, young women attended him whenever he went for a
walk, he wore women's clothes, and was forced to do everything else a
woman does in the same way. And to cap the climax, great honours and
boundless sums of money were actually offered to anyone who could
make a woman of him."[3]

Nero died within a year and a half of their marriage, but—astonishingly—Sporus was compelled to go on playing the role of Sabina. Even as
Nero's corpse was consumed on its funeral pyre, the boy passed into the
protection of Nymphidius Sabinus, the praetorian prefect who had betrayed his emperor and who now harbored imperial ambitions for him-

self, giving out that he was the bastard son of Caligula. Nymphidius treated Sporus as if they were married, and called him "Poppaea." This new husband was killed by the praetorians while attempting a coup against Galba, but Sporus next turns up in early 69, living intimately with, probably likewise "married" to, Galba's successor Otho, that is, Nero Otho, the former husband of Nero's Poppaea and would-be husband of Nero's Statilia.[4] The boy's sad career ended under Vitellius, in the late summer or autumn of 69. In the course of planning gladiatorial contests, even as the forces of Vespasian were invading Italy, someone proposed that the boy appear on stage, in the title role of the Rape of Persephone.[5] Sporus could not bear the shame, and he killed himself, little more than a year after the death of Nero. It is a pitiful story, with the quality of a nightmare, although the ancient authors, outraged by Nero's atrocities, have no pity to spare for the unhappy victim. He was probably not yet twenty years old when he died.

What is significantly missing in the relationship between Nero and Sporus is talk of love. Nowhere is it suggested that the emperor was besotted with the boyfriend whom he fondly kissed: his eternal love was pledged to Sabina. The fate of Sporus was to play the title role in Nero's elaborate mourning for his lost wife; his face was his misfortune. Did he for his part grow to love the man who had castrated him, who forced him to dress and act like a woman, and who longed to transform him surgically from male to female, an operation which would undoubtedly have killed him? No one thought to record his feelings. When Nero came to kill himself he wanted Sporus to join him in death, but the boy fled. Dio of Prusa asserts, obscurely, that Nero's mistreatment of him had angered Sporus into betraying the emperor's plans to his companions, who then forced him to suicide.[6] Earlier in that year, the boy had attended the usual New Year's ceremonies on January first. While Nero was solemnly taking the auspices, Sporus presented him with a gift, a ring with a gemstone depicting the Rape of Proserpina. This was of course subsequently taken as one of the many omens of Nero's fall and demise later in the year, but there is more to it. It was a singularly ill-timed gesture—to give a picture of a descent into hell to a man who was then ceremoniously consulting the gods about the future on the most ominous day of the year—and, unlike the many other portents of the coming disaster, this gesture was premeditated.[7] There is something dreadful about Sporus, the boy forced by his emperor to become a girl and a bride, giving Nero a representation of

Copy of Nero's official portrait, AD 64–68.

the ruler of the underworld forcing a young girl to become his bride. It was not by chance that the followers of Vitellius wanted him to play this very role of Proserpina/Persephone on stage the following year: Sporus himself had already suggested that he was the Queen of the Dead.

The Sporus affair is universally condemned as an abomination, one of the eternally infamous incidents in a life that set new standards in debauchery, and once condemned it is passed over. Yet the more closely it is examined, the less erotic, the more dramatic, the liaison appears. Other emperors had boyfriends, but none felt compelled to transform them with such obsessive thoroughness into the reincarnation of their dead wives. Again, Nero's motives may well have included the obvious ones, here exotic sexual pleasure (rather unlikely, as we shall see) and the chance to upset the moral majority (highly probable). But, yet again, there is good reason to suggest that he had something more in mind. When readers first encounter the story of Sporus, usually in the pages of Suetonius, they react with a mixture of emotions: shock, disgust, perhaps even horror, but inevitably, also, laughter—it is just too outrageous. Do we laugh, however nervously, at Nero's antics, or do we laugh with him?

The wedding itself may have been an intensely solemn ceremony, but it must have played as farce. All the good old Roman rituals were there—the dowry, the bridal veil, the crowd escorting the new wife to her husband's house, the prayer for legitimate children, perhaps even the vulgar jokes—but all were constantly undercut by the plain facts that the bride was not a woman, there would be no children, and the groom was already married, both to and as a wife.[8] Yet it was a Greek wedding as well, for there was a contract *(sumbolaion)*, which was a Greek legal form, not Roman; there was a "father" to give away the bride, that is, the *ekdosis* ("Tigellinus giving the bride away, as the law ordained"); and the ceremony took place not in Rome but during the tour of Greece and for the Greeks.[9] Nero was making it up as he went along.

His mood is clearly reflected in two aspects of the affair. Suetonius reports that when Nero had dressed Sporus as the empress he had him carried in a litter and escorted him around the fairs of Greece, *circa conventus mercatusque,* and around the Sigillaria at Rome, *circa Sigillaria,* kissing him constantly. The Greek fairs might be puzzling, but the Roman Sigillaria may help to explain them. Of all the public places at Rome in which he could have displayed his new bride, Nero is remembered as choosing the fair where goods were offered for sale as gifts for Saturnalia.[10] It took its name from the *sigilla,* the little gifts, originally humble pottery images, offered to friends and family during the great festival of the Saturnalia, a time when the normal rules of social conduct were suspended or even reversed in relaxation and merry-making. Sporus—the man turned into a woman, the freedman become empress—was a joke for Saturnalia, paraded around the Sigillaria.

Nero was the *Saturnalicius princeps:* the man who made the jests, the master of the revels. He had Sporus castrated before marrying his new Sabina, *exectis testibus.* Dio's version, translated literally, is this: "then, castrating a boy freedman—whom he called Sporus—because he too resembled Sabina . . ." "Whom he called Sporus": that is, *Nero* gave him the name Sporus. Sporus, in Greek *Sporos,* means "seed," "semen." It may not be to everyone's taste, but calling a boy Sporus after cutting off his testicles was meant as a joke.

SEVERAL of Nero's most outrageous actions look very different in the hard light of the great Roman festival of the winter solstice, the Saturnalia. Officially celebrated on 17 December, "the best of days" was so very popular that by Nero's time it was customarily extended to three, five, and even seven days. Then, at the darkest time of the year, everyone could take a well-earned break to relax, to have fun, to recreate for a brief time the happy Golden Age when Saturn had ruled Italy.[11]

It was a time of public celebration, with sacrifice at the temple of Saturn followed by a great banquet open to the people. It was also a time of freedom and public relaxation. Schools, courts, and businesses were closed. Men dressed not in the toga but in the comfortable, loose-fitting *synthesis,* the Greek garment worn at table, while on their heads they could wear the *pilleus,* the felt cap particularly associated with manumitted slaves. People could carouse all day: wine flowed, gambling flourished, the city was filled with noise.

Within the family and between friends it was also a time for the exchange of presents—originally wax candles and the clay statuettes or dolls that gave the Sigillaria its name, eventually all manner of luxury goods. Banquets could be held under the riotous leadership of a "king," normally chosen by lot, whose task as master of the revels was to keep up the merriment by issuing ludicrous, even humiliating, commands to his fellow diners. Above all, the Saturnalia was a time for the temporary suspension at home of social distinctions between masters and slaves: "at the Saturnalia, complete license is permitted to the slaves." Slaves might eat with their masters, in memory of the golden age of Saturn when no man owned a slave and there was no such thing as private property. Even more, status could be reversed: masters might serve their slaves, and within the miniature republic of the household, slaves might act as magistrates and judges.[12]

Saturnalia, then, connotes both the relaxation of social norms and even their temporary reversal. Its potential appeal to the leaders of society as a form of social control is clear: along with one or two other similar festivals in the Roman calendar it could offer a safety valve, a time when the normally unthinkable was possible, a time of leisure and amusement for everyone—even, above all, for slaves.[13] But the appeal of Saturnalia to Nero, it can be argued, went further: by freeing saturnalian behavior from its strict seasonal confines, by redefining it, by introducing it deliberately into other parts of Roman life, Nero not only amused himself, he drew emperor and people, ruler and ruled, closer together. Saturnalian behavior made him popular.

Ominously, he stepped into his new role by chance during the first Saturnalia after his accession, in December of 54, when he was chosen by lot from among his friends to play the king, *Rex Saturnalicius.* He duly gave the other boys orders that would make them blush. He commanded Britannicus to sing an extemporaneous song, but his not-so-innocent young brother turned the laugh on Nero by broadly hinting in song that he had been expelled from both his father's throne and his power. This rough give-and-take was well within the boundaries of Roman revelry, but Nero was already worried about the boy's advancing maturity and Agrippina's support for him. The incident sealed Britannicus' fate, and he was dead within two months.[14]

Early in his reign Nero took to the streets.[15] At nightfall he would put on the clothes of a slave, wearing a cap of freedom, the *pilleus,* or a wig, and then wander the streets of Rome, in and out of brothels and taverns and low eating-houses *(popinae),* looking for fun—he was particularly fond of relaxing in the area of the Milvian Bridge, which was then infamous for vice after dark. He and his gang would allegedly break into shops and houses and take their spoils back to the palace, where Nero divided the booty and sold it. They would molest men and women returning home from dinner. If anyone dared to resist, they would beat them and cast them into the sewers. The play was rough. After his nocturnal battles the emperor often had to apply a special ointment to soothe his bruises, and one man of senatorial rank whose wife Nero had molested beat him so severely and blacked his eyes so thoroughly that he was forced to spend several days in seclusion. The man was driven to commit suicide when he made the mistake of recognizing the emperor and begging forgiveness; thereafter Nero went out discreetly followed by soldiers and gladiators, who were under orders to interfere only if the resistance against him proved too fierce.

That was at night. During the day he would encourage violence in the theater, onstage and off, turning "theatrical license and the enthusiasm for the actors almost into pitched battles."[16] In this he was "at the same time leader and spectator," promising both rewards and impunity, forbidding his soldiers to interfere, and observing the fun from above. When the people began to brawl with fists and stones and pieces of the benches, he too would throw things down, on one occasion severely wounding a praetor in the head. So successful was the young emperor at rousing the rabble that, for fear of more widespread trouble, actors were banished from Italy and soldiers were assigned to maintain order in the theater.

Such escapades horrified genteel observers, but did everyone view them in quite the same way? Here was a young emperor, a tough brawler who actually joined and encouraged his people in their unrestrained pleasures—in the streets, in the brothels, taverns, and eating-houses, even in the theaters. He became one of them—dressing like them, carousing with them, leading them in riot. He stole from the propertied; he attacked senators. Why shouldn't he be popular? The emperor relaxed at night by relaxing the norms of society, upsetting all expectations of his character and his status. Freed from his role as ruler he put on the *pilleus,* and then it was Saturnalia, a brief respite from the serious business of life before he returned safe to the palace and became emperor again.

Roaming the streets at night, looking for violent fun with his gang, Nero was not alone: that was what uninhibited aristocratic youth did in the cities of the empire.[17] A century earlier Caelius Rufus had assaulted married ladies returning home from dinner parties. The future emperor Otho was accustomed to wander the streets at night and toss in a blanket anyone who was too feeble or too drunk to resist. The emperor Lucius Verus liked to wander at night as well, drinking, brawling, and breaking things, while Commodus resorted to taverns and brothels around town— and even the virtuous young Marcus Aurelius was exhilarated by scattering a flock of sheep and terrifying the shepherds. The student Augustine ran with a wild group known as the Wreckers who would assault innocent passersby, and one of the crucial incidents in the *Metamorphoses* of his African compatriot Apuleius is touched off by the hero's fear of the murderous rampages of a band of the noblest youths in town.[18]

What is interesting is the extent to which such behavior was tolerated: "In some cities," a third-century jurist lamented, "some people, who commonly call themselves 'the boys' *(iuvenes),* adapt themselves to the turbulent applause of the mob." The justification offered became a rhetorical commonplace—that boys will be boys, they were getting the wildness out of their system; one of Cicero's main defenses of his riotous young client Caelius Rufus was that this was a passing phase which every generation must indulge in its young men. Juvenal acknowledges just such a defense in his attack on the fictitious aristocrat who hangs around drinking in the lowest taverns all night: it was all right to protest that you had done the same when you were young, but you eventually gave it up, it was a brief phase, set aside with the first shaving of the beard; boys should be indulged, but Lateranus (the nobleman to whom Juvenal objects) was old enough to be commanding armies. This "boys will be boys" defense was probably raised on Nero's behalf: Suetonius says that although he at first indulged his various vices gradually and secretly and "as a sort of juvenile mistake," even then no one doubted that these vices were due to his innate character and not just to his age.[19]

His age is nevertheless significant, for these escapades were confined to the early years of his reign, between 55 and 58, when Nero was 18 to 21. There was no hint of recurrence thereafter, indeed nothing of the sort after the first shaving of his beard in 59.[20] Youthful folly was set aside as he turned to new ways of reaching across the vast social gulf between emperor and mob, of putting himself on a level with the common man.

THE APOGEE of Nero's reign as the King of Saturnalia came in 64 when, with Tigellinus as his entrepreneur, he celebrated the party of the century. Frightened by a vision from pursuing an intended journey to the East, he announced that his love for his homeland had forbidden him to leave it. The people of Rome wanted him to stay, so stay he would, setting up parties in public places (says Tacitus), treating the whole city as if it were his house, and preparing for the notorious dinner. The event so upset Tacitus that he stepped into his own narrative to comment in the first person: he would recount the infamous banquet of Tigellinus as an example, once and for all, of Nero's extravagance.[21]

Festivities centered on the Stagnum Agrippae, the great artificial lake or pool in the Campus Martius which had been constructed by Agrippa, the right-hand man and later the son-in-law of the emperor Augustus. Surrounded by parkland with trees, about 190 by 210 meters, it was fed by an aqueduct built for it in 19 BC (the Aqua Virgo), and it drained into the

Tiber through an 800-meter canal (the Euripus). The pool itself was an important part of the elaborate facilities for the pleasure and entertainment of the Roman people which Agrippa had laid out in the Campus Martius; Nero, his great-grandson and his successor as popular benefactor, incorporated it into his own new bath and gymnasium complex in the Campus.[22]

A great raft was now built for Nero's banqueters at the Stagnum—not the luxury yacht of a Ptolemy or a Caligula, but planks fixed on empty wine casks and covered with purple carpets and soft bedding. This was towed around the pool by other vessels adorned with gold and ivory. The rowers were male prostitutes, *exoleti,* who were arranged by their ages and their *scientia libidinum,* their sexual proficiency. The lake and its surroundings were stocked with exotic birds and beasts imported from distant lands and seas. On the banks of the lake stood taverns and brothels *(lupanaria, oikemata, porneia),* into which the people crowded while Nero and his companions floated about and dined in splendor. Tacitus suggests that on one side the brothels were filled with noblewomen, while on the other naked prostitutes disported in the open. Dio emphasizes the promiscuous availability of women of all kinds, noble and slave, professional prostitutes, matrons and virgins, all obliged to accommodate every request: here a slave had intercourse with his mistress in the presence of his master, there a gladiator enjoyed a noble maiden before her father's eyes. When night fell, all the surrounding groves and buildings echoed with songs and shone with lights (Tacitus); or there was chaos, pushing, blows, shouts, and for many, both men and women, death (Dio).

Then came what was perhaps the climax. A few days later, Nero himself was solemnly given in marriage to one of his band of perverts *(uni ex illo contaminatorum grege),* Pythagoras by name. The emperor was adorned with a bridal veil; witnesses attended; there were the usual preparations for dowry, marriage bed, and wedding torches. In short, everything was seen, comments Tacitus, which for a real woman is hidden by night. Without further comment, he and Dio (who does not mention Pythagoras or the marriage here) then pass to their accounts of the Great Fire.

The effect of this narrative is stunning: a society collapses in an orgy of sex and violence under an emperor who seems determined to pervert the course of nature.[23] Yet the significance of the notorious banquet shifts dramatically when it is placed in context.

First, the banquet of Tigellinus was not unique. Tacitus writes explicitly that he will offer it as an example, "to avoid too frequent a narrative of the same prodigality." And Dio does in fact briefly recount a remarkably similar occasion five years earlier. The elaborate celebration of Nero's Juvenalia in 59 had culminated with the emperor's performance as a citharode on stage, to the thunderous cheers of his Augustiani. After this triumph, he had feasted the people on boats in the Naumachia of Augustus. This naumachia was another, even larger, artificial basin surrounded by parkland across the river (in what is now Trastevere), where Augustus had staged his miniature version of the naval battle of Salamis, Greeks against Persians, in 2 BC. It too was fed by an aqueduct (the Aqua Alsietina, probably constructed for the purpose), and it likewise drained into the river through a canal. It was down this canal at midnight, after the success of his festival and his marine banquet in 59, that Nero sailed into the Tiber. Tacitus provides further details, without mentioning the floating banquet:

> Neither rank nor age nor previous high promotion hindered anyone from practicing the art of a Greek or Latin actor and even stooping to gestures and songs unfit for a man. Noble ladies too actually played disgusting parts, and in the grove, with which Augustus had surrounded the lake for the naval fight *(navali stagno)*, there were erected places for meeting *(conventicula)* and refreshment *(cauponae)*, and every incentive to excess was offered for sale. Money too was distributed, which the respectable had to spend out of sheer compulsion and which the profligate gloried in squandering.[24]

When the accounts of Tacitus and Dio are taken together, the shocking banquet of Tigellinus in 64 becomes little more than a repeat performance of the party in 59—the boats loaded with diners cruising around the lake, the degraded noblewomen, the temporary inns on the banks, crowded with people. Elsewhere both authors talk of noble men and women forced or cajoled to appear on stage and in the arena. Curiously, there is no hint of either force or persuasion here in Tacitus. People applied to participate; anyone could be an actor. Men even moved and sang in unmanly fashion, *gestus modosque haud virilis* (foreshadowing Nero and his bridegroom). Noblewomen practiced humiliating roles, *deformia meditari* (continues Tacitus), and inns and other meeting places were set up: this concatenation of degraded noblewomen and taverns on the bank suggests that their roles were not confined to the stage in 59, and that the scene in 64 may have been no less artificial. The idea of people being given money to spend in the celebration of 59, indeed being *forced* to spend it, gives the impression that everyone is acting on a large public stage.

But the banquet of Tigellinus is best appreciated in Suetonius' biography of Nero: he does not mention it at all. What he does say is important. In his account of the emperor's vices, Suetonius emphasizes his growing boldness and then proceeds, as usual, not chronologically but topically. First come excesses of gastronomic luxury. Nero would feast from noon until midnight. He would dine in public places, in the Naumachia, in the Campus Martius (which, incidentally, included the Stagnum Agrippae), in the Circus Maximus. Dancing girls and prostitutes from all over the city served at these parties. Whenever he floated down the Tiber to Ostia, or sailed along the gulf of Baiae (in the Bay of Naples), inns with taverns *(deversoriae tabernae)* were prepared along the banks and coasts; these were remarkable for their gourmandizing and for being kept by matrons who would imitate hostesses and urge Nero to put ashore. And he would impose the hosting of banquets on his close friends: one spent 400,000 sesterces on a dinner where the guests wore *mitellae,* oriental headdresses tied with ribbons under the chin (and a mark of effeminacy); another spent even more on roses.[25]

In short, not only were the banquets of 59 and 64 not unique, they were not unusual: their elements recur. Public banquets were a custom with Nero, not just an occasional popular gesture, and he enjoyed dining around the city. He took particular delight in eating while aboard ship, on the Naumachia, on the Stagnum, during expeditions down the Tiber and in the Bay of Naples. He liked ersatz inns to be set up on the shores, both artificial and real, which he passed. He liked to see Roman matrons running them—indeed, when they played the role of innkeepers for him they were assuming a social role not far from that of the prostitutes whom he also liked to have around. And he enjoyed lavish parties hosted by other men.

Elaborate feasting, sexual license, and messing about in boats make an arresting combination. Repeatedly indulged, it was not a passing whim, for Nero, always the showman with an artistic plan and an eye to his public, had another purpose. With these theatrical banquets he was deliberately recreating at Rome the notorious maritime delights associated with one place in the western Roman empire above all: Baiae, the pleasure capital of Italy.

Baiae was like nowhere else in the Roman world, a resort devoted entirely to luxurious relaxation.[26] Part of the territory of Cumae, it had no civic life of its own, yet it enjoyed a uniquely independent character. Maritime villas, palaces really, stretched out one after the other along the curving shore of the bay, rising up the hill and built out on piers over the sparkling waters. In this jewel-like setting the aristocrats and plutocrats of Rome energetically took their ease, enjoying the hot sulfur baths while seeking out love affairs and exotic entertainment. The entire Bay of Naples was ringed by resorts and pleasure villas, but Baiae and its gulf easily set the pace, and it was widely imitated around the empire: "no bay in the world outshines delightful Baiae"; "Baiae the golden shore of blessed Venus, Baiae the seductive gift of proud nature."[27] At the same time, it was notorious as a sink of corruption and prohibited pleasures. Details are usually lost in general, moralizing denunciations, but there is enough to form an impression in two famous passages of literature. In 56 BC Cicero defended his wild young friend Caelius Rufus against a complex of charges which included murder. Among the many allegations, the prosecutors hurled about accusations of "orgies, flirtations, adulteries, trips to Baiae, beach parties, dinner parties, drinking parties, musical entertainments and concerts, boating picnics."[28] Over a century later, Seneca, now in retirement from the excesses of Nero's court, visited Baiae. He left the place hurriedly the next day: it had some natural blessings, but luxury had chosen it as its headquarters. Baiae was becoming a lodging-house of vices, *deversorium vitiorum,* and Seneca had no wish, he writes, to see inebriated men wandering along its shores, drinking parties aboard ships, the lakes resounding with concert songs, and all the other indulgences by which luxury, freed from restraint, not only sins but proclaims its sin.[29] It was this luxury, the seaside luxury of Baiae, that Nero chose to import into Rome.

Nero loved the Bay of Naples.[30] The city of Naples itself offered him the first-class cultural amenities of a Greek city, and the artistic emperor visited it often. Pompeii he showered with favors: it may have been the home of his beloved Poppaea Sabina. But at Baiae he relaxed, sailing and feasting: "He often took delight in the sea near Puteoli and Misenum" (that is, in the Gulf of Baiae). Not only did he possess a villa there, so too did Poppaea (and Acte had property at Puteoli). He allegedly poisoned his aunt Domitia in 59, in his hurry to gain (among other things) her estate at Baiae, with its splendid fishponds. In 65, the Pisonian conspirators debated whether to murder the emperor at Piso's villa at Baiae, which Nero used to visit informally to bathe and to dine, captivated by its charm.[31] And it was at his Baian villa during the festival of Minerva that he held the banquet of reconciliation with his mother which was to prove her last meal.

This affection for Baiae is an element in two of Nero's largest, and most costly, construction projects. The first of these is mentioned by Tacitus as an appendix to his brief account of the Golden House. The architects of the new palace, Severus and Celer, had promised Nero to dig him a navigable canal from Lake Avernus, near Puteoli on the Bay of Naples, northward to the mouth of the Tiber. Suetonius likewise mentions the canal after describing the Golden House. He sensibly adds what Tacitus has omitted: that its course of 160 Roman miles would obviate the journey by sea, and it was to be built on such a scale that two ships with five banks of oars could pass each other. Today extensive cuttings near the Campanian coast attest to the grandiosity of the project, and a measured width of 60 to 65 meters confirms that two quinqueremes could indeed have passed with ease.[32] Other writers also mention this canal, but only Suetonius describes the emperor's second project. That was to be a vast covered pool, which would stretch from the port of Misenum to Lake Avernus, surrounded by colonnades. The work would pass through Baiae, and Nero intended to divert into it all the famous hot springs of the resort. Suetonius reports that he actually began construction, and something must have been accomplished, for two much later topographical sketches of the coast commemorate the Stagnum Neronis, Nero's lake, at Baiae.[33]

What we make of this depends on our point of view. Tacitus ignores any possible benefits, automatically condemning the canal, as he would the Golden House at Rome and the canal at Corinth, because it was Nero's, because it was against nature, and because it was extremely costly. To Suetonius it was an insane expenditure, while Pliny lamented its harmful effect on local viticulture. But a less jaundiced view can easily see the great benefit to the economy of the region and to the safety of Rome: the grain fleet from Alexandria always put in at the port of Puteoli, so now with the new canal the food of Rome would be safe from the great hazards and delays inherent in transshipment to Ostia by either land or sea. Securing the food supply of Rome would keep the people quiet and ensure the emperor's popularity in his capital.[34] But there is a further ideological aspect. Pliny gives a hint of it, writing clearly of "Nero's navigable ditch, which he had begun from the lake of Baiae up to Ostia." That is to say, when his projects were completed, the emperor would be able to float, if he wished, from the Lake of Agrippa (by then part of the Baths of Nero) in Rome, along the Euripus to the Tiber, down the Tiber to the newly re-built port of Ostia, thence by canal to Lake Avernus, and thence by the Lake of Nero to Baiae. His passage by ship from Rome to Baiae, from Baiae to Rome, would be quick, safe, and direct.[35]

His engineering projects thus sought to make real what he had already achieved symbolically: they brought Baiae to Rome. Baiae was the aristo-crat's playground *par excellence,* its diversions part of a universe unimagin-ably distant from the daily round of the man and woman on the dusty Roman street. Now their emperor brought his pleasures to Rome to share them with the people he loved. By treating the whole city as his house, he invited the people to be his guests. They too could watch and enjoy the exotic delights of Baiae, the elaborate feasting, the music, the lights at night, the seaside inns (and worse), the boating parties, the lavish expen-diture. The parties of 59 and 64 were politically astute pageants, bringing together the showman emperor and his people to enjoy in artificial form a revelry that was normally the prerogative of aristocrats. It is this very nov-elty, even more than the attendant scandals, that gives the banquet of Tigellinus its notoriety. The affair was a grand, outrageous paradox.

From beginning to end, the banquet overturned normal expectations.[36] The usual pleasure-skiffs of Baiae *(cumbae)* are replaced by a massive raft; a banquet more appropriate to land is held on the water; lowly tugboats are decorated with ivory and gold. These are manned not by professional rowers but by male prostitutes, chosen for their sexual rather than their nautical expertise and arranged not by skill but by age. Exotic wild birds and beasts stock a domestic park in downtown Rome, ocean creatures are imported into fresh water. Upper-class women are hidden inside brothels, naked prostitutes promenade in the open air. Night is turned into day, a man appears as a woman, an emperor marries a former slave, and the inti-macies of the marriage bed become a spectator sport. All this transpires in a city which has been transformed into a private house, before citizens who have become, as the emperor's edict proclaimed, his *necessitudines,* his intimate friends. It is a society turned upside down: the proud are humili-ated, the humble are treated to aristocratic pleasures. It is a Saturnalia unlike any seen before at Rome, and presiding over the great banquet is the *princeps Saturnalicius,* Nero himself.

PYTHAGORAS is a mystery. Tacitus closely links Nero's marriage to the freedman with the banquet of Tigellinus. Where Dio proceeds from the setting (inns with noble prostitutes) to the sexual atrocities that occurred there, Tacitus moves instead from the setting (the inns, the lights and music at night) to the single, perverse wedding: "Nero, who polluted himself by every lawful or lawless indulgence, had not omitted a single abomination which could heighten his depravity, till a few days afterwards *(paucos post dies)* he stooped to marry himself to one of that filthy herd, by name Pythagoras." It is unclear where in his narrative Dio treated the wedding—as represented in the surviving epitome of Xiphilinus he mentions it later twice, in passing—but for Tacitus, at least, Pythagoras marks the appropriate climax of the banquet of 64.[37] Why did Nero marry him? Did his wife Poppaea, the great love of his life, now pregnant with their second child, not object?

Yet again, matters are considerably complicated by Suetonius, with his very different, unchronological perspective. From description of the emperor's adventures in nautical gourmandizing, the biographer moves on to his sexual excesses. In what is probably his single most shocking escapade, we learn, Nero was assisted by a freedman named Doryphorus:

> He so prostituted his own chastity that after defiling almost every part of his body, he at last devised a kind of game, in which, covered with the skin of some wild animal, he was let loose from a cage and assaulted the private parts of men and women, who were bound to stakes, and when he had sufficiently worked off his savagery, he was despatched by his freedman Doryphorus. For he was married to this man in the same way that he himself had married Sporus, going so far as to imitate the cries and lamentations of maidens being deflowered. I have learned from some that it was his unshaken conviction that no man was chaste or pure in any part of his body, but that most of them concealed their vices and cleverly drew a veil over them; and that therefore he pardoned all other faults in those who confessed to him their lewdness.[38]

Not only does Suetonius ignore the banquet of Tigellinus as such, he misses the temporal link between banquet and wedding (of course) and he gives Nero's husband a different name. It is unimaginable that Nero was a bride twice without any ancient author remarking on it: the wedding that Suetonius describes must be the same as the wedding in Tacitus, which it resembles closely. Yet that took place in the spring or early summer of 64, whereas Doryphorus, one of the wealthiest and most powerful of Nero's freedmen, had died in 62.[39] Moreover, the appalling game played by Nero with his assistance is also noted by Dio under the year 67, with no mention of the late Doryphorus but immediately after naming Pythagoras and Sporus. (The concatenation of homosexual marriages and bestial games in both Suetonius and Dio suggests a common source.) In brief, the name "Doryphorus" must be a mistake in the text of Suetonius for "Pythagoras": this is the simplest solution to the dilemma, the solution commonly accepted and virtually inescapable, and the solution that will be followed here.[40] That is, Pythagoras was both Nero's husband and his partner in the game.

Pythagoras is central. It is difficult to separate truth from rumor in the stories about Nero's sexual crimes, but patterns or norms can be observed and, by any standard, Pythagoras lies beyond the pale. Indeed, if we could separate fact from innuendo, Nero's sexual life—but for Pythagoras—might appear disconcertingly regular for a Roman, despite its flamboyance. For a man who believed that everyone was completely corrupt, he lived a life of remarkable restraint.

Suetonius begins his account of Nero's sexual crimes bluntly: "Besides abusing freeborn boys and seducing married women, he debauched the Vestal Virgin Rubria."[41] Without elaborating on this, he moves on to concentrate in turn on Acte, Sporus, Agrippina, and Doryphorus/Pythagoras—a neat crescendo of horror, rising from the former slave woman he almost married, to the boy he castrated and did marry, to the mother he slept with, to the unspeakable acts with Doryphorus—and then on to his financial extravagance. Beyond these four shocking peaks of corruption there is very little but vague innuendo—and already we have seen in the case of Agrippina that the innuendo was probably not true.

As far as women are concerned, the key observation is that Nero did *not* play the rapacious tyrant, nor was he really portrayed as such. There are no salacious anecdotes about his philandering similar to those that attached themselves even to an Augustus—lists of adulterous liaisons, admitted by friends as well as foes, a wife who chose virgin sleeping partners for her elderly husband—not to mention a Caligula, who could rape a bride on her wedding day.[42] On the contrary, Nero appears to have been deeply romantic. Octavia, his wife from 53 to 62, he had never loved. Theirs had been a dynastic union, contracted when he was eleven, celebrated when he was fifteen. He loved only three women in his life: they happen to be the only women named as partners in adultery with him, and he married each one in turn.

In 55, at the age of 17, Nero fell deeply in love with the freedwoman Acte, and he probably set her up as a sort of second-class wife, affectionately but illegally, in a union known as *contubernium*. Suetonius says that their relationship was almost a full Roman marriage, *iustum matrimonium*. The objection to Acte was social rather than moral: she had been born into slavery, a slight which Nero countered by having distinguished friends swear that she was descended from the old kings of Pergamum in Asia Minor. More significantly, he was encouraged by his advisers in this passion which he worked so hard to make normal. Unnamed "senior friends" approved at the time, because Acte was inoffensive and satisfied his needs, because he abhorred Octavia, and because they were afraid that without Acte he would rush into sexual misconduct with noblewomen.[43] Such was her hold over Nero that Seneca supposedly chose her in 59 to warn the emperor about the impropriety of his relationship with his mother, and when she was supplanted by Poppaea her ties with her old flame remained at least outwardly affectionate: she grew vastly wealthy, she sacrificed in thanks for his deliverance from a conspiracy, she piously conducted his funeral.[44]

Only two other women are named as his lovers: Poppaea Sabina and Statilia Messalina, both of whom he did actually take in legal marriage. There is no record of Nero's feelings for Statilia, but he was extravagantly devoted to Poppaea, both before and after her death.[45] And he was prepared to play the ruthless tyrant in getting the woman he wanted. After allegedly insulting and attempting to murder Octavia, he divorced her for infertility, exiled her, and soon had her executed, in order to marry Poppaea in 62. As for Statilia, her penultimate husband, Vestinus Atticus, had been violent, headstrong, and an old crony of the emperor before the two had fallen out over Vestinus' bruising sense of humor. The Pisonian conspirators had not trusted the man to join their coup, but Nero pretended that Vestinus was implicated in it and forced him to commit suicide while still in office. What Tacitus omits, Suetonius says outright: "to possess [Statilia] he slew her husband Vestinus Atticus while he held the office of consul [in 65]." Within the year Nero had become Statilia's fifth husband.[46] She and Poppaea are the only married women whom Nero is said to have seduced.

Other than these three grand passions, adulteries which he felt impelled to convert, however violently, into regular marriages, Nero's relations with women are strikingly restricted. Two practices are marked out. During his nocturnal rampages about the city the teenage Nero, says Dio, made sexual attacks on women and boys. Tacitus too mentions the injuries inflicted on men and women of rank, and Suetonius remarks elsewhere on Nero's lewd handling of a married woman of senatorial rank during one of these escapades. Yet reports of these incidents are confined to the earliest years of the reign, to 55 and 56, and the abuse of women is incidental to their main purpose.[47] Beyond the isolated intrigue with the Vestal Virgin, a shocking capital offense which is undated, mentioned only by Suetonius, and extremely unlikely, Nero did *not* make a habit of indecent assaults against women.

For sexual gratification outside of marriage he turned not to rape but to concubines—a habit distasteful to his critics, perhaps, but one indulged in by other Roman aristocrats. A *concubina* was simply a man's sexual partner with whom there was no question of marriage, nor any legal ties. Socially acceptable, stable partnerships between male Roman aristocrats and lowborn concubines are on record, specifically for young bachelors and for widowers. Where lawyers and censors drew the line was at casual, multiple relationships, especially when the man was also married. Such unacceptable concubinage gives rise to standard invective against supposedly dissolute leaders of society: a consul who allegedly drank himself into a stupor with his troop of concubines, an emperor who was said to depilate his concubines personally (and to go swimming with common whores).[48] Conventions of abuse aside, how real such harems actually were is unclear; Nero's concubines are mentioned so casually—no critic makes anything of them—that one can conclude they probably did exist. Yet what little we hear of them makes them sound more like a theatrical troupe than a harem. One he chose and proudly exhibited because she resembled his mother. Another looked like his late wife, Poppaea. And near the end of his life, after the revolt of Vindex, as Suetonius tells it, "in pre-

paring for his campaign his first care was to select wagons to carry his theatrical instruments, to have the hair of his concubines, whom he planned
to take with him, trimmed man-fashion, and to equip them with Amazo-
nian axes and shields."[49] As so often with Nero, the appearance is more
significant than the reality.

This is not at first glance the case with Nero's sexual relations with men,
and here lies the real problem with Nero's sexuality and the harsh criticism
of it. Modern concepts of homosexuality or heterosexuality or bisexuality
are irrelevant here, as indeed are the subjective emotions of love and affection. What matters is the eye of the observer, the views of society. In what
we think of as homosexual relations, the crucial criterion for the Romans
in judging a man's conduct was not whether he indulged in them, but
whether he played the active or the passive role in intercourse, oral or
anal—more precisely, whether he penetrated or was penetrated, actions
which were clearly conceived of in terms of power, as dominant or submissive, male or female, superior or inferior:

> That is, a male who willingly allowed penetration by another was
> treated with contempt, and one who was compelled to allow it
> was thereby humiliated. But the penetrator himself was neither de-
> meaned nor disgraced; on the contrary, he had demonstrated his su-
> periority and his masculinity by making another serve his pleasure.[50]

So T. P. Wiseman describes it. In that view of the world, Nero was not in
any significant way homosexual.

Nero's practices as an active homosexual were peculiarly restricted.
Suetonius speaks vaguely of his *ingenuorum paedagogia,* his sexual abuse of
freeborn youths, a practice which Dio attributes only to his nighttime sor-
ties in 55, where it is quite clear that pederasty is not the main point. The
object then was precisely the flaunting of violent teenage machismo, part
of the larger demonstration that indiscriminately embraced attacks on
married ladies, robbery, burglary, stripping, beating, wounding, and murdering.[51]

But two quite different, and shocking, sexual attacks on freeborn youths
are recorded. In a section devoted to Nero's criminal mistreatment of all
his relatives, Suetonius includes among his victims

> the young Aulus Plautius, whom he forcibly defiled *(per vim conspur-*
> *casset)* before his death, saying "Let my mother come now and kiss

my successor," openly charging that Agrippina had loved Plautius and that this had roused him to hopes of the throne.

The point of Agrippina's kiss is, precisely, that Nero had forced Plautius to fellate him—the technical term is *irrumatio,* which generally connotes aggression, humiliation, and punishment.[52] His other victim was, again allegedly, his own adoptive brother Britannicus; as Tacitus puts it, several contemporary writers reported that some days before his brother's death Nero had sexually abused the boyhood of Britannicus, that is, sodomized him.[53] The two incidents are strikingly similar, particularly since Agrippina's denunciations of her own son and her threats to put Britannicus onto the throne had spurred Nero to the murder of his brother. Even if they are taken as true—and they are just the sort of charges that would be invented by enemies—the object in both attacks is again not sexual attraction but violent humiliation of a political rival before a society familiar with the idea of sexual assault as punishment.[54] Whether roistering with his gang or humiliating an adversary, Nero's repellent machismo has nothing to do with either desire or a homosexual way of life.

The apparently pederastic relationship with Sporus is unsatisfactory in a quite different way, in that it fits no norms. This was not a same-sex union but a marriage between a man and a mock-woman. Nero did not think of the eunuch Sporus as a male lover; he thought of him as a woman and wanted to change him physically into one. He did not take the boy for his own attractions but as a substitute for his dead wife, and he seems to have treated the affair as, at best, a simultaneously romantic and ironic homage to Poppaea, and, at worst, a joke.

Even more unusual, if that is possible, is the other and earlier relationship with Pythagoras, of which we are given two lurid glimpses. One is the elaborate wedding ceremony after which Nero, dressed as the bride, imitated the shrieks and moans of a virgin being deflowered. The other is the bizarre game in which Nero, dressed in animal skins, attacked the genitals of men and women who were bound to stakes, and then was "killed" by his freedman husband: "and, when he had sufficiently vented his rage, he would be finished off by the freedman Doryphorus" *(et, cum affatim desaevisset, conficeretur a Doryphoro liberto).* The verb *conficere* is ambiguous. It can mean both "kill" and "exhaust," and it joins other words for killing and dying in the vocabulary of sex, to connote excitement to orgasm: not only did the freedman "kill" the beast Nero, he brought the thoroughly aroused emperor to climax. That Suetonius knew what he was saying when he reported this is clear, for he immediately explains that "Doryphorus" ("the spear-carrier") was Nero's wedded husband.[55]

Pythagoras/Doryphorus does not fit. In every other relationship, real or alleged, with men or with women, Nero played the dominating male; here he took pleasure in playing the passive, the despised *cinaedus,* the *pathicus.* Even with his penchant for the outrageous and the unexpected onstage and off, it is difficult to imagine him in so submissive a role, and he himself had directed one of his famously wounding satires against a man notorious for his effeminacy.[56] Two elements of the relationship with Pythagoras stand out. One is that it is unique: no other similar partners are ever named, nor is it ever suggested that Nero, dissolute though he was, was essentially effeminate. The other is its theatricality: Pythagoras appears only as a supporting character in two dramas in which Nero takes on a role and its costume, transforming himself physically, from a man into a bride and into a beast. Why?

In an affair alleged to have occurred under Nero, a Roman nobleman named Gracchus (the name, at least, is fictitious), wearing a long dress and a veil, gave a huge dowry to his new husband, a trumpeter; they signed a contract; they received best wishes; and at the crowded wedding banquet the "bride" reclined in the bosom of his husband. This episode is recounted in Juvenal's second satire, part of a general attack on homosexual practices published in the early second century. A slightly earlier epigram of Martial tells a very similar story: bearded Callistratus was married to hard Afer, with torches, a veil, wedding songs, and even a dowry.[57] Juvenal concludes his account of such weddings with gratitude that all the fertility drugs and rites in the world will do nothing to help such brides— they die sterile. Martial ends his epigram: "Doesn't this seem enough to you, Rome? Are you waiting to see if he gives birth?" And of course when Nero married Sporus, some wit exclaimed what a good thing it would have been if Nero's father had taken a similar wife.[58] The joke wears thin with repetition, but Gracchus and Callistratus help to explain Nero.

The first skepticism about the wedding with Pythagoras was expressed fifty years ago in a long paper published by Jean Colin on the "wedding" of Gracchus. The episode in the second satire caps a Juvenalian tirade against effeminacy and transvestism, which are presented, remarkably, in a religious light. Men dress up as women for the rites of Bona Dea, the Good Goddess, whose ceremonies were normally for women only. Here only men can attend, wearing necklaces and a sort of turban *(mitra)* with ribbons hanging from it. One man applies eye makeup, one drinks from a phallic glass, another checks himself in a mirror, everyone chatters in falsetto.[59] With this context in mind, Colin showed in impressive detail how each item of dress and each action in the Bona Dea sequence and in the wedding of Gracchus, as well as in the wedding of Martial's Callistratus, could be seen as the distortion of a cultic act, and he concluded that the wedding ceremony was the acting out of a mystic marriage between man and goddess which for ancient religious cults was a supreme symbol of religious initiation. In the ceremony the place of the deity would be taken by one of her priests. The goddess who was thus receiving Gracchus into her worship, Colin argued, was Ma-Bellona, originally from Cappadocia, whose cult was associated with that of the better-known Cybele, the Great Mother. Nero's marriage to Pythagoras fits the pattern in detail, and just as Gracchus was the bride of a *tubicen,* a trumpeter, so Nero was the bride of a *doryphorus,* a spearman, both of which terms signified particular priesthoods in the cult of Cybele.[60]

Thus, perhaps, Nero was being initiated into one of the elaborate Eastern "mystery cults," those religions that revealed their secrets, their mysteries, only to the select few who had been initiated into them. Other scholars followed where Colin led. One suggested that Nero's marriage to Pythagoras was part of his known interest in Mithraism, and that it and other seemingly eccentric actions corresponded to the emperor's passing through various grades of initiation within the cult of the god Mithras. Another, more persuasively, drew attention to the banquet, mentioned by Suetonius, at which diners wore turbans, *mitellae,* coverings normally restricted to women: just such *mitellae,* or *mitrae,* were also worn by the male celebrants at the perverse rites of Bona Dea as described by Juvenal in the Gracchus poem.[61]

The idea that in being married to Pythagoras Nero was being initiated into an oriental cult is attractive, as long as we realize that it was not serious. By mid-64 Nero, the man who despised all cults, the man who would eventually urinate on the image of the only deity in whom he had ever believed, the Syrian Goddess, was, yet again, at play. The wedding was at best a parody of an initiation: the cries of a bride on her wedding night were not a part of any serious ceremony.[62] The name "Pythagoras" is as suspicious as that of Sporus: not attested in the inscriptions of Rome, and not otherwise known among the slaves and freedmen of the imperial household, it was surely chosen to recall the legendary ancient sage whose teachings on discipline included sexual abstinence. And a rather obscure poem of Martial, published some thirty years later, sets the marriage firmly within a familiar milieu:

> On the sumptuous feast days of the old Scythe-bearer [Saturn], over which King Dice-box rules, methinks you allow me, cap-clad (*pilleata*) Rome, to sport in toil-free verse. You smile. Permission granted then, I am not forbidden. Pale cares, get you far hence. Whatever comes my way, let me out with it and no moody meditation. Boy, mix me bumpers half [wine] and half [water], such as Pythagoras used to give Nero, mix them, Dindymus, and not too long between them. I can do nothing sober, but when I drink, fifteen poets will come to my aid. Give me kisses, Catullan kisses. If they shall be as many as he said, I will give you Catullus' Sparrow.[63]

To take the last part briefly: The poet has received permission from Rome to relax and let wine fuel his muse. The more he drinks, the better his poetry. His cup-bearer is to kiss him. If the kisses are as many as the myriads which Catullus asked from his mistress Lesbia (in his famous poem 7), Martial will present Dindymus with Catullus' *Passer* (that is, Catullus' second poem, on Lesbia's "sparrow"). These last three lines are purposely ambiguous. One meaning is poetic: the wine and the kisses of Dindymus will so stimulate the poet that he will produce a poem like that of Catullus. At the same time the lines are also patently obscene: wine and kisses will so arouse the poet that he will give the boy his *passer,* his phallus. *Passer* can have this lewd meaning, and the name of the cup-bearer, "Dindymus," confirms the obscenity, for it is also that of the eunuch priests of Cybele, the Great Mother, named after her sacred Mount Dindymus in Phrygia; elsewhere in his epigrams Martial employs the name invariably to refer to passive, effeminate males, objects of either the poet's ridicule or his lust.[64]

Yet again, Pythagoras presents a puzzle. Why Martial chose him for comparison is unclear. Perhaps because he was Nero's official cupbearer, *a potione;* certainly to give point to Dindymus' relations with Martial, because Pythagoras also shared Nero's bed, albeit in the more active role. But the context in which the poet calls him to mind is all-important: it is the time of Saturnalia, the luxurious days of the old scythe-bearer Saturn, when the dice-box reigns supreme and Rome wears the cap of liberty, the *pilleus.* It is the time for jests and particularly for indecent humor, when (as Martial says elsewhere) even a serious epic poet should lay aside his normal *severitas* and read without offense poems saturated with licentious jokes.[65] That is, when Martial—who was, after all, in Rome in 64—thought of Saturnalia and crude humor, he thought of Pythagoras. This really reveals nothing about Martial's sexuality, nor about Nero's; it does show what they and their audiences thought was witty.

Pythagoras' other role with Nero seems distinctly unfunny. Again, it was "a kind of game, in which, covered with the skin of some wild animal, he was let loose from a cage and assaulted the private parts of men and women, who were bound to stakes, and when he had sufficiently worked off his savagery, he was despatched by his freedman Doryphorus." Dio, following the same source here as Suetonius, embellishes pruriently: "binding naked boys and girls to stakes, he would put on the skin of a wild beast, and falling upon them he would act licentiously, as if he were devouring (them)."[66] Yet again, this is not what it first appears to be. Suetonius speaks of this as *quasi genus lusus* invented by Nero, a kind of game or—an equally possible translation—a kind of joke or prank. Just what kind of game it was, was noticed by Thomas Habinek.[67] Nero, dressed and acting like a beast, emerges from a *cavea*, a cage, to savage victims who are tied naked to stakes, before he is finished off, *conficeretur,* that is, killed by a *confector,* the attendant who delivered the *coup de grâce* to men and beasts in the arena. Nero's sport is not (or not just) the lustful whim of a demented tyrant; it is a would-be artistic rendering of the standard legal punishment called *damnatio ad bestias,* in which bound criminals were exposed, often naked, to mauling by wild beasts in the arena for the amusement and edification of the spectators.

Whatever happened, it looks as little like rough sex as it does a real execution; it is more a bizarre pantomime. The equation of sex with death is jejune: Nero attacking the genitals of criminals condemned to fatal mauling by wild beasts, Nero dying (in both senses) on the spear of his attendant. The reversal of norms is particularly Neronian—the emperor as a beast, the freedman as his master—but one of them is quite stunning. Nero's bestial act was surely meant to imply oral sex. Normally, to perform fellatio or cunnilingus, willingly or unwillingly, was to be degraded, to be viewed with the same contempt as the passive male. Here, however, the passive and active roles are inverted: the victim becomes the aggressor in the context of the arena, the mauling beast reverses the role.

Did the men and women at the stakes suffer, any more than Nero "died"? Neither Suetonius nor Dio says so; indeed there is nothing to suggest that the "victims" were not compliant actors in a bizarre piece of theater. Were they really innocents? When the refined voluptuary Petronius came to commit suicide in 66, Tacitus writes, he sent to the emperor a sealed codicil to his will, in which "he described fully the prince's shameful excesses, with the names of male and female prostitutes and their novelties in debauchery."[68] Tacitus speaks of *noctium suarum ingenia,* which has been well translated as "the ingenious varieties of his nightly revels": the elaborately theatrical *damnatio ad bestias* should be viewed as just one of these revels, sex as *tableau vivant,* sex as a game. Nero's partners were actors and players at least as much as they were concubines and whores. If we take that view, a male prostitute, *exoletus,* reporting for work of an evening, might just as easily find himself assigned to participate in another imperial wedding, to be tied naked to a stake, or to tow a dining barge around the Lake of Agrippa.

How seriously did Nero the libertine take all of this debauchery? In his account of the tour of Greece, Dio pauses to describe the wedding with Sporus. This reminds him of the concurrent marriage to Pythagoras and then of the attacks in the guise of a wild beast on naked boys and girls tied to stakes, and these remind him in turn (there is no break in the epitome of Xiphilinus) of Nero's disgracefully effeminate habits of dress. Senators who came to his *salutatio* would find him wearing a short, brightly colored tunic *(chitonion anthinon)* with a linen scarf or handkerchief *(sindonion)* around his neck, and he so far flouted custom as to wear unbelted tunics in public.[69] In his outrage Dio has ignored or quite missed Nero's point, which Suetonius' more precise version makes clear:

> He was utterly shameless in the care of his person and in his dress, so that during the trip to Greece he let his hair, which was always formed in steps, grow long and hang down behind, and he often appeared in public dressed in a dinner-gown with a handkerchief around his neck and without belt or sandals.[70]

The message in Nero's dress at the end of his reign is as unambiguous as that of the cap of freedom, the *pilleus,* which he wore at its start. The loose-fitting gown—Suetonius calls it *synthesina,* a variant of *synthesis*—was the correct dress for the casual relaxation of private dinner parties. A proper Roman could wear it out of doors on only one occasion without shocking his respectable fellow-citizens: during the Saturnalia.[71]

However outrageous they may appear, Nero's sexual escapades show calculation, not wild abandonment: they are calculated to amuse and to shock. Sensual pleasure is secondary to the intended effect on observers, both vulgar and refined, public and private, low and high. Even when radically innovative, they are rooted in one Roman tradition or another. It should not by now come as a surprise that Nero was in much of this "private" life following in the path of yet another legendary figure of the past.

W HEN HE COMES to recount the tale of Nero's increasing independence from his mother after his accession, and his growing indulgence in riot and murder, Cassius Dio is as short on fact as he is long on passionate rhetorical denunciation, yet into his account he slips unexpectedly an anecdote which is found nowhere else. Nero's excesses naturally ran to the wasteful expenditure of vast fortunes (usually other people's):

> He once ordered 250,000 [drachmas, = 1,000,000 sesterces] to be given at one time to Doryphorus, who was in charge of Petitions during his reign, and when Agrippina caused the money to be piled in a heap, hoping that when he should see it all together he would change his mind, he asked how much the mass before him amounted to, and upon being informed, doubled it, saying: "I did not realize that I had given him so little."[72]

Precisely the same story is told of the liberality of his great-grandfather, Mark Antony:

> He had given orders for 250,000 drachmas to be presented to one of his friends, a sum which the Romans call a *decies*. His steward was dumbfounded at this command, and in order to make Antony understand the sheer size of the gift, he had the money laid out in full view of his master. As Antony passed by, he asked what this heap of coins represented, and the steward then explained that this was the gift he had ordered for his friend. Antony saw that the man grudged the expense, and so he remarked: "I thought a *decies* amounted to more than that. This is just a trifle: you had better double it!"[73]

The anecdote, related here by Plutarch, is folkloric: it means to dramatize character and may well be fictional in both versions. (It can hardly be claimed that Nero cast a sentient Agrippina in the role of Antony's steward.) Yet it is an indication, a strong indication, of the tradition in which Nero was seen, and it could well be his own invention *after* his mother's death. For there should be no doubt that, in fashioning an image, Mark Antony was as important to Nero as his other ancestor, Augustus himself. In their common descendant, the two great rivals of the dying Republic, polar opposites in so many ways, could finally be reconciled.

Antony had something that Augustus would never achieve: the common touch. People liked him, liked the open, impetuous nature which he showed in public. The heap-of-coins story is told by Plutarch in his Life of Antony, where it forms part of an excursus on the man's popularity. His troops worshipped him not just for his swagger and his profanity, but for the delight he took in public carousing and his pleasure in eating with his men. Many found even his sexual appetites attractive, tempered as they were by a fondness for helping others in their love affairs and a willingness to laugh with others at his own. Again, his lavish generosity won him fervent supporters on the road to power.[74] Another man with such traits might be called a braggart, a libertine, and a spendthrift. Antony was forgiven much because he was well-liked.

Central to his character, in Plutarch's view, was Hercules. With his full beard, broad forehead, and aquiline nose, the virile Antony was thought to resemble portraits of the great hero, and his family, the Antonii, were indeed said to descend from Anto, a son of Hercules. This physical resemblance he deliberately cultivated, wearing clothes which were intended to recall those of Hercules when he appeared in public, and his behavior—comradely, generous, passionate—was similarly viewed as Herculean. Antony's identification with his heroic ancestor entered the intense propaganda wars of the triumviral period. It was commemorated on coins issued by a supporter of Antony, and on a gemstone which shows a statue of Hercules with Antony's features, or Antony with Hercules' features. Octavian's partisans seem to have countered with a conception of Antony as the hero of a less than flattering Herculean myth, in the thrall of the eastern Queen Omphale/Cleopatra; a widely circulated bowl of Arretine ware may allude to this, showing Hercules as he reclines in a chariot under a parasol dressed in women's clothes, while the masculine queen wears his lion skin, shoulders his club, and reaches for an enormous drinking cup.[75] That Octavian's partisans resorted to an aggressive parody of the Herculean image merely underscores the public impact of the original. The honest, affable, impulsive man of action with a weakness for pleasure was a powerfully attractive persona. A great man who candidly exhibited all too human characteristics was readily forgiven: the people of Alexandria not only liked Antony and enjoyed his escapades, they were proud that the stern Roman chose to relax in their city.[76] Antony and Hercules were popular in a way that Octavian/Augustus and Apollo could never be. Their common descendant Nero united the opposites in himself. It was no accident that the two gods with whom he identified himself were, as we have seen, Apollo/Sol and Hercules.[77]

Antony loved to be called a lover of Greece, and in his philhellenism he provided two paradigms for Nero. First there was his respect for the glories of old Greece: he loved above all to be called a philathenian. After the battle of Philippi, in 42, he proved a model guest at Athens, restrained and respectful, a frequenter of games, religious initiations, and scholarly disputes. The great temple of Apollo at Delphi, which had been damaged by fire in the 80s, he promised the town fathers to restore, and he went so far as to have it surveyed, though nothing came of the pledge—the actual work would only be undertaken by Nero, a hundred years later. Even more to the point is Antony's conduct in Athens when he arrived in 38 with his new bride Octavia, the sister of Octavian. Wintering there, he laid aside the character of a Roman general completely: he dressed like a Greek, he attended Greek lectures, he dined like the Greeks, he relaxed in Greek fashion, and he joined in Greek festivals. To celebrate a victory by one of his lieutenants over the Parthians he gave games in Athens, and the Panathenaic Games were apparently renamed after him, the Panathenaia Antonieia. He appeared at them clad in the dress of a gymnasiarch, the honorific superintendent of the gymnasium, but he went further than any previous Roman philhellene. He acted as umpire in wrestling matches, and physically intervened in them—astonishing conduct for a Roman general, but just what his great-grandson Nero would be noted for doing at wrestling contests in Greece a century later.[78] Indeed, no other Roman leader would so enthusiastically immerse himself in hellenic culture until Nero.

Falling in love with Cleopatra, Antony fell also under the spell of Alexandria. There too he dressed not as a Roman general but in the local Greek costume, to visit the temples, the gymnasia (he was also honorary gymnasiarch there), and professorial disputations. But the tenor of his life with Cleopatra in Alexandria was quite different from the sober decorum of his stay in Athens with Octavia. When in Egypt, the middle-aged triumvir would play the part of a much younger man with all the time in the world, as he plunged with the Egyptian queen and their band of "Inimitable Livers" into a riotous life of practical jokes, games, amateur dramatics, elaborate excursions, and lavish banquets.[79] The Alexandrians took him to their hearts and Antony returned their passion—a fatal mistake in his war of words with Octavian. Octavian would portray him as a Roman renegade, fallen under the sway of the Egyptian queen and the dog-headed gods of the Nile. Shocking and irrefutable proof was provided by Antony's own will, which Octavian seized in Rome: his children by Cleopatra were to receive massive gifts, and his body was to be buried with that of Cleopatra at Alexandria.[80]

Nero too wished to settle there, and it would indeed be rumored that he had fled in the end to the Egyptian capital. His interest in old Greece had been limited strictly to artistic and athletic games, and on his visit there he would ignore the cultural and religious centers which had no games to attract him. His heart lay rather in Alexandria, and much has been written about a veritable "Egyptomania" (both hellenistic and pharaonic) under his reign: hellenic Egyptians rose for the first time in significant numbers to positions of real political and cultural power; privileges were showered on Alexandria and Egypt generally; Rome, as it was rebuilt after the fire, has been seen as modeled on Alexandria, the Golden House as an imitation of the royal palace there; Egyptian motifs proliferated in art; even Nero's imitation of Apollo/Helios has been seen as derived in part from the solar theology of the ancient pharaohs.[81]

Against the cool, calculating figure of Octavian, Antony was the man of passion, the Roman general and magistrate who was also the lover of wine, women, low companions, spectacle, and practical jokes. One scandal drew the contrast sharply: Octavian might carouse all night, but he would never, as Antony did one morning after, stumble in to conduct a meeting in the Forum at Rome and vomit into his toga.[82] But that was precisely what attracted Nero to him so strongly. The casting aside of restraint, the upsetting of expectations, the reversal of roles—all these are key to his appeal for Nero and to the popularity of both men.

While at Alexandria, the triumvir would dress up as a slave at night, wander about the city, and mock the citizens through their open doors and windows. They would abuse him in return, sometimes beating him up before he returned to the palace, even though most people saw through the disguise. True or not, the behavior is a good model for the young Nero's bruising nighttime excursions, "disguised" as a freedman, and Plutarch's comment on this is invaluable: the people of Alexandria played along with Antony's fun because they liked him, and they would say that he wore a tragic mask for the Romans but a comic one for them. Enemies and later historians might be appalled, but what Antony did appealed to the people. A century later the population of Rome was a much more cosmopolitan one, and it was not necessary to go to Alexandria to relax.[83]

Antony was also a lover of maritime pleasures, infamous in Italy for his picnics in groves and on riverbanks, notorious in Egypt for his frolics with Cleopatra on the banks of Canopus and Taposiris. The spectacular arrival of Cleopatra in Tarsus for her first meeting with Antony prefigures the banquet of Tigellinus. The Queen of Egypt, dressed as Venus and surrounded by Cupids, sailed up the Cydnus River in a barge with gilded stern, purple sails, and silver-plated oars. To the throngs who followed the barge's progress along the shores, it would look as though the crew consisted of Nereids and Graces, for the most beautiful of Cleopatra's attendants were also in costume and seemed to be in charge of sails and rudder. Luxury and nautical role-playing are very Neronian, and again the popular reaction is telling. At the center of Plutarch's account of that first encounter lies the indelible image of the triumvir dressed in official uniform and sitting on his tribunal, waiting to receive Cleopatra, as the crowd slowly drifts away to watch the queen's spectacular progress up the Cydnus, until Antony is left sitting alone in stately Roman splendor in the marketplace of Tarsus.[84]

Exuberance and extravagance were not traditional Roman virtues, and popularity has a cost. Plutarch derives some of his most scandalous material about Antony from Cicero's rabid attack on the future triumvir in the autumn of 43 BC, a never-delivered speech known as the Second Philippic. To his enemy, Antony was of course a drunkard, a spendthrift, a robber, a murderer, but some of the incidental anecdotes have a special ring. Antony had once disguised himself as a slave messenger, to play a trick on his wife. The adolescent Antony had passed from being a male prostitute to being the "wife" of the younger Curio. And Antony had surrounded himself with low company. As tribune he had progressed around Italy in a two-wheeled chariot, with his official lictors escorting his actress-mistress in her open litter, a carriage full of pimps, his comrades, following him, and his poor mother bringing up the rear: "nowhere in the world has anything so shocking, scandalous, disgraceful, ever been heard of." He drank himself into a stupor at the wedding of an actor; he gave away whole cellars of wine to the most worthless of men; actors grabbed this, actresses grabbed that; gamblers and drunkards filled his house; the couches of his slaves were spread with purple coverings that had once belonged to Pompey; his bedrooms became brothels, his dining rooms taverns; in military fashion he billeted prostitutes and low musicians on ordinary citizens.[85]

So too the fondness for low company is really the principal charge brought against Nero, the lover of perverse roles and degraded disguises, the addict of the theater and the circus. Prostitutes and dancing girls served at his banquets; he too not only enjoyed but set up brothels and taverns; he all but married his freedwoman mistress; he intended to campaign with an army of concubines. He gave the estates of great generals to the lyre-player Menecrates and to the *murmillo* Spiculus, his favorite gladiator. He showered the money-lender Paneros with properties in both the city and the country, and buried him with near-regal splendor. The witty and deformed ex-cobbler from Beneventum, Vatinius, was for a time (we are told) the leading man at court in wealth and in evil influence. Tigellinus, the praetorian prefect, was allegedly an ex-prostitute, adulterer, poisoner, and forger, who had raised and trained racehorses before he entered the imperial service.[86] Tacitus sums up the negative image of Nero's courtiers memorably. After the defeat and death of Otho at Cremona, Vitellius, who made no secret of his admiration for Nero, marched south to Rome. The closer he came, wrote Tacitus, the more depraved his progress grew, swelled as it was by actors and gangs of eunuchs and the very essence of Nero's court.[87]

The line between truth and slander is neither clear nor particularly important. Even allowing for the thick layer of commonplaces in ancient rhetoric and historiography, the censure and the invective, there is enough in the record to see that Antony and his great-grandson shared an attitude to life not common among the Roman aristocracy, a mixture of philhellenism, so strong as to adopt Greek ways of life, with a fondness for pleasure among low company, so strong as to lead to identification with the masses. The behavior of Antony and Nero was often riotous; it was subversive; it outraged their critics. But for many more ordinary people, riotous subversion might be amusing—it might even be liberating.

In his last weeks, Nero vowed that if he remained safely in power he would celebrate victory games which would culminate with a personal appearance before his joyous people. It was something he had done at festivals before; critics would again be incensed by the spectacle of an emperor lowering himself to appear as a player on stage, the public would again be enchanted. He intended to perform on various musical instruments and, on the last day, he would dance the role of Vergil's Turnus. Turnus was of course the Latin prince whose bloody war with Aeneas dominates the last half of the *Aeneid,* and whose deeply disturbing death at the hands of Aeneas ends the poem.[88] But Nero's victory games would never be given. In his last hours, as he prepared to escape in June 68, he tried to persuade the officers of his guard to flee with him. Some prevaricated, some flatly refused, and one cried out, "Is it such a wretched thing to die?" The words were brilliantly apt, plucked from the last book of the *Aeneid.* In the final battle, losing, his strength and his spirits flagging, Turnus refuses to flee from the field: "Is it such a wretched thing to die? O you spirits of the dead be good to me, since the favor of heaven has turned away. A pure soul and without guilt I shall descend to you, in no way unworthy of my great ancestors."[89] The noble words were a stinging rebuke to the man who had wanted to play Turnus, just as real life intruded on his play. The officer who alluded to them might also have quoted the proverbial warning, the ultimate judgment on the subverter of Roman norms: *non semper Saturnalia erunt,* Saturnalia does not last forever.[90]

7

One House

As in private relationships the closest ties were the strongest, so the people of Rome had the most powerful claims and must be obeyed in their wish to retain him . . . And to confirm the belief that nowhere else in the world gave him such joy, he arranged banquets in public places and treated the whole city as if it were his house.

TACITUS

He had decided to call Rome Neropolis.

SUETONIUS[1]

On the night of 18/19 July 64 the city of Rome began to burn, and it burned fiercely, with one respite, for nine days. The fire broke out in the shops at the southeastern end of the Circus Maximus near the Palatine and the Caelian hills.[2] The merchandise there fueled the flames and, driven by a strong wind, they raced down the open 650-meter length of the circus. From there they spread out through the low-lying land and up the hillsides, roaring down the narrow and winding lanes of the old city. Over and around the Palatine the fire blazed, to engulf the new Domus Transitoria which Nero had built to connect the Palatine with the Gardens of Maecenas on the Esquiline.

Nero, who had been in Antium, returned to take immediate and effective measures to relieve popular suffering: he opened to the people the Campus Martius and the buildings of Agrippa there, and even his own gardens; he arranged for temporary shelters to be erected; he provided supplies from Ostia and the neighboring municipalities; he lowered the price of grain.[3]

On the sixth day, the fire was stopped on the lower slopes of the Esquiline hill after large numbers of buildings in its path were torn down. It broke out again, however, and spread across the more open spaces of the city, this time causing fewer casualties but overwhelming public temples and porticoes.[4] When the flames finally subsided three days later, they left behind four of the city's fourteen regions undamaged, three burned to the ground, and smoking ruins in the other seven. Houses, apartment buildings, temples, ancient works of art—the devastation was enormous.[5] Suetonius is eloquent: "At that time, besides an immense number of apartment houses, the private houses of leaders of old were burned, still adorned with trophies of victory, and the temples of the gods vowed and dedicated by the kings and later in the Punic and Gallic Wars, and whatever else interesting and noteworthy had survived from antiquity." After noting the ruin of the Palatine and the amphitheater of Taurus (in the Campus Martius), Dio adds simply that perhaps two-thirds of the city burned and countless people died.[6]

Nero's response to the disaster was magnificent. Along with the prompt relief of misery through temporary housing, emergency supplies, and cheap grain, he launched a careful and comprehensive long-term reconstruction of the city. Tacitus, who gives extensive details, sums up the situation admirably: those measures which were taken for utility also brought beauty to the new city. Moreover, acting as a good *princeps* should, Nero took care to appease the indignant gods with prayers and sacrifice. Even better, he discovered the arsonists to be a Jewish sect, infamous for its hatred of the human race, and he properly offered the perpetrators up as sacrifices to the offended gods, in the same gardens which were now home to so many of his displaced people.

Despite his best intentions, Nero also came in for heavy criticism. Some of it, whether truly contemporary or later invention, is trivial. Tacitus reports, for instance, that while the use and beauty of the new buildings and building codes were acknowledged, there were those who grumbled that the old, narrow streets and tall buildings were healthier than the new broad, unshaded spaces, exposed to the sun. Moreover, despite popular outrage at their crime, and despite popular enjoyment of a good spectacle, some felt the punishment of the Christians to be excessively cruel. Suetonius hints that Nero intended to loot the ruins; Dio asserts that he removed the free grain distribution.[7] But there were other, darker charges, far more damaging because they ran directly counter to his laudable actions, and taken together they suggested not merely callous indifference to the misery of his people but active hostility to their welfare: that Nero had intentionally started the fire, through his agents; that he sang while the city burned; that he built the fabulous Golden House amid the sufferings of the citizens; and that he extorted vast sums from them to pay for the recovery.

He certainly needed money. The cost of Nero's vigorous response to the disaster must have been enormous: the temporary feeding and housing of perhaps 200,000 homeless; the general clean-up; the rewards offered for quick rebuilding and the cost of the new, publicly funded colonnades for private houses; the repair and replacement of all the public buildings damaged or destroyed. There are clear signs of financial strain: distributions of free grain to some 150,000 to 200,000 citizens in Rome were indeed suspended temporarily, while the gold, silver, and bronze coinage were all permanently devalued.[8] Moreover, the emperor's ability to raise money must have been severely compromised by the social and economic dislocation caused by the fire. A highly plausible modern study has sketched the magnitude of the disaster: lost jobs, lost possessions, lost tools, lost stock, lost property, lost savings (which were often held in temples), in short, lost capital and lost income throughout society, from artisans to landlords; shortage of space for both business and housing; rising costs and rents, further overcrowding—in sum, increased misery.[9] And yet Nero needed money, desperately. Suetonius charges that "from the contributions which he not only received, but even demanded, he nearly bankrupted the provinces and exhausted the resources of individuals." Tacitus elaborates: the exactions wasted Italy, ruined the provinces and the so-called allied peoples and free cities, and ransacked temple treasuries in Rome and throughout Asia and Achaia (where even gifts and the statues of the gods were removed by the emperor's zealous procurators).[10] That is, the costs of the Fire of Rome fell on the rich, on communities outside of Rome (where and to what extent is unclear), and on temple treasuries. How much of this was passed onto and resented by the man and woman on the street is unknown, but the benefits of Nero's energetic response to the devastation must have been severely undercut by its inevitable costs.

Yet the central question is one more of belief than of economics. How people reacted to the economic devastation, direct and indirect, provoked by the Great Fire would depend very much on what they believed to be its cause. Rome was a firetrap, its people and buildings constantly prey to fires great and small. Accidents were part of life, however much one might resent the emperor's handling of the problem. But if he had deliberately set the fire, deliberately caused the death of thousands of his people and

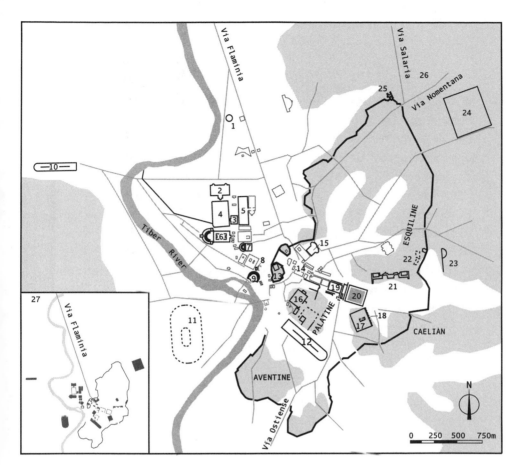

Nero's Rome

1. Mausoleum of Augustus
2. Baths of Nero
3. Baths of Agrippa
4. Lake of Agrippa
5. Saepta Iulia
6. Theater of Pompey
7. Theater of Balbus
8. Temple of Apollo Sosianus
9. Theater of Marcellus
10. Circus Vaticanus
11. Naumachia of Augustus
12. Circus Maximus
13. Temple of Jupiter Optimus Maximus
14. Roman Forum

15. Forum of Augustus
16. Domus Tiberiana
17. Temple of Divine Claudius
18. Golden House, Nymphaeum
19. Golden House, Vestibule
20. Golden House, Lake of Nero
21. Golden House, Oppian Complex
22. Gardens of Maecenas
23. Gardens of Lamia
24. Praetorian Camp
25. Gardens of Sallust
26. Villa of Phaon
27. Milvian Bridge

the deprivation of hundreds of thousands, that would indeed be monstrous. Did Nero start the Great Fire of Rome?

ANCIENT OPINION was initially divided. Tacitus tells us explicitly that some writers (now lost) attributed the Great Fire to accident, some to a plot of Nero. Yet one conviction soon came to dominate, for surviving opinion is virtually unanimous that Nero was indeed to blame—Tacitus is the only exception, and he professed to be unsure.[11] Certainly the Elder Pliny, who was in Rome at the time, and who detested Nero, was sure that he was guilty.[12] Similarly, Suetonius and Cassius Dio have no doubts, and the commonly accepted hostile version of Nero's actions can be reconstructed from them, as follows.

It was said that Nero had long desired the general destruction of both city and empire in his own lifetime: witness his claim to envy King Priam of Troy for having looked on the simultaneous destruction of his city and his reign; witness also his emendation of a Greek tragic line quoted by someone in conversation, from "when I am dead may the earth be overwhelmed by fire," to "while I am alive." He was also said to be offended by the ugliness of the ancient buildings and the narrow, winding streets, and a play written soon after his death claims that he wanted to take revenge on his people for their support in 62 of his discarded wife, Octavia.[13]

Nero therefore dispatched his agents to destroy the city, though here accounts of the actual arson differ. Dio presents his story as fact: Nero's men, pretending to be drunk or up to no good, set fire to different buildings in different parts of the city, causing general panic and chaos; later, some of those who should have been extinguishing the flames, soldiers and *vigiles* (the night watchmen), were seen actually to be kindling them. Suetonius' account is similar: several ex-consuls discovered Nero's own personal servants, his *cubicularii,* on their properties with tow and torches; and, later, since he coveted the space occupied by certain warehouses around the (future) Golden House, he had those warehouses destroyed and burned. Tacitus' story is also similar, but he presents everything as no more than rumor: rescue efforts were hampered by a number of unnamed people who either prevented the flames from being extinguished or openly hurled torches, shouting that someone had given them orders; when the fire broke out a second time, it was on a property of Tigellinus, and "it appeared" that Nero wanted the glory of founding a new city and calling it by his own name.

Not only did the emperor cause the destruction of his capital, he gloried in it, or—as a seventeenth-century accretion to the legend so memorably phrased it—Nero fiddled while Rome burned. Again, the accounts of what he actually did vary remarkably, as we have seen.

For later generations, rumors hardened into fact: "He set the city of Rome on fire in order that he might see the likeness of that spectacle which Troy once presented when it was captured and burned." Nevertheless, modern scholarship has generally absolved the emperor.[14] Three sorts of arguments have been made for Nero's innocence, relying on "general probability," on the problems presented by our sources, and on his continuing popularity.

As for the first, accidents were only too likely. The city of Rome, overcrowded, poorly constructed, and inadequately protected by fire-fighting forces, constantly suffered major fires. Moreover, the moon was almost full when the fire broke out, making it a poor night for arson. The energy and extent of Nero's measures for relieving the disaster might also argue against his responsibility for it, and the alleged motive of destroying the city so that he could rebuild it is a poor one: rational demolition and construction would have been far more practical than the uncontrolled conflagration which destroyed his own new palace, the Domus Transitoria, and in fact nothing like a complete urban renewal occurred afterward.

Second, in regard to the matter of sources, Tacitus tells us explicitly that some authors blamed chance and some blamed Nero, and he himself seems genuinely uncertain about the emperor's guilt. This hesitation on the part of Rome's greatest historian is easily the strongest argument in favor of Nero's innocence.[15] Moreover, the accounts of Suetonius and Dio, who are convinced of Nero's crime, are vague and tendentious throughout. The rumors they report as fact are inconsistent, and one of them surely reflects willful or ignorant misunderstanding of Nero's vigorous defensive actions: that is, the intentional destruction of buildings by his agents was the only way to create a firebreak. And two other contemporaries who mention Nero and the Fire and who had no reason to spare him, Martial and Josephus, do not accuse him of arson.[16] Moreover, for what it is worth, unlike his actions in other crises, such as the death of his mother, he certainly never accepted responsibility for the Fire, pinning the blame on others in spectacular fashion.

Third—and very interesting, however it is to be evaluated—it appears that the people of Rome did not blame Nero for their misery. Indeed, neither Tacitus nor Suetonius anywhere suggests that they did: both writers report that Nero was resented for taking advantage of the fire to sing and to build, both report that members of the elite accused him of setting it, but of *popular* blame they give no hint.[17] The only real indictment comes in Cassius Dio, and it is extremely interesting.

Dio asserts that the populace cursed Nero unreservedly—except that they did not mention his name, but rather called down curses on those who burned the city! Then he preserves a curious interchange between emperor and people. The people were alarmed by the memory of an oracle which had been current in Tiberius' day: "When thrice three hundred years have gone around, / civil discord will destroy the Romans." Nero, hoping to reassure them, proclaimed that no such words could be found anywhere; but they turned instead to another, supposedly Sibylline, prophecy: "Last of the race of Aeneas, a mother-slayer shall reign." As Dio solemnly comments, whether this was an actual prophecy or the people were divinely inspired, it was indeed true, for Nero was the last emperor of the Julian family, which was descended from Aeneas.[18]

This is a classic example of the Sherlockian dog not barking in the night. The people of Rome did *not* curse Nero: they blamed persons unknown. If they had believed that Nero was responsible for the fire, they would have let him know loudly and clearly in the theater and the circus, or through anonymous pasquinades. They did not. As his house burned he ran hither and thither unguarded, and he mixed freely with his homeless people in his gardens immediately afterward—neither action that of a man who feared popular outrage.[19] And thereafter there is no sign of waning popularity, indeed quite the opposite at several crowded and elaborate spectacles in the next few years. Could tens of thousands of bereaved and homeless citizens have forgiven him so easily?

Moreover, the first pseudo-oracle in Dio's narrative has nothing to do with the Great Fire. In fact it had originally surfaced in the year 19, just before the death of the prince Germanicus, and the emperor Tiberius, his uncle, had gone to considerable pains to show that the verses were spurious. The oracle clearly refers to civil war, and is part of a recurrent pattern

at Rome of prophesying doom after a 900-year cycle.[20] It is at worst a reaction to the fire and a rather clumsy one at that, not an assignment of
guilt. The other oracle about the mother-slayer being the last of the line
of Aeneas likewise prophesies doom, in a general sort of way, but it too
has no connection with arson. A similar pasquinade is to be found in
Suetonius: "Who denies that Nero comes from the great line of Aeneas? /
The one removed his mother, the other carried off his father."[21] But
Suetonius includes it in a collection of such gibes, making no connection
with the fire, and the obvious date for the attack would be 59, after the
death of Agrippina, and not 64.[22] If the lines were revived after the fire,
they were singularly inappropriate. Indeed, Suetonius devotes a section of
his biography to the remarkable patience with which Nero bore the curses
and abuses which people directed against him, being especially lenient toward those who attacked him *dictis et carminibus,* with gibes and lam-
poons—most of them refer to his matricide, none accuses him of arson.
The inventive people of Rome could do better than that. They and Nero
had something very different on their minds.

In short, general probability, the uncertainty of Tacitus along with the
inconsistencies of Suetonius and Dio, and Nero's continuing popularity
all speak strongly for his innocence—which he himself proclaimed by
identifying the true culprits. But this case for the defense, however rational, falls short of conviction. Two arguments could be used to undercut
much of it: that Nero's agents did indeed start the fire, but it ran out of
their control, and he was as horrified as anyone by the inadvertent destruction; or, that the fire did indeed begin by chance but it was fanned by
Nero's men for his own purposes, especially the second time, when it
flared up again in the property of his own praetorian prefect and showed a
propensity to attack public places. But there is no need to undermine the
case for the defense, since the case for the prosecution is damning: it looks
as if Nero was indeed responsible for the fire from the beginning.

THERE ARE two items of evidence, the first being the words of an eyewitness. In the following spring of 65, the dangerous conspiracy was betrayed which intended to murder Nero in the Circus Maximus on 19 April
and replace him with the supine nobleman Calpurnius Piso. It was dangerous precisely because it was led by several senior officers of the emperor's own praetorian guard: at least three centurions, no fewer than

three out of the twelve tribunes, and one of the two prefects were implicated, and in the aftermath four more of the tribunes were dismissed for their dubious loyalty. A ringleader of this astonishing plot at the heart of the palace was the tribune Subrius Flavus, one of the few individuals in his *Annals* whom Tacitus admires without reservation, portraying him as a strong-minded idealist who bravely died a martyr's death.[23] Betrayed by fellow-conspirators, he first denied the charge, but then "he embraced the glory of confession":

> Questioned by Nero as to the motives which had led him on to forget his oath of allegiance, "I hated you," he replied; "yet not a soldier was more loyal to you while you deserved to be loved. I began to hate you when you became the murderer of your mother and your wife, a charioteer, an actor, and an incendiary." I have given the man's very words *(ipsa rettuli verba)*.[24]

Thus Nero was accused of the arson to his face by a senior officer in his own guard some nine months after the fire. Subrius Flavus was not a man to act on popular rumor. He had spent much of his life at or near the emperor's side, and he was actually with Nero when Rome was burning.[25] The accusation of Subrius Flavus might be explained away by those who would prefer to believe in Nero's innocence, as just the sort of thing that a conspirator would say, but it still looks very much like a lone fact in a debate based on opinions about probabilities. Guilty or not, it assures us that the accusation against Nero was contemporary and not posthumous.

A stronger indication of his guilt lies in Nero's remarkable actions before the Great Fire. In the year 64, we are told by Tacitus, the emperor could no longer restrain his desire to race chariots and to sing and act in public. The urge to race he indulged in Rome; but he felt that he should make his artistic debut in a Greek city, where they appreciated such things—first at Naples, then in the cities of Achaia.[26] Accordingly, he set off for Greece. A packed performance in a theater in Naples narrowly missed disaster, when the building collapsed after the audience had departed. Nero celebrated with a song of thanks to the gods and proceeded with his entourage eastward toward the Adriatic, stopping in Beneventum to enjoy a gladiatorial show put on by his disreputable crony Vatinius. Then, for reasons unknown and not clear even at the time *(causae in incerto fuere)*, he abruptly abandoned the trip to Greece and turned back to Rome.

After this astonishing upset of imperial plans, something even more unusual happened: the emperor changed his mind again. He now announced his intention to visit the eastern provinces, particularly Egypt. In an edict he reassured the public that he would not be gone long and that the state would continue to prosper. He paid farewell visits to the temples of the gods, doubtless sacrificing for a safe return. After worshipping on the Capitol, he entered the Temple of Vesta at the eastern end of the Forum. There, in the words of Tacitus, he was suddenly seized with a trembling through all his limbs. He then again abruptly abandoned the projected journey altogether, repeatedly asserting that his own plans were of far less importance than his love for his country. Suetonius elaborates: he gave up the trip to Alexandria on the very day of departure, deeply upset by religious sentiment and by a sense of danger. Making the rounds of the temples, he had sat down in the shrine of Vesta, only to be subjected to two unsettling omens: when he stood up, the hem of his robe caught on something; and then such a darkness arose that he could not see through it. That was enough to keep him in Rome.

Tacitus continues the story, after talking of Nero's profession of love for his country, in what again reads like a paraphrase of the official edict explaining the emperor's latest change of plan:

> He had seen the sad countenances of the citizens, he had heard their secret complaints at the prospect of his entering on so long a journey, when they could not bear so much as his brief excursions, accustomed as they were to cheer themselves under mischances by the sight of the emperor. Hence, as in private relationships (*privatis necessitudinibus*) the closest ties were the strongest, so the people of Rome had the most powerful claims and must be obeyed in their wish to retain him.

To confirm the belief that nowhere else in the world gave him such pleasure, he arranged banquets in public places and treated the whole city as if it were his house. Thereupon followed the notorious banquet of Tigellinus, the infamous marriage with Pythagoras, and the fiery destruction of Rome, all apparently in quick succession. And out of the ashes rose the outrageous Golden House.[27]

Thus the events leading up to scandal and disaster are truly extraordinary. Not once but twice within a few months, the emperor abandoned an official journey to the East, the first time without explanation while actually en route, the second on the very day of his departure. On the second occasion Vesta herself, the goddess of the communal hearth of the city, plucked him back, a man who was otherwise said to have contempt for all cults. In the edict explaining his conduct, he referred ominously to the people taking comfort in their misfortunes from the sight of their emperor. Rome needed him.

The ancient, round Temple of Vesta stood at the eastern end of the Roman Forum, next to the Sacred Way at the foot of the Palatine. Together with the grove of the goddess and the large adjacent house of the Vestal Virgins, it formed a complex called the Atrium Vestae, the House of Vesta, which Augustus had expanded to absorb the official residences of two of the city's important priests, the *pontifex maximus* and the *rex sacrorum*. The temple itself, in the shape of an old Italic hut, was the hearth of Rome, holding the eternal fire of the city tended by the Virgins. It was also the very heart of Rome, for within it were preserved the *sacra* of the city, its sacred objects, including the Palladium, an image of Athena brought by Aeneas from Troy; the Penates, the household gods of Rome; and the *fascinus,* a phallus meant to ward off evil from the city.[28] According to Tacitus, the Regia (the house of the *pontifex maximus*) and the Temple of Vesta were both burned in the fire, along with the Penates of the Roman People. Afterwards, Nero showed a special affinity for his kinswoman Vesta. That he quickly rebuilt or repaired her temple is certain, although there is no archaeological trace: he displayed it on his gold and silver coinage, the only damaged building so depicted, presumably to reassure the public that the temple had been restored and the city's hearth was secure. He also extensively rebuilt the house of the Vestal Virgins on a much grander scale, as part of his general reconstruction of the adjacent Sacred Way, leading up to his new Golden House.[29]

The Fire of 64 was the fourth time in recorded history in which the Temple of Vesta, erected by the legendary King Numa more than seven centuries earlier, had burned. In 391 BC, a plebeian named Marcus Caedicius had received a warning that the Gauls were coming from a more than human voice "in the Nova Via, where the little shrine now stands above the Temple of Vesta" or, in another version, "from the grove of Vesta." The words of the unknown god, later identified as Aius Locutius, came "in the silence of the night." Vesta's temple was, it is assumed, burned in the Gallic sack, although the *sacra* were saved. In one of the best-loved legends of Rome, the pious plebeian Lucius Albinius, fleeing with his family across the Tiber, fell in with the Vestal Virgins toil-

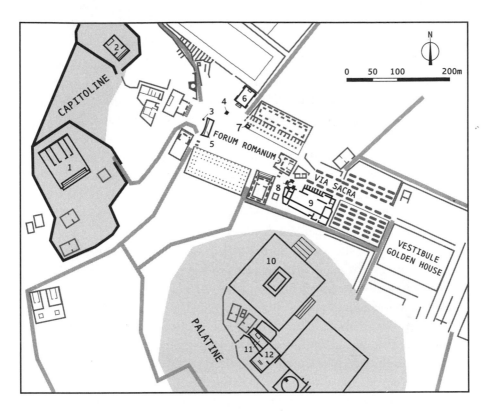

Nero's Rome: Central Area

1. Temple of Jupiter Optimus Maximus	7. Temple of Janus
2. Temple of Juno Moneta	8. Temple of Vesta
3. Mundus (?)	9. Atrium Vestae
4. Volcanal (approx.)	10. Domus Tiberiana
5. Rostra	11. House of Augustus
6. Curia Julia (Senate House)	12. Temple of Apollo Palatinus

ing along with their sacred objects, ejected his wife and children from the cart, and bore the priestesses and the *sacra* of Rome safely to neighboring Caere.

The next time the temple burned was in the year 241 BC, when, famously, the *pontifex maximus* Lucius Caecilius Metellus, who was in charge of the Vestal Virgins, braved the flames to save the *sacra*. Tradition emphasized two aspects of his story. One is that the day before the temple caught fire, Metellus was planning to leave town for his suburban estate at Tusculum. However, two crows flew in his face as if to impede his journey and, accepting the omen, he returned home—home at that time being perhaps the residence of the *pontifex maximus* in the *domus publica,* next to the precinct of Vesta. The other salient feature of the incident is that a story accepted as fact in Nero's day (but actually invented in the age of Augustus) had it that Metellus was struck blind, temporarily or permanently, for seeing and touching objects which no man should see or touch.

After some other brushes with disaster, the temple next burned (it appears) in 14 BC, when flames spread there from the nearby Basilica Paulli in the Forum. A brief notice in Dio tells us that the sacred objects were carried to the house of the priest of Jupiter on the Palatine by the Vestal Virgins—all but the Chief Vestal, who was blinded.[30]

The next time the temple burned was in the Great Fire of 64. Just before the fire, Nero abandoned his plans to leave Rome when the goddess Vesta physically restrained him, and he was plunged, temporarily, into blindness in her temple.

Again, Nero showed himself a close reader of the past, specifically of a past where warning and blindness were intimately connected with fire and a threat to the city. Like Caecilius Metellus, on the very day of his departure, Nero, who was also *pontifex maximus,* was supernaturally restrained from leaving Rome. Danger threatened his city, and what that danger would be was signaled by Nero's prophetic loss of sight in the presence of Vesta, just as Caedicius was warned at night by an invisible god, just as Metellus had been blinded, just as the Virgo Vestalis Maxima had been blinded: he was needed to save the *sacra* from fire.

Two particular themes should be stressed. One is the association of the precinct of Vesta with the preservation of Rome. Her eternal flame, *aeterni ignes,* symbolized the eternity of the city, and the sacred objects preserved in her temple guaranteed Rome's safety. Above all, the Palladium, the ancient image brought from Troy, was, in Cicero's words, "the pledge for our safety and our empire."[31] When Ilus had been marking out the boundaries of the future city of Ilium, or Troy, he had prayed for a sign, and discovered a wooden image half-buried in the ground. This turned out to be a statue of herself made by Athena in memory of her friend Pallas, whose name and character she took over, as Pallas Athena; this image the goddess had thrown to earth. When Ilus consulted Apollo as to the meaning of the omen, the god replied, "Preserve the heavenly goddess and you will preserve the city: she will transfer with herself the heart of empire, *imperium loci.*" This was the image preserved from the fiery destruction of Troy by Aeneas (or stolen by Diomedes and Odysseus), and eventually brought by the descendants of Aeneas to Rome: "as long as it is safe," said Cicero, "we shall be safe."[32]

Tied to this sense of preservation is a sense of danger, so powerful is the goddess concerned. The Palladium of Rome, which it was apparently *not* forbidden to behold, was assimilated into a Greek tradition of guardian statues: "each of these statues was small and portable by a single person, was imprisoned or bound, and caused blindness, madness, or sterility when gazed upon." The tradition connecting blindness with the saving of the Palladium from burning is a confused one, combining loss of sight as a warning of imminent peril with loss of sight as a punishment for seeing what must be saved. That the two were confused is evident from the double tradition that was uncertain whether Metellus' loss of sight was permanent or temporary, and from Nero's clear association of himself with Caecilius Metellus (supernatural retention of the *pontifex maximus* in Rome to save the *sacra* in the Temple of Vesta, and temporary blinding that was prophetic rather than after the fact).[33]

The abrupt and inexplicable abandonment of foreign travel (after considerable preparation), not once but twice; the suggestion in Nero's edict that he was needed to cheer his fellow-citizens in adversity; the significant omens of the Temple of Vesta (and perhaps of the collapsing theater in Naples); the fundamental connection between danger to the hearth of Rome and the conceptualization of Rome as a house and her citizens as his close relatives—all these point to one end: that Nero knew what was coming. A senior officer in his guard, a man who had been with him during the fire, accused him nine months afterwards, to his face, of being the arsonist. It looks as if Nero was responsible for the Great Fire after all, as his ancient critics maintained, and his motive can only have been the one alleged, that he wanted to rebuild the city.

BEFORE THE FIRE, Nero had indulged in highly populist rhetoric—the people of Rome were his nearest and dearest, the whole city was their house—and he had acted out the rhetoric with elaborate, Saturnalian banquets in public places. After the fire, the rhetoric and its enactment continued.

When the fire was over, the emperor solemnly undertook the great religious ceremonies necessary to appease the gods and to expiate the sin. The Sibylline Books were consulted, the remnants of the ancient collection of prophecies given by the Sibyl of Cumae to the king Tarquinius Priscus and deposited by Augustus in the Temple of Apollo on the Palatine. At the behest of these books, prayers were offered up to certain gods: as Tacitus tells us, supplication was made to Vulcan and to Ceres and Proserpina, and Juno was propitiated by the matrons of Rome. Why this god and these goddesses in particular? The standard explanation for the first three is that Vulcan was the god of fire, and that the temple of Ceres and Proserpina stood near the spot where the fire had broken out; no reason has been given for the prominent inclusion of Juno.[34] Yet more should be said.

As for the god of fire, we know that a vow was now undertaken to Vulcan, though not fulfilled until years after Nero's death: altars were to be set up in different parts of city, the areas of which were to be kept clear of buildings and plantings, and each year a magistrate was to offer prayer and sacrifice to the god on the day of his feast, the Volcanalia (23 August), "in order to ward off fires."[35] But in 64 the first sacrifice to him must have been made at his altar in the heart of Rome, the Volcanal in the Forum, which, thanks to the detective work of Filippo Coarelli, we can now place exactly: it was the monument known as the Niger Lapis, the black stone marking the place of Romulus' death or disappearance, part of a very sacred area within the Comitium, today directly in front of the Curia Julia, the still-standing senate house descended from the one built by Julius Caesar.[36]

The significance of this shrine of Vulcan emerges in juxtaposition with Ceres and Proserpina. These were in fact *not* the goddesses of the Temple of Ceres, Liber, and Libera (Proserpina), which stood on the lower slope of the Aventine near the Circus Maximus: that shrine lay near the northwest end of the Circus, whereas the fire had erupted at the southeast end, adjacent to the Palatine and the Caelian hills, and the temples of many other equally offended gods lay in between.[37] What the Sibyl was prescribing was supplication at the *mundus,* a vaulted ritual pit, divided into two parts: on three days in the year, days on which no public and little private business should be conducted, a cover was removed *(mundus patet)* to expose the Gates of Hell, through which the spirits of the dead might emerge to wander through the city. This pit was known as the *mundus Cereris,* the pit of Ceres, and it was likewise sacred to her daughter

Proserpina and to Dis Pater (Pluto), Proserpina's husband and king of the Underworld; in the words of the learned antiquarian Varro, "When the *mundus* opens, it is as if the doors of the sad and infernal gods are opened."[38] Where precisely the *mundus* lay is a matter of debate. Again, Coarelli has produced a brilliant answer, working from literary and archaeological fragments: the *mundus* was the round trench said to have been dug by Romulus in the Comitium, into which he threw different first-fruits (Ceres was goddess of the harvest), at the founding of the city of Rome; it is to be identified with the *umbilicus Romae,* the center of Rome; and the adjacent (as we know from ancient texts) Altar of Saturn is to be identified with the structure known today (confusingly) as the Volcanal.[39] Not all scholars have accepted this solution, but this much should be clear: that the *mundus* of Ceres was indeed also the *mundus* of Romulus the Founder, and that it lay in the Comitium, within (at most) thirty meters of the Volcanal.[40]

Volcanus and Ceres were dangerous gods who must be propitiated—Vulcan as the god of fire, Ceres as the goddess of punishment and the guardian of passage between this world and the next. But it is the Comitium that particularly binds them together. Vulcan's festival, the Volcanalia, was celebrated there at the Volcanal each year on 23 August, and each year the *mundus* of Ceres was opened for the first time *on the very next day,* 24 August. The Comitium, at the western end of the Forum, below the Capitol and next to the senate house, was an area particularly identified with the people of Rome, the original place of public assembly, and Vulcan and Ceres were both preeminently *popular* gods. Ceres the provider had been closely associated with the plebs from the foundation of her temple on the Aventine in the early fifth century; while of Vulcan we are told that the people themselves, not the priest, made the offerings to the god, and that before the rostra was built magistrates would address the people from the Volcanal itself, that is, in effect, it was at the Volcanal that popular assemblies were first convened.[41] The propitiation of the gods after the Great Fire was thus a pointedly populist act. At the same time it was conspicuously an act recalling the foundation of the city by Romulus: the *mundus* was the foundation trench dug by the first king, while the Volcanal was in one version founded by him (in another by his colleague Titus Tatius); it marked the site of his first military victory; and it was the site of his death or disappearance.[42] Thus the ceremonies of propitiation were also designed to remind the onlookers of the city's first founding. Nero's theme was the rebirth of their city by and with the people of Rome, celebrated a mere thirty days after the fire had burned itself out.

WHAT THEN of Juno, who was apparently the most offended of the deities? The matrons of Rome sought to propitiate her, first at her temple on the Capitoline, then at the seashore, whence they brought water to purify the temple and the statue of the goddess. Married women also held religious banquets to which the goddess was invited, as well as nightlong vigils. Why Juno, when there is no question that the Capitol had escaped the fire?

This was not, however, the Juno of the Capitoline triad who shared the temple of Jupiter Optimus Maximus with Jupiter and Minerva. It was Juno Moneta, whose temple also stood on the Capitol, but on the spur known as the Arx, and whose epithet was taken (erroneously) to derive from the word *monere,* "to warn," hence she was "Juno the Warner." Juno Moneta enjoyed a jumble of (historically unlikely) associations with the Gallic sack of 390 BC. Her temple had been vowed in 345 by the dictator M. Furius Camillus, the son and namesake of the dictator who had defeated the Gauls. It was erected in 344 on the site of the house of M. Manlius Capitolinus, the defender of the Capitol in 390 who had been warned by Juno's geese of the Gauls' sneak attack; Manlius had been convicted of aiming at tyranny, he was executed (in one account his enemy is the great Camillus), and his house was razed in 384. Or, in another version, there was a temple of Juno already on the spot in 390, Manlius' house stood nearby, and her geese aroused their neighbor, hence already she was Juno the Warner.[43] In a city where religion had such a deep-running sense of place, Juno Moneta recalled resistance to the Gauls. The Gallic sack, and the rebirth of the city after the defeat of the Gauls, became a major theme after the Great Fire of 64.

As Tacitus tells it, "There were some who observed that the beginning of this fire had occurred on the nineteenth of July [literally: the fourteenth day before the Kalends of Sextilis], and on that day the Senones had burned the captured city. Others even took such pains as to calculate that an equal number of years, months, and days had elapsed between the two fires."[44] As so often, to explain and justify the present, they and Nero reached back to stories from the past.

The Sack of Rome by the Gauls was the matter of legend, familiar to everyone.[45] Traditionally in the year 390 (actually in 387/386), as part of a general wave of Gallic migration into Italy, the tribe of the Senones descended on Rome. Not only did the leaders of Rome ignore the divine warning given to Marcus Caedicius, they contrived to remove the one man who might have saved the city, Marcus Furius Camillus, who withdrew into exile when wrongly accused of misusing plunder from his recent capture of the Etruscan city of Veii. The Gauls moved in and were met by a Roman army on the left bank of the Tiber at its confluence with the River Allia, a few miles north of Rome, on 18 July (*xv a.d. kalendas Sextiles*). This date, the day their troops were crushed by the Gauls, was forever after marked as the blackest day in the Roman year. A large part of the army fled to nearby Veii, which had been captured by Camillus only six years earlier. Rome itself lay undefended and the Gallic army entered unopposed—accounts vary as to when, but in Livy's version it was on 19 July, the day after the disastrous defeat (that is, the day the Great Fire broke out in 64).

The Gallic occupation gave rise to some of the best-loved legends of Roman history: the story of the pious plebeian Lucius Albinius, saving the Vestal Virgins and their *sacra;* the story of the senators, sitting stern and silent in official robes, each in the vestibule of his house, overawing the Gauls as if they were statues of the gods, until one of the invaders touched the beard of Marcus Papirius, Papirius struck him on the head with his ivory staff, and a general massacre ensued; the story of the Gauls' secret attempt on the party of Romans besieged in the Capitol, foiled by the cackling of Juno's sacred geese; the story of the Romans' effort to bribe the Gauls to withdraw, the measuring out of 1,000 pounds of gold, and the Gallic chieftain throwing his sword into the scales with the words ever after hateful to Roman ears: *Vae victis,* woe to the conquered! At that point in the legend the hero Camillus speeds to the rescue—Camillus the conqueror of Veii, the exile now appointed dictator by the senate. He breaks off negotiations and promptly annihilates the Gauls in battle. All these stories were familiar to every Roman.

After murdering Papirius and the other leading men of Rome, the Gauls had ransacked their houses and set them alight. This plundering and burning went on for several days, until in time the dry earth, the heat, and the clouds of ashes and dust proved harmful to the health of the invaders themselves—the city was, in short, half-ruined, *semiruta.* When the Romans reentered, a great debate took place. Much of the populace, stirred up by the tribunes, was strongly inclined to abandon the ruins and migrate to the newly won city of Veii, some ten miles to the north of Rome.[46] The senators, headed by the dictator Camillus, wanted to stay and rebuild.

At the heart of Camillus' speech to the people in Livy lay a passionate appeal to their ancestral religion and its overwhelming sense of place: "We have a city founded with all due rites of auspice and augury; not a stone of her streets but is permeated by our sense of the divine; for our annual sacrifices not the days only are fixed but the places too, where they may be performed: men of Rome, would you desert your gods—the tutelary spirits which guard your families, and those the nations prays to as its saviours?"[47] Livy remarks that Camillus moved his audience, especially when he touched on religious matters, and the matter was then clinched by a good omen: as a detachment of the garrison moved through the Forum nearby, the centurion called out, "Standard-bearer, set up the standard here; it looks like a good place to stay." But even before piety had convinced the people to remain, Camillus, "a most diligent observer of religious propriety," obtained a comprehensive decree of religious restoration from the senate. The first provision in that decree was that all the temples which had been occupied by the Gauls should be restored and their boundaries redefined, and that they should be purified in accordance with directions which were to be sought from the Sibylline Books.[48] After the gods had been honored and placated (and after the people had been persuaded to stay because of them), physical rebuilding could begin.

According to Livy, when Camillus entered Rome after defeating the Gauls, his troops hailed him as "Romulus, the father of his country *(parens patriae),* and the second founder of the city." Yet most of his deeds are fictitious, or so buried in fiction as to be all but irrecoverable. Indeed, most of the story of the Gallic invasion is patriotic invention, recasting Roman humiliation as triumph. In truth the city was only lightly damaged at worst—that is, some houses were razed, but there is no archaeological trace of the destruction; Rome did not lie in ruins. Likewise, the tradition that a hastily built, ramshackle new city replaced a planned, orderly old city on the Greek model is simply false. It is essentially a fiction meant to explain the chaotic layout of the city in the late Republic. Moreover, the Gauls may well have captured the Capitol also. They were almost certainly bought off, the ransom being recovered in a later battle.

And many of the antiquarian details such as the origins of the Capitoline
Games or the shrine of Aius Locutius, the Speaking Voice which had
warned Caedicius, are accretions to the tale.[49] But historical truth is irrelevant here; the legend that goes back at least to the second century BC is
what people believed. In noting Camillus' death some twenty-five years
after the Gallic invasion, Livy honored him with a laudatory obituary as a
man unique in fortune good and bad, the leading citizen *(princeps)* in
peace and war, worthy to be considered the second founder of the city of
Rome, after Romulus, *secundum a Romulo conditorem urbis Romanae.*[50]

The connection between the Great Fire of 19 July, AD 64, and the legendary fire of 19 July, 390 BC, was not merely a whim of antiquarian nu-
merologists. Tacitus' account of the fire is shot through with echoes of the
Gallic sack as narrated by Livy, from the *clades,* the disaster, to the building of *nova urbs,* the new city. Dio, who says nothing about the coinci-
dence of date, asserts that at the height of the fire people looked beyond
their individual disasters to mourn the common loss, recollecting how
once before most of the city had been destroyed by the Gauls. There is
even an unmistakable reference to the fire in Petronius' contemporary
novel, the *Satyricon.* And best of all, a pasquinade on the Golden House
makes sense only if the events of 390 were on people's minds: "Rome is
becoming a house: migrate to Veii, Romans, unless that house takes over
Veii as well."[51]

The primary use of the sack of 390 for Nero's purposes was that it
marked the birth of the old city of Rome in the popular mind. It did not
matter (and nobody knew) that the city had not really been destroyed by
the Gauls, nor that the irrational warren of narrow streets and shoddy
buildings had existed long before the sack. The story that explained the irregular layout of the city, apart from the public areas at least, was not interested in the huge immigration into the city in the last two centuries of
the Republic nor in the jerry-built apartment buildings erected to house
the growing populace. The legendary root of the problem was the hasty
popular rebuilding after the supposed Gallic sack. Livy pictures the bustle
in 390/389 vividly:

> The proposal for the migration was rejected, and the rebuilding
> of the city began. The work of reconstruction was ill planned. Tiles
> were supplied at the state's expense; permission to cut timber and
> quarry stone was granted without any restrictions except a guarantee

that the particular structure should be completed within a year. All work was hurried and nobody bothered to see that the streets were straight; individual property rights were ignored, and buildings went up wherever there was room for them. This explains why the ancient sewers, which originally followed the line of the streets, now run in many places under private houses, and why the general layout of Rome is more like a squatter's settlement than a properly planned city.[52]

Before Livy, Diodorus had told the same story—that people could build wherever they wished and the state supplied them with roof-tiles, hence the narrow and crooked lanes of later centuries. Plutarch gives just the same picture, writing of promiscuous building wherever people liked, which led to narrow, tortuous lanes and houses packed in together, and he too emphasizes that the new city, walls and all, stood within a year. Thus was the city born a second time (in Livy's view), even more fertile, from its old roots. The citizen body worked ceaselessly to rebuild it, too busy even to attend meetings called by their tribunes. The population boomed, and buildings sprang up everywhere. The state helped bear the costs, with the aediles urging people on as if these were public works, while private citizens expedited the work in their desire to make use of it. (Plutarch, too, shows the people encouraging each other.) Within a year, Livy concludes, the new city, *nova urbs*, was standing.[53]

This was the city ravaged by the Great Fire of 64: "The blaze in its fury ran first through the level portions of the city, then rising to the hills, while it again devastated every place below them, it outstripped all preventive measures; so rapid was the mischief and so completely at its mercy the city, with those narrow winding passages and irregular streets which characterized old Rome, *vetus Roma*."[54] The fire had destroyed Nero's new Domus Transitoria and devastated the valley between the Palatine and the roots of the Esquiline. He immediately began to erect his new palace, the Golden House, along with its park in the valley and on the slopes surrounding it—a project which involved not only large-scale construction but immense engineering efforts, a ruinously expensive fantasy, but one which must have provided employment for thousands of desperate workers. Elsewhere in the city, he rebuilt both quickly and rationally, as Tacitus tells it:

so much as was left unoccupied by his mansion, was not built up, *as it had been after the burning by the Gauls,* indiscriminately and at random, but with rows of measured streets, with broad thoroughfares, with a restriction on the height of houses, with open spaces, and the further addition of colonnades, as a protection to the frontage of the blocks of tenements.[55]

Nero promised both to pay for these colonnades from his own purse, and to hand over the cleared spaces to the owners of the adjacent buildings.[56] He also offered rewards for rebuilding to those who completed the task quickly, and arranged that the rubble should be transported down the Tiber in empty grain ships and deposited in the marshes around Ostia. He prescribed fire-resistant stone to be used in the new buildings; he appointed officers to restrict private (and dangerous) illegal siphoning of water from public aqueducts; he required all householders to maintain firefighting equipment in their courtyards; he forbade the construction of common walls. In short, he acted as the best of emperors might act, in giving careful thought and following sound advice, for the good of his people.

Whatever the reality, legend had it that, after the alleged fire of 390 BC, the alleged rebuilding of the city had been very much a popular movement, touched off by a *princeps,* Camillus, who was the second founder of Rome. Now it was going to be done properly, by the people but with the people's emperor in charge. As the authorities had done in 390, so Nero in 64 encouraged speedy action. Where chaos had ruled before, now wise and modest prescriptions guided private builders, but there were also significant material rewards for them: the free colonnades, and also an actual increase in property, in the form of the cleared areas around their buildings. There may have been other incentives of which we know nothing; it appears likely, for instance, that any informally manumitted freedman (a "Junian Latin") could win full citizenship if he were worth at least 200,000 sesterces, and if he spent at least half of his fortune in constructing a house in the city.[57]

Thus far, we can see an artistically satisfying, if lethal, consistency to Nero's plans and actions—the work of a man who, like the Periander of legend, considered that his ends justified his means and that he personally was above common morality. Rome would suffer as she had in the past and would spring reborn from the ashes in a form that drew the people and their *princeps,* the new Romulus, the new Camillus, even closer together. But there is one massive obstacle to this vision, the Golden House: Rome was indeed rebuilt, but only "so much as was left unoccupied by his mansion." To ancients and moderns alike, the Golden House has stood as the exemplar for the luxurious private retreat of a stupendously wealthy megalomaniac, but unlike Neuschwanstein or San Simeon it rose not on a distant hill, but on the side of a valley in the very heart of Rome. While his people camped out among the tombs, Nero "took advantage of the ruin of his country" (as Tacitus put it) to build his fabulous house. How can this outrageous fantasy be reconciled with his populist rhetoric?

O_F NERO'S many follies, none was more magnificent than his Xanadu, the legendary Domus Aurea, the Golden House. Suetonius, by far our most important source, captures its breathtaking "size and splendor" with fascinated disapproval:

> Its vestibule was high enough to contain a colossal statue of the Emperor a hundred and twenty feet high. So large was the house that it had a triple colonnade a mile long. There was a lake in it too, a sea surrounded with buildings to represent cities, besides tracts of country, varied with tilled fields, vineyards, pastures and woods, with great numbers of wild and domestic animals. In the rest of the house all parts were overlaid with gold and adorned with jewels and mother-of-pearl. There were dining-rooms with fretted ceilings of ivory, whose panels could turn and shower down flowers and were fitted with pipes for sprinkling the guests with perfumes. The main banquet hall was circular and constantly revolved day and night, like the heavens. He had baths supplied with sea water and sulphur water. When the edifice was finished in this style and he dedicated it, he deigned to say nothing more in the way of approval than that he was at last beginning to be housed like a human being.

Tacitus is much briefer, to the same effect:

> Nero . . . erected a mansion in which jewels and gold, long familiar objects, quite vulgarized by our extravagance, were not so marvellous

as the fields and lakes and artificial wildernesses with woods on one side, open spaces and extensive views on another.

One other important literary source for the Golden House survives, an epigram of Martial published in the year 80 to celebrate spectacles sponsored by the emperor Titus in the newly built Colosseum. Since the new amphitheater stood squarely in the grounds of the Golden House, the poet took the occasion to contrast the state of the area in 64 with its current condition:

Where the starry colossus sees the constellations at close range and lofty scaffolding rises in the middle of the road, once gleamed the odious halls of a cruel monarch [i.e., the vestibule], and in all Rome there stood a single house. Where rises before our eyes the august pile of the Amphitheater [the Colosseum], was once Nero's lake. Where we admire the warm baths [of Titus], a speedy gift, a haughty tract of land had robbed the poor of their dwellings. Where the Claudian colonnade [the portico of the Temple of the Divine Claudius] unfolds its widespread shade, was the outermost part of the palace's end. Rome has been restored to herself, under your rule, Caesar, the pleasances that belonged to a master now belong to the people.[58]

Part of the Golden House survives today, vast underground ruins on the Mons Oppius, a spur of the Esquiline Hill. Unfinished at Nero's death, later damaged by fire, it was filled in and built over by the emperor Trajan almost fifty years later to serve as the substructure of his great bath complex. Rediscovered in the Renaissance, its rooms, now "grottoes," served to stimulate generations of artists with their "grotesque" paintings. The shadowy subterranean ruins, and the dazzling literary accounts of what they once were, have fascinated kings, artists, and academics ever since. But the question is rarely asked directly: *why* did Nero build the Golden House? Or, in more romantic terms, what did he mean by saying "housed like a human being"? The answer to that lies in the answer to another question: *where* did he build the Golden House?

Suetonius tells us: "He made a palace extending all the way from the Palatine to the Esquiline, which at first he called the House of Passage, *Domus Transitoria,* but when it was burned shortly after its completion and rebuilt, the Golden House, *Domus Aurea.*"[59] Tacitus adds that Nero returned from Antium to Rome when the flames approached the *domus* by which he had connected, *continuaverat,* the Palatine and the *horti Maecenatis,* the Gardens of Maecenas (which lay on the Esquiline).[60] All this seems perfectly clear. By Nero's day, the formerly residential area of the Palatine Hill was dominated by two large imperial palace complexes: the Palatina Domus, the House of Augustus, in the southwest, overlooking the Circus Maximus; and to the north of it, the Domus Tiberiana, the House of Tiberius, which overlooked the Via Sacra and the eastern end of the Forum. The Esquiline Hill to the east, on the other hand, was particularly associated with "gardens," *horti,* that is, grand country villas of the inner suburb, most notably the large tracts of the Gardens of Maecenas and the Lamian Gardens, both now owned by the emperor. These were the areas that Nero now joined together, the public Palatine and the private Esquiline, through the valley where the Colosseum would later be built.

Despite these fairly precise indications, Nero's ancient critics would leave us in no doubt: the House was everywhere, it was taking over the city. As Tacitus sneered in passing, after the fire Nero rebuilt "so much [of the city] as was left unoccupied by his mansion." After the emperor's death, Martial (who had been in Rome when it was being built) complained that a single house stood in the whole city. The strongly disapproving Elder Pliny (who was also there) asserted explicitly, not once but twice, that the Golden House surrounded Rome. Why stop there? In Nero's own day the anonymous lampoon mentioned earlier continued: "Rome is becoming a house: migrate to Veii, Romans, / unless that house takes over Veii as well."[61] The spell of the Golden House seems to invite hyperbole. Did it really take over the whole city, occupy most of it, surround it? For that matter, did the *immensa domus* of Vedius Pollio, "the work of a city," really cover an area larger than many small towns, as Ovid maintained? Was Herodian strictly accurate in claiming that the later palace of the Severi was larger than a whole city?[62]

Modern scholars have been entranced by the supposed vastness of the fabulous Golden House. Elements of its predecessor, the Domus Transitoria, have long been identified in a marvelously elegant fountain-court on the Palatine, the so-called Bagni di Livia, certainly Neronian in date and covered over by the later Domus Flavia of the Flavian emperors; that is, it lay to the east of the House of Augustus. And since the splendid

Domus Tiberiana was revealed in the 1980s to be in essence a Neronian palace, it too has been claimed as part of the Golden House—indeed it has been grandly described as the Palatine nucleus of the Domus Aurea complex, a *domus-villa* balancing the celebrated *villa-domus* nucleus on the Oppian.[63] That is, the Golden House took over the Palatine. At the other extreme, it has been suggested that the Golden House engulfed the Gardens of Maecenas on the Esquiline, to the east.[64] It also included, so we have been told, a large tract on the Esquiline to the north and east of the Oppian ruins, to take in the cisterns of the Baths of Trajan at Sette Sale; it included the huge Temple of the Divine Claudius and a large expanse to the south of it on the Caelian Hill; the Servian Wall must have functioned as a boundary.[65] Unfortunately, there is no evidence for any of this.

The underlying scholarly assumption has been that *any* Neronian remains on or even near the Palatine, the Esquiline, or in the valley in between, must be part of the Golden House. As it happens, some of the remains confidently assigned to it have turned out not to be Neronian at all: the edifice beneath the Temple of Venus and Rome is now known to antedate Nero, while the cisterns of Trajan's Baths are now known to be Trajanic.[66] But what of the rich Neronian remains on the Palatine Hill? It is universally assumed by modern scholarship that the Golden House included the imperial residences on the Palatine. Yet there is no support at all for this assumption in the ancient sources, and good reason to doubt it.

By combining Suetonius' account with Martial's poem and with the archaeological evidence (some unearthed very recently), we can be sure that the grounds of the Golden House included the following: a huge vestibule intended for the Colossus on the Velia, its platform closely corresponding to the surviving platform of the Hadrianic Temple of Venus and Rome; a large, rectangular lake, surrounded by elaborate terraces and colonnades, in the floor of the valley of the later Colosseum; a grand nymphaeum, that is, a huge, spectacular, artificially "natural" fountain on the northeast slope of the Caelian Hill; the mansion sprawled along the Oppian; and an indeterminate open area dotted (apparently) with other, smaller buildings such as a Temple of Fortune, not to mention the "cities" and rustic scenes described by Suetonius. That is, what our sources describe is the entrance on the Velia, the mansion on the Oppian, and the open country below it. Both Suetonius and Tacitus speak clearly of only *one* house; indeed

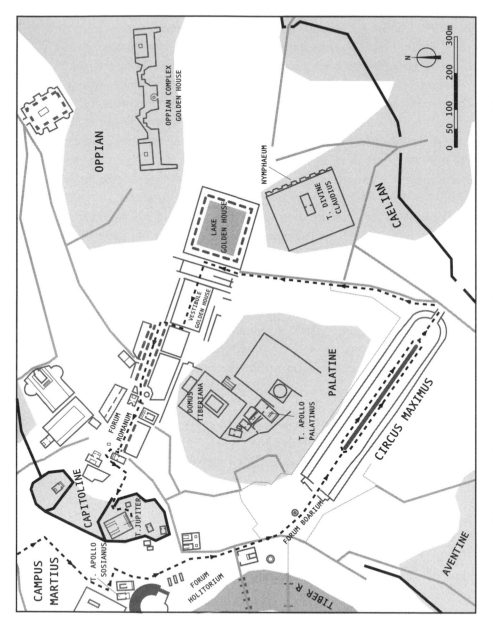

Nero's Rome: Golden House and Triumphal Route. The route of a Roman triumph is shown with dotted lines and arrows.

Suetonius describes just one house, one estate, however extravagant, however surrounded with open spaces, buildings, lakes, porticoes, and so forth. Of complexes of adjacent palaces such as existed on the Palatine, some of them new, some of them reconstructed under Nero, they say nothing. Neronian though such buildings undoubtedly were, there is no hint that Nero or anyone else thought of any palace on the Palatine as being part of the Golden House.

Moreover, as we have seen, Suetonius says, literally, that "he made a house from the Palatine all the way to *(usque ad)* the Esquiline," while Tacitus speaks of "the house by which he had joined *(continuaverat)* the Palatine and the Gardens of Maecenas [on the Esquiline]." Suetonius also clearly conceives of one house that was built, burned, and rebuilt: *domum . . . primo transitoriam, mox incendio absumptam restitutamque auream nominavit.* The Domus Transitoria (Nero's own name for it) is eclipsed by its golden namesake. What precisely did Nero mean by the bland *"transitoria"*? It should signify something that connects, a passageway between places. Can we then think of structures *on* the Palatine and the Esquiline hills as "transitional," *transitoria,* when those hills were just what was being connected? The name surely implies rather that the Golden House lay *between* the hills.

A precise analogy in the topography of Rome bears this out: the Forum of Nerva, which was widely known in Late Antiquity as the Forum Transitorium.[67] This narrow, elongated forum was essentially a magnificent passageway between the Subura district and the Forum Romanum, begun by Domitian and dedicated by Nerva. But if we applied to it the same criteria that have been applied to Nero's mansion, it would not just transitorially "lie between," "offer a passageway," "connect," it would also overrun and absorb all that it touched—the Forum of Augustus, the Forum of Julius Caesar, the Temple of Peace, the Forum Romanum, the Subura itself—which is absurd. By this analogy, the Domus Transitoria, and consequently the Domus Aurea, must *not* have included the Palatine, or the Esquiline, or any building on them: it lay *between* them; it connected them; it was a passageway between two areas. What Nero meant by this transition remains to be seen.

Behind modern inflation of its size there lies a fundamental assumption about the Golden House, that Nero wished to be private. Here the question of boundaries is central: wherever they may have lain, what *were* the boundaries? How was the Golden House defined? If there were walls over

open spaces or gates blocking off streets, no sign of them survives, and
this lack of clear boundaries (other than such obvious constructions as the
vestibule or the nymphaeum) has allowed free rein to scholarly imagination. Roads, some of them important, certainly crossed the area. Did
praetorian guards bar the way, forcing traffic to circumnavigate what was
by any measurement a huge swath of downtown Rome? Were the citizens
of Rome not to visit the Temple of Fortune, originally constructed under
the kings and now reconstructed by Nero on the grounds of his house?
The only scholar who has considered the matter of access seriously is Miriam Griffin, in her biography of Nero. She observed that the standard discussion of these matters fifty years ago "worked on two premises: that
Nero would follow the terrain as much as possible, and that he would
want to be isolated." Both assumptions, she pointed out, are incorrect,
disregarding Nero's notorious fondness for rearranging nature on a large
scale, and assuming contrary to the evidence that Nero wished for privacy.
Griffin's discussion and her conclusion, that "nothing suggests that Nero
meant to shut himself up in the Domus Aurea," have been largely ignored
by subsequent scholarship on the Golden House.[68] Yet the conclusion is
surely correct—that a man who "was carried away," in the words of
Suetonius, "by a craze for popularity," and whose popularity did not wane
after the fire, would do nothing to exclude his people.

In 64, just a few months before the Great Fire, Nero offered the most
elaborate portrayal yet of himself as the friend of the people, staging
through Tigellinus one of his great popular parties that pointedly recalled
the aristocratic pleasures of maritime Baiae. It was then too that he offered
the novel conceit that all Rome was his house and its citizens were his
family.[69] Again, how does the Golden House fit in?

When Nero came to the throne there were two large, permanent, artificial bodies of water in Rome, the Stagnum Agrippae in the Campus
Martius and the Naumachia Augusti across the Tiber. Both were fed by
aqueducts, both were surrounded by parks, around both Nero erected pavilions, and the area of the Lake of Agrippa (at least) he stocked with exotic birds and animals. Both were the scenes of elaborate nautical banquets and boating parties, reminiscent of Baiae. In 64 the emperor moved
to add a third large, permanent, artificial body of water to the city, one

surrounded by parkland, animals, and pavilions: the Stagnum Neronis, Nero's Lake, at the heart of the Golden House.

Two observations about the Stagnum Neronis link it and the Golden House to the Campus Martius. The first concerns its relationship with the later Baths of Titus (dedicated by that emperor in 80), which lay immediately to the west of the villa on the Oppian and which are the only other public buildings in Rome to share its precise east-west axis. Filippo Coarelli has suggested that they were originally conceived as the baths of the Golden House. As Inge Nielsen expressed the matter, this would solve two problems. First, it would explain why there is otherwise no trace of baths serving the huge Neronian complex on the Oppian: that is, the Baths of Titus, or their forerunner, were planned as the baths of the Golden House. And second, it would also explain why the Baths of Titus lacked the usual amenities of gardens, pool, porticoes: that is, the lake and gardens of the Golden House provided them. Thus the baths and the house complex would fit together very nicely.[70] If this were true—and it is, admittedly, purely speculative—the Domus Aurea baths would then have been intended as a strong and conscious echo of the very recent bath complex in the Campus Martius, erected by Nero himself. Certainly the Baths of Titus strikingly imitated on a smaller scale the new and innovative Baths of Nero in the Campus, with their great square palaestra; and where the Baths of Nero were integrated with the other facilities around the adjacent Lake of Agrippa in the Campus Martius, the Baths of Titus were or would be connected by a splendid staircase with the Lake of Nero in the Domus Aurea complex.[71]

There is more to be said about the Lake, as we have learned something astonishing about it in the last decade. Excavations at the Meta Sudans, the fountain later erected at the western end of the valley of the Colosseum, have revealed that the Stagnum Neronis, far from being an irregularly shaped rustic pond, surrounded by vegetation (as it has been universally conceived), was in fact a huge rectangle, bordered by elaborate porticoed colonnades: that is, it looked very much like the Stagnum Agrippae.[72] In short, the Domus Aurea offered another version of, a pendant to, a central complex of the Campus Martius. On this view, part of the Golden House was a clear image of one of the most public areas of Rome, an area where Nero meant to introduce the maritime pleasures of Baiae to the people of Rome.

Looking down on this rectangle of water fringed by colonnades was the great façade of the mansion on the Oppian, which has been defined as a porticus villa. The complex, as has often been observed, in many ways recalls the Campanian *villae maritimae,* those seaside villas familiar both from wall paintings and from archaeology, with their terraces, gardens, long cool porticoes, and (above all) grand panoramic views of the sea. Let us go further: the Domus Aurea *was* a Campanian seaside villa.[73] Like its counterpart in the Campus Martius, it was intended to recall the pleasures of Baiae in the heart of Rome. Is there any reason to think that it too did not welcome the people of Rome to forget their cares as their city rose from the ashes?

THE STANDARD charge against Nero, formulated during his lifetime and later echoed by Pliny and Martial, was that his house was taking over the city. Accordingly, the Flavians dismantled or built over the components of the Golden House and ostentatiously dedicated them to new public use: the Baths of Titus, the Temple of the Divine Claudius, the paintings removed to the Temple of Peace—and above all the Colosseum, a monument to military virtue at the heart of Nero's pleasure palace.[74] But here a basic principle must be stressed: criticisms of Nero are very often direct distortions of his own words and deeds. The idea of the city as house *originated* with Nero, not with his critics, who turned a popular act into one of tyranny. Yes, he treated the whole city as his house, as we know; yes, he even sought to make the city into his house: but his intention thereby was not to *ex*clude the people, as his critics claimed. It was to *in*clude them. The *princeps* and the *populus Romanus* were *necessitudines:* sharing the delights of Baiae, they would share the Campus Martius *and* the Domus Aurea.

How then do we define the Domus Aurea? In the last few years, the historical evolution of the *horti Romani* has been charted in a variety of modes—political, social, architectural, religious, philosophical, theatrical—and Nero surely understood them at least as well as we do. *Horti* have been defined as a singular unit, an urban villa with a park. They were luxurious, inner suburban dwellings of the Roman aristocracy which imitated in several respects the palace complexes of Hellenistic kings. One of the great markers separating *horti* from *domus,* or great townhouses, was the line between private and public, and the deepest luxury of the *horti* was their sense of privacy and space virtually within the city. Nero, with his Domus Transitoria, connecting the imperial *domus* on the Palatine with the great *horti* on the Esquiline, meant to cross that boundary between public and private and create something new: it was to be, as it were, a fusion of *domus* and *horti*. It must be emphasized: here alone, not everywhere. Public business would still be transacted in the *aulae,* the halls of the real *domus* on the Palatine. True privacy—or at least urban privacy—would still be found in the *horti* of Maecenas or Lamia or Servilius.

The Golden House should be conceived as something new, physically separate from the structures, public or private, which crowned the Palatine, the Caelian, and the Esquiline hills. In essence it was a bowl formed by the valley and the hillsides, and it seems designed for visual effect, calculating what a viewer would observe when looking around from the vestibule on the Velia, or up from the lake to the façade of the palace on the Oppian, or down from the palace to the lake: it is, in short, a theater, or rather an amphitheater. People were meant to look. Privacy was not an issue.

At least two spectacles were being presented simultaneously—the House of the Sun-God, and the Villa of the People—and actor/spectators were essential. Nero's association with Sol/Helios in the Domus Aurea is so much a part of his public solar ideology, and the visual effects of the exteriors (at least) of the Golden House are so calculated to impress spectators, and there are simply so many rooms in it, that it is hard to imagine the Palace of the Sun-God *not* being a place open to the public. At the same time, the Golden House conforms to Nero's fondness for consciously upsetting the hierarchies of Roman society, sharing pleasure with his people, staging at Rome riotous scenes of public license on sets reminiscent of a Campanian resort that was, until then, the playground of the rich. The godlike *princeps* is, after all, just a human being like the rest of us, and he invites us to share his house. It was indeed a private house, but it was the house of the whole Roman people as well.

Next to the glamorous Domus Aurea, its original name, the bland Domus Transitoria, the Connecting House, never draws a second glance. Yet it too was to be taken both literally and metaphorically. The adjective *transitorius* is extremely rare in Latin, and this is its earliest attestation.[75] It may be that Nero, ever creative, invented the word.

8

Triumph

The people erected scaffoldings in the . . . circuses, and round the forum, occupied other parts of the city which afforded a view of the procession, and witnessed the spectacle arrayed in white garments. Every temple was open and filled with garlands and incense, while numerous servitors and lictors restrained the thronging and scurrying crowds and kept the streets open and clear. Three days were assigned for the triumphal procession.

PLUTARCH

The grandest of all Roman spectacles and the highest of all possible honors was the triumph, the great victory parade of a successful general that wound its way through the streets and past the monuments of the city, ending with a sacrifice by the general to Jupiter in his temple on the Capitol. Celebrated by the leaders of Rome since the time of King Romulus, essentially voted by the Roman people at the senate's behest in the days of the Republic, it was the supreme honor, public recognition of outstanding military success through the favor of the gods.

Here is Plutarch's description of the triumph of Aemilius Paullus over Macedon in 167 BC:

Three days were assigned for the triumphal procession. The first barely sufficed for the exhibition of the captured statues, paintings, and colossal figures, which were carried on 250 chariots. On the second, the finest and richest of the Macedonian arms were borne along in many wagons. The arms themselves glittered with freshly polished bronze and steel, and were carefully and artfully arranged to look exactly as though they had been piled together in heaps and at random . . . After the wagons laden with armor there followed 3,000 men carrying coined silver in 750 vessels, each of which contained three talents and was borne by four men, while still other men carried mixing-bowls of silver, drinking horns, bowls, and cups, all well arranged for show and excelling in size and in the depth of their carved ornaments.

On the third day, as soon as it was morning, trumpeters led the way . . . After these were led along 120 stall-fed oxen with gilded horns, bedecked with fillets and garlands. Those who led these victims to the sacrifice were young men wearing aprons with handsome borders, and boys attended them carrying gold and silver vessels of libation. Next, after these, came the carriers of the coined gold, which, like the silver, was portioned out into vessels containing three talents, and the number of these vessels was 80 lacking 3. After these followed the bearers of the consecrated bowl, which Aemilius [Paullus, the conquering Roman general] had caused to be made of 10 talents of gold and adorned with precious stones, and then those who displayed the bowls known as Antigonids and Seleucids and Theracleian, together with all the gold dinner service of Perseus [the defeated King of Macedon]. These were followed by the chariot of Perseus, which bore his arms, and his diadem lying upon his arms. Then, at a little interval, came the children of the king, led along as slaves, and with them a throng of foster-parents, teachers, and tutors, all in tears, stretching out their hands to the spectators and teaching the children to beg and supplicate . . .

Behind the children and their train of attendants walked Perseus himself, clad in a dark robe and wearing the high boots of his country . . . He, too, was followed by a company of friends and intimates, whose faces were heavy with grief . . .

Next in order to these were carried wreaths of gold, 400 in number, which the cities had sent with their embassies to Aemilius as prizes for his victory. Next, mounted on a chariot of magnificent adornment, came Aemilius himself, . . . wearing a purple robe interwoven with gold, and holding in his right hand a branch of laurel. The whole army carried laurel, following the chariot of their general by companies and divisions, and singing, some of them songs intermingled with jesting, as the ancient custom was, and others with paeans of victory and hymns in praise of the achievements of Aemilius.[1]

Over the centuries certain rules and norms evolved, particularly in the granting of the prize, but less so in the exact route and components of the parade itself, which allowed for remarkable individual variation.² Under the Republic, when a victorious general returned to Rome with part of his army, he would wait in the Villa Publica, that is, in the Campus Martius and outside of the *pomerium,* the sacred boundary of the city. There he would apply to the senate for the right to hold a triumph, which necessitated a vote by the people to allow him to retain his military power, the *imperium,* within the *pomerium.* Certain conditions for holding a triumph developed over the years: victory must have been won in a properly declared war, a *iustum bellum,* against a foreign enemy; the Roman general must have been fighting under his own auspices, that is, he must have been a magistrate or promagistrate; at least 5,000 of the enemy must have been killed; and the war must have been ended. The senate might then grant the general's request. Or, if it felt that conditions did not warrant a full triumph, it might award him a "minor triumph" called an ovation. Or it might deny the request altogether, in which case the offended general might hold his own private triumph *in monte Albano,* ending with sacrifice at the Temple of Jupiter Latiaris on the Alban Mount, in the hills near Rome. The maneuvering that led to the senate's decision disappeared under the empire, when from an early date the emperor monopolized triumphal celebrations either for himself or for members of his immediate family; the generals who had won the victories for him were awarded *ornamenta triumphalia,* triumphal ornaments.

Two elements of a typical imperial triumph are of interest: its route and its components. The procession would form up in the Circus Flaminius, an open space in the Campus Martius. It would move off in a southeasterly direction, skirting the adjacent Theater of Marcellus, although in 71 the parade of Vespasian and Titus actually passed through the theater. Moving around the southern slopes of the Capitol, it passed through the Porta Triumphalis, not an actual gate but a freestanding double arch in the area of the present church of Sant'Omobono. It might next, as in Julius Caesar's case in 46 BC, move some distance up the Velabrum in the direction of the Forum, but would then double back to the Forum Boarium in order to pass through the Circus Maximus. The parade then turned north, skirting the foot of the Palatine along the Via Triumphalis (modern Via S. Gregorio), then northeast along the Sacred Way down through the Forum. After perhaps a pause to execute enemy leaders in the Carcer Tullianum at the foot of the Capitol, the procession would mount the Clivus Capitolinus to the Temple of Jupiter Optimus Maximus. There the victorious general would offer his spoils and sacrifice to the god who had brought him victory.

The route, a large ellipse, was short, perhaps 4 kilometers, but the procession was huge, it was very slow, and it stopped often, so a triumph might last for days. Temporary bleachers were erected for the crowds, and awnings in some places. It has been estimated that perhaps 300,000 to 400,000 spectators could have watched these parades, or roughly half the population of the city of Rome. The spectacle was worth it.

Her citizens were offered a tremendous paean to the might of Rome. The spoils were overwhelming: weapons piled in huge trophies on carts, gold and silver in coins and bullion, precious fabrics, gems, masterpieces of art and craft, all paraded by in fabulous amounts. In his triumph in the winter of 189 BC, for instance, Lucius Scipio, now known as Asiaticus for his defeat in Asia Minor of the King of Syria, displayed the following: 224 military standards, 134 *simulacra* (architectural representations) of captured towns, 1,231 ivory tusks, 234 gold crowns, 137,420 pounds of silver, 224,000 Attic 4-drachma pieces, 321,700 cistophori (Asian coins), 140,000 gold coins of Philip (of Macedon), 1,423 pounds of embossed silver vases, 1,023 pounds of gold vases—and that was early days.[3] At the same time, great towers might lumber by, some three or four stories high, representing the capture of cities; large paintings depicted battles, sieges, slaughter, significant moments in the campaign, and the terrain in which they all took place, scenes reminiscent of those on the surviving columns of Trajan and Marcus Aurelius. These were accompanied by *tituli,* placards with the names of conquered peoples or with slogans like Julius Caesar's *veni vidi vici.* Thus the important incidents of the war were captured in words and pictures. These were carried on wagons or borne by soldiers on litters, *fercula,* which would presumably stop often to allow observers to "read" the glorious story, like a primitive newsreel.

The parade included several standard elements. Sacrificial victims, white oxen, were driven along, adorned for offering to Jupiter. Important prisoners of war were displayed along with their families, often in chains and either walking or forming part of tableaux on wagons. While they might be spared for a comfortable retirement, some of their leaders might be abused by soldiers and spectators and put to death in the Tullianum. Musicians such as trumpeters or citharodes played as they marched in the parade. Incense-bearers passed by, as did the general's lictors, dressed in red tunics and carrying their *fasces,* the rods and axes of his office, bound with laurel. The magistrates and senators of Rome marched in their dignity; the general's officers and his older relatives rode by on horses. The triumphator himself drove in a chariot, accompanied by his younger children, and followed by his aides, his secretaries, and his armor-bearers, also perhaps by Roman citizens who had been freed from the enemy, wearing the cap of freedom, the *pilleus*. Then the soldiers marched by in their units and with their standards, wearing their parade uniforms and decorations, and bearing laurel wreaths and branches. In the holiday atmosphere they would sing victory songs and praise and abuse of their officers, even obscene verses. All along the route, temples were open, lit up, and decorated. Spectators, dressed in their holiday best, cheered and threw flowers. And after the culminating sacrifice to Jupiter the general held a banquet for his friends, while his fellow-citizens celebrated their good fortune at home.

The center of the triumphal spectacle was of course the triumphator. He entered the city riding in a high, two-wheeled chariot, the *currus triumphalis,* drawn by four horses and decorated with laurel branches. All of Augustus' successors in fact used the first emperor's own, elaborately decorated chariot. Beneath it, for the purpose of warding off evil, was slung a large phallus, which might be adorned with bells and whips. The general himself was a blaze of color in his triumphal garb, the *vestis triumphalis.* Normally he wore a purple tunic embroidered with gold palm branches, the *tunica palmata,* and over this a purple toga embroidered with gold stars, the *toga picta.* On his head he might wear a laurel wreath, the *corona laurea,* as did some of his suite, or a public slave might hold a heavy gold wreath, the *corona triumphalis,* over him. In his right hand, he would carry a laurel branch; in his left, an ivory scepter topped by an eagle. Around his neck he wore a *bulla,* a protective amulet, and, in the old days at least, he would have his face painted red.[4]

There is no question that the triumphator, the successor of the kings of old, was meant to represent Jupiter. Riding with him in the chariot, the slave would periodically remind him who he was: *Respice post te, hominem te esse memento,* Look behind you, and remember that you are a man. But the whole point was that he *was* Jupiter, for a day.

Three interrelated aspects of the triumph should be emphasized. First, although there were certain set elements of the victory parade which ended with sacrifice to the god, the form and components were far from rigid. The order of the elements might shift; some might be dropped or added; others might grow ever more elaborate or exotic, especially as the parade expanded over the centuries, thanks to escalating individual ambitions and rivalries and to ever grander victories. Similarly, the route might be varied, as the triumphator chose to pass by or through monuments or locations significant to him. Second, aspects of the triumphal procession were mirrored in other elements of Roman public life, most notably in the parades inaugurating many games and in funeral parades: in the former triumphal garb was worn on occasion by the magistrates in charge, even by the relatively junior tribunes and aediles.[5] And third, triumphal apparatus was absorbed specifically into the emperor's role as bringer of victory, as he gradually stepped into the continuous exercise of the rights, the robes, and the equipment of the triumphator, and public images came to portray even the mildest of emperors in military dress and surrounded with the paraphernalia of victory.[6] In short, the triumph itself permitted creative variation, and triumphalism was an accepted part of both public life and the developing image of the emperor.

EVEN THOUGH he was never to see an army in peace or in war, and would visit only one of his provinces—an unarmed one at that—militarism and triumphalism marked Nero's life as a prince in Rome. Indeed, they were imposed upon him from an early age. Especially noteworthy are the honors and celebrations associated with his early adoption of the toga of manhood in 51. The emperor Claudius, we are told, gladly complied with the flatteries of the senate, which designated Nero to hold the consulship in his twentieth year. In the meantime they granted him proconsular *imperium,* the power of a general, outside of the city, along with the title *princeps iuventutis,* leader of the youth of Rome, an honor sometimes held by princes of the blood. A cash donative was given in his name to the soldiers, along with largesse to civilians, and he led a parade of the Praetorian Guard with a shield in his hand:

> At the games too of the circus which were then being celebrated to win for him popular favour, Britannicus wore the dress of boyhood, Nero the triumphal robe, *triumphali veste,* as they rode in the procession. The people would thus behold the one with the decorations of

a general, the other in a boy's habit, and would accordingly antici-
pate their respective destinies.[7]

Nero was 13.

At the end of 54, soon after his accession, the Parthians invaded Armenia, but before Rome could respond a dynastic crisis at home prompted
the invaders to withdraw. The senate's reaction to this unexpected resolution of the crisis was one of startling excess. Public thanksgivings to the
gods were decreed, and on the days of these supplications Nero was to
wear the *vestis triumphalis;* he was also to enter the city in an *ovatio,* that
is, in the lesser triumph; and his statue was to be placed in the Temple of
Mars Ultor, of the same size as that of the god. Soon after, Nero ordered
it proclaimed that because of the successes of Domitius Corbulo and
his rival, Ummidius Quadratus, the governor of Syria, laurel would be
added to the *fasces* of the emperor.[8] He was 17. The young Nero had undertaken no military action to warrant these marks of distinction—indeed, no one had.

As a result of the Parthian disturbance, Nero appointed a real general,
Corbulo, to secure the frontier, and Corbulo's real success in Armenia,
ending with the destruction of its capital, Artaxata, led to further celebration four years later, in 58:

> For all of this Nero was unanimously saluted "imperator," and by the
> senate's decree a thanksgiving *(supplicationes)* was held; statues also,
> an arch and successive consulships were voted to the *princeps,* and
> among the holy days were to be included the day on which the vic-
> tory was won, that on which it was announced, and that on which
> the motion was brought forward. Other proposals too of a like kind
> were carried, on a scale so extravagant, that Cassius Longinus, after
> having assented to the honours, argued that if the gods were to be
> thanked for the bountiful favours of fortune, even a whole year
> would not suffice for thanksgivings.[9]

Another four years later, in 62, after the stunning humiliation of a Roman army under Caesennius Paetus, Corbulo negotiated a settlement
with the Parthians. Despite this, the arch decreed in 58 was erected "in
the center of the Capitol Hill," along with trophies of the Parthian War.
This arch is well known from coins: it was topped by a statue of Nero in

triumphal toga and carrying his eagle-tipped scepter, as he drove four
prancing horses in his triumphal chariot. Victory accompanied him with
a palm branch and Peace with a cornucopia, while soldiers saluted from
the four columns. The location of the arch has been identified as that of
a podium standing next to the Temple of Jupiter Optimus Maximus,
where it formed a sumptuous entrance into the piazza for all future
triumphatores to see.[10] Victory was thus claimed in the midst of retreat
and negotiation, and for an emperor who had never seen an army.

The cheapening of triumphal vocabulary and paraphernalia, the divorce of these attributes from the triumph itself, their assignment to
purely civilian non-combatants, the general mixing of military and civilian, and the ready acquiescence, even spontaneous enthusiasm, of the senate and people of Rome: all help us to understand several extraordinary
Neronian episodes, most notably the strange aftermath of the unmasking
of the Pisonian conspiracy in 65.

As Tacitus tells the story, in the midst of executions, suicides, and ban-
ishments there was public rejoicing, real or feigned, as victims were sacrificed on the Capitol, thanks rendered to the gods, and private homes
adorned with laurels. At a public meeting, Nero gave a donative of 2,000
sesterces to each soldier and an award of free grain. And then,

> as if he were going to describe successes in war, he summoned the
> Senate, and awarded triumphal honours to Petronius Turpilianus, an
> ex-consul, to Cocceius Nerva, praetor-elect, and to Tigellinus, com-
> mander of the praetorians. Tigellinus and Nerva he so distinguished
> as to place busts of them in the palace in addition to triumphal stat-
> ues in the Forum. He granted a consul's decorations to Nymphidius
> [Sabinus].

Suetonius adds, without referring precisely to the events of 65, that Nero
awarded the *ornamenta triumphalia* even to ex-quaestors (very junior senators) and to a few men of the equestrian order, and not for any military deed. And Dio, in epitome, mentions the excessive honors voted to
Nero and his friends in 65.[11] It was also around this time that Nero was
saluted as Imperator for the tenth time, an honor normally marking a
claim to military success, now probably awarded for the detection of a
conspiracy.[12]

Epigraphy has confirmed just how far this peacetime appropriation of military honors extended. Thus, a fragmentary inscription from his native Umbria records the senatorial career of M. Cocceius Nerva, the praetor-elect of 65, who went smoothly on through the Year of the Four Emperors to be consul in 71, and who himself would reign in his old age as emperor, from 96 to 98. The *triumphalia ornamenta* of 65 are duly included on the inscription, but with no mention of the reason for which they were won or the emperor who had granted them to him. There is also a fragmentary inscription from Rome showing that the imperial freedman Epaphroditus was granted military honors, *dona militaria,* including the *hasta pura,* a headless spear presented for valor, and golden crowns for general gallantry. It was to Epaphroditus, Nero's secretary in charge of petitions and a servant who would be with him until the end, that a freedman of one of the plotters revealed the conspiracy of Piso. It was highly irregular for a freedman like Epaphroditus to win military honors, since ex-slaves could not serve in the regular army, although again there was a precedent in the emperor Claudius, who had presented his freedman Posides with the headless spear at his British triumph in 43.[13]

More alarming is the case of the senator L. Nonius Calpurnius Asprenas (consul c. 72), as recorded in an inscription erected during his proconsulship of Africa in 83. His career was that of a patrician already favored by birth and promoted by Nero, serving as the emperor's quaestor, and proceeding smoothly upward to serve in turn the short-lived emperors of 68/69 and the Flavian dynasty. In the middle of this progress, which is set down in chronological order, there is a very curious item, inserted after his quaestorship and before his praetorship and the subsequent governorship of Galatia in 69, en route to which he would capture and execute the first False Nero. In the latter years of Nero's reign Asprenas was "centurion of the Roman knights," and he was showered with an array of military honors: eight spears; four banners; two mural crowns, *coronae murales* (awarded to the first Roman soldier over an enemy's city walls); two rampart crowns, *coronae vallares* (for the first soldier to cross the ramparts of an enemy's camp); and one gold crown. The astonishing thing is that this young senator, one of the most decorated men in the history of Rome, had never served a day in the army. What he actually did to deserve these awards is unclear, but the most likely explanation is that they were among the honors handed out for services rendered in the discovery and suppression of the Pisonian conspiracy, as if for deeds done in war, in Tacitus' words, *gesta bello.*[14]

The events of 65 confirm two observations. One is the growing appropriation of military images and vocabulary for civilian achievements. An attack on the emperor was an act of war, his salvation a matter of state rejoicing: just as after a war, statues of men in triumphal dress were erected in the Forum, military honors were distributed, gifts and thanks to the gods were decreed, a new temple was proposed.[15] The other element to be noted is the complicity of society. This is not just a matter of public rejoicing and thanksgiving, although it is perhaps wrong to dismiss such popular reactions in hindsight, with Tacitus, as the outpourings of servile flattery: who is to say that some people were not genuinely relieved at the salvation of their emperor from real danger? It is rather a matter of the memorials. Long after Nero's death, two senators and an imperial freedman proudly recorded military honors as part of their resolutely civilian careers. As is common on such inscriptions, when the emperor whom they served was disgraced after death, he is not named, but this is not a matter of falsifying reality: no observer could be in any doubt that it was a Nero or a Domitian who had awarded the office or the honor recorded, and if falsification were the point, inconvenient facts would be suppressed altogether. The service—the fact that one had served as the emperor's quaestor—was important, not the emperor served. It is all the more interesting then that these three men continued to proclaim their military honors proudly after Nero's death. We may dismiss them as the ridiculous awards of a deluded tyrant to his obsequious cronies, just as Tacitus would have us do, but that would be to miss the point: they were proud of them, and they could assume that the public would accept them. Two lessons are to be drawn: that loyal service to the emperor was worth commemorating, whoever that emperor might be; and that the expression of imperial gratitude in military terms was an acceptable currency of public honor. If the people could tolerate that, they could tolerate triumphs that had nothing to do with real war.

On three public occasions Nero and his people went further than mere triumphal trappings, to produce elaborate spectacles that may or may not have been real triumphs. The first came in the tumultuous year of 59.

For three months after his mother's murder near Baiae, the emperor skulked in Campania, worried about the public mood and working to reconcile it to the deed. His courtiers assured him, according to Tacitus, that people had loathed Agrippina and that he was now more popular than ever. Preceding him on the road to Rome,

> they found greater enthusiasm than they had promised, the tribes coming forth to meet him, the Senate in holiday attire, troops of their wives and children arranged according to age and sex. Tiers of the seats used at spectacles were erected, in the manner used for watching triumphs. From here the arrogant victor over the servility of his people proceeded to the Capitol, discharged his thanks to the gods, and than plunged into all the excesses, which, though ill-re-strained, some sort of respect for his mother had for a while delayed.

Dio adds that the people of Rome rejoiced at the news of the murder, since now Nero would be destroyed, while the senate pretended to rejoice and voted much in his honor: which is to say, stripped of Dio's comment, that the senate and the people rejoiced. When he returned to the city and Agrippina's statues were removed, everyone flattered him in public, but he was attacked in private, and various pasquinades appeared around the city; yet Nero refused to prosecute anyone accused of speaking against him. Sacrifices were decreed for his safety from Agrippina's plots, but they were marred by an eclipse. Elephants drawing the chariot of Augustus entered the Circus but stopped at the seats of the senators and refused to go further. And Nero presented the lavish Ludi Maximi in five or six places "on account of his mother," that is, to celebrate his salvation from her.[16]

Even at the age of 21, the young emperor was practicing his triumphal skills. The courtiers preceding him into the city, the holiday clothes, the formal divisions of the crowd by tribe, rank, age, and sex, the temporary bleachers, the procession to sacrifice on the Capitol, the public rejoicing, the chariot of Augustus entering the Circus, the celebratory games—all are meant to recall the elements of a formal triumph. Tacitus understood the message, with his reference to the bleachers erected "in the manner used for watching triumphs," and he added his own editorial comment: that Nero was indeed a victor ascending the Capitol, but he had con-quered his people's servility. The Arval Brothers too caught the spirit. Ac-cording to their records, the priests sacrificed in three temples on 23 June for the safety and return of Nero Claudius Caesar Augustus Germanicus: on the Capitol, to the Capitoline trinity of Jupiter, Juno, and Minerva, as well as to Public Safety (Salus Publica), Good Fortune (Felicitas), and a third goddess whose name has been lost; at the New Temple (of the Divine Augustus) near the Forum, to Nero's ancestors the Divine Augustus and the Divine Augusta (Livia), and to the Divine Claudius, his predecessor; and in the Forum of Augustus to Mars the Avenger (Mars Ultor) and to Nero's own guardian spirit (Genius). All of these are appropriate to celebrate the averting of this particular danger, but Mars the Avenger gives the celebration a deliberately military cast. The temple of the god of war in the Forum of Augustus was very much "War Central" in Rome, the place where maturing boys were enrolled among the youth of military age, where provincial commanders embarked on their commands, where the senate debated the granting of triumphs, where triumphatores dedicated their scepters and their crowns to Mars, where they and the winners of triumphal ornaments were commemorated by bronze statues, and more. When the Arval Brothers sacrificed there to Mars Ultor and to the emperor's Genius there could be no doubt: his preservation was publicly treated as a military victory. Thus, in the early summer of 59, did Nero celebrate an informal triumph over his dead mother.[17]

Nero's next triumph was a pageant designed to mark the successful negotiation of peace with Parthia, a peace that would last almost sixty years. The ovation of 54 and the triumphal arch of 58/62, even the triumphal celebration of his salvation from his mother's plots, were modest next to the stunning theatrical coup produced in 66.

After the Roman disgrace of 62, Corbulo brought the war back to Armenia in 63, at Nero's orders. Tiridates, the Parthian prince who had been installed as King of Armenia by his brother, the King of Parthia, requested a meeting. Corbulo chose the place—Rhandeia, where the legions of Caesennius Paetus had surrendered—and an elaborate charade was played out. As Tacitus recounts the event, Corbulo arrived in Tiridates' camp with a small escort and dismounted; Tiridates likewise dismounted and approached him; and the two joined their right hands. After conciliatory speeches on both sides, the king agreed to lay his diadem before an image of Nero and to receive it back only from Nero's hands, thus acquiescing to a compromise which up until then one or the other party had rejected: a Parthian prince installed as King of Armenia by the emperor of Rome. Accordingly, some days later in a grand pageant staged before both armies, and with images of the gods arrayed as if in a temple, Tiridates approached a tribunal on which stood a magistrate's chair bearing an image of the emperor; he sacrificed; and then he placed his crown before the image. The epitome of Dio gives an abbreviated version of the same affair, concluding with the remark: "In honour of this event Nero was saluted as *imperator* a number of times and held a triumph, contrary to precedent."[18] In fact the triumph was not to take place for another three years: it needed a lot of preparation.

After submitting at Rhandeia and enjoying Corbulo's subsequent hospitality, Tiridates begged leave to see his mother and his brothers before embarking on the long journey to Rome; in the meantime he handed over his daughter as a hostage, and he wrote dutifully to Nero. After meeting with Tiridates, his brother Vologeses, the King of Parthia, wrote to Corbulo to demand special treatment for Tiridates: he should suffer no sign of subjection, he should not surrender his sword, he should not be denied the embrace of provincial governors en route or be kept waiting at their doors, and at Rome he should be shown the same honor as that shown to consuls. Tacitus scoffs at Vologeses' concerns, but they were clearly part of the negotiations and were accepted by the Roman side. Tiridates was going to Rome "for the emperor's Armenian triumph over himself," in Pliny's words, but he was explicitly to be treated with honor, not as a defeated enemy. Indeed, Dio says, the king's journey from the Euphrates to Rome was itself "like a triumphal procession":

> Tiridates himself was at the height of his reputation by reason of his age, beauty, family and intelligence; and his whole retinue of servants together with all his royal paraphernalia accompanied him. Three thousand Parthian horsemen and numerous Romans besides followed in his train. They were received by gaily decorated cities and by peoples who shouted many compliments. Provisions were furnished them free of cost, a daily expenditure of 800,000 sesterces for their support being thus charged to the public treasury. This went on without change for the nine months occupied in the journey. The prince covered the whole distance to the confines of Italy on horseback, and beside him rode his wife, wearing a golden helmet in place of a veil, so as not to defy the traditions of her country by letting her face be seen. In Italy he was conveyed by a two-horse carriage sent by Nero, and met the emperor at Neapolis, which he reached by way of

Picenum. He refused, however, to obey the order to lay aside his dagger when he approached the emperor, but fastened it to his scabbard with nails. Yet he knelt upon the ground, and with arms crossed called him master and did him obeisance.

Thus the subjected enemy king, far from being abused, was treated with such honor that he himself seemed to be on a triumphal progress. As for Domitius Corbulo, the architect of victory, we hear of no rewards. Tiridates, who is said to have admired Corbulo and despised Nero, remarked to the emperor one day, "Master, you have in Corbulo a good slave." The Greek he used was not the usual word for slave, *doulos,* but *andrapodon,* which meant specifically a person captured in war and sold as a slave. Tiridates as triumphator and Corbulo as war booty: Nero's Armenian triumph promised to be most unusual. Dio comments that the emperor did not understand Tiridates' observation.[19]

They proceeded together from Campania to Rome sometime in late May of 66. The citizens poured out to welcome their emperor and to see the king. Their city had been adorned with lights and garlands and was packed: on the night before the ceremony the Forum filled with people carrying laurel branches, and the very rooftops of adjacent buildings were covered with spectators. Nero arrived at dawn, accompanied by the senate and the Praetorian Guard, whose cohorts were then stationed around the temples of the Forum, resplendent in their parade uniforms. The emperor, dressed in triumphal robes, ascended the Rostra, the speakers' platform at the western end of the Forum, and sat in a magistrate's chair, surrounded by military standards. Tiridates and his companions then appeared, passing through a lane formed by armed soldiers and stopping near the Rostra, where they made obeisance. A huge roar from the crowd seemed to terrify the king. He addressed Nero as a god who would determine his fate. Nero thanked him in return, and granted him the kingship of Armenia. The king ascended the Rostra on a ramp built for the occasion, and sat at the emperor's feet. Nero then raised him with his right hand and kissed him, before removing his tiara and setting a diadem on his head. An ex-praetor translated the words of the suppliant king to the crowd, which roared its approval. From there they proceeded to the Theater of Pompey, which had been gilded, hence marking the day as the Golden Day; a purple awning over the theater portrayed Nero driving his chariot among golden stars. There Tiridates again performed obeisance, and the emperor placed him at his right side. For these actions, Suetonius concludes, Nero was saluted as Imperator and, after carrying a laurel branch to the Capitol, he closed the doors of the Temple of Janus, to signify that the Roman world was now at peace. Dio, who omits these last details, concludes his account with a celebratory banquet, followed by Nero singing in public and racing a chariot in the costume of the Green faction.[20]

Again, the records of the Arval Brothers provide valuable confirmation. First, probably in May, they sacrificed on the Capitol "because of the laurel" of Imperator Nero Claudius Caesar Augustus Germanicus, to the gods Jupiter, Juno, Minerva, Jupiter Victor, as well as to a goddess whose name has been lost, and to Peace. Later they sacrificed again on the Capitol because the senate had decreed thanksgivings, to Jupiter, Juno, Minerva, Good Fortune (Felicitas), and Mercy (Clementia). And later still, but before 17 June, again because of the emperor's laurel but now in the new temple of the Divine Augustus, they sacrificed to the Divine Augustus, the Divine Augusta (Livia, his wife), the Divine Claudius, the Divine virgin Claudia (Nero's short-lived daughter), the Divine Poppaea Augusta, the Genius of Nero, and the Juno of Messalina (his new wife). The themes are clear: victory, good fortune, and peace are proclaimed because of the end of war, and mercy because of the reception of Tiridates, while the triumphal laurel is celebrated both as a public honor, on the Capitol, and as a family glory, at the Temple of Augustus, among the emperor's family and ancestors. There may also be a reference to Arval activity "before the arch [of Janus Geminus]," but the text is uncertain. However that may be, several coins from about 64 to 67 bear a legend proclaiming that "when the peace of the Roman people had been imposed on land and sea, he closed Janus." It is also likely that now not only was Nero saluted as Imperator for the eleventh time, but he took the name "Imperator," essentially "General," as his *praenomen,* in imitation of Augustus—something his predecessors had refused to do.[21] And it seems that some sort of triumphal monument was erected which included a depiction of Tiridates submitting to the image of Nero at Rhandeia in 63.[22]

These events of the spring of 66 should be viewed from three related perspectives: the triumphal, the Parthian, and the spectacular. For Nero, the extraordinary pageant of the Golden Day was a high-wire tour de force, combining two very different ceremonies—triumph over a defeated enemy, and the reception and coronation of a foreign potentate. This was extraordinary, but was it a triumph at all? In their detailed descriptions neither Suetonius nor Dio (in epitome) calls it one, and they give no hint of one of the two central, defining actions of the triumph, the parade through the streets of Rome, with its visual reminders of conquest. Moreover, the submission of a suppliant to an emperor, and his coronation as king by the emperor, have nothing to do with the traditional Roman triumph. On the other hand, Pliny, without a hint of irony, refers to Nero's Armenian triumph, and the epitome of Dio's account of Rhandeia in 63, which seems to telescope events, concludes with Nero's consequent salutation as emperor many times (the number is exaggerated, but in any event the next salutation did not come before April 65) and his triumph "contrary to custom," which must refer to the ceremony of May 66.[23] Custom is the key. Once a triumph was formally decreed by the senate and voted by the people, there were no legal rules to bind the triumphator in how he celebrated his victory. Custom dictated the parade and its components, but in the details creative and competitive variety was already the norm under the Republic. Certainly the atmosphere in May of 66 was one of triumph: the lighting and decoration of the city, the citizens bearing laurel branches in the Forum, the armed soldiers in parade uniforms, the subdued foreign potentate and his retinue, the emperor in triumphal robes, his salutation as Imperator, the supplications to the appropriate deities, the concluding banquet and games, the rare closing of the doors of the Temple of Janus—and above all, the dedication of the laurel branch to Jupiter on the Capitol. That, combined with the explicit testimony of Pliny and Dio, should mean that this indeed was, and was perceived as, a formal triumph, however new and strange.

What made it uniquely exotic was the strong Parthian atmosphere that marked Tiridates' venture into the Roman world. The whole occasion reflects serious negotiation and ingenious compromise between two very different traditions, and from the beginning it is clear that the Parthians were equal partners in the invention of the pageant. Tiridates came as a suppliant but on his own terms, treated with the highest honor due a foreign potentate as he made his triumphal progress westward from the Euphrates, with 3,000 Parthian cavalrymen as retinue. One of the earlier obstacles to his coming to Rome had been his religious duty as a priest, *sacerdotii religione,* in the words of Tacitus. Tiridates was in fact a *magus,* a Zoroastrian priest, and, as Pliny tells us, he refused to travel by sea, since *magi* could not pollute the sea by any bodily excretion. He therefore

crossed from Asia into Europe over the Hellespont, and rode overland
through Illyricum and into Italy from the north. When at last he met
with Nero, again he showed himself the suppliant on his own terms, performing obeisance with the brilliant compromise of not surrendering his
dagger but rendering it harmless in the emperor's presence. Nero was captivated by this and arranged various entertainments, particularly a gladiatorial show at Puteoli which was produced with exceptional magnificence
by one of his freedmen, Patrobius. "By way of showing Patrobius some
fitting honour, Tiridates shot at wild beasts from his elevated seat, and—if
one can believe it—transfixed and killed two bulls with a single arrow."
Believable or not, the killing of two beasts with a single arrow was a mark
of princely virtue in ancient Iran.[24] Nero had met a kindred spirit in a
Parthian prince.

The understanding between Parthia and Rome is best seen in the cli-
mactic ceremony in the Forum. First there is the central exchange, recorded apparently verbatim in Dio, between Tiridates and Nero, as the
king stood at the foot of the Rostra. Tiridates spoke first:

> Master, I am the descendant of Arsaces, brother of the kings Vologeses
> and Pacorus, and your slave. I have come to you, my god, worship-
> ping you as I do Mithra. The destiny you spin shall be mine, for you
> are my Fate and my Fortune.

To which Nero replied:

> You have done well to come here in person, so that you might enjoy
> my grace in person. For what neither your father left you nor your
> brothers gave and guarded for you, this I give you freely and I make
> you King of Armenia, so that you and they may understand that I
> have the power to take away kingdoms and to bestow them.[25]

The dialogue has been carefully crafted, for this, it has been pointed out,
is not the traditional surrender of an enemy to Roman protection, *deditio
in fidem;* it is rather the acceptance by Rome of a Parthian form of submission. Moreover, minutes later, at the defining moment, when Nero removed Tiridates' tiara and replaced it with a diadem, he was removing the
symbol of Armenian kingship and replacing it with the mark of the independent Hellenistic king, a sign of *international* recognition as the legiti-

mate monarch.[26] That is, we are watching the complex interplay of two very different interests, as both Rome and Parthia maintain their dignity.

The personal relationship between Tiridates and Nero is central to the story. Nero is portrayed by the sources, especially Dio, as being enchanted by the Armenian king. Tiridates is depicted as the wise barbarian who enlightens the emperor's court with the honest truth, is disgusted by Nero's singing and his charioteering, tells him that in Corbulo he has a good slave, actually admires Corbulo for his stern treatment of himself, and protests against a fallen athlete being struck by his opponent. At the same time, he is shown as the consummate flatterer, rebuilding his capital city of Artaxata as "Neronia" and worming his way into the emperor's esteem, so successfully that Nero was said to have given him enormous gifts. There are problems with the figures named, but it appears that contemporaries believed that the visit of Tiridates cost Rome at least 300 million sesterces at a time when the entire imperial budget was perhaps 800 million: the expense of the emperor's pageant was staggering.[27]

What fascinated Nero about his friend was that Tiridates was a *magus*. The Parthian prince was not only a worshipper of Mithra but also a priest, Mithra being the god of light who led the struggle against the forces of darkness in the dualistic Zoroastrian religious system of his native land. But to the Romans *magi* were magicians, and the emperor, if we are to believe Pliny, wished to learn their secret arts, "in fact his passion for the lyre and tragic song was no greater than his passion [for magic]." Tiridates "had brought *magi* with him and had initiated him into their magic banquets; yet the man giving him a kingdom was unable to acquire from him the magic art." Nero found all their methods of divination and their ability to speak with the dead, especially his late mother, to be empty lies.[28] Pliny goes on to inveigh against magic and against Nero at wearisome length, but the central fact remains, stripped of Roman misconception, that Nero was initiated by his friend Tiridates into the religion of Zoroaster and Mithra.

What binds together Roman triumph and Parthian ceremonial is the third aspect of the Golden Day, the theatrical nature of the great occasion. We have already seen the drama of the Day of the Sun as Nero composed it: the planned effect of the rising sun on the white robes of the citizens and the glittering arms and armor of the soldiers as they packed the Forum, and the repetition of the scene in the Theater of Pompey under a canopy that showed Nero driving the chariot of the Sun. But beyond the inherent drama there is a deliberate, even explicit, theatrical aspect as well. Suetonius, who progresses by topic through his biographies of the emperors, remarks when he comes to consider the various games produced by Nero: "I may fairly include among his *spectacula* the entrance of Tiridates into the city." As he must have known, Nero himself treated the event as a show. Dio notes that the people in the Forum were arranged by rank (or division) and clad in white: this was surely intended to replicate the regulations governing the theater, the one place in Rome where the audience was required to sit in groups according to various social criteria, including rank, age, sex, and marital status, and to wear (at least in the majority of the seats) white clothing, which would be togas in the case of men.[29] The effect would be heightened by the crowds of people on the rooftops of all the surrounding buildings, looking down on the pageant like spectators in the upper rows of the theater. That is, the subsequent performance in the actual theater (of Pompey) physically mirrored the virtual theater of the Forum.

Here the role of the Sun in both places is yet again central. In the Theater of Pompey, the purple awning, which presented Nero as the Sun among the gleaming stars, looked down on the dazzling gilt interior. In the Forum, we are told, all the spectators arrived during the night, and Nero in his purple triumphal robe appeared at dawn, followed by Tiridates, just as the rising sun hit the white clothing of the crowd, the shining armor of the soldiers, the flashing weapons and standards. Both actors presumably made their entrances from the eastern end of the Forum to proceed through the crowd to the Rostra. When Nero entered with the senators and the guard, he ascended the Rostra and sat in his chair of state, looking back down the Forum in an east-southeasterly direction. That is, as Tiridates approached him through the ranks of soldiers, the rising sun would have hit Nero full on the face, in all his triumphal splendor.

The prince then addressed the emperor from the ground, looking up to him on the Rostra: "I have come to you, my god, worshipping you as I do Mithra." The important point—something Nero would know as an initiate, whether others did or not—is that for Zoroastrians the sun was the eye of Mithra, and Mithra was often so closely associated with the sun as to be identified with it: "the Sun whom they call Mithres," as Strabo puts it. Moreover, when Zoroastrians prayed in the open air, they turned toward the sun, since their religion bound them to pray facing fire. Thus, when Tiridates stood in the open Roman Forum facing the sunlit emperor, and worshipping him as he did Mithra, he was in essence worshipping the sun. An ex-praetor translated his words and proclaimed them to the crowd. At this stage in Rome's history, very few of those present would have known who Mithra was, but there is a good likelihood that the interpreter relayed Tiridates' words as "I have come to you, my god, worshipping you as I do the Sun." For Nero, the marriage of Roman triumph and Parthian ceremony culminated in a splendid theatrical affirmation of his role as the new god of the Sun.[30]

N ERO'S STRANGEST triumph was his last, celebrated on his return to Rome from his athletic conquest of Greece, in late 67.[31] His journey back took him first to Naples, to honor the city which had witnessed his first appearance in public as an artist. He entered it driving white horses through a breach made in the city's walls, "as was customary for victors in sacred games" (Suetonius). In the same manner, as he progressed northward, he entered Antium, then his Alban villa, and then Rome itself. Again, part of the city wall there was torn down and a gate broken in, as "was customary upon the return of crowned victors from the games" (Dio)—but with this difference, that into Rome he drove the chariot in which Augustus had celebrated his triumphs almost a century before.

The victor was preceded and followed by attendants and soldiers. First came men bearing the crowns he had won, accompanied or followed by others bearing on spears wooden placards, *tituli,* on which were inscribed the names of the different games in which the crowns had been won, the contests, the competitors defeated, and even the subjects of the songs and plays successfully performed. For some of the contests, there were placards claiming that Nero Caesar was the first of all Romans to win them since the beginning of time. Next came Nero himself in the chariot of Augustus. He wore a purple robe under a Greek cloak, a *chlamys,* which bore golden stars. On his head he wore a wreath of wild olive, the mark of a victor in the Olympic games, while in his right hand he carried one of laurel, the crown of a Pythian victor. And standing with him in the chariot was the citharode Diodorus, whom he had defeated in contest. Following Nero's chariot came his claque, crying out, "We are the Augustiani and the soldiers of his triumph." Knights and senators accompanied them.

The city through which they passed was in festive spirit, hung with garlands and bright with lights. As the emperor proceeded, sacrificial animals were killed everywhere, saffron perfume was sprinkled on the streets, and the parade was showered with birds, ribbons, and sweets. The crowds, led by the senators, chanted praise of the triumphant emperor, which Dio quotes verbatim:

> Hail, Olympian victor! Hail, Pythian victor! Augustus! Augustus! To Nero Hercules! To Nero Apollo! The only victor of the grand tour, the only one from the beginning of time! Augustus! Augustus! Divine voice: blessed are those who hear you!

The victory parade followed an unusual route. The broken gate through which Nero entered was presumably the Porta Capena over the Via Appia, the road leading in from Alba and the south. From there he proceeded to the nearby Circus Maximus, where he had an arch removed, thence through the Velabrum between the Capitol and the Palatine, and into the Forum. From there he may have gone up to the Capitol (according to Dio; not in Suetonius), presumably to sacrifice in the Temple of Jupiter Optimus Maximus, and from there back through the Forum to the Palatine and the Temple of Apollo. Where and when exactly the parade ceased to be a parade is unclear. Suetonius tells us that Nero placed the sacred crowns (for music and tragedy, presumably) around the couches in his private apartments (on the Palatine), along with statues of himself dressed as a citharode. Neatly balancing this is the report of Dio, who declares that after the parade Nero announced horse races, had all the crowns he had ever won for charioteering (some 1,808!) carried into the Circus and arrayed around the obelisk of the Sun, and then raced around them.

Again, as with the triumph over Tiridates a year and a half before, the events of late 67 can be viewed from three different perspectives, here the triumphal, the Greek, and the spectacular. For Nero, his splendid return to Rome was another tour de force, yet again combining two quite different ceremonies—the triumph over defeated enemies, and the homecoming reception and celebration of a victor in Greek sacred games. And again, the first question to be asked is whether this was a triumph at all. Did it further expand the elastic boundaries of what was permissible in a triumph, or did it at last cross over into deliberate parody?[32] The parade was plainly intended to look like a triumph: the accompanying senators and knights, the men bearing crowns and *tituli,* the triumphal chariot of

Augustus drawn by white horses, the purple robe and the gold stars of the conqueror, the crown (albeit olive) on his head and the laurel (albeit a crown) in his hand, the "soldiers" (who helpfully identify themselves as "the soldiers of his triumph"), and apparently the visit to the Capitol. Yet, despite the familiar elements, neither Dio nor Suetonius actually calls the parade a triumph: both authors mention the chariot in which Augustus had once triumphed, and Suetonius quotes the Augustiani calling themselves the soldiers of the emperor's triumph, but that is all. And no outraged later commentator like Pliny or Martial decries a triumph formally awarded by senate and people for purely non-military reasons, without even the salvation of the emperor as an excuse. In fact, a sentence of Suetonius appears decisive: "His claqueurs followed his chariot after the fashion of those celebrating a triumph and shouted out that they were the Augustiani and the soldiers of his triumph." "After the fashion" should mean that to Suetonius this was *not* a triumph; and their unnecessary explanation that they were the "soldiers of his triumph" further suggests that neither the Augustiani nor the spectators were under any illusion.[33] Indeed, if Suetonius is to be preferred to Dio, the culmination of a regular triumph, sacrifice to Jupiter on the Capitol, was simply omitted; and even if we accept Dio's version, Apollo replaces Jupiter as the eventual goal of the parade.[34] This was not a triumph.

In fact, it was ostentatiously not a triumph. The route of the parade, whether or not it included the Capitol, not only deviates from the norm, it looks to be a deliberate reversal. A triumph always started from the Circus Flaminius to the northeast and proceeded in a *counter-clockwise* direction around the Palatine, that is, through the Velabrum, the Circus Maximus, and the Forum Romanum, on its way to the Capitol. Nero's parade began at the Porta Capena to the southeast and proceeded *clockwise* around the Palatine through the Circus Maximus, the Velabrum, and the Forum, and then presumably up the Clivus Palatinus to the Palatine (after possibly deviating to the Capitol)—and he even continued on, back to the Circus Maximus. Not only was this not a triumph, it looks like a deliberate anti-triumph.

Triumph or not, there could be no doubt about the Greek nature of the occasion. As several have observed, it was in fact a glorious *eiselasis,* the entry into his native city of a *hieronikes,* the victor in one of the great sacred games of old Greece (Suetonius makes the comparison explicit); elements of this were the festive dismantling of part of the city wall, the chariot with four white horses (again), the Greek *chlamys,* the crown of Pythian laurel and the crown of Olympic olive, the dedication of the crowns, and especially the chants of victory, which precisely reflect the praise accorded to real champions in the sacred games.[35] Moreover, Suetonius tells us that, among other things, the emperor was showered with *lemniscos* along his route. *Lemnisci,* the latinized version of Greek *lemniskoi,* were ribbons that were attached to and hung down from honorific garlands or crowns as a sign of exceptional honor. Thus, when Flamininus, Nero's predecessor in the liberation of Greece, proclaimed the freedom of the Greek states at the Isthmian Games of 196 BC, he was almost killed when the crowds rushed to shake his hand and to throw on him crowns and ribbons, *coronas lemniscosque.*[36] The people of Rome were now playing their part.

Here the matter of the entries into different cities should be emphasized. Why four of them, each of which entailed the dismantling of some walls?[37] The reason for Naples we know because, as Suetonius reports, that was where "he had made his debut as an artist." Antium we might presume was chosen because that was where Nero was born, and Rome was likewise his hometown. But why Alba? It has been suggested that he had his favorite imperial residence there, but in fact this is the only time he showed any interest in the place; his suburban villas at Antium and Sublaqueum were the homes on which he lavished attention, and his presence at them is well attested. It has also been suggested that there may be some reference here to the private triumph *in monte Albano,* but the site of the cult of Jupiter Latialis on the Alban Mount is a few miles away from the villa, and Suetonius uses the word "Albanum" with precision: this was the standard way to refer to a villa, in this case to the imperial villa at Alba, inherited from Augustus.[38] The ancient city of Alba Longa had in fact disappeared long ago, and the *ager Albanus* was the scene of the Roman *villeggiatura,* Domitian's later grand villa rising on the site of Alba itself. The location of Nero's villa is uncertain—there were several imperial properties in the area—but the important point is the absence of Alba Longa. By tearing down some of his villa's wall and entering through the gap, Nero was coming as close as he could to an eiselastic entry into Alba itself. The reason then becomes clear: it was common knowledge that the Iulii Caesares were natives of Alba Longa, descended from Aeneas and the old royal house of Alba, and Nero was their heir, through Agrippina and Augustus. Thus, in his progress to Rome he moved from the city where he had been born as an artist to the city where he had actually been born, then to the city of his ancestors, finally to the city where he lived and ruled: Nero played the homecoming of the victor in the sacred games to the hilt.

In its fourth and last version, at Rome, the manner in which Nero blended Roman triumph with Greek *eiselasis* was brilliantly clever. The standard triumphal *tituli* now recorded details of artistic, not military, victories. The triumphal robe merged the garb of Roman general and Greek artist, the laurel crown of the general became the olive crown of the Olympic victor, but both victor and general carried laurel. The role of the slave in the triumphator's chariot was played by a defeated competitor; the claque of Augustiani played the triumphant soldiers; Palatine Apollo and Sol of the Circus replaced Capitoline Jupiter as the goal of the parade. In fact, this merging of Greek and Roman was not entirely new, since there are signs that, even before Nero, Romans might view the eiselastic entry in triumphal terms, and Greeks the triumph in eiselastic terms. By blending the two Nero was putting into resplendent practice a Graeco-Roman rapprochement. It was, as his best biographer has concluded, "the triumph of an artist."[39]

Yet, as with the Tiridates affair, it is the spectacle that makes something unique of this artistic triumph. Our sources are by no means as forthcoming about this occasion,[40] but there is one clear hint of what Nero had in mind in an innocuous passage in Suetonius: "All along the route beasts were sacrificed, the streets were sprinkled from time to time with saffron perfume, while birds, ribbons, and sweetmeats were showered upon him."[41] Sacrificial victims aside, none of this has anything to do with a Roman triumph. At Nero's parade the ribbons, the *lemnisci*, are clearly meant to honor his athletic and artistic victories, appropriate pendants to the many crowns he brought back with him. But why birds *(aves)* and sweets *(bellaria)*? Indeed, why is anything thrown upon the passing emperor? These favors are surely meant to recall the *sparsiones*, the well-attested scattering of all manner of gifts to the crowd by the emperor at his games. As it happens, Nero's presents to his people at the Ludi Maximi of 59 had included food and a thousand birds of all kinds every day, while at games given during a later Saturnalia, among many different and exotic gifts, Domitian is recorded as distributing sweets, *bellaria*, and birds of every kind.[42]

With the imperial games in mind, the setting becomes all-important— the fragrant streets through which the parade passes. *Sparso per vias identidem croco:* the streets were constantly sprinkled with saffron. The perfumed juice of the crocus or saffron plant was used publicly for one purpose and one purpose only at Rome: it was sprayed to refresh both the stage and the audience in theaters.[43] Taken in conjunction with the showering of gifts, this should suggest that the imperial artist was making explicit the implicit theatricality of the parade. In the triumph over Tiridates, the Forum had been turned into a stage. Now the very streets of Rome were for a time one vast theater, and Nero was again the star performer.

THE TRIUMPH of late 67 is the last authentically Neronian spectacle on record. If we look forward, there is little left to tell. Tacitus has failed us; Dio is fragmentary; Suetonius is caught up in his tale of the end. The only event of 68 is the revolt of Vindex, a drama not produced by Nero. The story of his last days and death, for all its circumstantial detail, is so weighted with literary flourishes and folkloric motifs, not to mention "Neronian" apothegms, that it is hard to credit beyond the driest of its facts. But if we look backward, we can see how his conception of the triumph fits in with the increasingly audacious self-dramatization of an indefatigable artist and performer who happened also to be emperor of Rome—a man who presented his role in the deaths of his mother and his wife in the most grandiose terms of myth and legend; one who acted in public as Apollo and Sol, as Hercules and the King of Saturnalia, as the heir of both Augustus and Mark Antony; one who proclaimed himself the intimate friend of all the people of Rome, sharing the city as one house with everyone, refounding a new and better city, and inviting everyone in that city to share in his fabulously artificial new palace; and one who paraded in an ever more resplendent aura of most unwarlike military glory. The triumph of 67 was not a real Roman triumph, nor was it a parody mocking that greatest of Roman honors. It was rather something consciously new and artificial: a performance. It was a gaudy, impressionistic spectacle fusing Greek and Roman culture, the celebration of art and athletics with the celebration of war, and it was a spectacle presented in a city turned for the day into a theater, a performance with thousands of citizen-actors. It was indeed the triumph of an artist.

Epilogue

In the year AD 221 a figure claiming to be Alexander the Great proceeded peacefully down the Danube through the provinces of Moesia and Thrace, accompanied by 400 men in Bacchic dress. When he arrived at Byzantium he crossed by ship to Chalcedon on the Asian shore of the Bosporus, performed certain nocturnal rituals there, buried a wooden horse—and disappeared. The narrative of Cassius Dio, who was a contemporary, sketches a world in a trance.[1] Alexander and his entourage were actually fed and lodged at public expense, and no one, Dio tells us—no magistrate, no soldier, no procurator, not even the governors of the provinces—dared to oppose his progress. This was remarkable, as Alexander the Great had been dead for over five hundred years.

Some years ago I was asked to present a seminar on the image of the ideal prince in Late Antiquity, and it was then that I first appreciated the endlessly fascinating, richly complex afterlife of Alexander the Great, throughout antiquity, into the Middle Ages, and even into the modern period, from Britain to India, as each generation and many different nations claimed him and reinterpreted him for their own needs. No other figure from Greek antiquity is remotely like him, repeatedly evoking memories so intense that he might even, sometimes, be recalled to life. Did he, I wondered, have any counterpart in the Roman world? Only one, at first glance a surprise: Nero. Not that he was universally admired in Late Antiquity, but he was the only Roman who, like Alexander, was a living presence for centuries after his death, one whose return was expected with hope or with fear. And in one aspect Nero has surpassed Alexander: of all the non-Christian men and women of classical antiquity, his name surely arouses the widest interest today. Why?

There is no shortage of excellent works on Nero.[2] Readers of the present book will have little idea of the events of Nero's day or the fortunes of the Roman Empire under him; they will have little idea of the variety of literary discourses that evolved to deal with him and the fact of empire, during his lifetime and posthumously; they will have little knowledge of the outrage vented by the aristocracy after his death, none of the attitude of the army which he ignored to his ultimate peril in his life, and none of the day-to-day workings of the empire which were barely affected by the pyrotechnics at Rome. Readers will have learned nothing about the various mechanisms of accommodation to tyranny, nothing about dissidence and dissimulation, nothing about modes of representation. All of this can be found in the best of the ever-flowing stream of modern literature on Nero. Yet good as these works are, they seem little interested in what to me is the fundamental question: why is Nero so fascinating?

Nero has remained notorious for two millennia because of a series of extravagant public gestures, usually outrageous, often repellent, always riveting: murdering the mother with whom he may have slept, killing his pregnant wife in a rage, castrating and marrying a young freedman, mounting a public stage to act a hero driven mad or a woman giving birth, racing a ten-horse chariot at the Olympic Games, fiddling while Rome burned, burning Christians to light up the night, building the vast Golden House, and so forth. My purpose in this book has been restricted: to explain what Nero might have meant by the deeds and misdeeds that have made him so notorious for so long. I have not tried to justify his actions or to rehabilitate his character, and I have not attempted to discern any large program, political or artistic. I have assumed that his actions were rational—that is, he was not crazy—and that much of what he did resonated far more with contemporary social attitudes than our hostile sources would have us believe. The Nero who has emerged in the preceding pages, whatever his many faults as an emperor and a human being may have been, was a man of considerable talent, great ingenuity, and boundless energy. He was an artist who believed in his own abilities and vision, and an aesthete committed to life as a work of art.[3] He was a historian with a keen sense of the sharp reality of the past (real, legendary, mythical) in daily life at Rome, and a public relations man ahead of his time with a shrewd understanding of what the people wanted, often before they knew it themselves. From all of this, I would make two general observations about Nero's relations with posterity: one concerns the author of his reputation, the other its text.

The first springs from the intense theatricality not just of his life but especially of his most notorious actions, the actions that have defined his reputation. So much has been written, not least in this book, about the transgression of the boundary between actor and audience, between life and art, that it has become almost a cliché. What I mean here is something more limited and precise, and it is a theme that has arisen repeatedly in each chapter. It is the conviction that for most of Nero's actions, even the most notorious, from the framing of debate over the death of his mother to the construction of the Golden House, we can find a purpose which may have nothing to do with the motives ascribed to him. However monstrous or bizarre or even irrational his behavior might appear, there was a purpose to it. He constantly calculated the effects of his actions on an audience. If the melodramatic highlights of his life have fascinated posterity, however grimly, however distorted by tradition, it is because Nero himself was the original dramaturge.

The second observation concerns the omnipresence of myth. It is no accident that Greek and occasionally Roman mythology and legend have recurred so frequently in the preceding pages. Anyone with a passing knowledge of Roman life will appreciate the ubiquity of myth, in art and literature, in public places and private homes, on stage and in paintings and sculpture, on the earthenware pots in your house and in the graffiti on your wall and on the coins in your marketplace, in the names you gave to your children and in the tales told them by old wives. So common was the vocabulary of myth in daily life, high and low, that it was one of the hardest currencies in public debate: it provided simple, universal codes which everyone could comprehend. Nero was neither the first nor the last Roman dynast to realize this, but he probably went further than any other to stage his deeds in mythological costume or in a setting derived from myth. It justified him, it raised him above normal human constraints, and it struck a deep chord in its audience, one that has echoed down through the centuries.

"He had a longing," we are told, "for immortality and undying fame."[4] He succeeded, though not quite in the manner he intended, as he was transformed from the hero of his own story into the monster of history. Our image of Nero was reworked for eternity by hostile sources and by the popular imagination, but they did not create it. It remains so vivid because it was created by an artist.

Note on Sources

Our three major extant sources for the life and reign of Nero are the biographer Suetonius and the historians Tacitus and Cassius Dio. They and their works are discussed in Chapter 2, but readers interested in pursuing them may find the following remarks useful.

Suetonius: References in this book are to the standard modern text divisions in Suetonius' *Life of Nero (Nero)*, for example, Suetonius 35. 1. Other lives by him are referred to in full, for example, Suetonius *Augustus* 35. 1. Translations are those of Joseph Gavorse in Suetonius, *The Lives of the Twelve Caesars* (New York: Modern Library, 1931).

Tacitus: References are to the books and the standard modern text divisions and sections of Tacitus' *Annals (Annales)*, for example, Tacitus 15. 3. 2. Other works by him are referred to in full, for example, Tacitus *Historiae* 1.6.3. Translations are those of Alfred John Church and William Jackson Brodribb in *The Complete Works of Tacitus* (New York: Modern Library, 1942).

Cassius Dio: As explained in more detail in Chapter 2, the text of Dio's Histories for the Neronian years is lost. What we call "Dio" in fact is mostly represented by two Byzantine epitomes compiled centuries after his death. The ordering and numbering of the fragments recovered from these epitomators may cause mild confusion. The standard edition of Dio is that of U. Boissevain, published by Teubner in Leipzig, 1895–1901. In presenting the small fragments and large chunks in epitome that constitute the last quarter of Dio's huge work (Books 61 through 80), Boissevain broke with the traditional presentation of Dio's text, assigning new book divisions and rearranging the order of some chapters and fragments. His principle was simple: he followed one of the Byzantine epitomators, Xiphilinus, in ordering these books to conform with the reigns of the emperors. There is, however, no authority for this. As a result, scholars use Boissevain's text but refer to the old divisions. Unfortunately, the confusion is compounded by the Loeb Classical Library text and translation of Earnest Cary in nine volumes (Cambridge, Mass.: Harvard University Press, 1914–1927), upon which most people rely and which is used here. Cary chose to present his text in Boissevain's book division. Thus, Book 62 in the Loeb edition covers the events of Nero's reign from 58 to 68. The old and still standard book and chapter divisions appear in the margins of the left-hand pages of Cary's text. Loeb "Book 62" in fact contains material from 61. 11. 2 through 63. 21. 3. Readers should ignore the captions at the top of the right-hand pages of the Loeb edition (for example, "Epitome of Book LXII"), since all references in the present book will be to the old book and chapter divisions.

Bibliography

This list does not pretend to be a general bibliography for Nero's life and times. It does include most of the books and articles that I have found useful in exploring the themes of this book. Abbreviations, where not explained, are those used by the annual bibliography of classical studies, *L'Année Philologique.*

Adams, J. N., *The Latin Sexual Vocabulary* (Baltimore, 1982).

———— "Words for 'Prostitute' in Latin," *RhM* 126 (1983): 321–358.

Ahl, F. M., "Lucan's *De Incendio Urbis, Epistulae ex Campania* and Nero's Ban," *TAPA* 102 (1971): 1–27.

———— *Lucan: An Introduction* (Ithaca, N.Y., 1976).

Aiardi, A., "Sulla pretesa iniziazione di Nerone ai misteri di Mithra," *AIV* 134 (1975–1976): 225–236.

———— "Per un'interpretazione della Domus Aurea," *PP* 33 (1978): 90–103.

———— "Interessi neroniani in Oriente e in Africa. L'idea di Alessandro Magno," *AIV* 138 (1979–1980): 563–572.

Alföldi, A., "Die Ausgestaltung des monarchischen Zeremoniells am römischen Kaiserhofe," *RM* 49 (1934): 1–118.

———— "Insignien und Tracht der römischen Kaiser," *RM* 50 (1935): 1–171. [Alföldi 1934 and 1935 were republished together as *Die monarchische Representation im römischen Kaiserreiche* (Darmstadt, 1970).]

———— "Gewaltherrscher und Theaterkönig. Die Auseinandersetzung einer attischen Ideenprägung mit persischen Repräsentationsformen im politischen Denken und in der Kunst bis zur Schwelle des Mittelalters," in K. Weitzmann, ed., *Late Classical and Medieval Studies in Honor of Albert Mathias Friend, Jr.* (Princeton, 1955), 15–55.

———— *Die zwei Lorbeerbäume des Augustus* (Bonn, 1973).

Alföldi, A., and E. Alföldi, *Die Kontorniat-Medaillons*, 1–2 (Berlin, 1976, 1990).

Allen, W., "Nero's Eccentricities before the Fire (Tac. Ann. xv, 37)," *Numen* 9 (1962): 99–109.

Allison, P., "Nero and the Development of the Insula in Roman Architecture," *Architectural Association Quarterly* 13 (1981): 11–18.

Amandry, M., *Le monnayage des duovirs Corinthiens* (Paris, 1988).

Ameling, W., "Tyrannen und schwangeren Frauen," *Historia* 35 (1986): 507–508.

Arciprete, G., "Macchina o Macellum Augusti? Considerazione sul dupondio neroniano," *Bollettino di Archeologia* 16–18 (1992): 279–285.

Auhagen, A., "Nero—ein 'Phaethon' in Rom? Eine politische Deutung des Apennin-Exkurses in Lukans *Bellum Civile* (2, 396–438)," in T. Baier and F. Schimann, eds., *Fabrica. Studien zur antiken Literatur und ihrer Rezeption* (Stuttgart, Leipzig, 1997), 91–102.

Baldwin, B., "Petronius and the Fire of Rome," *Maia* 28 (1976): 35–36, = *Studies on Greek and Roman History and Literature* (Amsterdam, 1985), 147–148.

———— "Nero and His Mother's Corpse," *Mn* 32 (1979): 380–381, = *Studies,* 280–281.

Balensiefen, L., "Überlegungen zu Aufbau und Lage der Danaidenhalle auf dem Palatin," *RM* 102 (1995): 189–209.

———— "The Greek-Egyptian Progeny of Io: Augustus' Mythological Propaganda," in N. Bonacasa, M. C. Naro, E. C. Portale, and A. Tullio, eds., *L'Egitto in Italia dall'antichità al medioevo* (Rome, 1998), 23–32.

Ball, L. F., "A Reappraisal of Nero's *Domus Aurea,*" *JRA,* Supplementary Series 11, *Rome Papers* (1994): 182–254.

Balland, A., "*Nova urbs* et 'neapolis.' Remarques sur les projets urbanistiques de Néron," *MEFR* 77 (1965): 349–393.

Bardon, H., "Les poésies de Néron," *REL* 14 (1936): 337–349.

———— *Les empereurs et les lettres latines d'Auguste à Hadrien*² (Paris, 1968).

Barrett, A. A., *Agrippina: Sex, Power, and Politics in the Early Empire* (New Haven, London, 1996).

Barrett, D. S., "Nero in Jewish Tradition," *Prudentia* 8 (1976): 37–39.

Bartsch, S., *Actors in the Audience: Theatricality and Doublespeak from Nero to Hadrian* (Cambridge, Mass., 1994).

Bastet, F. L., "Nero und die Patera von Aquileia," *Babesch* 44 (1969): 143–161.

———— "Domus Transitoria, I," *Babesch* 46 (1971): 144–172.

———— "Domus Transitoria, II," *Babesch* 47 (1972): 61–87.

Bastomsky, S. J., "The Emperor Nero in Talmudic Legend," *Jewish Quarterly Review* 59 (1969): 320–325.

Baudot, A., *Musiciens romains de l'antiquité* (Montreal, 1973).

Baudy, G. A., *Die Brände Roms. Ein apokalyptisches Motiv in der antiken Historiographie* (Hildesheim, Zürich, New York, 1991).

Bauer, R., "Nero de inferno levatus," *Euphorion* 66 (1972): 238–257.

Beacham, R. C., *The Roman Theatre and Its Audience* (London, 1991).

Beagon, M., *Roman Nature: The Thought of Pliny the Elder* (Oxford, 1992).

Beaujeu, J., *L'incendie de Rome en 64 et les Chrétiens* (*Coll. Latomus* 49, Brussels, 1960), = *Latomus* 19 (1960): 65–80, 291–311.

Bélis, A., "Néron musicien," *CRAI* 1989, 747–763.

Bellen, H., *Die germanische Leibwache der römischen Kaiser des julisch-claudischen Hauses* (Mainz, 1981).

Bercé, Y.-M., *Le roi caché. Sauveurs et imposteurs. Mythes politiques populaires dans l'Europe moderne* (Paris, 1990).

Bergmann, M., "Der Koloss Neros, die Domus Aurea und der Mentalitätswandel im Rom der frühen Kaiserzeit," *Trierer Winckelmannsprogramme* 13 (1993): 3–37.

———— *Die Strahlen der Herrscher. Theomorphes Herrscherbild und politische Symbolik im Hellenismus und in der römischen Kaiserzeit* (Mainz, 1998).

Bergmann, M., and P. Zanker, "*Damnatio memoriae.* Umgearbeitete Nero- und Domitiansporträts. Zur Ikonographie der flavischen Kaiser und des Nerva," *JDAI* 96 (1981): 317–412.

Besombes, P.-A., "Les miroirs de Néron," *RN* 153 (1998): 119–140.

Bessone, L., "Pitagora e Sporo, non dorifori," *GFF* 2 (1979): 105–114.

———— "Nerone nel tardo antico," *AFLM* 21 (1988): 51–61.

Bianchi, L., "*Palatiolum* e *palatium Neronis:* topographia antica del Monte di Santo Spirito in Roma," *BCAR* 95, 2 (1993): 25–46.

———— "L'estremità settentrionale del Gianicolo. Questioni di topografia antica e medioevale," in E. M. Steinby, ed., *Ianiculum-Gianicolo. Storia, topografia, monumenti, leggende dall'antichità al rinascimento* (*Acta Instituti Romani Finlandiae*, vol. XVI, Rome, 1996), 29–51.

Bizarri Vivarelli, D., "Un ninfeo sotto il parco di Traiano," *MEFR* 88 (1978): 719–757.

Blaison, M., "Suétone et l'*ekphrasis* de la *Domus Aurea* (Suét., *Ner.* 31)," *Latomus* 57 (1998): 617–624.

Blake, M. E., *Roman Construction in Italy from Tiberius through the Flavians* (Washington, 1959).

Bodinger, M., "Le mythe de Néron, de l'Apocalypse de Saint Jean au Talmud," *Revue de l'Histoire des Religions* 206 (1989): 21–40.

Boethius, A., "The Neronian 'nova urbs,'" *Corolla archeologica principi hereditario regni Sueciae Gustavo Adolpho dedicata* (Rome, 1932), 84–97.

———— "*Et crescunt media pegmata celsa via* (Martial's *De spectaculis* 2,2)," *Eranos* 50 (1952): 129–137.

———— *The Golden House of Nero: Some Aspects of Roman Architecture* (Ann Arbor, 1960).

Bollinger, T., *Theatralis licentia. Die Publikumsdemonstrationen an den öffentlichen Spielen im Rom des früheren Kaiserzeit und ihre Bedeutung im politischen Leben* (Winterthur, 1969).

Bolton, J. D. P. "Was the *Neronia* a Freak Festival?" *CQ* 42 (1948): 82–90.

Bonaria, M., *I mimi Romani* (Rome, 1965).

Boriello, M., and A. D'Ambrosio, *Baiae-Misenum (Forma Italiae Regio I*, vol. XIV, Florence, 1979).

Born, H., and K. Stemmer, *Damnatio memoriae. Das Berliner Nero-Porträt* (vol. V, *Sammlung Axel Gutmann,* Berlin, 1996).

Boschung, D., "Die Bildnistypen der iulisch-claudischen Kaiserfamilie: ein kritischer Forschungsbericht," *JRA* 6 (1993): 39–49.

——— *Die Bildnisse des Augustus* (Berlin, 1993).

Boschung, D., and W. Eck, "Ein Bildnis der Mutter Traians? Zum Kolossalkopf der sogenannten Agrippina Minor vom Traiansforum," *AA* 1998, 473–481.

Bousset, W., *Der Antichrist in der Überlieferung des Judentums, des neuen Testaments und der alten Kirche. Ein Beitrag zur Auslegung der Apokalypse* (Göttingen, 1895; repr. Hildesheim, Zürich, New York, 1983).

Boyce, M., and F. Grenet, *A History of Zoroastrianism,* vol. 3, *Zoroastrianism under Macedonian and Roman Rule* (Leiden, 1991).

Braccesi, L., and A. Coppola, "Il matricida (Nerone, Agrippina e l'*imitatio Alexandri*)", *DHA* 23 (1997): 189–194.

Bradley, K. R., "The Chronology of Nero's Visit to Greece A.D. 66/67," *Latomus* 37 (1978): 61–72.

——— *Suetonius' Life of Nero: An Historical Commentary* (Brussels, 1978).

——— "Nero's Retinue in Greece, A.D. 66/67," *ICS* 4 (1979): 152–157.

Brenk, F. E., "From rex to rana: Plutarch's Treatment of Nero," *Il protagonismo nella storiografia classica (Pubblicazioni dell'Istituto di Filologia Classica e Medievale dell'Università di Genova* 108, 1987), 121–142.

Brind'Amour, P., "L'horoscope de l'avènement de Néron," *CEA* 25 (1991): 145–151.

Bruun, C., "The Name and Possessions of Nero's Freedman Phaon," *Arctos* 23 (1989): 41–53.

Bryson, N., "Xenia," in *Looking at the Overlooked: Four Essays on Still Life Painting* (Cambridge, Mass., 1990), 16–59.

Buecheler, F., "Νεόψηφον," *RhM* 61 (1906): 307–308.

Burke, P., *The Historical Anthropology of Early Modern Italy: Essays on Perception and Communication* (Cambridge, 1987).

——— *The Fabrication of Louis XIV* (New Haven, 1992).

Cameron, A., *Circus Factions: Blues and Greens at Rome and Byzantium* (Oxford, 1976).

Campanile, D., "*Praecipua cenationum rotunda,*" *Athenaeum* 78 (1990): 186–191.

Campanile, M. D., "L'iscrizione neroniana sulla libertà ai Greci," *Studi Ellenistici* 3 (1990): 191–224.

Carafa, P., *Il Comizio di Roma dalle origini all'età di Augusto* (*BCAR Supplemento* 5, Rome, 1998).

Carandini, A., *Schiavi in Italia. Gli instrumenti pensanti dei Romani fra tarda Repubblica e medio Impero* (Rome, 1988).

———— "Il giardino Romano nell'età tardo repubblicana e Giulio-Claudia," in Morganti 1990, 9–15.

Carcopino, J., "Un procurateur méconnu de Néron," *BSNAF* 1960, 150–158.

Carettoni, G. F., "Costruzioni sotto l'angolo sud-occidentale della Domus Flavia," *NdS* 1949, 48–79.

Carroll, K. K., *The Parthenon Inscription* (Durham, N.C., 1982).

Castagnoli, F. "Note sulla topografia del Palatino e del Foro Romano," *Arch. Clas.* 16 (1964): 173–199.

Cavallaro, M. A., *Spese e spettacoli. Aspetti economici-strutturale degli spettacoli nella Roma giulio-claudia* (Bonn, 1984).

Ceauçescu, P., "ALTERA ROMA—Histoire d'une folie politique," *Historia* 25 (1976): 79–108.

Cesaretti, M. P., *Nerone e l'Egitto: messaggio politico e continuità culturale* (Bologna, 1989).

Champlin, E., "God and Man in the Golden House," in Cima and La Rocca 1998, 333–344.

Charles, R. H., "The Antichrist, Beliar, and Neronic Myths, and Their Ultimate Fusion in Early Christian Literature," in *A Critical and Exegetical Commentary on the Revelation of St. John* (London, 1920), II, 76–87.

Charlesworth, J. H., *The Old Testament Pseudepigrapha,* 1–2 (Garden City, N.Y., 1983–1985).

Charlesworth, M. P., "Nero: Some Aspects," *JRS* 40 (1950): 69–76.

Chevallier, R., "La survie de Néron dans la toponymie et la légende en Italie et en France," *Neronia V* (1999): 339–358.

Chilver, G. E. F., *A Historical Commentary on Tacitus' Histories I and II* (Oxford, 1979).

Cima, M., and E. La Rocca, eds., *Horti Romani* (*BCAR Supplemento* 6, Rome, 1998).

Cizek, E., *L'époque de Néron et ses controverses idéologiques* (Leiden, 1972).

———— *Néron* (Paris, 1982).

———— "L'expérience néronienne: réforme ou révolution," *REA* 84 (1982): 105–115.

———— "La Nova Urbs e la riforma assiologica neroniana," *Neronia III:* 31–39.

———— "L'idéologie antonienne et Néron," in *Marc Antoine, son idéologie et sa descendance* (Lyon, 1993), 107–126.

Clauss, M., *The Roman Cult of Mithras: The God and His Mysteries* (Edinburgh, 2000).

Clay, C. L., "Die Münzprägung des Kaisers Nero in Rom und Lugdunum. Teil 1: Die Edelmetellprägung der Jahre 54 bis 64 n. Chr.," *NZ* 96 (1982): 7–52.

Coarelli, F., "La Porta Trionfale e la Via dei Trionfi," *DdA* 2 (1968): 55–103.

———— *Il Foro Romano,* I: *Periodo arcaico* (Rome, 1983).

———— *Il Foro Romano,* II: *Periodo repubblicano e augusteo* (Rome, 1985).

———— *Il Foro Boario: dalle origini alla fine della Repubblica* (Rome, 1988).

———— "Aedes Fortis Fortunae, Naumachia Augusti, Castra Ravennatium: La Via Campana Portuensis e alcuni edifici adiacenti nella pianta marmorea severiana," *Ostraka* 1 (1992): 39–54.

———— *Il Campo Marzio: dalle origini alle fine della Repubblica* (Rome, 1997).

Cohen, N. G., "Rabbi Meir, a Descendant of Anatolian Proselytes," *JJS* 23 (1972): 51–59.

Cohn, N., *The Pursuit of the Millennium: Revolutionary Millenarians and Mystical Anarchists of the Middle Ages*[2] (New York, 1970).

Coleman, K. M., "Fatal Charades: Roman Executions Staged as Mythological Enactments," *JRS* 80 (1990): 44–73.

———— "Launching into History: Aquatic Displays in the Early Empire," *JRS* 83 (1993): 48–74.

———— "Ptolemy Philadelphus and the Roman Amphitheater," in Slater 1996, 49–68.

Colin, J. "Juvénal, les baladins et les rétiaires d'après le manuscrit d'Oxford," *Atti Accad. Scienz. Torino, Classe Sci. Mor.* 87 (1952/53): 315–386.

———— "Juvénal et le mariage mystique de Gracchus," *Atti Accad. Scienz. Torino, Classe Sci. Mor.* 90 (1955/56): 114–216.

Colini, A. M. *Storia e topografia del Celio nell'Antichità* (*Atti della Pontificia Accademia Romana d'Archeologia,* ser. 3, *Memorie,* vol. VII, Rome, 1944).

———— "La villa di Faonte," *Capitolium* 33 (1958): 3, 3–5.

———— "La tomba di Nerone," *Colloqui del Sodalizio tra Studiosi dell'Arte* 5 (1975–1976): 35–40.

Colini, A. M., and L. Cozza, *Ludus Magnus* (Rome, 1963).

Constans, L. A., "Les jardins d'Epaphrodite," *MEFR* 34 (1914): 383–387.

Correra, L., "Graffiti di Roma," *BCAR* 22 (1894): 89–100.

Courtney, E., *The Fragmentary Latin Poets* (Oxford, 1993).

Cramer, F. H., *Astrology in Roman Law and Politics* (Philadelphia, 1954).

Crawford, J. S., "A Portrait of Alexander the Great at the University of Delaware," *AJA* 83 (1979): 477–481.

Crescenzi, L., S. Gizzi, and P. Vigilante, *Anzio. Villa di Nerone. Restauri 1989–1992* (Rome, 1992).

Cresci Marrone, G., "Alessandro in età neroniana. Victor o praedo?," *AIV* 142
 (1983–1984): 75–93.

Crowther, N. B., "Slaves and Greek Athletics," *QUCC* 40 (1992): 35–42.

Crum, R. H., "Petronius and the Emperors," *CW* 45 (1951/52): 161–167, 197–201.

Cumont, F., "L'iniziazione di Nerone da parte di Tiridate d'Armenia," *RFIC* 11
 (1933): 145–154.

Dacos, N., "Fabullus et l'autre peintre de la Domus Aurea," *DdA* 2 (1968): 210–
 226.

Dahmen, K., "Ein Loblied auf den schönen Kaiser. Zur möglichen Deutung der
 mit Nero Münzen verzierten römischen Dosenspiegel," *AA* 1998, 319–345.

D'Arms, J. H., *Romans on the Bay of Naples* (Cambridge, Mass., 1970).

Darwall-Smith, R. H., *Emperors and Architecture: A Study of Flavian Rome*
 (Brussels, 1996).

Daugherty, G. N., "The *cohortes vigilum* and the Great Fire of 64 AD," *CJ* 87
 (1991/92): 229–240.

Davidson, H. R. E. "Folklore and History," in *Patterns of Folklore* (Ipswich,
 1978), 1–20, = *Folklore* 85 (1974): 73–92.

Dawson, A., "Whatever Happened to Lady Agrippina?" *CJ* 64 (1968/69): 253–
 267.

de Caro, S. "The Sculptures of the Villa of Poppaea at Oplontis: A Preliminary
 Report," in E. B. MacDougall, ed., *Ancient Roman Villa Gardens*
 (Dumbarton Oaks Colloquium on the History of Landscape Architecture
 10, Washington, 1987), 77–133.

de Fine Licht, K., *Untersuchungen an den Trajansthermen zu Rom 2, Sette Sale*
 (*Analecta Romana Instituti Danici,* Suppl. 19, Rome, 1990).

de Vos, M., "Nerone, Seneca, Fabullo et la Domus Transitorio al Palatino," in
 Morganti 1990, 167–186.

Delcourt, M., *Oedipe ou la légende du conquérant* (Liège, 1944; repr. Paris, 1981).

—— *Oreste et Alcméon. Étude sur la projection légendaire du matricide en Grèce*
 (Paris, 1959).

Della Corte, M., *Case ed abitanti di Pompeii*³ (Naples, 1965).

Dewar, M., "Nero and the Disappearing Tigris," *CQ* 41 (1991): 269–272.

di Lorenzo, E., "A proposito dell'espressione neroniana 'qualis artifex pereo'
 (Suet. *Nero* 49)," in I. Gallo, ed., *Studi salernitani in memoria di R.
 Cantarella* (Salerno, 1981), 523–535.

Domus Tiberiana. Nuovi ricerche. Studi di ristauro (Zürich, 1985).

Dowling, L., "Nero and the Aesthetics of Torture," *The Victorian Newsletter* 66
 (Fall 1984): 1–5.

Dubourdieu, A., *Les origines et le développement du culte des Pénates à Rome*
 (Rome, 1989).

Dumortier, J., "Le châtiment de Néron dans le mythe de Thespeios (De sera numinis vindicta 31, 567E-568A)," *Association Guillaume Budé, Actes du VIIIe Congrès* (Paris, 1969), 552–560.

Duncan-Jones, R. P., *Money and Government in the Roman Empire* (Cambridge, 1994).

Dunkle, J. R., "The Greek Tyrant and Roman Political Invective of the Late Republic," *TAPA* 98 (1967): 151–171.

——— "The Rhetorical Tyrant in Roman Historiography: Sallust, Livy and Tacitus," *CW* 65 (1971–1972): 12–20.

Dupont, F., *L'acteur roi, ou le théâtre à Rome* (Paris, 1985).

Duret, L., "Néron-Phaéthon, ou la témérité sublime," *REL* 66 (1988): 139–155.

Dzielska, M., *Apollonius of Tyana in Legend and History* (Rome, 1986).

Eck, W., "Neros Freigelassener Epaphroditus und die Aufdeckung der Pisonischen Verschwörung," *Historia* 25 (1976): 381–384.

——— *Agrippina die Statdgründerin Kölns. Eine Frau in die frühkaiserzeitlichen Politik* (Cologne, 1993).

——— "Kaiserliche Imperatorenakklamation und ornamenta triumphalia," *ZPE* 124 (1999): 223–227.

Edmondson, J. C., "Dynamic Arenas: Gladiatorial Presentations in the City of Rome and the Construction of Roman Society during the Early Empire," in Slater 1996, 69–112.

Edwards, C., *The Politics of Immorality in Ancient Rome* (Cambridge, 1993).

Elsner, J., and J. Masters, eds., *Reflections of Nero: Culture, History and Representation* (London, 1994).

Equini Schneider, E., *La tomba di Nerone sulla via Cassia. Studio sul sarcofago di Publio Vibio Mariano* (Rome, 1984).

Evans, H. B., "Nero's Arcus Caelimontanus," *AJA* 87 (1983): 392–399.

Eyben, E., *Restless Youth in Ancient Rome* (London, 1993).

Fabbrini, L., "Domus Aurea. Il piano superiore del quartiere orientale," *Memorie della Pontificia Accademia Romana di Archeologia* 14 (1982): 5–24.

——— "Domus Aurea: una nuova lettura planimetrica del Palazzo sul Colle Oppio," in K. de Fine Licht, ed., *Città e architettura nella Roma imperiale* (*Anal. Rom. Suppl.* 10, Odense, 1983), 169–185.

——— "I corpi edilizi che condizionarono l'attuazaione del progetto del Palazzo Esquilino di Nerone," *Atti della Pontificia Accademia di Archeologia, Rendiconti* 58 (1985–1986): 129–179.

Fabia, P., "Néron acteur," *Bulletin de la Société des Amis de l'Université de Lyon* 19 (1905): 24–51.

Faraone, C., *Talismans and Trojan Horses: Guardian Statues in Ancient Greek Myth and Ritual* (New York, 1992).

Favro, D., "The Street Triumphant: The Urban Impact of Roman Triumphal

Parades," in Z. Çelik, D. Favro, and R. Ingersoll, eds., *Streets: Critical Perspectives on Public Space* (Berkeley, 1994), 151–164.

Fears, J. R., "The Solar Monarchy of Nero and the Imperial Panegyric of Q. Curtius Rufus," *Historia* 25 (1976): 494–496.

———— *Princeps a diis electus. The Divine Election of the Emperor as a Political Concept at Rome* (Rome, 1977).

Feo, M., "Nerone e il cuculo nella fantasia medioevale (*Babio*, 236)," *ASNP* 1 (1971): 87–107.

Finley, M. I., and H. W. Pleket, *The Olympic Games: the First Thousand Years* (London, 1976).

Firpo, G., "Le tradizioni giudaiche su Nerone e la profezia circa il 'regnum Hierosolymorum,'" in M. Sordi, ed., *La profezia nel mondo antico* (Milan, 1993), 245–259.

Fishwick, D., *The Imperial Cult in the Latin West: Studies in the Ruler Cult of the Western Provinces of the Roman Empire*, 2 (Leiden, 1991).

Fittschen, K., review of H.-G. Niemeyer, *Studien zur statuarischen Darstellung der römischen Kaiser* (Berlin, 1976), *BJ* 170 (1970): 541–552.

Flaccelière, R., "Rome et ses empereurs vus par Plutarque," *AC* 32 (1963): 28–47.

Fletcher, R., *The Quest for El Cid* (New York, 1990).

Frayn, J., *Markets and Fairs in Roman Italy: Their Social and Economic Importance from the Second Century BC to the Third Century AD* (Oxford, 1993).

Frazer, R. M., "Nero the Artist-Criminal," *CJ* 62 (1966/1967): 17–20.

———— "Nero, the Singing Animal," *Arethusa* 4 (1971): 215–218.

Frey, M., *Untersuchungen zur Religion und Religionspolitik des Kaisers Elagabal* (Stuttgart, 1989).

Friedlaender, L., *Darstellungen aus der Sittengeschichte Roms in der Zeit von Augustus bis zum Ausgang der Antonine*[9/10] (Leipzig, 1920–1923); English translation of the 7th edition: *Roman Life and Manners* (London, 1907).

Fuchs, M., "Besser als sein Ruf: Neue Beobachtungen zum Nachleben des Kaisers Nero in Spätantike und Renaissance," *Boreas* 20 (1997): 83–96.

Fuchs, M., P. Liverani, and P. Santoro, *Caere* 2, *Il teatro e il ciclo statuario giulio-claudio* (Rome, 1989).

Gagé, J., *Apollon romain. Essai sur le culte d'Apollon et le développement du "ritus Graecus" à Rome des origines à Auguste* (Paris, 1955).

———— "Commodien et le moment millénariste du IIIe siècle (258–262 ap. J.-C.)," *Revue d'histoire et de philosophie religieuses* 41 (1961): 355–378.

Gallivan, P. A., "Nero's Liberation of Greece," *Hermes* 101 (1973): 230–234.

———— "The False Neros: A Re-examination," *Historia* 22 (1973): 364–365.

Garson, R. W., "The Pseudo-Senecan Octavia: A Plea for Nero?" *Latomus* 34 (1975): 754–756.

Gatti, G. "Studi neroniani II: gli Augustiani," *CRDAC* 8 (1976–1977): 83–121.

———— "Culto imperiale e *inclinatio imperii* in età neroniana," *Neronia III:* 179–
187.

Gavazzi, L., "Alcuni aspetti della *popularitas* di Nerone," *AIV* 134 (1975–1976):
421–437.

Geer, R. M., "The Greek Games at Naples," *TAPA* 66 (1935): 208–221.

Geertz, C., *Negara: The Theatre-State in Nineteenth Century Bali* (Princeton,
1980).

Geffcken, J., "Studien zur älteren Nerosage," *NGG* (1899): 441–462.

Geraci, G., "Suet., *Nero,* 47, 2, e la presunta 'regalità' del governo Romano in
Egitto," *Quaderni Catanesi di Cultura Classica e Medioevale* 2 (1989): 79–
115.

Ghini, G., "Terme Neroniano-Alessandrine," in *Roma. Archeologia nel centro*
(Rome, 1985), 395–399.

———— "Le terme Alessandrine nel Campo Marzio," *Monumenti Antichi* ser.
misc. 3. 4 (1988): 121–177.

Giordani, R., "'. . . *in templum Apollonis . . .'* A proposito di un incerto tempio
d'Apollo in Vaticano menzionato nel *Liber Pontificalis,*" *RAC* 64 (1988):
161–188.

Gizzi, S., "Villa di Nerone ad Anzio: perderla o restaurla?" *BA* 96/97 (1996): 97–
126.

Goldsmith, R. W., "An Estimate of the Size and Structure of the National Product of the Early Roman Empire," *Review of Wealth and Income* 30 (1984):
263–288.

Gonfroy, R., "Homosexualité et idéologie esclaviste chez Cicéron," *DHA* 4
(1978): 219–262.

Gorlin, A. C., "The Domus Aurea, the Golden House of Nero," *The Princeton
Journal* 2 (1985): 6–21.

Graf, A., *Roma nella memoria e nell'immaginazione del Medio Evo,* 1 (Turin,
1882).

Grant, M., *Nero: Emperor in Revolt* (New York, 1970).

Grenade, P., "Un exploit de Néron," *REA* 50 (1948): 272–287.

Griffe, E., "La persécution des chrétiens de Rome en l'an 64," *BLE* 65 (1964): 3–
16.

Griffin, J., "Augustan Poets and the Life of Luxury," in *Latin Poets and Roman
Life* (London, 1985), 1–31 (rev. = *JRS* 66 [1976]).

Griffin, M. T., *Seneca: A Philosopher in Politics* (Oxford, 1976).

———— *Nero: The End of a Dynasty* (London, 1984).

Grimal, P., "Sur deux mots de Néron," *Pallas* 3 (1955): 15–20.

———— "L'éloge de Néron au début de la Pharsale est-il ironique?" *REL* 38
(1960): 296–305 = *Rome. La littérature et l'histoire,* I (Rome, 1986), 125–134.

———— *Les jardins romains²* (Paris, 1969).

———— "Le *De Clementia* et la royauté solaire de Néron," *REL* 49 (1971): 205–217, = *Rome,* 625–630.

Guarducci, M., "I pomi delle Esperidi in un epigramma di Lucillio," *RAL* 24 (1969): 3–8.

Gwyn, W. B., "Cruel Nero: The Concept of the Tyrant and the Image of Nero in Western Political Thought," *History of Political Thought* 12 (1991): 421–455.

Gyles, M. F., "Nero Fiddled While Rome Burned," *CJ* 42 (1946–1947): 211–217.

———— "Nero, qualis artifex?" *CJ* 57 (1961–1962): 193–200.

Habinek, T. N., "Lucius' Rite of Passage," *Materiali e discussioni per l'annalisi dei testi classici* 25 (1990): 49–69.

Halfmann, H., *Itinera principum. Geschichte und Typologie der Kaiserreisen im Römischen Reich* (Stuttgart, 1986).

Halliday, P. J., "Roman Triumphal Painting: Its Function, Development, and Reception," *The Art Bulletin* 79 (1997): 130–147.

Halsberghe, G. H., *The Cult of Sol Invictus* (Leiden, 1972).

Hannestad, N., *Roman Art and Imperial Policy* (Aarhus, 1986).

———— "Nero, or the Potentialities of an Emperor," in N. Bonacusa and G. Rizzo, eds., *Ritratto ufficiale e ritratto privato (Atti della II conferenza internazionale sul ritratto romano,* Rome, 1988), 325–329.

Harris, B. F., "Domitian, the Emperor Cult and *Revelation*," *Prudentia* 11 (1979): 15–25.

Häuber, R. C., "Zur Topographie der Horti Maecenatis und der Horti Lamiani auf dem Esquilin in Rom," *Kölner Jahrbuch für Vor- und Frühgeschichte* 23 (1990): 11–107.

Hays, R. S., "Lucius Annaeus Cornutus' 'Epidrome' (Introduction to the Traditions of Greek Theology): Introduction, Translation and Notes" (Diss., University of Texas at Austin, 1983).

Heaney, S., "The Interesting Case of Nero, Chekhov's Cognac and a Knocker," *Shenandoah* 87.3 (1987): 3–15.

Heinz, K., "Das Bild Kaiser Neros bei Seneca, Tacitus, Sueton und Cassius Dio. Historisch-philologische Synopsis" (Diss., Bern, 1948).

Hemsoll, D., "Reconstructing the Octagonal Dining Room of Nero's Golden House," *Architectural History* 32 (1989): 1–17.

———— "The Architecture of Nero's Golden House," in M. Henig, ed., *Architecture and Architectural Sculpture in the Roman Empire* (Oxford, 1990), 10–38.

Henderson, G., "The Damnation of Nero, and Related Themes," in A. Borg and A. Martindale, eds., *The Vanishing Past: Studies of Medieval Art, Liturgy and Metrology Presented to Christopher Hohler* (BAR internat. ser. III, Oxford, 1981), 39–51.

Herington, C. J., "Octavia Praetexta: A Survey," *CQ* 11 (1961): 18–30.

Hermansen, G., "Nero's Porticus," *GB* 3 (1975): 159–176.

Hickson, F. V., "Augustus *triumphator:* Manipulation of the Triumphal Theme in the Political Program of Augustus," *Latomus* 50 (1991): 124–138.

Hiesinger, U. W., "The Portraits of Nero," *AJA* 79 (1975): 113–124.

Higgins, J. M., "Cena rosaria, cena mitellita: A Note on Suetonius Nero 27, 3," *AJP* 106 (1985): 116–118.

Hild, F. "Eirenupolis in der Kilikia Pedias," in G. Dobesch and G. Rehrenbeck, eds., *Die epigraphisch und altertumskundlich Erforschung Kleinasiens: Hundert Jahre Kleinasiatische Kommission der österreichischen Akademie der Wissenschaften* (Vienna, 1993), 221–225.

Hind, J. G. F., "The Middle Years of Nero's Reign," *Historia* 20 (1970): 488–505.

——— "The Death of Agrippina and the Finale of the 'Oedipus' of Seneca," *AUMLA* 38 (1972).

Hölscher, T., "Denkmäler der Schlacht von Actium. Propaganda und Resonanz," *Klio* 67 (1985): 81–102.

——— "Augustus and Orestes," *Travaux du centre d'archéologie méditerranéene de l'Académie Polonaise des Sciences, Études et Travaux* 15 (1991): 164–168.

——— "Mythen als Exempel der Geschichte," in F. Graf, ed., *Mythos in mythenloser Gesellschaft. Das Paradigma Roms* (Colloquium Rauricum 3, Stuttgart, Leipzig, 1993), 67–87.

Holt, J. C., *Robin Hood* (rev. ed., London, 1989).

Homolle, T., "Le temple de Delphes. Son histoire," *BCH* 20 (1896): 641–654, 677–701, 702–732.

Hopkins, K., *Conquerors and Slaves: Sociological Studies in Roman History,* 1 (Cambridge, 1978).

——— *Death and Renewal: Sociological Studies in Roman History,* 2 (Cambridge, 1983).

Horsfall, N. M., "From History to Legend: M. Manlius and the Geese," in J. N. Bremmer and N. M. Horsfall, *Roman Myth and Historiography* (*BICS* Supplement 52, 1987), 63–75.

——— "Cleaning up Calpurnius," *CR* 43 (1993): 267–270.

——— "Criteria for the Dating of Calpurnius Siculus," *RFIC* 125 (1997): 166–196.

Horváth, I. K., "Perse et Néron," *StudClas* 3 (1961): 337–343.

Howell, P., "The Colossus of Nero," *Ath* 46 (1968): 292–299.

Hughes-Hallett, L., *Cleopatra: Histories, Dreams and Distortions* (New York, 1990).

Humphrey, J. H. *Roman Circuses: Arenas for Chariot Racing* (Berkeley, Los Angeles, 1986).

Huss, W., "Die Propaganda Neros," *AC* 47 (1978): 129–148.

Huttner, U., "Marcus Antonius und Herakles," in C. Schubert and K.

Brodersen, eds., *Rom und die griechische Osten. Festschrift für Hatto H. Schmitt zum 65. Geburtstag* (Stuttgart, 1995), 103–112.

——— "Hercules und Augustus," *Chiron* 27 (1997): 369–391.

Instinsky, H. U., "Kaiser Nero und die Mainzer Jupitersäule," *JRGZ* 6 (1959): 128–141.

Isager, J., *Pliny on Art and Society: The Elder Pliny's Chapters on the History of Art* (London, New York, 1991).

Jakob-Sonnabend, W., *Untersuchungen zum Nero-Bild der Spätantike* (Hildesheim, Zürich, New York, 1990).

Johannowsky, W., "Appunti su alcune infrastrutture dell'annona romana tra Nerone e Adriano," *Boll.Arch.* 4 (1990): 1–13.

Jones, B. W., "C. Vettulenus Civica Cerialis and the False Nero of A.D. 88," *Ath* 61 (1983): 516–521.

Jones, C. P., *Plutarch and Rome* (Oxford, 1971).

——— *The Roman World of Dio Chrysostom* (Cambridge, Mass., 1978).

——— "Greek Drama in the Roman Empire," in R. Scodel, ed., *Theater and Society in the Classical World* (Ann Arbor, 1993), 39–52.

Jucker, H., "Porträtminiaturen von Augustus, Nero, und Trajan," *GNS* 13–14 (1963–1964): 81–92.

——— "Der grosse Pariser Kameo. Eine Huldigung an Agrippina, Claudius und Nero," *JDAI* 91 (1976): 211–250.

——— "Iulisch-Claudische Kaiser- und Prinzenporträts als 'Palimpseste,'" *JDAI* 96 (1981): 236–316.

Kaufmann, M., *Das Sexualleben des Kaisers Nero* (Leipzig, n.d. [c. 1915]).

Kay, N. M., *Martial Book XI: A Commentary* (London, 1985).

Kelly, H. A., "Tragedy and the Performance of Tragedy in Late Roman Antiquity," *Traditio* 35 (1979): 21–44.

Kennell, N. M., "ΝΕΡΩΝ ΠΕΡΙΟΔΟΝΙΚΗΣ," *AJP* 109 (1988): 239–251.

Kierdorf, W., *Sueton: Leben des Claudius und Nero* (Paderborn, Munich, Vienna, Zurich, 1992).

Kiss, Z., "Néron jeune," *Études et Travaux* 10 (1978): 234–250.

——— *Études sur le portrait impérial romain en Egypte* (Warsaw, 1984).

Kleiner, F. S., *The Arch of Nero in Rome: A Study of the Roman Honorary Arch before and under Nero* (Rome, 1985).

Kloft, H., *Liberalitas principis. Herkunft und Bedeutung. Studien zur Prinzipatsideologie* (Cologne, Vienna, 1970).

Koestermann, E., *Cornelius Tacitus: Annalen, III, Buch 11–13* (Heidelberg, 1967).

——— *Cornelius Tacitus: Annalen, IV, Buch 14–16* (Heidelberg, 1968).

Kolendo, J., "Le projet d'expédition de Néron dans le Caucase," *Neronia 1977:* 23–30.

König, I., "Der Titel 'Proconsul' von Augustus bis Traian," *GNS* 21 (1971): 42–54.

Konrad, R., "Kaiser Nero in der Vorstellung des Mittelalters," in *Festiva lanx. Studien zum mittelalterlichen Geistesleben J. Spoerl dargebracht aus Anlass seines 60. Geburtstages,* ed. K. Schnith (Munich, 1966), 1–15.

Korver, J., "Néron et Musonius. À propos du dialogue du Pseudo-Lucian 'Néron, ou sur le percement de l'isthme de Corinthe,'" *Mn* 3 (1950): 319–329.

Kragelund, P., "Vatinius, Nero and Curiatius Maternus," *CQ* 37 (1987): 197–202.

———— "The Prefect's Dilemma and the Date of the *Octavia,*" *CQ* 38 (1988): 492–508.

Krappe, A. H., "La fin d'Agrippine," *REA* 42 (1940): 466–472.

Krause, C., "La Domus Tiberiana e il suo contesto urbano," in Voisin 1987, 781–798.

———— "Wo residierten die Flavier? Überlegungen zur flavischen Bautätigkeit auf dem Palatin," in F. E. Koenig and S. Rebetz, eds., *Arculiana, receuil d'hommages offerts à Hans Bögli* (Avenches, 1995), 459–468.

Kreitzer, L., "Hadrian and the Nero redivivus Myth," *ZNTW* 79 (1988): 92–115.

Kruse, T., "BGU III 981 und der Monat Νερώνειος," *ZPE* 107 (1995): 85–94.

Künzl, E., *Der römische Triumph. Siegesfeiern im antiken Rom* (Munich, 1988).

Lahusen, G., and E. Formigli, "Die römischen Kaiserbildnisse der Biblioteca Vaticana," *MDAI(R)* 100 (1993): 177–184.

Lanciani, R., "Miscellanea Epigrafica," *BCAR* 5 (1877): 161–183.

———— *Pagan and Christian Rome* (Boston, New York, 1893).

———— *Wanderings in the Roman Campagna* (Boston, New York, 1909).

La Rocca, E., *Amazzonomachia. Le sculture frontonali del tempio di Apollo Sosiano* (Rome, 1985).

———— "Il lusso come espressione di potere," in M. Cima and E. La Rocca, *Le tranquille dimore degli dei. La residenza imperiale degli horti Lamiani* (Venice, 1986), 3–35.

———— "'Disiecta membra Neroniana.' L'arco partico di Nerone sul Campidoglio," in H. Froning, T. Hölscher, and H. Mielsch, eds., *Kotinos. Festschrift für Erika Simon* (Mainz, 1992), 400–414.

Lefèvre, E., *Das Bild-Programm des Apollo-Tempels auf dem Palatin* (Xenia 24, Konstanz, 1989).

Lega, C., "Il Colosso di Nerone," *BCAR* 93 (1989/1990): 339–378.

Lemosse, M. "Le couronnement de Tiridate . . . Remarques sur le statut des protectorats romains," *Mélanges G. Gidel* (1960), 455–468 = *Études romanistiques* (Clermont-Ferrand, 1991), 219–232.

Lepore, E., "Per la storia del principato neroniano," *PP* 3 (1948): 81–100.

Lepper, F. A., "Some Reflections on the Quinquennium Neronis," *JRS* 47 (1957): 95–103.

Leppin, H., *Histrionen. Untersuchungen zur sozialen Stellung von*

Buhnenkünstlern im Westen des römischen Reiches zur Zeit der Republik und des Prinzipats (Bonn, 1992).

Lesky, A., "Neroniana," *AIPhO* (*Mélanges Grégoire,* I) 9 (1949): 385–407 = *Gesammelte Schriften* (Bern, 1966), 335–351.

Leuze, O., "Metellus caecatus," *Philologus* 64 (1905): 95–115.

Levi, M. A., "L'idea monarchica fra Alessandro e Nerone," *Neronia 1977*: 31–39.

Levick, B. M., "Nero's Quinquennium," in C. Deroux, ed., *Studies in Latin Literature and Roman History,* 3 (*Collection Latomus* 180, 1983): 211–225.

——— "The *Senatus Consultum* from Larinum," *JRS* 73 (1983): 97–115.

——— *Claudius* (New Haven, London, 1990).

Levy, B., "When Did Nero Liberate Achaea—and Why?" *Achaia und Elis in der Antike* (Athens, 1991), 189–194.

Liebeschuetz, J. H. W. G., *Continuity and Change in Roman Religion* (Oxford, 1979).

LIMC = *Lexicon Iconographicum Mythologiae Classicae* (Zurich, Munich, 1981–).

Linderski, J., "Games in *Patavium*," *Ktema* 17 (1992): 55–76.

Lohmeyer, E., "Antichrist," *RAC* I (1941): 450–455.

Longo, V., "Nerone o Vespasiano? (Anth.Pal. xi, 185)," *Tetraonyma. Miscellanea Graeco-Romana* (*Pubblicazioni dell'Istituto di Filologia Classica di Università di Genova,* 25, Genova, 1966), 175–179.

L'Orange, H. P., "Domus aurea, der Sonnenpalast," *Serta Eitremiana* (*SO Suppl.* 11, 1942), 68–100 = *Likeness and Icon: Selected Studies in Classical and Early Mediaeval Art* (Odense, 1973), 278–297.

——— "Le Néron constitutionnel et le Néron apothéosé," *From the Collections of the Ny Carlsberg Glyptothek* 3 (1942) = *Likeness and Icon,* 247–267.

Lorenz, T., "Römische Prinzen als Allegorien der Jahreszeiten," in T. Lorenz, ed., *Thiasos* (Amsterdam, 1978), 113–134.

LTUR = E. M. Steinby, ed., *Lexicon Topographicum Urbis Romae,* I (Rome, 1993); II (1995); III (1996); IV (1999); V (1999).

Lugli, G., "Saggio sulla topografia dell'antica Antium," *RIA* 7 (1940): 153–188.

McCloskey, P., and E. Phinney, "Ptolemaeus Tyrannus: The Typification of Nero in the Pharsalia," *Hermes* 96 (1968): 80–87.

McDaniel, W. B., "Some Greek, Roman and English Tityretus," *AJP* 35 (1914): 52–66.

MacDonald, W. L., *The Architecture of the Roman Empire,* I: *An Introductory Study* (rev. ed., New Haven, 1982).

MacDowall, D. W., "The Numismatic Evidence for the Neronia," *CQ* 8 (1958): 192–194.

——— *The Western Coinages of Nero* (New York, 1979).

McGann, M. J., "The Authenticity of Lucan, fr. 12 (Morel)," *CQ* 7 (1957): 126–128.

McGinn, B., *Antichrist: Two Thousand Years of the Human Fascination with Evil* (San Francisco, 1994).

MacMullen, R., "Roman Attitudes to Greek Love," *Historia* 31 (1982): 484–502 = *Changes in the Roman Empire: Essays in the Ordinary* (Princeton, 1990), 177–189, 344–351.

Maggi, S. "Il ritratto giovanile di Nerone. Un esempio a Mantova," *RdA* 10 (1986): 47–51.

———— "'Palinsesto' Libarnese," *Athenaeum* 79 (1991): 260–264.

Maiuri, A., "Fossa Neronis," *Babesch* 29 (1954): 57–61.

Makin, E., "The Triumphal Route, with Particular Reference to the Flavian Triumph," *JRS* 11 (1921): 25–36.

Malavolta, M., "I Neronia e il lustrum," *MGR* 6 (1978): 395–415.

Manning, C. E., "Acting and Nero's Conception of the Principate," *G&R* 22 (1975): 164–175.

Martin, H. G., "Zur Kultbildgruppe im Mars-Ultor-Tempel," *WZRostock* 37 (1988): 55–64.

Martin, J. P., "Néron et le pouvoir des astres," *Pallas* 30 (1983): 63–74, 137.

Mastino, A., and P. Ruggieri, "*Claudia Augusti liberta Acte,* la liberta amata da Nerone ad Olbia," *Latomus* 54 (1995): 513–544.

Mavrojannis, T., "Apollo Delio, Atene e Augusto," *Ostraka* 4 (1995): 85–102.

Maxfield, V. A., *The Military Decorations of the Roman Army* (London, 1981).

Mayer, R., "Neronian Classicism," *AJP* 103 (1982): 305–318.

———— "What Caused Poppaea's Death?" *Historia* 31 (1982): 248–249.

Megow, W.-R., *Kameen von Augustus bis Alexander Severus* (Berlin, 1987).

———— "Zum Florentiner Tituskameo," *AA* (1993): 401–408.

Meissner, B., "*Meris VI ad ludum Neronianum:* Beobachtungen und Überlegungen zu einer Inschrift des Katasters von Orange," *ZPE* 90 (1992): 167–191.

Meslin, M., *La fête des kalendes de janvier dans l'empire romain. Étude d'un rituel de Nouvel An* (Brussels, 1970).

Meyboom, P. G. P., and E. M. Moormann, "Domus Aurea. Appunti sul padiglione della Domus Aurea neroniana sul Colle Oppio," *Bollettino di Archeologia* 16–18 (1992): 139–145.

Meyer, H., *Prunkkameen und Staatsdenkmäler Römischer Kaiser. Neue Perspektiven zur Kunst der frühen Prinzipatszeit* (Munich, 2000).

Millar, F., *A Study of Cassius Dio* (Oxford, 1964).

Miller, J. F., "*Triumphus in Palatio,*" *AJP* 121 (2000): 409–422.

Momigliano, A., "Literary Chronology of the Neronian Age," *CQ* 38 (1944): 96–100 = *Secondo contributo alla storia degli studi classici* (Rome, 1960), 454–461.

Montevecchi, O., "Nerone e l'Egitto," *Neronia 1974:* 48–58.

Moormann, E. M., "'Vivere come un uomo.' L'uso dello spazio nella *Domus Aurea*," in Cima and La Rocca 1998, 345–361.

———— "Das goldene Haus Neros in Rom: eine orientalische Erfindung?" *Veröff. Joachim Jungius-Ges. Wiss. Hamburg* 87 (1998): 689–701.

Morelli, C., "Nerone poeta e i poeti intorno a Nerone," *Athenaeum* 2 (1914): 117–152.

Morford, M. P. O., "The Distortion of the Domus Aurea Tradition," *Eranos* 66 (1968): 158–179.

———— "Nero's Patronage and Participation in Literature and the Arts," *ANRW* II. 32. 3 (Berlin, New York, 1985), 2003–2031.

Morgan, M. G., "The Three Minor Pretenders in Tacitus, *Histories* II," *Latomus* 52 (1993): 769–796.

Morganti, G., ed., *Gli Orti Farnesiani sul Palatino* (Rome, 1990).

Morricone, M. L., "Edificio sotto il Tempio di Venere e Roma," *Studi per Laura Breglia,* III: *Archeologia e storia* (*Bollettino di Numismatica,* suppl. no. 4, Rome, 1987), 69–82.

Most, G. W., "Cornutus and Stoic Allegoresis: A Preliminary Report," *ANRW* II. 36. 3 (Berlin, New York, 1989), 2014–2065.

Mourgues, J.-L., "Les augustians et l'expérience théâtrale néronienne," *REL* 66 (1988): 156–181.

———— "Néron et les monarchies hellénistiques: le cas des Augustians," *Neronia IV* (1990): 196–210.

Murison, C. L., *Galba, Otho and Vitellius: Careers and Controversies* (Hildesheim, Zurich, New York, 1993).

Murray, O., "The Quinquennium Neronis and the Stoics," *Historia* 14 (1965): 41–61.

Néraudau, J.-P., "La parole et la voix," *Neronia III:* 101–124.

———— "Néron et le nouveau chant de Troie," *ANRW* II. 32. 3 (1985): 2032–2045.

Neronia 1974. Relazioni presentate al I Convegno di Studi S.I.E.N. (Soc. internat. d'études néroniennes) = *PdP* 30 (1975): 5–101.

Neronia 1977. Actes du 2e colloque de la Société internationale d'études néroniennes (Clermont-Ferrand, 27–28 mai 1977), ed. J. M. Croisille and P. M. Fauchère (Clermont-Ferrand, 1982).

Neronia III. Actes du IIIe colloque international de la Société internationale d'études néroniennes (Varenna, juin 1982) = *Atti Ce.R.D.A.C* 12 (1982–1983).

Neronia IV. Alejandro Magno, modelo de los emperadores romanos. Actes du IVe colloque internationale de la SIEN, ed. J. M. Croisille (*Collection Latomus,* vol. 209, Brussels, 1990).

Neronia V. Néron: histoire et légende. Actes du Ve colloque international (Clermont-Ferrand et St. Étienne, 2–6 novembre 1994), ed. J. M. Croisille, R. Martin, and Y. Perrin (*Collection Latomus*, vol. 247, Brussels, 1999).

Neudecker, R., *Die Skulpturenaustattung römischer Villen in Italien* (Mainz, 1988).

Neverov, O., *Antique Cameos in the Hermitage Collection* (Leningrad, 1971).

——— [Névéroff] "À propos de l'iconographie julio-claudienne. Les portraits de Néron à l'Hermitage," *GNS* 24 (1974): 79–87.

——— *Antique Intaglios in the Hermitage Collection* (Leningrad, 1976).

——— "Nero-Helios," in M. Henig and A. King, eds., *Pagan Gods and Shrines of the Roman Empire* (Oxford, 1986), 189–194.

Newbold, R. F., "Some Social and Economic Consequences of the A.D. 64 Fire at Rome," *Latomus* 33 (1974): 858–869.

Nicol, D. M., *The Immortal Emperor: The Life and Legend of Constantine Palaiologos, Last Emperor of the Romans* (Cambridge, 1992).

Nielsen, I., *Thermae et Balnea: The Architectural and Cultural History of Roman Public Baths* (Aarhus, 1990).

Nisbet, R. G. M., "The Dating of Seneca's Tragedies, with Special Reference to *Thyestes*," *Papers of the Leeds International Latin Seminar* 6 (1990): 95–114.

Ogilvie, R. M., *A Commentary on Livy Books 1–5* (Oxford, 1965).

Ostrow, S. E., "The Topography of Puteoli and Baiae on the Eight Glass Flasks," *Puteoli* 3 (1979): 77–140.

Palmer, R. E. A., "Jupiter Blaze, Gods of the Hills, and the Roman Topography of *CIL* VI 377," *AJA* 80 (1976): 43–56.

——— "Severan Ruler-Cult and the Moon in the City of Rome," *ANRW* II. 16. 2 (1978): 1088–1120.

Palombi, D., "Gli *horrea* della Via Sacra: dagli appunti di G. Boni ad un ipotese su Nerone," *DdA* 8 (1990): 53–72.

Panella, C., "La valle del Colosseo nell'Antichità," *Boll.Arch.* 1–2 (1990): 34–88.

——— ed., *Meta Sudans*, I. *Un area sacra in Palatio e la valle del Colosseo prima e dopo Nerone* (Rome, 1996).

Paratore, E., "Nerone (Nel xix centenario della morte)," *StudRom* 17 (1969): 269–287.

Paribeni, R., "Nuovi monumenti del Museo Nazionale Romano," *Bollettino d'Arte* 8 (1914): 278–287.

Parke, H. W., and D. E. W. Wormell, *The Delphic Oracle* (Oxford, 1956).

Pascal, C., *Nerone nella storia aneddotica e nella leggenda* (Milan, 1923).

Pavan, M., "Nerone e la libertà dei Greci," *PP* 39 (1984): 342–361, ?=? *Neronia III*: 149–165.

Pavolini, C., *Caput Africae*, I. *Indagini archeologiche a Piazza Celimontana (1984–1988). La storia, lo scavo, l'ambiente* (Rome, 1994).

Perrie, M., *The Image of Ivan the Terrible in Russian Folklore* (Cambridge, 1987).

Perrin, Y., "Êtres mythiques, êtres fantastiques et grotesques de la Domus aurea de Néron," *DHA* 8 (1982): 303–338.

———— "Néron et l'Égypte: une stèle de Coptos montrant Néron devant Min et Osiris (Musée de Lyon)," *REA* 84 (1982): 117–131.

———— "Le règne de Néron, une monarchie tribunicienne? (À propos du changement apporté au comput des puissances tribuniciennes en l'année 60)," *Centre Jean Palerme. Mémoires, VII: Recherches épigraphiques. Documents relatifs à l'histoire des institutions et de l'administration de l'empire romain,* ed. B. Rémy (1986), 55–83.

———— "La domus aurea et l'idéologie néronienne," *Le système palatial en Orient, en Grèce et à Rome. Actes du colloque de Strasbourg, 19–22 juin 1985,* ed. E. Lévy (Leiden, 1987), 359–391.

———— "Néronisme et urbanisme," *Neronia III:* 65–78.

———— "D'Alexandre à Néron: le motif de la tente d'apparat. La salle 29 de la Domus Aurea," *Neronia IV:* 211–229.

———— "Néron, Antoine, Alexandre. Quelques notes sur une paradoxe," in *Marc Antoine, son idéologie, sa descendance* (Lyon, 1993), 93–106.

———— "*Turris Maecenatiana:* une note d'histoire et de topographie," *Latomus* 55 (1996): 399–410.

Peters, W. J. T., and P. G. P. Meyboom, "The Roots of Provincial Roman Painting: Results of Current Research in Nero's Domus Aurea," in J. Liversidge, ed., *Roman Provincial Wall Painting of the Western Empire* (Oxford, 1982).

———— "Decorazione ed ambiente nella Domus Aurea di Nerone," *Babesch,* Suppl. 3 (1993): 59–63.

Phillips, E. J., "Nero's New City," *RFIC* 106 (1978): 300–307.

Picard, G.-C., *Augustus and Nero* (New York, 1964).

———— "Les peintures théâtrales du IVe style et l'idéologie néronienne," *Neronia 1977:* 55–60.

Plantzos, D., "Nero and Poppaea on a Cornelian Ringstone," *OJA* 12 (1993): 355–360.

Poinsotte, J.-M., "Un *Nero redivivus* chez un poète apocalyptique du IIIe siècle (Commodien)," *Neronia V:* 201–213.

Pollini, J., "Damnatio Memoriae in Stone: Two Portraits of Nero Recut to Vespasian in American Museums," *AJA* 88 (1984): 547–555.

Potter, D., *Prophecy and History in the Crisis of the Roman Empire: A Historical Commentary on the Thirteenth Sibylline Oracle* (Oxford, 1990).

Preller, L., *Griechische Mythologie,* 4th ed., rev. by C. Robert (Leipzig, 1894–1921).

von Premerstein, A., "Lex Tappula," *Hermes* 39 (1904): 327–347.

Prückner, H., and S. Storz, "Beobachtungen im Oktagon der Domus Aurea,"
 RM 81 (1974): 323–339.

Purcell, N., "Town in Country and Country in Town," in E. B. MacDougall,
 ed., *Ancient Roman Villa Gardens* (Washington, 1987), 187–203.

Putnam, M. C. J., *Virgil's Epic Designs: Ekphrasis in the Aeneid* (New Haven,
 1998).

Quilici, L., and S. Quilici Gigli, *Fidenae* (*Latium Vetus* V, Rome, 1986).

Rainbird, J. S., and F. B. Sear, "A Possible Description of the Macellum Mag-
 num of Nero," *PBSR* 39 (1971): 40–46.

Rawson, E., "Chariot-Racing in the Roman Republic," *PBSR* 49 (1981): 1–16 =
 Roman Culture and Society: Collected Papers (Oxford, 1991), 389–407.

———— "Theatrical Life in Republican Rome and Italy," *PBSR* 53 (1985): 97–113
 = *Roman Culture,* 468–487.

———— "*Discrimina Ordinum:* the *Lex Julia Theatralis,*" *PBSR* 55 (1987) 83–114
 = *Roman Culture,* 508–545.

Reece, B. R., "The Date of Nero's Death," *AJP* 90 (1969): 72–74.

Reed, N. J., "The Sources of Tacitus and Dio for the Boudiccan Revolt,"
 Latomus 33 (1974): 926–933.

Reynolds, R. W., "Criticism of Individuals in Roman Popular Comedy," *CQ* 37
 (1943): 37–45.

Riasanovsky, N. V., *The Image of Peter the Great in Russian History and Thought*
 (New York, Oxford, 1985).

RIC = C. H. V. Sutherland and R. A. G. Carson, *The Roman Imperial Coinage,*
 I. *From 31 BC to AD 69,* rev. ed. by C. H. V. Sutherland (London, 1984).

Richardson, L., Jr., *A New Topographical Dictionary of Ancient Rome* (Baltimore,
 1992).

Rickman, G., *The Corn Supply of Ancient Rome* (Oxford, 1980).

Ritter, S., *Hercules in der römischen Kunst von den Anfängen bis Augustus* (Heidelberg, 1995).

Robert, I., *Études épigraphiques et philologiques* (Paris, 1938).

———— "Dans l'amphithéâtre et dans les jardins de Néron. Une épigramme de
 Lucillius," *CRAI* 1968: 280–288 = *Opera Minora Selecta. Epigraphie et
 antiquité grecques* 5 (Amsterdam, 1989): 552–560.

———— "Deux concours grecques à Rome," *CRAI* 1970: 6–27 = *Opera Minora
 Selecta* 5 (1989): 647–668.

Rocca-Serra, G., "Exégèse allégorique et idéologie impériale: l'*Abrégé* de
 Cornutus," *Neronia 1977:* 61–72.

Rocco, G., "Alcune osservazioni sul valore architettonico della antica
 decorazione parietale: la *Domus Aurea* di Nerone," *Palladio* 1 (1988): 121–
 134.

Rodríguez-Almeida, E., "Marziale in marmo," *MEFR* 106 (1994): 197–217.

Rogers, R. S., "Freedom of Speech in the Empire: Nero," in *Laudatores temporis acti: Studies in memory of Wallace Everett Caldwell,* ed. M. F. Gyles and E. W. Davis (Chapel Hill, 1964), 91–98.

Roper, T. K., "Nero, Seneca and Tigellinus," *Historia* 28 (1979): 346–357.

Roscher, W. H., ed., *Ausführliches Lexikon der griechischen und römischen Mythologie* (Berlin, 1884–1937).

Rose, C. B., *Dynastic Commemoration in the Julio-Claudian Period* (Cambridge, 1997).

Rose, K. F. C., "Problems of Chronology in Lucan's Career," *TAPA* 97 (1966): 377–396.

——— *The Date and Author of the Satyricon* (Leiden, 1971).

Rosenmeyer, T. G., *Senecan Drama and Stoic Cosmology* (Berkeley, Los Angeles, 1989).

Rostowzew [Rostovtzeff], M., *Römische Bleitesserae. Ein Beitrag zur Sozial-und Wirtschaftsgeschichte der römischen Kaiserzeit* (*Klio,* Suppl. 3, Leipzig, 1905).

Rostovtzeff, M., "Commodus-Hercules in Britain," *JRS* 13 (1923): 91–109.

Rotolo, V., *Il pantomimo. Studi e testi* (Palermo, 1957).

Rougé, J., "Néron à la fin du IVe et au début du Ve siècle," *Latomus* 37 (1978): 73–87.

Royo, M., *Domus imperatoriae. Topographie, formation et imaginaire des palais impériaux (IIe siècle av. J.-C.–Ier siècle ap. J.-C.* (Rome, 1999).

RPC = A. M. Burnett, M. Amandry, and P. Ripolles, eds., *Roman Provincial Coinage,* I. *From the Death of Caesar to the Death of Vitellius (44 B.C.–A.D. 69)* (London, Paris, 1992).

Rudich, V., *Political Dissidence under Nero* (London, New York, 1992).

——— *Dissidence and Literature under Nero: The Price of Rhetoricization* (New York, 1997).

Ruggeri, P., "I *ludi Ceriales* del 65 d.C. e la congiura contro Nerone: *C.I.L.* XI 1414 = *I.L. Sard.* 309 (Pisa)," *MGR* 18 (1994): 167–176.

de Ruyt, C., *Macellum. Marché alimentaire des Romains* (Louvain-la-Neuve, 1983).

Sabbatini Tumolesi, P., "Pyrricharii," *PdP* 25 (1970): 328–338.

Sablayrolles, R., *Libertinus miles. Les cohortes de vigiles* (*Collection de l'École Française de Rome,* 224, Rome, 1996).

Salaç, A., "ΖΕΤΣ ΚΑΣΙΟΣ," *BCH* 46 (1922): 160–189.

Salzmann, D., "Vespasian statt Nero. Ein numismatischer Palimpsest," *AA* 99 (1984): 295–299.

Sande, S., "Qualis Artifex! Theatrical Influences on Neronic Fashions," *SO* 71 (1996): 135–146.

Sanford, E. M., "Nero and the East," *HSCP* 48 (1937): 75–103.

Sansone, D., "Nero's Final Hours," *ICS* 18 (1993): 179–189.

Santa Maria Scrinari, V., and M. L. Morricone Matini, *Mosaici antichi in Italia. Regione prima. Antium* (Rome, 1979).

Scheid, J., "La mort du tyran. Chronique de quleques morts programmées," *Du châtiment dans le cité. Supplices corporels et peine de mort dans le monde antique* (Rome, 1984), 177–190.

———— *Romulus et ses frères. Le collège des frères arvales, modèle du culte publique dans la Rome des empereurs* (Rome, 1990).

Schmidt, P. L., "Nero und das Theater," in J. Blänsdorf, ed., *Theater und Gesellschaft im Imperium Romanum* (Tübingen, 1990), 149–163.

Schumann, G., *Hellenistische und griechische Elemente in der Regierung Neros* (Leipzig, 1930).

Scott, K., "Greek and Roman Honorific Months," *YCS* 2 (1931): 201–278.

———— *The Imperial Cult under the Flavians* (Stuttgart, Berlin, 1936; repr. New York, 1976).

Shiel, N., "Nero citharoedus," *Euphrosyne* 7 (1975–1976): 175–179.

Simon, E., *Die Portlandvase* (Mainz, 1957).

———— *Augustus. Kunst und Leben in Rom um die Zeitwende* (Munich, 1986).

Simpson, C. J., "Thoughts on the Ceremonial 'Opening' of Secular Buildings at Rome," *Historia* 45 (1996): 376–382.

Sinn, U., "L'attività dell'imperatore Nerone ad Olympia. Risultati e prospettive dei nuovi scavi," in A. Mastrocinque, ed., *I grandi santuari della Grecia e l'Occidente* (Trento, 1993), 137–147.

Slater, N. W., "Nero's Masks," *CW* 90 (1996–1997): 33–40.

Slater, W. J., ed., *Roman Theater and Society. E. Togo Salmon Papers,* I (Ann Arbor, 1996).

Smith, R. R. R., "The Imperial Reliefs from the Sebasteion at Aphrodisias," *JRS* 77 (1987): 127–132.

———— "Nero and the Sun-god: Divine Accessories and Political Symbols in Roman Imperial Images," *JRA* 13 (2000): 532–542 [review of Bergmann 1998].

Solin, H., "Anthroponymie und Epigraphik. Einheimische und fremde Bevölkerung," *Hyperboreus* 1. 2 (1994/1995): 93–117.

Solin, H., and R. Volpe, "I graffiti della Domus Aurea," *Tituli* 2 (1981): 81–93.

Speidel, M., *Riding for Caesar: The Roman Emperor's Horse Guards* (London, 1994).

Sperti, L., *Nerone e la "submissio" di Tiridate in un bronzetto di Opitergium* (Rome, 1990).

Speyer, W., "Kaiser Nero in einer christlichen Legend," *JbAC* 18 (1975): 87–89.

Stemmer, K., *Untersuchungen zur Typologie, Chronologie und Ikonographie der Panzerstatuen* (Berlin, 1978).

Strazzulla, M. J., *Il principato di Apollo. Mito e propaganda nelle lastre "Campana" del tempio di Apollo Palatino* (Rome, 1990).

Strocka, V.-M., ed., *Die Regierungszeit des Kaiser Claudius* (Mainz, 1994).

Sullivan, J. P., "Ass's Ears and Attises: Persius and Nero," *AJP* 99 (1968): 159–170.

———— *Literature and Politics in the Age of Nero* (Ithaca, N.Y., 1985).

Sumner, G. V., "Germanicus and Drusus Caesar," *Latomus* 26 (1967): 413–435.

Sutherland, C. H. V., *Roman History and Coinage 44 B.C.–A.D. 69* (Oxford, 1987).

Sydenham, E. A., *The Coinage of Nero* (London, 1920).

Syme, R., *Tacitus* (Oxford, 1958).

———— *The Augustan Aristocracy* (Oxford, 1986).

———— *Roman Papers,* I–II (Oxford, 1979); III (1984); IV–V (1988); VI–VII (1991).

Tamm, B., *Neros Gymnasium in Rom* (*Stockholm Studies in Classical Archeology* 7, Stockholm, 1970).

Tengstrom, B., "Theater und Politik in kaiserlichen Rom," *Eranos* 75 (1977): 43–56.

Thiele, W., "Martial III, 20," *Philologus* 70 (1911): 539–548.

Thompson, L., "Lucan's Apotheosis of Nero," *CP* 59 (1964): 147–153.

Thompson, S., *Motif-Index of Folk-Literature*[2] (Bloomington, Indianapolis, 1953).

Tomei, M. A. "La villa di Nerone a Subiaco: scavi e ricerche," *Archeologia Laziale* 6 (1984): 250–259.

———— "La villa detta di Traiano ad Arcinazzo," *Archeologia Laziale* 7 (1985): 178–184.

———— "Le tre 'Danaidi' in nero antico del Palatino," *Bollettino di Archeologia* 5–6 (1990): 35–48.

———— "Nota sui giardini antichi del Palatino," *MEFR* 104 (1992): 917–951.

———— *Il Palatino* (Rome, 1992).

———— "La Domus Tiberiana dagli scavi ottocenteschi alle indagini recenti," *RM* 103 (1996): 165–200.

Townend, G. B. "The Circus of Nero and the Vatican Excavations," *AJA* 62 (1958): 216–218.

———— "The Sources of the Greek in Suetonius," *Hermes* 88 (1960): 98–120.

———— "Traces in Dio Cassius of Cluvius, Aufidius and Pliny," *Hermes* 89 (1961): 227–245.

———— "The Reputation of Verginius Rufus," *Latomus* 20 (1961): 337–341.

———— "Some Rhetorical Battle Pictures in Dio," *Hermes* 92 (1964): 467–481.

———— "Cluvius Rufus in the *Histories* of Tacitus," *AJP* 85 (1964): 337–377.

———— "The Earliest Scholiast on Juvenal," *CQ* 22 (1972): 376–387.

———— "Tacitus, Suetonius and the Temple of Janus," *Hermes* 108 (1980): 233–242.

Toynbee, J. M. C., "Nero *Artifex:* The *Apocolocyntosis* Reconsidered," *CQ* 36 (1942): 83–93.

———— "Ruler-Apotheosis in Ancient Rome," *NC* 7 (1947): 126–149.

Traina, G., "L'impossibile taglio dell'Istmo (Ps. Lucian, *Nero* 1–5)," *RFIC* 115 (1987): 40–49.

Treggiari, S., "Concubinae," *PBSR* 49 (1981): 59–81.

Tucker, R. A., "Lucan and Phoebus," *Latomus* 42 (1983): 143–151.

Tuplin, C., "The False Neros of the First Century," in C. Deroux, ed., *Studies in Latin Literature and History* 5 (1989): 364–404.

Van Buren, A. W., "Pompeii—Nero—Poppaea," in G. E. Mylonas and D. Raymond, eds., *Studies Presented to David Moore Robinson,* II (Saint Louis, 1953), 970–974.

Van Deman, E. B., "The Sacra Via of Nero," *MAAR* 5 (1925): 115–126.

van der Horst, P. W., *Chaeremon, Egyptian Priest and Stoic Philosopher* (Leiden, 1984).

van Essen, C. C., "La topographie de la Domus Aurea Neronis," *Mededelingen der Koninklijke Nederlandse Akademie van Wetenschappen, Afd. Letterkunde,* n.s. 17, 12 (Amsterdam, 1954), 371–398.

———— "La découverte du Laocoon," ibid., n.s. 18, 12 (Amsterdam, 1955), 291–308.

van Henten, J. W., "*Nero redivivus* Demolished: The Coherence of the Neronian Traditions in the *Sibylline Oracles*," *Journal for the Study of the Pseudepigrapha* 21 (2000): 3–17.

Vassileiou, A., "Sur la date des thermes de Néron," *REA* 74 (1972): 94–106.

Verdière, R., "À verser au dossier sexuel de Néron," *Neronia 1974:* 5–22.

Vermaseren, M. J., *Cybele and Attis, the Myth and the Cult* (London, 1977).

Vermeule, C. C., G. M. A. Hanfmann, W. J. Young, and H. Jucker, "A New Trajan," *AJA* 61 (1957): 223–253.

Vernant, J. P., "The Lame Tyrant: from Oedipus to Periander," in J. P. Vernant and P. Vidal-Naquet, *Myth and Tragedy in Ancient Greece* (New York, 1988), 207–236.

Versnel, H. S., *Triumphus: An Enquiry into the Origin, Development and Meaning of the Roman Triumph* (Leiden, 1970).

———— *Inconsistencies in Greek and Roman Religion,* 2: *Transition and Reversal in Myth and Legend* (Leiden, 1994).

Veyne, P., *Le pain et le cirque: Sociologie historique d'un pluralisme politique* (Paris, 1976). Abridged English translation: *Bread and Circuses: Historical Sociology and Political Pluralism* (London, 1990).

———— "Le folklore à Rome et les droits de la conscience publique sur la conduite individuelle," *Latomus* 42 (1983): 3–33 = "Les droits de la conscience publique sur la conduite individuelle: un constat ethnologique," in *La société romaine* (Paris, 1991), 57–87.

———— "Homosexuality in Ancient Rome," in P. Ariès and A. Béjin, eds., *Western Sexuality: Practice and Precept* (Oxford, 1985), 26–35.

———— "Histoire de Rome. Le voyage de Néron en Grèce," *Annuaire du Collège de France* 86 (1985–1986): 705–737.

———— "The Roman Empire," in *A History of Private Life,* I: *From Pagan Rome to Byzantium* (Cambridge, Mass., 1987), 5–234.

Ville, G., *La gladiature en Occident des origines à la mort de Domitien* (Rome, 1981).

Vittinghoff, F., *Der Staatsfeind in der römischen Kaiserzeit. Untersuchungen zur "damnatio memoriae"* (Berlin, 1936).

Voisin, J.-L., *"Exoriente sole* (Suétone, *Ner.* 6). D'Alexandrie à la *Domus Aurea,"* *L'Urbs: Espace urbain et histoire (Ier siècle av. J. C.–IIIe ap. J. C.* (Rome, 1987): 509–543.

Wankenne, J., "Faut-il réhabiliter l'empereur Néron?" *LEC* 49 (1981): 135–152.

———— "Encore et toujours Néron," *AC* 53 (1984): 249–265.

Ward-Perkins, J. B., "Nero's Golden House," *Antiquity* 30 (1956): 209–219.

———— *Roman Imperial Architecture* (Harmondsworth, Middlesex, 1981).

Warden, P. G., "The Domus Aurea Reconsidered," *JSAH* 40 (1981): 271–278.

Wardle, D., "Cluvius Rufus and Suetonius," *Hermes* 120 (1992): 466–482.

———— *Suetonius' Life of Caligula: A Commentary* (Brussels, 1994).

Watt, W. C., "666," *Semiotica* 77 (1989): 369–392.

Webster, T. B. L., *The Tragedies of Euripides* (London, 1967).

Weinstock, S., *Divus Julius* (Oxford, 1971).

Weir, R., "Nero and the Herakles Frieze at Delphi," *BCH* 123 (1999): 397–404.

Whitmarsh, T., "Greek and Roman in Dialogue: The Pseudo-Lucianic *Nero,"* *JHS* 119 (1999): 142–160.

Wiedemann, T., *Emperors and Gladiators* (London, New York, 1992).

Wilkes, J. J., "Julio-Claudian Historians," *CW* 65 (1971/1972): 177–203.

Wille, G., *Musica Romana. Die Bedeutung der Musik im Leben der Römer* (Amsterdam, 1967).

Williams, C. *Roman Homosexuality: Ideologies of Masculinity in Classical Antiquity* (New York, 1999).

Williams, M. H., "'Θεοσεβὴς γὰρ ἦν'—The Jewish Tendencies of Poppaea Sabina," *JTS* 39 (1988): 97–111.

Wiseman, J., *The Land of the Ancient Corinthians* (Goteborg, 1978).

Wiseman, T. P., "Legendary Genealogies in Late-Republican Rome," *G&R* 21

(1974): 153–164 = *Roman Studies Literary and Historical* (Liverpool, 1987), 207–218.

———— "Topography and Rhetoric: The Trial of Manlius," *Historia* 28 (1979): 32–50 = *Roman Studies,* 225–243.

———— "A World Not Ours," *Catullus and His World: A Reappraisal* (Cambridge, 1985), 1–14.

———— "*Conspicui postes tectaque digna deo.* The Public Image of Aristocratic and Imperial Houses in the Late Republic and Early Empire," *L'Urbs: Espace urbain et histoire (Ier siècle av. J. C.–IIIe ap. J. C.* (Rome, 1987): 395–413 = *Historiography and Imagination: Eight Essays on Roman Culture* (Exeter, 1994), 98–115, 154–161.

———— *Flavius Josephus: Death of an Emperor* (Exeter, 1991).

Wistrand, M., *Entertainment and Violence in Ancient Rome: The Attitudes of Roman Writers of the First Century* A.D. (Göteborg, 1992).

Wittke, C., "Persius and the Neronian Institution of Literature," *Latomus* 43 (1984): 802–812.

Woodman, T. [= A. J.] "Nero's Alien Capital. Tacitus as Paradoxographer (*Annals* 15. 36–7)," in T. Woodman and J. Powell, eds., *Author and Audience in Latin Literature* (Cambridge, 1992), 173–188, 251–255 = Woodman 1998, 168–189.

Woodman, A. J., "Amateur Dramatics at the Court of Nero: *Annals* 15. 48–74," in T. J. Luce and A. J. Woodman, eds., *Tacitus and the Tacitean Tradition* (Princeton, 1993), 104–128 = Woodman 1998, 190–217.

———— *Tacitus Reviewed* (Oxford, 1998).

Wuilleumier, P., "Cirque et astrologie," *MEFR* 44 (1927): 184–209.

Yavetz, Z., *Plebs and Princeps* (Oxford, 1969; rev. ed. New Brunswick, N.J., 1988).

———— "Forte an dolo principis (Tac. Ann. 15. 38)," in *The Ancient Historian and His Materials. Essays in Honour of C. E. Stevens,* ed. B. Levick (Farnborough, 1975), 181–197.

Zahn, R., "Otho, Nero und Poppaea auf einer Karneolgemme," *Staatliche Museen zu Berlin. Forschungen und Berichte* 14 (1972): 173–181.

Zanker, P., "Galba, Nero, Nerva, drei barocke Charakterstudien," *Stud. Blanckenhagen* (1979): 305–314.

———— "Herrscherbild und Zeitgesicht," *Wissenschaftliche Zeitschrift der Humboldt-Universität, Ges.-Sprachw. R.* 31 (1982): 307–312.

———— "Der Apollontempel auf dem Palatin. Ausstattung und politische Sinnbezüge nach der Schlacht von Actium," *Città ed architettura nella Roma imperiale (Analecta Romana Instituti Danici,* Suppl. 10, Odense, 1983): 21–40.

———— *The Power of Images in the Age of Augustus* (Ann Arbor, 1988).

Zecchini, G., "L'immagine di Nerone nel lessico Suda (con una postilla sulla *Lettera di Anna a Seneca*," *Neronia V*: 214–224.

Zevi, F., "Nerone, Baiae e la *Domus Aurea*," in B. Andreae and C. Parisi Presicce, *Ulisse. Il mito e la memoria* (Rome, 1996), 320–331.

Zinserling, G., "Studien zu den Historiendarstellung der römischen Republik," *Wissenschaftliche Zeitschrift der Friedrich-Schiller-Universität Jena* 9 (1959/60): 403–448.

Notes

1. The Once and Future King

1. *The False Nero,* translated by Edwin and Willa Muir (1937), chapter 54. From Lion Feuchtwanger, *Der Falsche Nero* (1936), book 3, chapter 12 (Fischer Taschenbuch edition, Frankfurt, 1984), 260–261.

2. This account rests largely on the remarkably detailed record of Nero's last days to be found in the biography by Suetonius, *Nero* 40–50, conflated with the surviving excerpts of the history of Cassius Dio, book 63. They derive from a single source; cf. Chapter 2 below. (A comparison of the two accounts can be found in Heinz 1948, 61–66.) Details gleaned from other authors will be noted. Precise chronology is very unsure: see generally Bradley 1978, Murison 1993 (with bibliography). It was claimed that Nero heard the news of the Gallic uprising on the anniversary of his mother's death, that is, 19/23 March: Suetonius 40. 4. Scheid 1984 and Sansone 1993 offer fascinating interpretations of the ancient account of Nero's last days, the one religious, the other literary.

3. These military preparations are, significantly, not recounted in the death narratives. See particularly Tacitus *Hist.* 1. 6, and Chilver 1979, *ad loc.*

4. Dio 63. 28. 5. The line has been garbled in Suetonius 46. 3, as "Wife, mother, father drive me to death": Delcourt 1944, 204, n. 1. Dio's version is clearly superior.

5. See Chilver 1979, 8–12, on the very unsure chronology. The legate of the North African legion III Augusta, Clodius Macer, also defected. It *may* be that Nero had already received news of the Battle of Vesontio: there Vindex had been defeated and committed suicide, but afterwards the victorious general, Verginius Rufus, legate of Upper Germany, refused to declare his loyalty to either Nero or Galba, leaving the senate to decide. The German army also at some point deserted from Nero: Tacitus *Hist.* 1.8.

6. Cf. Pliny *NH* 37. 29.

7. Plutarch *Galba* 2. 1–2.

8. Neophytus appears only in the late *Epitome de Caesaribus,* 5. 7. The number of four, from Suetonius, is confirmed by Josephus *BJ* 4. 493.

9. Reece 1969. Against the standard dating of 9 June, Reece argues for Dio's date of 11 June, citing among other evidence the partial horoscope of an anonymous man who was born at sunrise on 15 December, A.D. 37 and died on 11 June 68: Vettius Valens 5. 11 Kroll = V. 7. 20–35 Pingree, with the translation and commentary by O. Neugebauer and H. B. van Heusen, *Greek Horoscopes* (Philadelphia, 1959), 78–79. Sumner 1967, at 416–418, had expressed doubts as to the year of Nero's birth.

10. *Qualis artifex pereo* (Suetonius 49. 1). Perhaps the most misunderstood statement in antiquity: see Chapter 2 below.

11. Eutropius 7. 15 expands on Suetonius' account.

12. Curiously, Suetonius' account seems to suggest inhumation rather than cremation. But cremation was overwhelmingly the norm in the first century; in his last hours Nero had twice indicated that he wished to be cremated; Plutarch alludes to the burning of his corpse (*Galba* 9. 3); and, despite the apparent contradiction in terms, ashes have been found within Roman sarcophagi (J. M. C. Toynbee, *Death and Burial in the Roman World* [Ithaca, N.Y., 1971], 40, n. 107). The presence or absence of a body might prove important later. Nero was the first emperor to be buried in a porphyry sarcophagus.

On the location of the tomb, see Colini 1975–1976, who guesses that it stood with other monuments along the Via Salaria Vetus (Via Francesco Crispi), rather than near the Porta del Popolo, where medieval legend believed Nero's ghost to lurk (Graf 1882, 349–356). Colini's suggestion might indeed better suit Suetonius' description of the solemn sacrifices made by Vitellius to Nero's shade *medio Martio campo,* in the middle of the Campus Martius (*Vitellius* 11. 2).

13. *Hist.* 1. 4; cf. Suetonius 50, Dio 63. 29. 1.

14. This glimpse of savagery comes from Plutarch *Galba* 8.

15. Suetonius 57. 1; Tacitus *Hist.* 1. 4.

16. Plutarch *Galba* 16–17.

17. The accounts of Tacitus (*Hist.* 1. 78), Plutarch (*Otho* 3. 1–2), and Suetonius (*Otho* 7) are so close in formulation and details that they must derive from a common source, and that source should be Cluvius Rufus (on whom see Chapter 2 below); as governor of Hispania Tarraconensis, the historian had received one of the dispatches from Nero Otho (Plutarch).

18. Suetonius *Vitellius* 11. 2; Tacitus *Hist.* 2. 95.

19. Pliny: see Chapter 2 below; the *Octavia:* Chapter 4.

20. For aspects of Nero's vigorous afterlife, both in antiquity and after, see Graf 1882, 332–361; Geffcken 1899; Konrad 1966; Feo 1971, Rougé 1978; Bodinger 1989; Jakob-Sonnabend 1990; Gwyn 1991; Chevallier 1999 (a rather haphazard selection of evidence); and, above all, Pascal 1923.

21. Millar 1964, 214–218.

22. Suetonius 40. 2.

23. Tacitus *Hist.* 1. 8; Dio of Prusa *Or.* 21. 9–10. Dio died sometime (probably not long) after 110; on the date of this oration, possibly after 88, see Jones 1978, 50, 135.

24. The most recent and exhaustive discussion is that of Tuplin 1989. There has been some arid debate as to the number of false Neros: two or three? Tacitus *Hist.* 2. 8. 1 (cf. 1. 2. 1) should be decisive for three: see Gallivan 1973, and Tuplin, 382–386.

25. The main source is Tacitus *Hist.* 2. 8–9, supplemented by Zonaras 11. 15, cf. Dio 64. 9. 3. Tuplin 1989 analyzes the incident at great length, 364–371. Comparison will show that the following account differs from his in several ways; I discount the presence of Asprenas as being due to chance.

E. Woeckner pointed out in seminar the curious fact that Tacitus' account here ("Sub idem tempus Achaia atque Asia falso exterritae velut Nero adventaret . . .") is strikingly similar to his report, written later, of the appearance of a False Drusus in 31 (*Ann.* 5. 10 [cf. Dio 58. 25. 1, differing in details and assigning the incident to 34]: "Per idem tempus Asia atque Achaia exterritae sunt acri magis quam diuturno rumore, Drusus Germanici filium apud Cycladas insulas, mox in continento visum"). In both cases, the Cyclades islands are involved, Egypt and Syria are named as intended destinations, and a governor deals with the pretender in person. How much this doublet is due to similar historical circumstances and how much to Tacitus' descriptive powers is unclear, but there is no reason to doubt the essential historicity of the two imposters.

26. Calpurnius Asprenas, the man who executed the claimant, had been an intimate of the emperor: for his remarkable career, see below, Chapter 8.

27. Dio 66. 19. 3, from Zonaras 11. 18 and John of Antioch fr. 104M; Tuplin 1989, 372–377.

28. Suetonius 57. 2; cf. Jones 1983; Tuplin 1989, 377–382. In the later second century, Lucian refers to the false Nero in the days of our forefathers, *Adv. Ind.* 21. 10. It is uncertain to which of the known pretenders he refers.

29. On Nero and the East in general, see Sanford 1937.

30. *Oracula Sibyllina* 4. 119–124, 1137–139. All translations are those by J. J. Collins, "Sibylline Oracles," in Charlesworth 1983, 317–472. The Greek text can be consulted in J. Geffcken, *Die Oracula Sibyllina* (Leipzig, 1902; repr. New York, 1979). On Nero in the Sibyllines see the summation of McGinn 1994, at 46–48.

31. Lines 93–110 do not seem to fit Nero.

32. *Ascension of Isaiah* 3. 13 – 4. 22. The best text of the Martyrdom and Ascension survives in Ethiopic, supported in part of this section by a papyrus fragment of the Greek original of the Ascension. The translation here is that of M. A. Knibb, "Martyrdom and Ascension of Isaiah," in Charlesworth 1985, 143–176,

preceded by an excellent introduction. On Nero in the Ascension and in St. John, see in general McGinn 1994, 48–54.

33. On the complicated reasons why 666 must be read as Nero, see the fascinating paper by W. C. Watt, 1989.

34. See Charles 1920 for an elaborate dissection.

35. See Gagé 1961; and, most recently, Poinsotte 1999, adding little.

36. *Instructiones* 41; *Carmen de duobus populis* 823–936. McGinn 1994, 65–66.

37. Victorinus *In Apocalypsin* 13. 2, 3.

38. Sulpicius Severus *Chronica* 28–29; *Dialogi* 2. 14.

39. *De mortibus persecutorum* 2. 7–9.

40. *Commentarium in Danielem* 11. 28/30. Cf. *Epistulae* 121. 11.

41. *De Civitate Dei* 20. 19. 3. As Rougé 1978, 86, demonstrates, for the contemporary St. John Chrysostom, who mentions Nero often, neither was the emperor Antichrist nor would he return; rather, he had embodied the *image* of what the Antichrist would be.

42. Thompson 1953, motifs A 570 and A 580.

43. See Davidson 1978, and now the excellent, wide-ranging Bercé 1990.

44. In Nero's case, during the Middle Ages demons lived in a walnut tree on the supposed site of his grave in Rome; or perhaps he himself lay in golden armor under the Neroberg in Hesse: *Handwörterbuch des deutschen Aberglaubens* 6 (1934/35): 1007; cf. Graf 1882, 353ff. Lanciani remarked in 1909 of Anzio, the town where the emperor and his only child were born, "Nero is still the popular hero, and the subject of many legends in the folk-lore of Antium" (Lanciani 1909, 340). Compare tales of Poppaea's milk-bath still told in the region of Nero's suicide north of Rome: Quilici 1986, 102, n. 125.

45. Cohn 1970, 89–93 (quotation from p. 93).

46. Ibid., 111–126, 142–143; cf. McGinn 1994, 152–157.

47. See Charlesworth 1950, 73, an invaluable paper.

48. Neronias: Hild 1993; cf. *PW* 17 (1936): 148–149. Neroneios at Amaseia: *AE* 1992. 1671 (AD 252/253). The flasks, dated to the later third or fourth century: Ostrow 1979, 89–91, 136–137.

Suetonius assures us (55) that in his quest for undying fame, Nero "took their former appellations from many things and numerous places and gave them new ones from his own name." His memory persisted in four forms: personal names, place-names, month-names, and portraits. Surviving and posthumous portraits will be considered at length below.

Names: The personal name Nero is found almost exclusively in the East: Solin 1994/1995 (from which the following examples are drawn). Some instances are clearly contemporary with the emperor, such as *CIG* 2942d (Caria), the dedication of a Tiberius Claudius Nero to Nero himself, and 4714 = *IGRR* I. 1148

(Panopolis), the inscription from AD 109 of a military tribune whose father was a Tiberius Claudius Nero, presumably born before 68.

Nevertheless the name does crop up after 68, when it can only have been intended as a memorial to the emperor: a soldier from Beirut serving in the legio III Augusta, in Africa, L. Ulpius Nero, *ITG* 337; an Aurelius Nero at Athens in the mid-third century, *IG* III. 758; a Neronianus at Flaviopolis in Cilicia, *SEG* XXVIII. 1271; a Macarius Nero at Tanais in the Kingdom of the Bosporus in AD 244, *CIRB* 1287 (not in Solin). Most suggestive, as Solin notes, are the two ephebes named together on an Athenian ephebe list of the mid-third century, *IG* II². 2243: Aurelius Nero (presumably the same as the man cited above), followed by an Aurelius Hadrianus—surely named for the two philhellenic Roman emperors.

Toponyms: For the (understandably) obscure and uncertain history of cities named after Nero, see L. Keppie, "Colonisation and Veteran Settlement in Italy in the First Century A.D.," *PBSR* 52 (1984): 77–114, at 81–90; Y. Meshorer, "Sepphoris and Rome," *Greek Numismatics and Archaeology: Essays . . . M. Thompson* (New York, 1979), 159–163; *RPC*, 488–490, 670–671. During his lifetime, the Armenian capital Artaxata was named Neroneia in his honor: Dio 63. 7.

Around AD 100 a military way station in Thrace, probably on the Via Egnatia, continued to be known as *ta Neronos stabla*, the stables of Nero: *BE* 1972. 443. And Gallia Narbonensis had two cities called Forum Neronis, "Nero's Forum": Carpentorate (Ptolemy *Geography* 2. 10. 8) and Luteva (Pliny *NH* 3. 37). The "Nero" in question need not be the emperor, and in the case of Luteva it was certainly Tiberius Claudius Nero, the father of the emperor Tiberius.

However, besides the *stagnum Neronis* at Baiae in Italy, there was a way-station called Neronia on the Via Popillia north of Ravenna, which was surely named after him as well; it lay next to the canal known as the Fossa Flavia (cf. Pliny *NH* 3. 120) and is listed in the medieval itinerary/map known as the Peutinger Table, based on a fourth-century source (which had in turn absorbed earlier sources). And an official document of the second century refers to what must have been a large, imperially owned *saltus Neronianus*, the Neronian estate, in the hinterlands of Carthage, in North Africa: *CIL* VIII. 25943 (Ain-el-Djemila). This certainly is to be referred to Nero and his confiscations in the area: note the names of other nearby estates on the inscription, which preserve the names of Nero's victims, along with the comment of the elder Pliny at *NH* 18. 35, that he had six African landowners killed who owned half the land in the province.

Most striking of all, the great baths in the center of Rome continued to be known commonly as the *thermae Neronianae* for at least four centuries after his death: *LTUR* IV 1999, 60–62, *s.v. Thermae Neronianiae / Alexandrinae* (G. Ghini). Sidonius Apollinaris refers to them at *Carmen* 23. 495. Martial (7. 34. 4–5) notably sums up the dilemma of posthumous nomenclature: "What was worse than Nero? What is better than the Neronian baths?"

Honorary months: The basic survey is Scott 1931. Again, there are difficulties, since months named Neronaios or Neroneios are attested for both the emperor Tiberius (Claudius Nero) and for Nero the brother of Caligula. In Rome, the senate changed April to Neroneus to commemorate the unmasking then of the Pisonian conspiracy of AD 65: Tacitus 15. 74; Suetonius 55 (attributing the change to Nero himself). The month is attested in Pompeian graffiti (*CIL* IV. 8078a; 8092), undated, but presumed Neronian. In Egypt it was the month of Choiak, 27 November to 26 December, Nero's birth-month, that was changed to Neroneios, very early in the reign. It is attested on some twenty-two papyri, collected and discussed by Kruse 1995. One of these seems to be dated to 78, well after Nero's death: *BGU* III. 981. Unfortunately, it is very lacunose and difficult to decipher. Kruse accordingly emends it to remove the month, which may well be correct. But he starts from the first principle that the month cannot have survived Nero, which is by no means certain and may blind us to the fact that Neronian names, place-names, months, and portraits did indeed survive.

Months and toponyms: Cf. Suetonius 55 on the emperor's desire for undying fame: "With this in view he took their former appellations from many things and numerous places and gave them new ones from his own name. He also called the month of April Neroneus and was minded to name Rome Neropolis."

49. Josephus *AJ* 20. 154. It is the latter tradition which of course had prevailed: cf. Chapter 2 below.

50. *Epigram* 7. 34, 8. 70. The context for the latter is Martial's praise of the emperor Nerva: Nero, no mean critic, had recognized the merits of Nerva's verse, calling him "the Tibullus of our day" (not a wholly favorable assessment).

In the early third century, the most learned scholar of the age, Serenus Sammonicus, related the story of the discovery of memoirs of the Trojan War written by a participant, Dictys Cretensis. They had been found by shepherds looking for treasure in his tomb near Cnossus on the island of Crete. The language of the manuscript proved to be Greek, written in Punic letters. The shepherds' master then had it transliterated and offered it to "Nero, the Roman Caesar, for which he was showered with presents." The forgery, which apparently deceived Serenus himself, was in fact probably concocted in Greek in the second century AD. The interesting point is that its creator chose to have the learned Nero as its supposed recipient. On Serenus and Dictys, see "Serenus Sammonicus," *HSCP* 85 (1981): 189–212.

51. *Epitome de Caesaribus* 5. 2; Aurelius Victor 5. 2: their common source, and that source's source, are a mystery. For a good recent discussion, see Levick 1983. Much has been written on the identity of Nero's "quinquennium," with most favoring the (roughly) five years of "good government" from 54 to the

murder of Agrippina in 59. R. Syme made the attractive suggestion (summarily rejected by Levick) that "Trajan" meant *a* quinquennium, that is, any five years under Nero, and not *the* Quinquennium, a period presumably known to all: *Emperors and Biography* (Oxford, 1971), 106–110. Murray 1965 offers a fine example of speculation spun out far beyond the breaking point.

52. A good case has been made recently that one of the worst of emperors, Elagabalus (218–222), deliberately imitated Nero by driving a chariot drawn by four elephants around Nero's own circus in the Vatican, an area which he had to clear of tombs that had encroached in the interim (*HA Elagabalus* 23. 1): Humphrey 1986, 552–557. The incident may, however, be fictional. The same emperor's Antoninian Games were probably an imitation of the Neronian Games: Robert 1970, 6–27.

53. For Plutarch's views of Nero, see Jones 1971, 18–19. The quotation is from Plutarch, *Marcus Antonius* 87. 2, translated by I. Scott-Kilvert, Plutarch, *Makers of Rome* (Harmondsworth, Middlesex, 1965).

54. Plutarch *Moralia* 56 F, 462 A, 810 A. Plutarch's contemporary, Dio of Prusa, is harsher on Nero, showing contempt for his artistry (3. 135, 32, 60, 71. 9) and blaming his downfall on his treatment of Sporus (21. 9), but even he can remind the Rhodians that whereas Nero and his agents had looted Olympia, Delphi, Athens, and Pergamum, they had spared Rhodes (31. 147–150).

55. *De Sera Numinis Vindicta, Mor.* 567 E–F.

56. Brenk 1987 offers a long, not uniformly convincing interpretation of the passage to argue that Plutarch's image of Nero is thoroughly negative. More interestingly, Frazer 1971 suggests that the frog imagery is not original to Plutarch, but that he refers to some well-known caricature of Nero which, together with Nero's acclaimed performance of Canace in Childbirth and possibly with various folkloric elements, may lie behind the medieval Golden Legend of Nero giving birth to a frog through his mouth. Moreover, Adrienne Mayor has pointed out to me the froggy details of Nero's last hours, from the reedy marsh to the bulging eyes (a folkloric identifier of the frog), which further suggest that Nero the frog is not Plutarch's own invention.

57. Robberies: 5. 25. 9, 5. 26. 3, 9. 27. 3, 10. 7. 1, 10. 19. 1–2. Dedications: 2. 17. 6, 5. 12. 8

58. Isthmus: 2. 1. 5. Crimes: 9. 27. 3–4. Liberation: 7. 17. 2.

59. Most recently, see Whitmarsh 1999 on the intellectual background of the dialogue.

60. Philostratus *Apollonius* 4. 35–39, 5. 7.

61. *Apollonius* 5. 7, 5. 41, translated by C. P. Jones, Philostratus, *Life of Apollonius* (Harmondsworth, Middlesex, 1970).

62. *Gittin* 56a, translated by M. Simon, *Gittin* (London, 1936). For a literal translation, see G. Stemberger, *ANRW* II. 19. 2, 347.

63. Bastomsky 1969. Barrett 1976 takes issue with Bastomsky, but seems to me to be wrong on every point. Cohen 1972 points out that "Meir" is not a legitimately attested Jewish name, and suggests that it is a hebraïzed transliteration of an unfamiliar gentile name, the Phrygian "Meiros." Firpo 1993 offers a survey of the Jewish traditions about Nero, but adds little.

64. Malalas *Chronographia* 10. 29–40, translated by E. Jeffreys et al., *The Chronicle of Malalas* (Melbourne, 1986).

65. Cf. Zecchini 1999. There is a rich vein to be mined in the Byzantine sources. In the seventh-century *Chronicon Paschale* the christianizing Nero dies, again at the age of 69, the victim of Jewish plots. The eighth-century chronographer Syncellus relates as fact that Nero was killed on his way back from Greece to Rome, but he was unsure whether the emperor died in a palace plot or through suicide.

66. Portraits modeled on Nero's after his death: e.g., Born and Stemmer 1996, 99. Posthumous mirror boxes: Dahmen 1998, 331–332.

67. Fishwick 1991, 562–563. The flowers and the statues are a powerful indicator of a popular cult of a "martyr." Compare Plutarch on reaction to the violent death of Gaius Gracchus in 121 BC, *Gaius Gracchus* 18, and Tacitus on reaction to the death of Otho in AD 69, *Histories* 2. 55.

68. *CIL* VI. 34916. The point was made by Lanciani 1893, 185–190. Using the detailed account by Suetonius of Nero's last itinerary, he was able to pinpoint the impressive ruins in which the epitaph was discovered as the villa of Phaon where Nero died. Accepted by Colini 1958; Quilici and Quilici Gigli 1986, 191–194, 263, 265, 285–288 dispute Lanciani, but unpersuasively.

69. On this and much of what follows, see the classic work, Vittinghoff 1936. Recently, see C. W. Hedrick, *History and Silence: Purge and Rehabilitation of Memory in Late Antiquity* (Austin, Texas, 2000), especially chapter 4, "Remembering to Forget: The *Damnatio Memoriae*," 89–130.

70. An informal but very instructive search of standard epigraphical collections has suggested that Nero's name was vandalized on roughly 12 percent of his inscriptions: J. M. Paillier and R. Sablayrolles, *"Damnatio memoriae: une vraie perpétuité,"* *Pallas* 40 (1994): 13–55, at 22, with n. 47. Not an impressive figure at all: Domitian (the subject of the paper referred to) runs to about 35 percent.

71. Bergmann and Zanker 1981; Pollini 1984; Maggi 1991. The proper term should be "palimpsest": Jucker 1981.

72. Megow 1987, 202, 210–220, 225–226, 230, 241, 308; and Megow 1993. Meyer 2000 has added several startling reworkings of Nero's portrait: the emperor on the Grand Camée de France is Nero, reworked as Constantine (11–28); the figure in a breast-plate on the relief from San Vitale in Ravenna is Nero, reworked as Vitellius (35–48); the central figure on Frieze A of the Cancelleria Reliefs is Nero,

reworked as Domitian and then as Nerva (125–140). Meyer also argues (41–47) that the statue of Mars Ultor currently in the Capitoline Museum orginally bore the head of Nero, and is in fact the statue voted to him by the senate in 55 (Tacitus 13. 8. 1).

73. Besombes 1998, 125: from graves nos. 15 (mid-second century), 22 (turn of the first and second centuries), 35 (Flavian). Note also nos. 24 and 30 (undated graves), 33 (a temple of Janus near Autun), and 34 (a villa).

74. Fittschen 1970, 549; Stemmer 1978, 17, n. 62; Sperti 1990, 10. The inscription is republished as *I. Tralleis* 40.

75. So, convincingly, argues Fuchs 1997, 83–90, reacting against Lahusen and Formigli 1993, 180–182. A striking carnelian, destroyed in Berlin at the end of the Second World War, shows Otho in the center with smaller facing busts of Nero and Poppaea below him, all labeled, with the Dioscuri in the upper left-hand corner and a snake at the bottom: Zahn 1972. Alas, this remarkably rich piece of Othonian propaganda is likely to be a modern fake, in the opinion of my colleague Hugo Meyer.

76. Alföldi 1990.

77. Ibid., 34–40; vs. A. Cameron, in introduction to Alföldi 1990, 70.

78. *Variae* 3. 51. 9, translated by S. J. B. Barnish, *The Variae of Magnus Aurelius Cassiodorus Senator* (Liverpool, 1992), 69–70. The cameo is discussed in Megow 216, no. A104, with Tafel 35. 6.

79. See Megow 1987, 214–215, no. A99, with Tafel 35. 3, with description, full bibliography (including the authority of A. Furtwängler, G. Lippold, E. Simon, and H. Jucker), and speculation as to the origin of the piece. Add the posthumously published remarks of H. Möbius, who had inspected it carefully: *ANRW* II. 12. 3 (1985): 67–68.

80. Megow asserts that, since Nero underwent *damnatio memoriae*, a posthumous honoring is unthinkable; reasons have been given above to show why this is untenable. For the eagle's role and significance in consecration, see Vittinghoff 1936, 106–108; S. Price, "From Noble Funerals to Divine Cult: The Consecration of Roman Emperors," in D. Cannadine and S. Price, eds., *Rituals of Royalty: Power and Ceremonial in Traditional Societies* (Cambridge, 1987), 94–95, with 73–77.

81. Cohn 1970, 73.

82. Perrie 1987, 62. The remarks on Ivan here are no more than a distillation of chapter 3 (pp. 45–65) in this admirable study of folklore in history. Contrast with Ivan the folkloric image of Peter the Great as presented by Riasanovsky 1985, 74–85. Peter, a generally laudable figure to western eyes, was condemned almost immediately after his death for destroying the old Russia: absentee, besotted with foreigners and foreign ways, blasphemous, debauched, filicidal, and an enemy of

the church, in one of the three basic versions of his legend it is assumed that he must be the Antichrist. Here then is one figure of terror who was not a peasant-tsar.

83. Perrie 1987, 117.

2. Stories and Histories

1. Epigraphs: Josephus *AJ* 20. 154; Martial 3. 20. 1–4 (Loeb Classical Library translation by D. R. Shackleton Bailey, considerably modified). Martial's Latin could equally be rendered as: "Or does he emulate the compositions that a mendacious writer ascribed to Nero or the fables of rascal Phaedrus?" (as preferred by Shackleton Bailey, who notes the alternative); but it is difficult to see why Canius Rufus would want to imitate writings falsely attributed to Nero. Josephus' *Jewish Antiquities* was published in 93/94; the third book of Martial's *Epigrams* was published in 87.

2. Herz 1948; cf. Syme 1958, 688–692, and for a summary statement, Griffin 1984, 235. Whether Suetonius knew and criticized Tacitus' *Annals* is much debated, and hinges in part on the uncertainty as to when each author was writing. If Suetonius was indeed familiar with the *Annals,* its traces are exceedingly faint.

3. E.g., Suetonius *Otho* 10. 1 (on the year 69).

4. E.g., in Tacitus, respectively: 15. 74; 13. 31, cf. 16. 22.

5. The best introduction is Wilkes 1971/1972, on which the following depends heavily. The fragments of lost historians are collected by H. Peter, *Historicorum Romanorum Reliquiae* 2 (Leipzig, 1906): Corbulo, 99–101; Pliny, 110–112; Fabius Rusticus, 112–113; Cluvius Rufus, 114–115; Junius Rusticus, 116.

6. Tacitus 4. 53. Barrett 1996, 198f.

7. Cited at Tacitus 15. 16. 1.

8. Arulenus: Suetonius *Domitian* 10. 3, Tacitus *Agricola* 2. 1. Fannius: Pliny *Epp.* 5. 5.

9. Tacitus 13. 20. 2–4.

10. Eyewitness in Rome: e.g., *NH* 14. 56, 12. 10, 9. 117, 9.4. History of Rome: Pliny *Epp.* 3. 5. 6; mentioned by his uncle in the *NH* at Pref. 20.

11. *NH* 7. 45 (enemy of mankind); cf. 34. 45, 35. 51, 22. 96, 37. 50, et al.

12. Syme 1958, 291–295. It is assumed, for instance, that Tacitus criticizes Pliny at 13. 31 without naming him: "When Nero for the second time and L. Piso were consuls [57] little happened worth remembering, unless one enjoys filling volumes with praise for the foundations and timbers with which Caesar had raised his tremendous amphitheatre in the Campus Martius, since it is clearly appropriate to the dignity of the Roman people that important affairs be assigned to histories, such matters to the *acta diurna urbis.*" Yet it is hard to associate praise with Pliny's feelings about Nero, and the use of "Caesar" rather than "Nero" sug-

gests the writing of a favorable contemporary, or even the *acta urbis* themselves. Similarly, the "curious" numerological inquiry into the date of the Great Fire (15. 41) need not come from Pliny.

13. Tacitus 15. 53.

14. As established by R. Syme in "Pliny the Procurator," *HSCP* 73 (1969): 201–236 = Syme 1979, II. 742–773.

15. Tacitus 14. 2; Suetonius 28.

16. Seneca's death: Tacitus 15. 61. Not necessarily a historian: Townend 1964.

17. For an excellent account of his career and the nature and extent of his work, see Wiseman 1991, 111–118. Cluvius as Nero's herald: Suetonius 21. 2; Dio 63. 14. 3. Pliny's letter: *Epp.* 9. 19. 5.

18. Townend 1960, 1961, 1980; Wardle 1990.

19. Tacitus *Hist.* 4. 43 (AD 70).

20. Tacitus 13. 14; Pliny 22. 92; *Octavia* 164–165. Mushroom jokes: Suetonius 33, cf. 39; Dio 60. 35. 4; Martial 1. 20; Juvenal 5. 148. There is no mushroom in Seneca, *Apocolocyntosis* (it was a bowel problem), or in the official edict, Suetonius 47.

21. Suetonius *Claudius* 44. 2–3; Tacitus 12. 66–67; Dio 60. 34. 2–3. "Dio" also omits Halotus, but that is presumably the choice of the epitomator. Note that Suetonius knows of Locusta, but in not in this context: *Nero* 33, 47.

22. As modern scholars generally recognize: see Levick 1990, 77, with references. Claudius' eating habits and ill health: Suetonius *Claudius* 31–33. Our sources agree that Claudius died during the night or at dawn, but the official version was that he died between noon and 1:00 P.M. the next day: Tacitus 12. 68 (assuming a cover-up); Seneca *Apocolocyntosis* 2. Seneca tells us (c. 4) that he was taken ill while watching comic actors; Suetonius claims (*Claudius* 45) that the actors were brought in after his death, as part of the cover-up.

23. Tacitus *Historiae* 1. 13; Suetonius *Otho* 3; Plutarch *Galba* 19. 2 – 20. 1; Dio 61. 11. 2. The story as Suetonius presents it is particularly intriguing. From one angle, Nero is shown as the sad and angry figure of the *exclusus amator* in love po etry, shouting at his mistress's closed door: *ipsum etiam exclusisse quondam pro foribus astantem miscentemque frustra minas ac preces ad depositum reposcentem.* At the same time, there is an elegant legal color, punning on two kinds of contract. Nero made a temporary loan, in that Sabina was *demandatam interim* to Otho: a *mandatum* was a contract whereby one party agreed to perform a service gratuitously for another. But when he came to demand her back, he asked for his *depositum: a depositum* involved the handing over of a thing for safekeeping but not for use. That is, literarily and legally this is a very clever tale, and Suetonius was probably not its inventor.

24. Tacitus 13. 45–46; cf. 13. 20. For embroidery, literary and legal, of the first version, see the previous note. The second version likewise has a legal joke: if

Poppaea had stayed with Nero for three nights she would then be married to him *cum manu,* and in his legal power. Moreover, both versions have folkloric aspects and literary coloring. The conclusion quoted is that of Syme 1958, 290.

25. The idea arose in the seventeenth century: Gyles 1946–1947. It was lushly recalled by A. C. Swinburne, in "Dolores," *Poems and Ballads* (First Series, London, 1866):

> When, with flame all around him aspirant,
>   Stood flushed, as a harp-player stands,
> The implacable beautiful tyrant,
>   Rose-crowned, having death in his hands;
> And a sound as the sound of loud water
>   Smote far through the flight of the fires,
> And mixed with the lightning of slaughter
>   A thunder of lyres.

26. Townend 1960, 105; Wiseman 1991; Wardle 1992; Sansone 1993, 189. (*Pace* Griffin 1984, 236 and 1976, 429, n. 2, this very passage should show that Dio did use Cluvius Rufus: Suetonius and Dio clearly follow a common source here, and that source [cf. Sansone] is very unlikely to have been Pliny or Fabius Rusticus.)

27. Literary artist: Wiseman 1991. Sansone 1993, 179 cites the opinions of such eminent Latinists as G. B. Townend on Suetonius' retelling of Nero's death ("perhaps the most successful piece of continuous narrative in the *Caesars*") and F. R. D. Goodyear ("perhaps the best thing he ever wrote"); the praise should of course be assigned to Cluvius. Sansone's outstanding contribution was to reveal the underworldly aspect of the narrative, which he believed "contained a substantial admixture of fiction." The folkloric aspect was pointed out to me by Adrienne Mayor.

28. Egypt: Dio 63.27. 2. No killer: Suetonius 47. 3, Dio 63. 29. 2 (at a later point in the narrative). Boiled water: Suetonius 48. 3, Dio 63. 28. 5; cf. Pliny 31. 40 for his original habit. Self-reproach and exhortation: Suetonius 49. 3. Homer: 49. 3. Centurion: 49. 4.

29. Suetonius 49. 1 (Gavorse translation, modified). Cf. Dio 63. 29. 2.

30. Nero's meaning has sparked much comment: e.g., Gyles 1962; Bradley 1978, 277; di Lorenzo 1981; et al. Cf. Griffin 1984, 164ff., "What an artist dies with me"; Kierdorf 1992, 229, "Was für ein Künstler geht mit mir zugrunde"; et al.

3. Portrait of the Artist

1. Epigraphs: Pliny *Panegyricus* 46. 4; Juvenal 8. 198–199; Suetonius 53 (Gavorse translation, modified).

2. For Nero's itinerary in Greece, and its chronology, see Halfmann 1986,

173–177. Rescheduling the games and adding artistic contests: Suetonius 23. 1; Philostratus *Apollonius* 5. 7. Nero's building at Olympia: Sinn 1993; Sinn also shows, at 139–140, that the so-called House of Nero at Olympia is a modern fiction. The empty 211th Olympiad: Pausanias 10. 36. 9, with Habicht 1985, 83.

3. This assertion merely restates the conclusion to N. Kennell's invaluable paper (Kennell 1988, 251): "Nero did not go to Greece to admire the monuments of Classical Greek culture, but to be admired himself."

4. Dio 63. 8. 3, 10. 1. On all of this, including the precise meaning of Nero's titles, Kennell 1988 is fundamental. Compare the elder Philostratus' *Nero* 2: "Nero had been brought to Greece by the call of music and his own exaggerated conviction that even the Muses could not surpass the sweetness of his song."

Nero or others offered excuses for his avoidance of Athens and Sparta: see Kennell 246–247, and Chapter 4 below. His presence is attested in only a few other places in Greece, each of them associated with one of the five circuit cities: the Isthmus of Corinth, for the canal; Lerna, in the Argolid (Pausanias 2. 37. 5); possibly but by no means certainly Thespiae (Pausanias 9. 27. 3), which he could have passed through on the way from Corinth to Delphi.

5. For what is known, see Bradley 1978, who has Nero leave Rome early in August 66 and return there early in December 67.

6. Singing to the lyre: Suetonius 23. 1–3 (Olympia); Dio 63. 8. 2, 63. 8. 4 (competitors, cf. 63. 20. 3); Schol. ad Juv. 8. 226 (Isthmia); Philostratus *Apollonius* 4. 24 (Isthmia), 5. 8 (Olympia); Jerome *Chron.* 65 (Olympia), 66 (Isthmia, Pythia, Actia).

Tragic acting: Suetonius 24. 1; Dio 63. 8. 2; [Lucian] Nero 8; Philostratus *Apollonius* 4. 24, cf. 5. 8 (Olympia), 5. 9 (Pythia); Jerome *Chron.* 65 (Olympia), 66 (Isthmia, Pythia, Actia).

Chariot-racing: Suetonius 24. 2 (Olympia); Dio 63. 8. 2, 14. 1 (Olympia); Jerome *Chron.* 65 (Olympia).

Acting as herald: Suetonius 24. 1; Dio 63. 8. 2, 9. 2; Dio of Prusa *Or.* 71. 9; Philostratus *Apollonius* 4. 24 (Isthmia); Jerome *Chron.* 65 (Olympia), 66 (Isthmia, Pythia, Actia).

7. Prizes for non-competition in Rome (all at the first or second Neronia): Suetonius 12. 3; Dio 61. 21. 1; Tacitus 14. 21. 8, 16. 4 (Nero declined). Prizes sent from Greece: Suetonius 22. 3, Dio 61. 21. 2, with Bradley 1978, 138.

8. Dio 63. 9. 4–6; Suetonius 23. 2–24. 1; Philostratus *Apollonius* 5. 7.

9. Tacitus 16. 4. 2–3; Suetonius 23. 2.

10. Suetonius 20. 1; Pliny 34. 166, 19. 108.

11. Feeble voice: Suetonius 20. 1; Dio 61. 20. 2. Frog: Plutarch *Moralia* 568A. Melodious voice: *Oracula Sibyllina* 5. 141–142. Sang well: Suetonius 39. 3, cf. Philostratus *Apollonius* 4. 42. False Neros: Tacitus *Histories* 2. 8; Dio 66. 19. 3b.

Modest natural gifts improved by training: Pseudo-Lucian *Nero* 6 (Loeb Classical Library translation by M. McLeod). "[Nero's] voice deserves neither admiration nor yet ridicule, for nature has made him tolerably and moderately tuneful. His voice is naturally hollow and low, as his throat is deep set, and his singing has a sort of buzzing sound because his throat is thus constituted. However, the pitch of his voice makes him seem less rough when he puts his trust not in his natural powers but in gentle modifications, attractive melody and adroit harp-playing, in choosing the right time to walk, stop and move, and in swaying his head in time to the music."

12. Suetonius 41. 1.

13. Dio 63. 14. 4 (Cary translation, modified). According to Philostratus *Apollonius* 5. 7, it was the suggestion of his flatterers that Nero proclaim Rome the victor.

14. Three master citharodes are named as Nero's competitors. Pammenes, who was too old: Dio 63. 8. 4. Terpnus: Suetonius 20. 1; cf. Philostratus *Apollonius* 5. 7. Diodorus: Dio 63. 20. 3. Terpnus and Diodorus were later the stars, along with the actor Apelles, at Vespasian's dedication of the restored stage of the Theater of Marcellus, for which occasion each citharode earned 200,000 sesterces: Suetonius *Vespasian* 19. 1.

15. Rivalry: Suetonius 23. 2 (where *condicionis eiusdem* should mean not "of the same rank," but "of the same talent"); Dio 63. 8. 5, 9. 2. Statues into latrines: Suetonius 23. 1. Citharode's statues vandalized: Dio 63. 8. 5. Murder: Philostratus (Pseudo-Lucian) *Nero* 9–10: the story reads like fiction, with folkloric elements; indeed the second-century dialogue in which it appears was probably never meant to be taken as fact.

16. Pythicus: Dio 63. 18. 2. Paris: Dio 63. 18. 1 for the first motive, Suetonius 54 for the second, uncertainly ("et sunt qui tradunt . . .").

17. Suetonius 24. 2; Dio 63. 14. 1. The quotation and the description of the Olympic course are taken from Finley and Pleket 1976, 29.

18. Fear: Suetonius 23. 2; Dio 63. 9. 2; Philostratus *Apollonius* 5. 7. Address to the judges: Suetonius 23. 3. Rewards: Dio 63. 14. 1; Suetonius 24. 2.

19. Tacitus 14. 15; Dio 61. 20. 3 (AD 59); Suetonius 20. 3 (AD 64). On the Augustiani see Gatti 1976–1977; Mourgues 1988 (fundamental) and 1990.

20. Audience control: Suetonius 23. 2; Tacitus 16. 5. 1. Enthusiasm required: Dio 63. 10. 1; Suetonius 25. 3, *Vespasian* 4. 4; Tacitus 16. 5. 4–5. Prosecutions: Philostratus *Apollonius* 5. 7. Suetonius alleges that Vespasian withdrew into an obscure city of the province, but the severity, indeed the reality, of the emperor's displeasure is highly dubious, since he very soon appointed him commander-in-chief of the war against the Jews, in winter 66/67: Josephus *BJ* 3. 64 with 3. 1–7.

There is a problem of chronology here. Tacitus describes the control and abuse of the audience, including the insult to Vespasian, in his account of the Second Neronia at Rome, in 65, whereas Suetonius and Dio explicitly assign the same

events to the tour of Greece in 66/67. These two versions may reflect two different sources. The problem is not too important here: what is significant is that the
context is one of public performance in the last three years of the reign.

21. Dio 63. 10. 1–3.

22. The bibliography has grown massive over the last thirty years. See especially Friedlaender, Wistrand (very traditional but intelligent), Cameron,
Hopkins, Coleman. Returns are diminishing.

The following pages are intended for readers little acquainted with the nature
of Roman spectacles, and they make no claim to originality.

23. Far less important in Rome, and new in Nero's day or even later, were
such Greek buildings as gymnasiums for athletics, stadiums for running, and
small odeons for recitation and declamation.

24. Plutarch *Pompey* 52. 4; Dio 39. 38.

25. *Sat.* 10. 77–81, with the commentary of E. Courtney (1980) *ad loc.,* for
other references. Fronto, *Principia Historiae* 17 (Loeb Classical Library translation
by C. R. Haines, slightly modified).

26. *Pro Sestio* 106, translated by D. R. Shackleton Bailey, *Cicero Back from
Exile: Six Speeches upon His Return* (Chicago, 1991). For the following see Bollinger 1969, and especially Cameron 1976, 157–190 ("the emperor and his people
at the games"); cf. Hopkins 1983, 14–20 ("gladiatorial shows as political theater"),
Veyne 1990, 398–419. It should be noted that the term "theater" could signify for
the Romans not just theaters but amphitheaters (the sites of gladiatorial combats)
and circuses (the sites of chariot races) as well.

27. 13. 24. The theme recurs in Tacitus, cf. Cameron 1976, 160, n. 4: *theatri
licentia,* 1. 77. 1; *theatralis populi lascivia,* 11. 13. 1; *ludicra licentia,* 13. 25. 4.

28. The evidence is very difficult to decipher, the rules themselves complex;
see above all Rawson 1987.

29. Seneca *Epistulae* 47. 17. On the attitudes of intellectuals (i.e., writers) to
performers—actors and dancers were immoral, gladiators were contemptible,
charioteers were a matter of indifference—see the thorough collection of evidence by Wistrand 1992. On performers as sports heroes and popular stars, see
Friedlaender 1907; Hopkins 1983, 20–27.

30. Levick 1983, 108, writing of the theater; Tacitus *Dialogus* 29.

31. See Levick 1983, 105–108, for an excellent account of "restrictions on public performance by members of the upper classes, 46 B.C. – A.D. 15."

32. Noble Romans are occasionally on record as competing as charioteers at
the victory games presented by Sulla (Asconius 93C), Julius Caesar (Suetonius
Julius 39. 2) and (probably) Augustus (Suetonius *Augustus* 43. 2): Rawson 1981,
398–399. Also as competitors at the Olympics, although in most cases it is not
clear whether they themselves or hired charioteers actually drove: Cameron 1976,
202–205. Nero's father, Domitius Ahenobarbus, was exceptional in his devotion

to *ars aurigandi* (Suetonius 4), and Vitellius as a young man recommended himself to Caligula by his skill (Suetonius *Vitellius* 4), but Nero seems to be the first Roman aristocrat to have driven as a regular competitor, and for a particular racing faction, at Rome. That Caligula was a charioteer (as distinct from a zealous fan) rests only on the dubious testimony of Dio 59. 5. 5.

33. Tacitus 14. 14; Rawson 1981.

34. Burrus: Tacitus 14. 15. Vitellius: Tacitus *Histories* 2. 71, cf. Suetonius *Vitellius* 11. 2. Valens: Tacitus *Histories* 3. 62. Cluvius Rufus: Suetonius 21. 2; Dio 63. 14. 3. Thrasea: Tacitus 16. 21; Dio 62. 26. 3–4. Piso: Tacitus 15. 65 (he was likewise adept at playing the lyre: *Laus Pisonis* 166). On Thrasea's stage appearance, see Linderski 1992, dating it to 57 or 56.

35. Chariot-racing in 59: Tacitus 14. 14. Neronian Games in 65: this account combines Tacitus 16. 4; Suetonius 21. 2; Suetonius *Vitellius* 4.

36. Tacitus 14. 13; Dio 63. 20. 4–5.

37. Pliny *Panegyricus* 46. 4–5. Decorum was reestablished after Nero's death, entailing disapproval of his extravagances by later writers. But some of his style survived: cf. Juvenal 4. 136–137, on a counselor of Domitian, *noverat ille / luxuriam imperii veterem noctesque Neronis.*

38. *Civilitas*, civility, is the ability of the emperor to act as an ordinary citizen, or at least as an ordinary Roman nobleman.

39. Dio 61. 9. 1.

40. Tacitus 13. 22.

41. Tacitus 13. 31.

42. Suetonius 12. 1, cf. 11. 1.

43. Suetonius 12. 1. On the history of the *pyrrichae* dance, see Sabbatini Tumolesi 1970.

44. Dio 61. 9. 5.

45. Suetonius 12. 2. His *curator ludorum* was almost certainly Q. Veranius, consul in 49, who went out in 57 to govern the province of Britain, where he died the following year. Veranius' partially preserved epitaph seems to mention *ludi* of which he was in charge. The original publication of that inscription proposed a connection with Nero's *ludis [maximis]*, repeated at *AE* 1953. 251 (Rome); the best and most recent version, *CIL* VI. 41075, suggests the following restoration, based on line lengths: *Ludis / [maximis praefectus est, cum honorem non p]etierit ab Augusto principe, cuius liberalitas erat minister.* But the Ludi Maximi (on which see below) took place in 59, the year after Veranius' death: cf. Bradley 1978, 83. The games must be those of 57; Nero's *liberalitas*, of which Veranius was the agent, should be the *congiarium*, the public largesse, referred to by Tacitus (13. 31. 2) and on coins; and the full restoration of the lacuna in Veranius' epitaph remains unsure.

46. *Ludis, quos pro aeternitate imperii susceptos appellari maximos voluit* (Suetonius 11. 2).

47. Suetonius 12. 1. Balcony: see Kelly 1979, 30, n. 36.

48. Dio 61. 11. 1, 61. 15–16; cf. Tacitus 14. 12–13.

49. Dio 61. 16. 1–3; cf. Suetonius 39. 2.

50. Dio 61. 16. 4–5; cf. Tacitus 14. 22. 4, dating the lightning to 60, and Philostratus *Apollonius* 4. 43.

51. Dio 61. 17. 1–2; cf. Suetonius 34. 5.

52. Dio 61. 17. 2 – 18.2. Dio's opinions and the rhetorical embellishments to his narrative should be ignored throughout: e.g., the pasquinades represented true public opinion; Nero did not bring charges because he was contemptuous of what people did; the lightning bolt represented divine displeasure; the upper classes performed in public like the dregs of society. Similarly to be dismissed are the supposed comments by the audience (Macedonians pointing to a descendant of their conqueror, Aemilius Paulus, et al.); the comment that by these games Nero introduced his own disgrace; the comment that any thinking person bemoaned the vast expenditure, and that thinking people could foresee that his need for money would lead to crime; and so on. The eclipse which marred the sacrifices occurred on 30 April: Pliny *NH* 2. 180; Tacitus also mentions it in the context of thanksgiving, 14. 12. 3.

53. The standard English translation of Dio in the Loeb Classical Library is misleading in three places. At 61. 16. 4, ʼεν μέσαις ταῖς θυσίαις ταῖς ἐπὶ τῇ Ἀγριππίνῃ is rendered "in the midst of the sacrifices that were offered in Agrippina's honour," and at 61. 17. 2, Ἐπὶ δὲ δὴ τῇ μητρὶ καὶ ἑορτὴν μεγίστην κ.τ.λ. is rendered "In honour of his mother he celebrated a most magnificent and costly festival." Both lead to confusion, suggesting that Nero, years after the break with his mother and indeed after her death, is suddenly paying her honor. But in both cases, this is not honoring her but celebrating her death, and the Greek ʼεπί + the dative is simply causal, "on account of": the point obscured by the translation is that Dio's order is perfectly chronological. Moreover, ʽεορτὴν μεγίστην, rather than merely "magnificent festival," is surely meant to convey the Latin "Ludi Maximi."

54. Tacitus 14. 11. 2; Quintilian 8. 5. 15. For these passages, the Arval Brothers, and more on the aftermath of Agrippina's death, see especially Chapters 4 and 8 below.

55. Dio 61. 17. 3–5.

56. Tacitus 14. 14. 5–6.

57. A character in Epictetus (1. 12. 18) debates whether to take part in Nero's spectacle *(theoria)*, by playing in a tragedy. This must be the Ludi Maximi, the only games in which dramas were performed. If he does not, he will be be-

headed—this is standard anti-tyrannical rhetoric in a Stoic text, and in fact no one was executed.

58. Nero's Juvenalia may have had a small effect on later literary history. R. Syme suggested (Syme 1958, 774–775; repeated in Syme 1984, 1125) that the poet Juvenal was born in the year 67, and hence turned sixty in 127. The argument was based on the occurrence of two consular dates in Juvenal's corpus: one, at 15. 27, refers to an incident in Egypt as recent in the consulship of Juncus (October–December 127), a very rare dating by suffect consul in literature, and Egypt being of special interest to the poet; the other, at 13. 16–17, is addressed to a sixty-year-old friend born in the consulship of Fonteius. "Which Fonteius? Not the *ordinarius* of 59, but the Fonteius Capito of 67 . . . as Borghesi divined," and "Juvenal may himself have reached sixty in 127." This is all of course highly speculative. As Syme points out, c. 55 and c. 60 (rather than 67) are the years most favored by scholars for Juvenal's birth, and E. Courtney prefers c. 60 in a careful review of the evidence, in *A Commentary on the Satires of Juvenal* (London, 1980), 1–2. Perhaps the Fonteius consul in 59 was significant to Juvenal after all, if his patriotic father named him in honor of the emperor's unique celebration of the Juvenalia in that year. For similar significant cognomina, compare the telling contemporary examples (Innocens, Laetus, Tranquillus, Sospes) produced by Syme in another context: Syme 1984, 1053.

59. Tacitus 14. 15; Dio 61. 19–20.

60. Compare Tacitus' *Histories* 3. 62, recording, as mentioned earlier, that Fabius Valens, a man of senatorial rank, took part in the mimes *ludicro Iuvenalium,* at first "as if from necessity, but soon of his own free will."

61. Suetonius 11. 2.

62. A problem is raised by the text of Suetonius and its ordering by topic rather than chronology, which must be faced here. At 11. 2, as reported, he mentions simply that consulars and matrons participated in the Juvenalia. In 12. 3–4 he considers in detail the Neronian games, established in 60, the first games in the Greek style at Rome, which included "musical," "gymnastic," and "equestrian" contests. On the gymnastic contests, he writes that they were held in the Saepta—a large rectangular area in the Campus Martius, used for voting and appropriate to such contests, before Nero built his own Greek-style gymnasium—and that amidst sacrifice of oxen Nero shaved off his first beard and dedicated it on the Capitol in a golden casket decorated with valuable pearls; also that he began athletic contests and invited the Vestal Virgins to watch them just as the priestesses of Ceres watched the Olympic Games. Here Suetonius has inadvertently transferred the shaving and dedication from the un-Greek Juvenalia (59) to the Neronia (60). Bradley and Kierdorf note the discrepancy between Suetonius and Dio, but make no further comment. However, the whole point of the

Juvenalia was to celebrate the rite of passage, cutting the first beard, and it fits in with the anecdote at 34. 5. Suetonius tells how Nero arranged the death of his aunt Domitia: once, when he visited the lady on her sickbed, she stroked his fluffy beard and said lovingly, "When I receive this, I wish to die," to which he replied jokingly "I shall shave at once," had her doctors kill her with an overdose, and seized her property. Dio, as mentioned above, gives the correct temporal order: death of Agrippina, Nero's triumphant return to Rome, death of Domitia, Ludi Maximi, first shave and dedication, Juvenalia—all in 59.

63. Suetonius 12. 3.

64. No pantomimes: Tacitus 14. 21. 7. Baths and gymnasium, and oil distribution: Suetonius 12. 3; Dio 61. 21. 2. Greek dress: Tacitus 14. 21. 8. At 14. 20–21 Tacitus gives a long account of what purports to be popular reaction, pro and con, to the innovation, concluding rather regretfully that no exceptional disgrace occurred during the games.

65. Suetonius 12. 4. Tacitus' anonymous commentators grumble about the idleness and shameful love affairs that came with gymnasia. The ancient scholiast to Juvenal 4. 53 mentions a Palfurius Sura, son of a consul, who wrestled at an "agon," allegedly against a girl from Sparta. This unlikely event might have occurred at either of the two Neronia, but there is no reason to assume it, and such buffoonery does not sit well with Nero's elevated conception of his Greek games (with Vestals in attendance and pantomimes banned).

66. Suetonius 12. 3; Tacitus 14. 21. 8.

67. *Vita Lucani.* The Life of Lucan attributed to Vacca adds the detail about the theater.

68. Suetonius 12. 4; Dio 61. 21. 2.

69. Dio 61. 21. 2; Suetonius 22. 3.

70. Tacitus 15. 32.

71. Dio 62. 15. 1.

72. Dio 62. 15. 2–6; Tacitus 15. 37.

73. Tacitus 15. 44. 7.

74. Suetonius 21. 1–2.

75. Bolton 1948, Bradley 1978, 129–131, and Malavolta 1978 believe, following Suetonius 21, that the Second Neronia was begun in 64, then suspended and resumed in 65; this view is dismissed, rightly, by Griffin 1984, 161, 280, who assigns it all to 65.

Suetonius continues (21. 2–3) that Nero presented himself in public on occasion. He also thought of performing in private *spectacula,* and a praetor offered him one million sesterces for his services. He acted in tragedies as well; Suetonius then talks about his roles and his performances. Dio, however, discusses these roles and performances in the context of the Greek tour of 67 (63. 9), and assigns the offer of one million sesterces to the year 68 (63. 21. 2; he also names as the would-be donor a Larcius Lydus, who was certainly not a praetor). Since Suetonius offers no chronology, Dio's sequence should be accepted.

76. Tacitus 16. 2. 3–4.

77. Tacitus 16. 4.

78. The Second Neronia is not mentioned explicitly in the epitome of Dio. However, at 62. 29. 1, after his account of the Pisonian conspiracy and its aftermath in 65, Dio does remark that at a certain public festival Nero descended into the orchestra of the theater and recited some of his own poems called *Troica.* This might be the same as the *carmen* which he recited *in scaenam* before leaving the theater and then being called back to perform to the lyre.

Tacitus 16. 5 also assigns to this occasion the notorious harassment of the audience which Suetonius (23) and Dio (63. 15. 1–3) refer to the Grecian tour of 66/67.

Pliny 37. 19 mentions Nero practicing *(praeludit)* in his Vatican gardens before his public debut in the Theater of Pompey. An anonymous graffito referring to the Roman Apollo (Nero) tuning his lyre should be dated between the defeat of Caesennius Paetus by the Parthians in 62 and Corbulo's humbling of them in 63.

79. Dio 63. 1. 1.

80. Suetonius 13. 1. Date: Scheid 1990, 404–406.

81. Dio 63. 6. 1–3.

82. Dio 63. 21. 2. For the chronology, see the varying arguments of Bradley 1978, Halfmann 1986, Levy 1991. There is still considerable uncertainty, much of it depending on the date of the liberation of Achaia, which the Acraephia decree assigns to 28 November: 66 or 67? Since the arguments are complex, inconclusive, and not very relevant here, I will simply state two convictions; interested readers should follow up with the three papers cited above, none of which agrees with the others. First, when the Acraephia decree confusingly seems to name Nero as "in his 13th *tribunicia potestas* designate," "designate" has the looser sense of "chosen" (that is, actually *in* his 13th t.p.) rather than the normal "chosen but not yet in office" (indeed, if that were the case, why the needless circumlocution for "12th"?). And second, Clay 1982 has shown (at 9–16) that Nero's tribunician power was dated from 13 October throughout his reign (and not from early December in the latter years). Therefore, Nero proclaimed the liberation of Greece in his 13th year of tribunician power (13 October 66 – 12 October 67), on 28 November 66. (So, in the end, Halfmann and Levy.) His return to Italy can be dated to (?) early autumn of the next year, 67 (Halfmann, with other considerations).

83. Terpnus, Naples, Rome: Suetonius 20–21. On his early interest in singing, cf. Tacitus 13. 3. 7. The Naples and Rome appearances dated to 64: Tacitus 15. 33ff.

84. Early obsession with the circus: Suetonius 22. 1–2; cf. Tacitus 13. 3. 7. Vat-

ican racing in 59: Tacitus 14. 3–5; Suetonius 22. 2. First public racing: Dio 62. 15. 1; with Suetonius 22. 2. He also befriended Vitellius because of his skill at charioteering, among other virtues (Suetonius *Vitellius* 4), and Tigellinus for his skill at breeding horses for four-horse chariots (*Schol. ad Iuvenalem* 1. 155).

85. From the beginning of the reign he had allowed the people to watch him exercise in the Campus Martius; he often declaimed in public; and he had read his own poems not only at home but in the theater "to such universal joy" that a supplication to the gods was decreed and the poems themselves were inscribed in letters of gold and dedicated to Jupiter Capitolinus: Suetonius 11. 2. These were the actions of an affable emperor, the *civilis princeps.*

86. "Attis": Dio 61. 20. 2 (possibly referred to or quoted in Persius' first satire). "Niobe": Suetonius 21. 2. Sack of Troy: Suetonius 38. 2; Tacitus 15. 39; Dio 62. 18. 1.

To start off his Greek tour, Nero sang at the altar of Zeus Casios in Corfu, presumably a hymn of praise to the god: Suetonius 22. 3. Similarly, at the inauguration of the excavation of the Corinth canal he sang hymns in honor of the marine deities Amphitrite and Poseidon, and of Melicertes (in whose honor the Isthmian Games had been founded) and his mother Leucothea: [Philostratus] *Nero* 3. (For the complicated tale of Melicertes [later the god Palaemon] and his mother Ino [later Leucothea, the White Goddess], see R. Graves, *The Greek Myths* [London, 1955], 225–229.) Whether to include these performances as citharody is uncertain.

87. Favorite roles, presumably from a common source: Dio 63. 9. 4–5, 10. 2; Suetonius 21. 3. At 63. 22. 6, Dio repeats the names Thyestes, Oedipus, Alcmaeon, and Orestes in the contemptuous speech by the rebel Vindex; at 46. 3, Suetonius refers to Oedipus in exile, which should be the same as or related to Oedipus blinded; and at 39. 2 he records a graffito in Greek naming Nero "Orestes Alcmaeon." At 39. 3, a contemporary refers to his singing of *Naupli mala;* for the argument that this must concern his role as Orestes, see Chapter 4 below.

88. Philostratus *Apollonius* 5. 7; Juvenal 8. 228. Creon and Antigone are both associated with the blinded Oedipus. If he really played both characters, were these separate tragedies, or did Nero play different roles at different times, or even on the same occasion? At *Apollonius* 4. 39, Philostratus implies that Nero wrote an *Oresteia* and an *Antigone* for singing by a citharode (and presumably performed them himself).

89. Suetonius 54.

90. Suetonius 10. 2; Tacitus 16. 4. 2, Dio 62. 29. 1 (where, *contra* the Loeb translation, *orchestra* is to be understood as "stage": Kelly 1979, 30, n. 36).

91. The following depends heavily on Lesky 1949 and especially on Kelly's excellent paper of 1979. The Greek word *citharoedia* is used here for convenience, although it does not appear in classical Latin.

92. Suetonius 25. 2. What is actually shown on the reverse of coins issued from c. 62 to 68 is Apollo Citharoedus in flowing robes, holding his lyre in
his right hand: *RIC* nos. 73–82, 121–123, 205–212, 380–381, 414–417, 451–455.
Whether this is meant to depict Apollo or Nero as Apollo is unsure.

93. Masks: Dio 63. 9. 4–5, Suetonius 21. 3. Props: Suetonius 24. 1 (scepter);
Suetonius 21. 3, Dio 63. 9. 6 (chains). Like the citharode, the tragic actor wore
high boots.

94. Lucian *De Saltatione* 29 (masked with closed lips); 27 (criticism of actor's
high boots, not to mention use of padding as needed).

95. Pantomimic contests: Dio 61. 17. 3 (59); Tacitus 14. 15, Dio 61. 19. 2
(Juvenalia, 59). Took up dancing late in reign: Dio 63. 18. 1; Suetonius 54.

96. Same story danced and acted: Suetonius *Caligula* 57. 3. Common vocabulary: *histrio* can refer to both actor and singer (e.g., Suetonius 54); *canere,* to
sing, can refer to both singing and tragic acting (e.g., Tacitus 15. 65).

97. Arias: Lesky 1949, 345–346. Concert tragedies: Kelly 1979, 34–38. The essential source for the latter is Dio of Prusa 19. 4–5. Lesky rightly draws attention to the Roman taste for pathos, and compares these performances to the
"Ovidische Pathosmonologie" such as one finds in Ovid's *Heroides* and scattered
through his *Metamorphoses.*

98. Tacitus 15. 65. 2. The remark presumably would have no point if Nero
was also known as a tragic actor. The emphasis placed on actions and remarks by
Subrius Flavus, one of the leaders of the conspiracy (Tacitus 15. 50. 6–7, 58. 4, 65.
1–2, and especially 67), suggests that he was the subject of a hagiography like
those mentioned in Chapter 2 above. On Nero's late turn to tragedy, see Lesky
1949, 397–399; Kelly 1979, 28–29.

99. See Kelly 1979, 22–27, on the complicated history. The classic instance of
a role both danced and acted is the "Cinyras" which Neoptolemus acted before
the assassination of Philip of Macedon and Mnester danced before the murder of
Caligula: Suetonius *Caligula* 57. 4. Whether the spoken text differed according to
the type of performance is by no means clear. Lucian states that the same subjects
were treated by both pantomime and tragedy, illustrating with a long list of
mythological examples: *De Saltatione* 31, 37–61.

Note that by Nero's day, poets of the caliber of Statius and Lucan were not
above writing texts for pantomimes: Juvenal 7. 82–87 (Statius' *Agave*) and Vacca
Vita Lucani (his *fabulae salticae*). They did it, in part at least, because it paid well:
see Juvenal on Statius, cf. Ovid *Tristia* 2. 507, *scaena est lucrosa poetae* (on writing
mimes).

100. Suetonius 24. 1; Dio 63. 8. 2, 9. 2; Dio of Prusa 71. 9; Philostratus
Apollonius 4. 24.

101. See Suetonius 54 for his interests. Water organ: Suetonius 41. 2; Dio 63.
26. 4 (cf. 59. 5. 5, for a similar story about Caligula). Pipes: Dio of Prusa 71. 9.

102. For the different *Neroniani ludi,* see Meissner 1992, 172–175. On the glad-

iator (Tib. Claudius) Spiculus as not only an officer in (*ILS* 1730) but the commander of Nero's bodyguard, see Speidel 1994, 29. Rewards: Suetonius 30. 2. He met a gruesome end: Plutarch *Galba* 8. 5.

103. Philostratus *Apollonius* 4. 36 (influenced by Commodus?); Suetonius 53.

104. Tacitus 14. 47; Dio 61. 17. 1; Philostratus 4. 42; Suetonius 12. 3 (Neronia), 40. 4 (Naples), 45. 1 (court). His intent to wrestle: Suetonius 53; Dio of Prusa 71. 9.

105. Suetonius 25. 3, 41. 1–2; Dio 63. 26. 1–2.

106. Weeping and victory songs: Suetonius 43. 2, apparently verbatim. Alexandria: Dio 63. 27. 2. His dream of Alexandria may well be true. Suetonius reports (47. 2) that after Nero's death a speech was discovered among his writings, which he planned to deliver on the Rostrum in the Forum, dressed in black, seeking pardon for his past deeds *maxima miseratione,* with the utmost pathos, or at least an appointment to the prefecture of Egypt.

107. Easy versifier: Suetonius 52, apparently taking exception to the sentiments expressed by some, like Tacitus at 14. 16. 1–2, that Nero's *studium carminum* ran to the production of prepared or extempore verse which other poets fleshed out for him. His poems read under Vitellius (Suetonius *Vitellius* 11. 2); Domitian (Martial 8. 70, on the reader *carmina qui docti Neronis habet:* Martial's 8th book was published in 94, R. Syme, *Some Arval Brethren* [Oxford, 1980], 44); Hadrian (Suetonius 52, *Domitian* 1); and around the year 400 (Servius *ad Aen.* 5. 370, *ad Georg.* 3. 36).

108. Satires: Suetonius 24. 2 (probably); 42. 2; *Domitian* 1; Tacitus 15. 49; Martial 8.70, cf. 9. 26. Hymns: Tacitus 15. 34 (Naples); Suetonius 22. 3 (Corcyra); Philostratus *Nero* 3 (Isthmus). Epic: Dio 62. 29. 1–2; *et alibi.*

109. Sullivan 1985, 91 92. The fragments with commentary are given in Courtney 1993, 359; discussed at Morelli 1914, 135–138; Bardon 1936 adds little.

4. The Power of Myth

1. Epigraphs: Dio 63. 9. 4 – 10. 1 (from Xiphilinus); Suetonius 21. 3.

2. The main source is Tacitus, 13. 1 – 14. 13, supplemented with passages from Suetonius, especially 34. 1–4, and the excerpts from Dio 61. 1. 1 – 16. 5. For comparison of the three authors, see Heinz 1948, 30–33. The narrative here, beginning with the astrologers' prediction (Tacitus 14. 9), does not claim to represent historical fact.

3. The precedent for a grant of lictors (or rather one lictor) and a priesthood of her late husband had been set for Livia, the widow of Augustus: Koestermann 1967, 237.

4. On the incest, see Suetonius 28. 2; Tacitus 14. 2; Dio 61. 11. 3–4. Dio at 61. 8. 5 speaks vaguely of rumors of incest in 55, but this is his retrojection: all other reports refer to 58/59 and the threat of Poppaea.

5. See Dio 61. 3. 2 on the litter occasionally shared in 54. Thereafter Nero kept his distance.

6. This bald report can hardly replace the cinematic brilliance of Tacitus' account. There are many versions of Agrippina's last action and words, all centering on her offering for the fatal stroke the womb that bore Nero: Tacitus' lapidary "ventrem feri" (cf. *Octavia* 269f.) is the most dramatic, but not necessarily the correct version.

7. Quintilian 8. 5. 18. The same source quotes (8. 5. 15) a line from a response by the orator Julius Africanus: "Your Gallic provinces beg, Caesar, that you bear your felicity with fortitude."

8. The inscribed records of the priestly college of the Arval Brothers record on 5 April 59 various public sacrifices which they undertook because of the thanksgivings decreed for the safety of Nero Claudius Caesar Augustus Germanicus; on 23 June they sacrificed for his safety and return: *ILS* 230. On the nature and significance of his reentry into Rome, see Chapter 8 below.

9. Dio 61. 14. 2; Suetonius 34. 4; Tacitus 14. 9. The plaintive "I did not know that I had so beautiful a mother" cannot be taken as evidence that there had been no incest: Delcourt 1944, 204, rightly compared it to Nero's remark at the death of Rubellius Plautus, that he did not know he had so big a nose (Dio 62. 14. 1)! Baldwin 1979 suggests that in handling his mother's limbs, Nero, a son who had knowingly killed his mother, was reversing the situation of the *Bacchae* of Euripides, where a mother who has unknowingly killed her son handles his mangled body.

10. *Octavia* 593ff., Agrippina as Fury with torch and scourge. Cf. Statius *Silvae* 2. 7. 116–119, where the ghost of Lucan is granted a vision of Nero in Tartarus, "pale in the light of his mother's torch": she pursues him still in hell.

11. Dio 61. 16. 1–3; Suetonius 39.

12. Dio 61. 16. 1; Suetonius 45. 2. The two incidents may of course be one, but there is no reason to assume so. Bradley 1978, 239, dates all of the pasquinades to the period after Agrippina's death, but popular memory was not so brief: a pseudo-Sibylline verse circulated after the Great Fire of 64 predicting that "Last of the family of Aeneas, a matricide will rule" (Dio 62. 18. 4). The meaning of the inscription "What could I do? But you have deserved the sack" remains unsure, despite emendation and interpretation: perhaps a dialogue?

13. Suetonius 39. 2. Dio and others have a slightly different version of the first line only: "Nero, Orestes, Alcmaeon, mother-slayers" (cf. Philostratus *VS* 1. 481, and Sopater, *Prolegomena in Aristidem*, p. 740, Dindorf). This is the standardly accepted version, but by making the noun plural these writers have lost the joke of the original iambic line, which transformed the *tria nomina* "Nero Claudius Caesar"—standard nomenclature on inscriptions—into "Nero Orestes Alcmaeon."

14. Suetonius 39.

15. See the splendid paper of Wiseman, 1974.

16. For an excellent introduction to the whole question of "myth as example of history," see Hölscher 1993.

17. See Zanker 1988, especially 33–77, on the rival mythological images of Antony and Octavian (Augustus) expressed visually in coins, freestanding and relief sculpture, gems, earthenware, and monumental architecture.

18. See Zanker 1988, 192–215, based on P. Zanker, *Forum Augustum* (Tübingen, 1968).

19. Hölscher 1993, 80. On Augustus as Orestes, a figure of interest to his descendant Nero, see also Hölscher 1991.

20. Examples can be found in Cameron 1976, 158–161, 171–172, and Reynolds 1943.

21. Laberius: Macrobius *Saturnalia* 2. 7. 4. Caligula: Suetonius *Caligula* 27. Cicero: *Pro Sestio* 120–122. Marcus: *HA Marcus* 29. Nero: above. Commodus: *HA Commodus* 3. Gallienus allegedly burned some impudent actors alive: *HA Gallieni* 7–9. Rawson 1985, 470, points out that the tradition of the political double entendre goes back at least into the 90s BC, citing two examples.

22. Cicero *Ad Familiares* 7. 1, with Beacham 1991, 156–158. For other examples of plays produced for their contemporary relevance, see Cameron 1976, 171.

23. Reynolds 1943, 40.

24. Suetonius *Augustus* 53, *Galba* 13.

25. It should be noted that the myths discussed here are those which Nero *acted*, not those which he sang about: for the difference, see Chapter 3. That his roles were relevant to his real life is not a new idea, but their nature and purpose have been little explored.

26. Details for this and the following stories, with full references to the ancient sources, may be found in L. Preller, *Griechische Mythologie*, 4th ed., rev. C. Robert (Leipzig, 1894–1921), and W. H. Roscher, ed., *Ausführliches Lexikon der griechischen und römischen Mythologie* (Berlin, 1884–1937). The two major ancient collections are Hyginus' *Fabulae* and Apollodorus' *Bibliotheca*.

27. Delcourt 1959, 65–67, is central to what follows.

28. *Choephoroi* 299–304, translated by Richmond Lattimore. The brace of women is Clytemnestra and the womanish Aegisthus, who had not gone to war at Troy.

29. The parallel is suggested in Krappe 1940, 471–472, but cf. Delcourt 1959, 66–67.

30. Suetonius 34; see Pliny *NH* 30. 14–17, for the date and for Nero's disgust.

31. Dio may be confused: Athens should have been a place of refuge for the new Orestes.

32. Convincingly argued by Kennell 1988: cf. Chapter 3 above. Dio 63. 14. 3. Athens was something of a backwater at the time, and Nero made no effort even to visit a city far more attractive to him, Alexandria. Nor is it at all clear why the

Furies should have kept him from Athens: Athena had after all been the goddess who had saved Orestes from them there, and in her Italian form as Minerva she had saved Nero.

33. And Alcmaeon is routinely linked with Orestes in standard attacks on Nero: Suetonius 39. 2, Dio, Philostratus *Apollonius.*

34. Besides Hyginus and Apollodorus, the main sources are Pausanias and two plays by Euripides which survive only in fragments. The story clearly had greater resonance in antiquity than now. The only known representation of Alcmaeon in Roman art (if it is Alcmaeon) appears in a Pompeian fresco contemporary with Nero ("third quarter of the first century"): *LIMC* I. 1, 549, 552.

35. Juvenal 8. 215–221; Philostratus *VA* 4. 38; Pseudo-Lucian [Philostratus the Elder] *Nero* 10; Suetonius 39. 2. I am not sure what to make of the late scholiast's note on Lucan, *Bellum Civile* 5. 113 (cf. 139, 178), which claims that the Delphic oracle replied to Nero, "I do not respond to parricides": that is precisely what it *had* done to Orestes and Alcmaeon. The rhetorical response is not at all Delphic.

36. See, e.g., Crum 1951/1952, building on a point made by R. S. Rogers, *CW* 35 (1945/1946), 53–54: in one version of the myth Palamedes was first lured down a well by a false report of treasure there, then stones were tossed down on him. This is taken by Crum as an allusion, made in a *Nauplius* written by Nero, to the hunt for Dido's treasure (Suetonius 31. 3, et al.). Frazer 1966/1967 prefers the version that has Palamedes murdered by drowning while on a fishing expedition. Nero would then be dramatizing his own disposal of his young stepson while the boy was fishing (Suetonius 35. 5). *Mala Naupli:* Suetonius 39. 3.

37. Dio 63. 9. 4–10; 22. 6; Suetonius 21. 3.

38. Philostratus *Apollonius* 5. 7.

39. Dio 63. 9. 4; Suetonius 46. 3. The idea that the ghost of Laius pursued his murderous son first appeared in a horrific scene of necromancy in Seneca's near-contemporary play *Oedipus.*

Webster 1967, 242–243, suggested that "*excaecatum* could hardly refer to self-blinding," hence that Nero was following a tradition much less familiar to us but central to the (lost) *Oedipus* of Euripides, wherein Oedipus was exposed as the murderer of Laius and blinded at the order of Creon *before* it was revealed that he was Laius' son. This alternative Oedipus, more dignified and more passive, was sent into exile with Antigone after the deaths of his fratricidal sons, Polyneices and Eteocles, at the end of Euripides' (surviving) *Phoenissae:* Nero's line would be appropriate for such an ending, although there is nothing like it in Euripides. Whichever the case may be, I presume that Juvenal's association of Nero with the mask of Antigone (8. 229) refers to his *Oedipus Exul.*

40. Again, the following depends on Delcourt 1944, especially 190–213.

41. According to Plutarch *Caesar* 32. 6. Suetonius *Divus Iulius* 7. 2 places the incident much earlier in Caesar's career, making explicit the interpretation that

"mother . . . is no other than the earth, which is considered the parent of all." For other instances, see Delcourt 1944, 192–203.

42. The death of Jocasta in Seneca's *Oedipus* poses an interesting problem. On the verge of suicide, she debates where to stab herself, in the breast or in the throat, but settles on the place where all the troubles began, her womb (*Oedipus* 1032–1039). As Hind 1972 pointed out, her suicide by striking the womb appears in no extant Greek tragedy, but it does strongly recall Agrippina's *ventrem feri*. Unfortunately the date of Seneca's play is unknown. Hind canvasses three possibilities: it was written before Agrippina's death, and she was playing a role; it was written after her death, and Seneca was perhaps implying that she killed herself; or it was written before her death, and popular rumor embroidered her death with a Senecan reminiscence. All three are quite possible, with a variant of the third being more likely, that is, the literary embroidery shows the hand of Nero, who controlled the story of his mother's death.

43. *Annals* 13. 45–46, 14. 1, 14. 60–61, 16. 6–7.

44. *Octavia* 125, cf. 186. Compare Tacitus 14. 60, *paelex et adultera;* Dio 62. 13. 1, *pallikida.*

45. Tacitus 13. 45. The whole description is meant to recall, sometimes to echo, Sallust's description of another wild and immoral noblewoman, Sempronia, in *Catilina* 25: Syme 1958, 353.

46. Milk baths: Pliny 11. 238, 28. 183 (and favorite mules were shod with gold: Pliny 33. 140); *Scholia ad Juvenalem* 6. 462; Dio 62. 28. 1 (along with the prayer for early death). Amber-colored hair *(sucini):* Pliny 37. 50. It is usually thought that this comes from an erotic poem by the emperor; it may reflect an amber craze which sprang up in the reign (Pliny 37. 45–46). A face cream, *pinguia Poppaeana,* was named after her: Juvenal 6. 462.

47. Astronomy: *Anthologia Palatina* 9. 355 = D. L. Page, *Further Greek Epigrams* (Cambridge, 1981), 535–536, Leonides xxxii. Judaism: Josephus *Jewish Antiquities* 20. 189–195, *Vita* 16. Williams 1988 showed conclusively what should never have been doubted—that Josephus was both precise and accurate in calling the empress *theosebes,* pious (that is, in her support for the pious).

48. *Scholia ad Juvenalem* 6. 434. It might argued that his third marriage was part of his extravagant plan to keep Poppaea alive (see below). As graffiti attest, Poppaea and Nero were both highly popular at Pompeii, which may well have been her native town: Van Buren 1953; Della Corte 1965, 72–80; Carcopino 1960, 153–154; add the laudatory *AE* 1977, 217–218.

49. She appears as such, or as *diva Claudia virgo,* on coins and inscriptions: *PIR²* C 1061. There seems to be no trace of the temple.

50. Tacitus 16. 6; Suetonius 35. 3; Dio 62. 27. 4.

51. Funeral: Tacitus 16. 6. Perfume: Pliny 12. 83. Deification: Tacitus 16. 21; Dio 62. 26. 3; RPC (Corinth/Patrae); AFA (AD 66); *ILS* 232, 8902. Temple: see

Dio 63. 26. 3, observing that most of the money had been extorted. The temple appears to have escaped notice in *LTUR* and Richardson 1992, and Sabina Venus does not seem to appear on coins or inscriptions. However, note the close connection between Poppaea, Nero, and Venus on the Pompeian graffiti, *AE* 1977, 217–218.

52. Dio 62. 28. 2–3, 63. 9. 5, 63. 12. 3 – 13. 2. On the boy Sporus, see Chapter 6 below.

53. Suetonius 21. 3; Dio 63. 9.4, 10. 2.

54. Ovid *Heroides* 11. 121ff. For Euripides' *Aeolus,* see Webster 1967, 157–160. In this version Macareus rapes his sister and she bears his child in secret. He then persuades his father to let the twelve siblings marry each other, which they do by lot, and Canace marries another brother. Aeolus discovers the truth and sends Canace the sword; Macareus confesses and persuades his father to forgive Canace, but it is too late. He finds his sister dying and kills himself with the same sword. But it appears that the child survives (Webster 1967, 159), and neither that nor the rape would be to Nero's purpose.

55. Suetonius 21. 3; cf. Dio 63. 10. 2 (soldier), 63. 9. 5 (golden chains). Dio at 63. 9. 4 mentions Nero playing a madman, and that Hercules was one of his favorite roles. The young soldier's impetuous act was presumably a shrewd tribute to the emperor's acting genius.

Two other roles are attributed to Nero for which it is hard to find any contemporary relevance: Thyestes (Dio 63. 94. 4, 22. 6; Juvenal 8. 227–230) and Melanippe (Juvenal 8. 229).

56. There is an echo of the theme of the loss of the heir in the tale of Canace, as her father Aeolus destroys mother and child in his fury but soon repents of the deed—in part at least because, in the Euripidean version, he has earlier expressed "his desire for male grandchildren who will be good fighters and wise counselors": Webster 1967, 158.

57. The parallels were first noted by the folklorist A. H. Krappe: Krappe 1940, 470–471; cf. Delcourt 1944, 203. See also Mayer 1982 ("It does not seem to have been noticed . . .").

58. Diogenes Laertius, *Lives of the Philosophers* 1. 96. His *Life of Periander,* 1. 94–100, is the main ancient source for the tyrant. Cf. Plutarch *Moralia* 146D.

59. Diogenes Laertius 1. 94.

60. Herodotus 5. 92. Explained as the historicizing of myth by J. Stern, "Demythologization in Herodotus: 5. 92. ε," *Eranos* 87 (1989): 13–20.

61. Nero's extortion: Dio 63. 26. 3–4. Diogenes Laertius offers a doublet of the clothing/enforced dedication story at 1. 96. Periander vowed a golden statue if he won the chariot race at the Olympic Games. He won but, being short of gold, he helped himself to the ornaments which he had seen the women wearing at a festival.

62. Gerster 1884; Traina 1987. Pliny *NH* 4. 10, grumbling about impiety, gives the standard list of names of those who dared (without Periander); each is confirmed by other sources.

63. Discussed in connection with Nero, Periander, and the standard image of the tyrant by Ameling 1986. On the death, the trial, and the extravagant mourning, see W. Ameling, *Herodes Atticus* I, *Biographie* (Hildesheim, Zürich, New York, 1983), 100–107.

64. Herodotus 5. 92; Diogenes Laertius 1. 100.

65. Diogenes Laertius 1. 98–99.

66. The point is made by Coleman 1990, 62–63, 66.

67. Thompson 1953, motifs K 2111. 5; M 344; N 365. 1; T 412 passim.

68. Vernant 1988 brilliantly compares the legendary kings of Thebes, the Labdacids, the family of Oedipus, with the historical tyrants of Corinth, the Cypselids, the family of Periander. Concluding at 226–227: "in the way that the Greeks imagined the figure of the tyrant, as projected in the fifth and fourth centuries, he took on the features of the hero of legend, an individual at once elect yet accursed," and so on. And quoting Gernet about the tyrant as a "natural" product of the past: "His excesses had their models in legends." Rejecting social norms, he is "relegat[ed] to an isolation comparable both to that of a god, who is too far above men to come down to their level, and to that of a beast, so dominated by its appetites that it can brook no restraint. The tyrant despises the rules that control the ordering of the social fabric and, through its regularly woven mesh, determine the position of each individual in relation to all the rest, in other words—to put it more crudely, as Plato does—he is perfectly prepared to kill his father, sleep with his mother, and devour the flesh of his own children."

Also relevant to Nero's interests in performance and Periander is R. P. Martin, "The Seven Sages as Performers of Wisdom," in C. Dougherty and L. Kurke, eds., *Cultural Poetics in Archaic Greece: Cult, Performance, Politics* (Cambridge, 1993), 108–128.

5. Shining Apollo

1. Epigraphs: Cornutus *Epidrome* 32. 3 (translated in Hays 1983); Seneca *Apocolocyntosis* 4.

2. Tacitus 14. 14–15; Dio 61. 19–20, at 19. 5.

3. The argument is set out in my paper "Nero, Apollo, and the Poets," forthcoming in *Phoenix* 57 (2003). The controversy over the date of Calpurnius Siculus is clearly detailed in Horsfall 1993 and 1997.

4. *Civil War* 1. 47–50.

5. Transcribed twice by an admiring Galen, in his *De antidotis* (1. 6) and *De theriaca ad Pisonem* (6). Edited by E. Heitsch, in *Die griechischen Dichter-*

fragmente der römischen Kaiserzeit, II (*Abh.Ak.Wiss.Gött., Phil.-hist. Kl.* 3. 58, Göttingen, 1964), 8–15. Nero (named in line 3) is addressed in the second line as Caesar, giver of freedom: this dates the work to between late November of 66 (the liberation of Greece: Levy 1991) and mid-June of 68 (Nero's death).

6. *Apoc.* 4, quoted in the epigraph at the beginning of this chapter.

7. Suetonius 21. 2, 39. 2. A Niobid, presumably part of a larger group, was discovered in Nero's suburban retreat at Subiaco: Neudecker 1988, 223–225.

8. Radiate obverses: *RIC* 185, 192, 197, et al. Radiate reverses with scenes of sacrifice and victory: *RIC* 44–45 and 46–47. Apollo Citharoedus: *RIC* 74–82, 205–212, 380–381, 384–385, 414–417, 451–455; with Suetonius 25. 2.

9. *RPC* 1195–1196 (Corinth); 1275 (Patras); 1371–1376 (Nicopolis); 1439 (Thessalian League); 1752–1753 (Perinthus: 1752 "?54/59??"); 2060–2061 (Nicaea); 2383 (Thyatira).

The coinage of Alexandria in Egypt, the second city of the empire, represents a very different world with its own elaborate and often unique symbols (*RPC* 706–710). Here Nero appears radiate on a throne with a scepter and baton(?) on the reverse of tetradrachms from the years 56/57 through 59/60; other reverses in these years present Agrippina, Octavia, the Roman People, Demeter, Justice, Peace, Concord, Rome, and the Agatho Daimon. From 63/64 to 67/68 Nero's radiate head or bust appears on the obverse of all coins. Clearly the reverses of 56–60 reflect Egyptian concerns with the Pharaoh as Sun King (cf. Grimal 1971; the Agatho Daimon is very local); but the obverses of 63 to 68 may reflect images being propagated from Rome in just these years. Similarly independent are the reverses of the coins of 66/67 and 67/68 which refer to the deities connected with the games in which the emperor competed in Greece. Thus busts of Actian Apollo and Pythian Apollo appear, to represent the Actian and the Delphic games, but not Apollo Citharode.

10. *SIG*[3] 814. Text, Italian translation, and good commentary by Campanile 1990.

11. *AE* 1929. 75 (Athens); *AE* 1971. 435 (Athens); *AE* 1994. 1617 (Athens); *IGR* III. 345 (Sagalassus); *AE* 1961. 22 (Prostanna).

12. Dio 63. 1. 1, 6. 3.

13. This account amalgamates Suetonius 25 and Dio 63. 19–21, both based on a good source. Suetonius omits the Capitol stopover. See further Chapter 8 below.

14. *CIL* VI. 701, repeated on two sides of the obelisk, which now stands in the Piazza del Popolo.

15. It must be admitted that the statues dedicated to Nero as the New Apollo may have had non-solar Apolline attributes and that the coins showing Apollo Citharoedus may indeed have been intended to depict Nero, or statues of Nero; but what representations survive are exclusively solar. Much material is collected by Neverov in a stimulating paper on Nero-Helios (Neverov 1986), but most of

his attributions of specific images to Nero are open to doubt. See the reservations expressed by H. Jucker at the end of Neverov 1974.

16. It is said to be either an authentic ancient work or a baroque copy of a lost original: G. A. Mansuelli, *Galleria degli Uffizi. Le Sculture,* II (Rome, 1961), 68–69; *LIMC* IV, *Eros-Herakles* (1988), *s.v.* Helios/Sol 445 (C. Letta). A lost relief panel from the great portico of the Sebasteion at Aphrodisias juxtaposed images of "Nero Claudius Drusus Caesar Augustus" and "Helios": J. Reynolds, *ZPE* 43 (1981): 317–327, at 324. How they were portrayed is unknown.

17. M. Fuchs, *Untersuchungen zur Ausstattung römischer Theater in Italien und den Westprovinzen des Imperium Romanum* (Mainz, 1987), 81, 170–171. For the late antique cameo, see Chapter 1 above; on Nero's other appearance as the Sun, the notorious Colossus, see below.

18. Dio 63. 6. 2.

19. An ancient relief plaque might give us an impression of what the awning looked like. In the surviving fragment, Nero's large head in his first portrait type is crowned with fifteen rays; three stars can be seen in the background; and the top of a smaller female head can be discerned at the lower left: Paribeni 1914, 283–285, fig. 6. However, Bergmann has shown convincingly (1998, 167–169) that the image should derive from a private funerary monument, which set the deceased among the stars and portrayed him, as many other private citizens were portrayed, in a manner that recalls the imperial image (what Paul Zanker has termed the *Zeitgesicht*).

20. Tertullian *De Spectaculis* 8. On the temple and its appearance, see *LTUR* IV, 333–334, "Sol (et Luna), Aedes, Templum" (P. Ciancio Rossetto).

21. See the fascinating article of Wuilleumier 1927: he points out (p. 104) that, while most of the information comes from late antique authors, the elaborate learning of Suetonius seems to lie behind it, and that elements certainly date from the time of the republic.

22. Tacitus 15. 74. The Temple of Sol (and Luna) in the Circus: Humphrey 1986, 91–93.

23. Suetonius 6. 1, Dio 61. 2. 1: in these sections of their works the two authors clearly draw on a common source.

24. Note also the relief portrait of a very Julio-Claudian Sun on a dedication to Sol and Luna from one Eumolpus, slave of Caesar, who identifies himself as none other than the man in charge of the furnishings of the Golden House, that is, after 64: photograph of Eumolpus relief at Bergmann 1993, plate 5.3; inscription at *ILS* 1774.

25. For the Great Fire and its repercussions, see Chapter 7 below. The following brief account is mainly that of Tacitus 15. 38–44.

26. Tacitus 15. 44; my translation. Note *hortos suos ei spectaculo Nero obtulerat et circense ludicrum edebat, habitu aurigae permixtus plebei vel curriculo insistens.*

27. Publicity of punishment: Wiseman 1985. Capital punishments at Rome:

T. Mommsen, *Das römische Strafrecht* (Leipzig, 1899), 916–928. Fatal charades: Coleman 1990.

28. This paragraph merely distills Palmer 1978, 1108–1109. Palmer is ignored by the article in *LTUR* III, 198, "Luna, Aedes" (M. Andreussi).

29. Altar: *CIL* VI. 30837 abc, cf. *LTUR* IV, 76–77, "Arae Incendii Neroniani" (E. Rodríguez Almeida, doubting whether the altars mark the boundaries of the Fire: *contra* Palmer 1978, F. Coarelli, *Roma* [new ed., Rome, 1995], 272). Varro *RR* 5. 68. Luna Noctiluca: *LTUR* III, 345, "Noctiluca, Templum" (J. Aronen). Tacitus' choice of words may give a hint. The Christians were burned *in usum nocturni luminis,* for use as a nightlight. The singular *nocturni luminis* might look odd for a mass of victims, but not so if we hear in it an echo of *noctiluca.*

30. Palmer 1978.

31. So argues Coleman 1990, 73, cf. 65–66 with full discussion of the text of Clement I *Cor.* 5–6, and reflecting general scholarly opinion. There is no call for emendation, and there is no doubt that the context is Neronian.

32. Especially in the papers of Zanker 1983 and Lefèvre 1989; cf. *LTUR* I, 54–57, "Apollo Palatinus" (P. Gros).

33. Tomei 1990.

34. Lefèvre 1989, 12–19, suggested (vs. Zanker) that the Danaids were shown holding not the jars of their punishment but the daggers of just vengeance (in a version of the story known from Euripides and Hyginus, among others): that would make excellent sense if Octavian meant to show Greece defending itself once more against Egyptian invasion. While this is the most satisfying of explanations for the program, it has been pointed out that the Augustan poets uniformly presented the deed of the Danaids as a crime (P. Hardie, *CR* 40 [1990]: 520), and the three statues identified after Lefèvre wrote were undoubtedly water-carriers. Tomei 1990, 47–48, suggests that they were deliberately meant to be ambiguous, representing both punishment and catharsis in the uncertain climate after 31, but that too is hard to reconcile with the universally negative depiction of the losers at Actium. Balensiefen 1998 sees the Danaids as completely negative images of the defeated Egyptians (which may be, but her remarks on the genealogy of the Danaids, the Dardanids, the Ptolemies, the Antonii, et al. seem far too complex to be convincing or apparent). A fine discussion of the Danaids under Augustus in Putnam 1998, 195–201, suggests an unresolved difference of opinion between the emperor and the poets.

Thus the programmatic purpose remains unclear: even in the hands of a master like Octavian, not all propaganda is uniformly successful or readily intelligible.

35. Tacitus 15. 39; Dio 62. 18. 2. Cf. Bastet 1971, 167; Carettoni 1949. Tacitus names the Temple of Jupiter Stator as one destroyed in the Fire; M. A. Tomei has identified a podium on the Palatine near the Domus Flavia as the base of

that shrine: "Sul Tempio di Giove Stator sul Palatino," *MEFRA* 105 (1993): 621–659 (*contra LTUR* III, 155–157, "Iuppiter Stator, Aedes, Fanum, Templum" [F. Coarelli], ignoring Tomei). The Palatine house of the Republican orator L. Crassus also suffered in the Fire: Pliny 17. 2–5.

36. To be recognized by the audience, the martyrs must have been provided with jugs, preferably leaking. If they were iconographically faithful to the Palatine statues, this would mean that the latter were indeed shown as water-carriers.

37. Dio 62. 18. 2. No remains have yet been identified with any certainty: *LTUR* I, 36–37, "Amphitheatrum Statilii Tauri" (A. Viscogliosi).

38. It should be stressed that if Tacitus' last sentence is taken at face value, the punishment of the Christians and the circus game happened simultaneously.

39. Tacitus 16. 1–3 and Suetonius 31. 4–32. 5, both depending on the same source.

40. Hemsoll 1990, 36, n. 87, gives a long list of golden items connected with Nero.

41. On gold as the attribute of the Sun, see L'Orange 1973, 292–294.

42. The prime sources are Dio 63. 1–6 and Suetonius 13; cf. Pliny 33. 54, Tacitus 16. 23–24.

43. In a carefully staged ceremony, complete with dialogue, Tiridates proclaimed himself to be Nero's slave who had come to worship him as a god, as he did Mithras. For the solar aspect of this, see Chapter 8 below.

44. Dio 63. 3. 4–6; Suetonius 13, noting the postponement *propter nubilem;* Pliny 33. 54 (and possibly 19. 24, though he writes there of the sky-colored, star-strewn awnings as being over the *amphitheatrum Neronis*). On the wearing of white clothes at public spectacles, see, e.g., Martial 4. 2, 14. 137.

45. Pliny 33. 54, cf. 36. 111. On the Golden House, see Chapter 7 below.

46. Petronius *Satyrica* 120. 87; Seneca *Epistulae Morales* 115. 12–13, cited in Hemsoll 1990, 31. Blaison 1998 argues that Suetonius' description of the Golden House should be taken not literally but literarily, suggesting that it was heavily influenced by Ovid's description of the House of the Sun; but the Ovidian lens was provided by Seneca, who actually knew the Golden House.

47. Seneca *Epistulae Morales* 115. 15.

48. Tacitus 15. 60: *caedes Annaei Senecae, laetissima principi.*

49. Seneca *Epistulae Morales* 115. 6–7.

50. Martial *De Spectaculis* 2. 3; Suetonius 31; Pliny *NH* 36. 163. On the complex history of the Fortune of Sejanus, see Coarelli 1988, 265–288; cf. *LTUR* II, 278, "Fortuna Seiani, Aedes" (L. Anselmino and M. J. Strazulla).

51. Martial *De Spectaculis* 2. 1. The Colossus remained a byword for its huge size even to those who had never seen it: *CLE* 1552 A, 82–83 (from Cillium, in Tunisia, c. AD 150).

52. The large bibliography on the Colossus is collected and superseded by

the paper of Lega 1989–1990 (cf. her article in *LTUR* I, 295–298, "Colossus: Nero"), and by the book of Bergmann 1993.

53. See Smith 2000, 536–538, on Pliny 34. 45 and Suetonius 31.

54. Dio 66. 15. 1. Note also Martial *De Spectaculis* 2, which works a series of contrasts between the contemporary valley of the Colosseum in 80 and its state in 64, when the Golden House occupied the area. Where the Colosseum now stands, was Nero's Lake; where the Baths of Titus now stand, was once a stretch of open country after the houses of the poor were removed; where now the Colonnade of the Temple of the Divine Claudius stands, was the boundary of the House; and (beginning the list of contrasts) where the Colossus itself now stands were the halls of the tyrant: *if* we were to follow Martial to the letter, this *should* mean that the Colossus, like the Colosseum, the Baths, and the Temple, was raised after Nero's death.

55. Lega 1989–1990 discusses the evidence. The quote is from Martial (1. 70), writing under Domitian. The Colossus stood in the same location for half a century, until in the later 120s the emperor Hadrian, needing to clear the area for his new Temple of Venus and Rome, moved the statue to a site next to the Colosseum (which was built by the Flavians and took its name from the statue). The statue itself disappeared sometime after the fourth century, but its new base survived until it was demolished as late as 1933.

56. The case is summarized in Lega 1989–1990, 349–351, and Bergmann 1993, 4–6, 14–17.

57. What the post-Neronian Colossus looked like can be deduced from coins or medallions of the third-century emperors Severus Alexander and Gordian III. Those of Alexander are difficult to decipher, but Gordian's clearly show next to the Colosseum a standing nude figure with radiate head, his right hand held forward and resting on the rudder of Fortune, his left arm perhaps bent with the hand holding a globe: *LTUR* I, fig. 17. Moreover, very happily, Bergmann has drawn attention to a carved amethyst, now in Berlin, which seems to present the figure of Helios in precisely the same way as the medallion of Gordian. On the rudder, see J. Gagé, "Le colosse et la Fortune de Rome," *MEFR* 45 (1928): 109–122, arguing cleverly but unconvincingly for a transformation of the statue into the symbol of Rome's fate.

58. In fact, where one might expect to discover just such a scene painted in a vestibule, one would see a reality—a double *trompe l'oeil.*

59. The following paragraph depends heavily on Voisin 1987, 509–519.

60. Voisin 1987 suggests fascinating astrological intentions. There certainly does seem to be a singular prominence accorded to the *oculus,* the large circular opening in the dome of the great central octagonal hall. At noon on the equinoxes, the circle of light cast by the *oculus* precisely touches the four corners of the door leading into the great nymphaeum: the circle is, as it were, squared. Un-

fortunately, a cupola stood over the dome (Hemsoll 1989, 1990): unless it were ingeniously opened or removable in some way, the light would have great difficulty penetrating.

61. It should be noted that the extent of the Golden House has been exaggerated by both ancients and moderns: see Chapter 7 below. The practical effect of properly recognizing its size, which will be relevant to the argument here, is that the so-called Oppian or Esquiline "wing" (as the residence is known) was at the periphery of the area.

62. Tacitus 15. 42; Suetonius 31. On the surprising form of the lake, revealed by excavation, see Chapter 7.

63. Suetonius 31: see Chapter 7 below. The house was far from finished: Suetonius *Otho* 7, confirmed by archaeology. We can also imagine a large empty pedestal in the vestibule.

64. L'Orange's conception of Nero's reign as developing into a solar theocracy, argued particularly in L'Orange 1942 (= 1973), has been decisively rejected, most thoroughly by Toynbee 1947 and Boethius 1960; cf. Fears 1976, Griffin 1984. Boethius wrote (1960, 119), "His suggestion that the whole Domus Aurea complex was a palace of Nero-Helios, a palace of the Sun, must, as far as I can see, be discarded as completely unverified. Again, I emphasize its obvious connection with the Hellenized late Republican villas." Yet it is not obvious why it could not be *both* sun-palace and villa. We may discount L'Orange's theocratic concerns: although Nero *presented* himself as a god, there is no reason to assume that he or anyone claimed he *was* that god, any more than they thought of earlier *principes* or Hellenistic monarchs as "being" the deities with whom they wished to be associated. But once we assume that Nero and his audience were concerned with metaphor, not reality, L'Orange was essentially right, and his *Sonnenpalast* has been returning to favor; witness the important recent contributions of Voisin, Hemsoll, and Bergmann noted earlier.

65. Refusal of divine honors: O. Montevecchi, *Aegyptus* 50 (1970): 5–33 (AD 54/55); Tacitus 15. 74 (AD 65); cf., in general, M. P. Charlesworth, "The Refusal of Divine Honours, an Augustan Formula," *PBSR* 15 (1939): 1–10. Tacitus gives as Nero's reason the fear that some might turn the conception of *divus Nero* into a bad omen for his death, "since an emperor did not receive the honor of the gods until he had ceased to live among human beings." *Religionum contemptor:* Suetonius 56.

The standard picture of the godless tyrant appears very soon after his death, in the play *Octavia*, e.g., line 89, *spernit superos hominesque simul;* 240–241, *hostis deum hominumque;* cf. 449. In fact there is very little substance to it, beyond the allegation that Nero raped a Vestal Virgin (found only in Suetonius 28), and that he bathed in the source of the Aqua Marcia (Tacitus 14. 22). On the other side, there is a lot of evidence for careful observation of cult acts: e.g., Suetonius 19, 22,

34, 46, 56; Tacitus 14. 4, 13, 15. 36, 44, 74, 16. 21; Dio 62. 18. 3; and the *Acta* of the Fratres Arvales, passim.

66. For what follows, see Rocca-Serra 1977; Hays 1983 (with translation); Most 1989. Hercules is discussed at *Epidrome* 31, Apollo at 32. Banishment in 65: Dio 62. 29. 2–4.

67. The sources for this are late: Sopater *Prolegomena in Aristidem* (Aristides III. 740 Dindorf); and the scholia on Aeschines, *Contra Ctesiphontem* 3. 116 (Aeschines, *Orationes*, p. 334 Schultz).

68. Combining Suetonius 40. 3 and Dio 63. 14. 2. Galba, who was 73 and notorious for his lack of humor, recovered the money from Delphi when he won the throne. This and the next paragraph depend heavily on Parke and Wormell 1956, I. 283–284, with texts at II. 99, 187, 231.

69. "Nero Orestes Alcmaeon mother-slayers": [Lucian] *Nero* 10; Philostratus *VS* 1. 481; Sopater *Prolegomena in Aristidem*. Dio has the same version of the line at 61. 16. 2, but assigns it to Rome, not Delphi. The full and correct original is in Suetonius 39. 2.

70. *Scholia ad Lucanum* 5. 113, 139, 178; Sopater *Prolegomena in Aristidem*.

71. Pausanias 10. 7. 1, 10. 19. 2; Dio of Prusa 31. 148.

72. Duret 1988, with earlier bibliography, relying on Seneca *NQ* 6. 2. 8–9, 3 Praef. 1, 3–4. Ovid offers the epitaph of Phaethon as a greathearted failure, in *Metamorphoses* 2. 327–328: *Hic situs est Phaethon currus aurigi paterno / quem si non tenuit magnis tamen excidit ausis.* Aufhagen 1997, who does not cite Duret, argues unconvincingly that the brief story of Phaethon in the Apennine excursus of Lucan's second book (*BC* 2. 396–438) is anti-Neronian.

73. Duret 1988, 149–152, points also to the elaborate painting in the Golden House of Phaethon standing before his father at the moment his wish is granted: if it were to be taken as especially meaningful to the owner of the house, the picture should refer not to the standard view of Phaethon as the usurper, but to Phaethon as the successor.

74. Pliny 37. 45–46, 50.

75. E.g., Ovid, *Metamorphoses* 2. 340–366; Pliny *NH* 37. 31; Hyginus 152.

76. Suetonius 38. 1. On the Fire, see Chapter 7.

77. Suetonius 53. *Aequiperare* can be translated as either "to equal" or "to be compared."

78. Dio 63. 20. 5.

79. So asserts Robert 1938, 111–12, observing that this has nothing to do with notions of divinity.

80. Coins: *RPC* 1278, cf. 1275–1281. Hercules frieze: persuasively argued by Weir 1999. The Heraion at Argos: Pausanias 2. 17. 6. Dio 63. 9 seems to suggest that he played Hercules Furens in Greece.

81. Suetonius 44. 1. Neudecker 1988, 131–134, mentions a statue of Hercules from Nero's villa at Anzio.

82. See Weinstock 1971, 142–145, with references. For Nero's partly favorable posthumous reputation among Greek intellectuals, see Chapter 1.

83. Philostratus *Nero* 5; cf. Korver 1950; Traina 1987.

84. O. Zwierlein, *Kritischer Kommentar zu den Tragödien Senecas* (Stuttgart, 1986), 313–343; *Der Neue Pauly* 5 (1998): 406, "Hercules Oetaeus" (C. Walde).

85. [Seneca] *Hercules Oetaeus* 82–84: *si iungi iubes, / comittat undas Isthmos, et iuncto salo / nova ferantur Atticae puppes via.* Grenade 1948, 276–280, first noticed the reference and tried to connect it also with Nero's construction of the canal from Lake Arvernus to the Tiber.

86. See Wiseman 1978, 48–50, with photographs. D. G. Romano, currently excavating at Corinth, confirms, *per litteras,* that the relief does indeed depict Hercules.

87. Apollodorus 2. 6. 2; Hyginus 32; et al.

88. Rostovtzeff 1923, 102–104, drew attention to a quite undated votive inscription erected by Hilarus, an imperial freedman who served in the *tabularium,* or public archives, at Aquileia, apparently offering the attributes of Hercules (*Tirynthia munera*) to Apollo: "He conquered the earth, you, Phoebus, gave it peace" (*ILS* 3228 = *CLE* 1841). In a romantic mood the great historian attributed the four lines of verse to Nero: "Such sentiments could not have been expressed by a modest slave. Probably the verses were copied from some famous monument dedicated by the emperor himself."

89. E.g., Sanford 1937; Aiardi 1979–1980; Voisin 1987; et al.

90. For example, the proposed expedition to the Caspian Gates, in the footsteps of Alexander, ensured that a newly enrolled legion was called "the phalanx of Alexander": Suetonius 19. 4. Nero possessed and had gilded a famous equestrian statue of the young Alexander by Lysippus: Pliny 34. 63. Reference is generally made to A. Bruhl, "Le souvenir d'Alexandre le Grand et les Romains," *MEFR* 47 (1930): 202–231, who calls Nero a fanatical admirer of Alexander at 211–212, but who cites only these two passages. Nero also always carried with him a favorite statuette as a lucky charm, as had Alexander, but then so had many others: Suetonius 56, Pliny 34. 48 and 82. Against the general acceptance of Roman "*imitatio Alexandri,*" note the salutary skepticism of E. S. Gruen, "Rome and the Myth of Alexander," in T. W. Hillard, R. A. Kearsley, C. E. V. Nixon, and A. M. Nobbs, eds., *Ancient History in a Modern University,* 1: *The Ancient Near East, Greece, and Rome* (Grand Rapids, 1998), 178–191 (with bibliography).

91. Suetonius 10. 1. The imitation of Augustus has been emphasized by some scholars (listed in Most 1989, 2036; add especially Gagé 1955, 650).

92. Cameo: Neverov 1974, 80; cf. Tacitus 12. 69 (Agrippina). Battle of Athenians and Persians: Dio 61. 9. 5 (Nero), 55. 10. 7 (Augustus); cf. 61. 20. 5 (feast for people on boats in naumachia, 59). Coins: see Grant 1950, 79–87, and further below. In Grant's opinion, the fiftieth anniversary of Augustus' death was the occasion for Nero's great reform and revival of the state's bronze coinage. Janus coins

(with slightly variant legends): *RIC* 50–51, 58, 263–271, 283–291, 300–311, 323–328, 337–342, 347–350, 353–355, 421, 438–439, 468–472, 510–512, 537–539, 583–585.

93. On Nero's closing, see especially Townend 1980. On Augustus and Janus, Syme III (1984), 1179–1197.

94. Refusals: Suetonius *Tiberius* 26; Dio 57. 2, 59. 5; Suetonius *Claudius* 12. On *Imperator* as *praenomen,* see Syme I (1979), 361–377.

95. Suetonius *Augustus* 94. 4, cf. Dio 45. 1. Mavrojannis 1995 throws some new light on the familiar theme of Apollo and Augustus.

96. Suetonius *Augustus* 5, 94.6.

97. What follows depends on La Rocca 1985.

98. Zanker 1983.

99. For the wealth of Apolline evidence, see Zanker 1989, Simon 1986, and especially Simon 1957, 30–44. For a survey of Augustus and Apollo, see K. Galinsky, *Augustan Culture: An Interpretive Introduction* (Princeton, 1996), 215–221, 297–299.

100. Alföldi 1973, 53–54.

101. Arretine ware: A. Oxé, "Römisch-italisch Beziehungen der früharretinische Reliefgefässe," *BJ* 138 (1938): 81–98, at 92–93. Carnelian: Simon 1986, 21. Sol and Apollo: see esp. Propertius 2. 31 (*supra fastigia* at verse 12).

102. Suetonius *Augustus* 70. Valerius Maximus (1. 5. 7) suggests that the association went back at least to the battle of Philippi in 42.

103. Pseudo-Acro on Horace *Ep.* 1. 3. 17, *habitu et statu Apollinis;* cf. Servius on Vergil *Ecl.* 4. 10, *cum Apollinis cunctis insignibus* (not located by Servius, but surely the same statue). Augustus appears as the New Apollo on the inscription from a statue base in Athens, and was presumably shown accordingly: D. Peppas-Delmousou, "A Statue Base for Augustus. *IG* II² 3262 + *IG* II² 4725," *AJP* 100 (1979): 125–132.

104. Suetonius 12. 3; cf. Dio 61. 21, Tacitus 14. 20.

105. Grant 1950, 80–83.

106. La Rocca 1985, 24, 89; Strazulla 1990, 17–20. The ideological importance of Hercules to Augustus is discussed by Ritter 1995, 129–148, and contested by Huttner 1997, passim, especially at 385–386, n. 77. The issue seems to be, in large part, one of exclusivity: could a Roman statesman claim connection with more than one god or hero? (Augustus' identification with Apollo is well known); and could two statesmen both claim the same god or hero? (Hercules was already associated closely with Augustus/Octavian's great rival, Mark Antony). The answer to both questions should be yes: Augustus, for instance, was not committed exclusively to Apollo, and indeed he can be shown to have laid claim to Dionysus, the other divine associate of Mark Antony: D. Castriota, *The Ara Pacis Augustae and the Imagery of Abundance in Later Greek and Early Roman Imperial Art* (Princeton, 1995), 87–123. And as we shall see in Chapter 6, the claims by two

men to one god can be to different aspects of that god. Be that as it may, the question of Augustus' intentions may not be too important. Huttner 1997 shows convincingly, 369–383, that the Augustan poets were eager to equate Augustus with Hercules; Nero, who knew the literature well, would not care about, might not even be aware of, the difference between what Augustus wanted and what his poets claimed of him.

Note also that Nero's interest in Apollo's punishment of Niobe is prefigured by her remarkable prominence on the other pediment of Apollo Sosianus and on the doors of Apollo Palatinus.

107. See Chapter 8 below.

108. On the significance of the laurel, see especially Simon 1957, 38–42. Pliny 15. 136–137; Propertius 4. 6. 53; Tibullus 2. 5. 5.

109. Suetonius 25; Dio 63. 20. 1 – 21. 1.

110. Suetonius *Galba* 1. Pliny *NH* 15. 136 relates the same tale, but says that the grove actually survived.

6. Saturnalia

1. Epigraphs: Suetonius 28. 1 (Gavorse translation, modified); Tacitus 15. 37 (translation by A. J. Woodman, in Woodman 1992, 175).

2. Dio 62. 28. 2–3; 63. 12. 3 – 13. 2. Both passages are from the epitome of Xiphilinus, showing that Dio discussed Sporus in his accounts of the events of 65 and of 67. Tacitus *Hist.* 1. 73.

3. Dio of Prusa 21. 6–7 (the translation is that of the Loeb Classical Library by J. W. Cahoon, but modifies the last phrase which was incorrectly rendered as "to anyone who should make him his wife").

4. Plutarch *Galba* 9. 3; Dio 64. 8. 3 (on Otho, using the word *suneinai*, to be with, commonly with a marital and sexual connotation).

5. Dio 65. 10. 1: ’εν Κόρης ’αρπαζομένης σχήματι. In the Loeb edition, E. Cary translates "in the role of a maiden *(kore)* being ravished," but this surely refers to *the* Kore, Persephone/Proserpina and her rape by Hades/Pluto.

6. Suetonius 48. 1, 49. 3; Dio 63. 29. 2 (in the versions of Zonaras and John of Antioch). Dio of Prusa 21. 9 is obscure, but he seems to be talking only of Nero's final hours, the truth about which (he goes on to claim) remains unknown. What Nero's plans were (for himself, for Sporus, for the group?), and whether it was his actions then (including the suicide pact) or his general treatment that angered "the eunuch," are unclear.

7. On the significance of January first for the emperor, with its oaths of loyalty, public vows, exchange of gifts, and omens, see Meslin 1970, 27–36.

8. Suetonius 28. 1; Dio 63. 13. 1. Jokes: Suetonius and Dio (62. 28. 3a) report variant versions of the same joke, which was essentially the wish that Nero's father

had had such a wife. Both authors gloss it, to make it an attack on Nero, Dio even suggesting that it was the reply of a philosopher to a demand by the emperor for his opinion of the marriage. But it is both witty and risqué, as it simultaneously flatters Sporus, denigrates Agrippina, and pokes fun at Nero—just the sort of joke one might expect at a Roman wedding.

9. *Sumbolaion* and *ekdosis:* Dio 63. 13. 1, cf. *sungraphe* at 62. 28. 3. At 63. 13. 1 Dio says explicitly that the marriage took place in Greece. The sequence in Suetonius (28. 1–2) obscures but does not contradict this: marriage—father joke—travels in Greece, *then* Rome. The Greek custom of contract did not invade Roman law before c. AD 100: see briefly J. F. Gardner, *Women in Roman Law and Society* (London, 1986), 49–50.

10. On the meaning of *conventus mercatusque,* see Frayn 1993, 9, 133; on the Sigillaria, ibid., 136–138. The significance of the Sigillaria was noted in a paper delivered by C. Vout at Neronia VI, 1999 (forthcoming), and was independently suggested in versions of the present chapter circulated in 1994.

11. The following paragraph is nothing more than a précis of the classic article by M. P. Nilsson, *PW* 2. 2. 1 (1921): 201–211, *s.v.* "Saturnalia": extensive references can be found there, and discussion of the origins and significance of the festival, which are omitted here. See more recently the stimulating essay of Versnel 1993, 136–227.

12. Macrobius *Saturnalia* 1. 7. 26 (license); Seneca *Epistulae* 47. 14 (magistrates, judges, miniature republic).

13. The Romans were well aware of this aspect: see K. R. Bradley, *Slaves and Masters in the Roman World: A Study in Social Control* (Oxford, 1987), 42–44.

14. Tacitus 13. 14 is the only account of Britannicus' death which mentions the preceding Saturnalia.

15. The following combines Tacitus 13. 25, 47; Dio 61. 8. 1–4, 9. 24; and Suetonius 26. They all clearly depend on the same source, possibly Pliny, who mentions the ointment in his *Natural History* 13. 126. Dio's rhetorical embellishments may be discounted, as when he speaks of murder, about which the other authors say nothing, or when he says that the disguised Nero was recognized because no one else would have dared to commit such excesses.

The account in the common source owed as much to art as to life. Compare, as does Kierdorf 1992 *ad loc.,* Suetonius' *siquidem redeuntis a cena verberare assueverat* and *uxorem tractaverat* with Cicero at *Pro Caelio* 20, deflecting accusations against his wild young client: *qui dicerent uxores suas a cena redeuntis attrectatas esse a Caelio.*

16. The references are the same as those in the previous note, again reflecting the common source. *Ludicram licentiam* (in Tacitus) here refers to the leeway allowed actors and audience within the theater. Onstage: Suetonius mentions the

seditionibus pantomimorum, which, on the face of it, refers to the pantomimes themselves, not their supporters.

17. McDaniel 1914; Eyben 1993.

18. Cicero *Pro Caelio* 20; Suetonius *Otho* 2. 1; *HA Verus* 4.6 and *Commodus* 3. 7 (possibly influenced by the stories about Nero); Fronto *Ad M. Caesarem* 2. 16 (van den Hout); Augustine *Confessions* 3. 3; Apuleius *Metamorphoses* 2. 18. The historical veracity of each anecdote is less important than the expectations of society.

19. *Digest* 48. 19. 28. 3 (Callistratus); Cicero *Pro Caelio* 39–42; Juvenal 8. 146–182, at 163–170; Suetonius *Nero* 26. 1. Mark Antony, a real general who was also old enough to know better, liked to wander around at night in disguise, playing jokes and fighting, to the great enjoyment of the people of Alexandria, who were delighted that he could relax away from the strictures of Rome: Plutarch *Antony* 29. 2–4, on which see below.

20. Sources are given in note 15 above. Pliny mentions the ointment as being used by Nero at the beginning of his reign.

21. Tacitus 15. 33–37, with Dio 62. 15. 1–6.

22. Coleman 1993, 50–51.

23. The accounts of Dio and Tacitus differ strikingly. Tacitus describes the towboats, their outrageous rowers, and the menagerie of exotic birds and beasts; Dio does not. Dio describes the structure of the raft; Tacitus does not. Tacitus clearly reports the separation of the noblewomen from the prostitutes; Dio strongly implies a promiscuous mixing of all classes. Tacitus mentions only brothels; Dio has equally well-patronized taverns and brothels. Where Dio offers a detailed picture of social meltdown, Tacitus has the scene end quietly with lights and song. Above all, and related to this, Tacitus caps the narrative with the wedding to Pythagoras, while Dio appears to have been silent on the matter.

The other major discrepancy between the two historians concerns the location. Without naming the site or the occasion (probably the fault of his epitomator), Dio tells of Nero staging a beast-hunt, then flooding "the theater" to mount a sea-battle, draining it for a gladiatorial show, and then flooding it again for Tigellinus' great public banquet. This can hardly be the lake of Agrippa: presumably Dio or the epitomator has telescoped separate but related festivities.

As a reader has pointed out, Tacitus and Dio seem to be following two different accounts of the same event.

24. Dio 61. 20. 5; Tacitus 14. 15. Tacitus, perhaps for artistic reasons, puts the emperor's performance after the scene at the naumachia. On the naumachia, see Coleman 1993, 51–54; Coarelli 1992.

25. Suetonius 27. Although the sense is clear, the Latin describing what Nero saw as he sailed down the Tiber or along the coast is all but impossible to trans-

late as it stands, and the text must be corrupt: *dispositae per litora et ripas dever-soriae tabernae parabantur insignes ganea et matronarum institorio copas imitan-tium atque hinc inde hortantium ut appelleret.*

Suetonius' omission of the banquet of Tigellinus as such is not particularly sig-nificant, since he ignores Tigellinus altogether in the Life of Nero. This was a conscious decision on his part, right or wrong, for he omits other significant fig-ures of the reign such as the generals Corbulo and Verginius Rufus, the writers Petronius and Lucan, and the prefect Nymphidius Sabinus; cf. R. Syme, "Domitian: The Last Years," *Chiron* 13 (1983): 121–146, at 125–126 = Syme IV (1988), 252–277, at 256–257.

26. The following depends on D'Arms 1970, especially 42–43, 119–120.

27. Horace *Epistulae* I. 1. 83; Martial II. 80. 1–2.

28. Cicero *Pro M. Caelio* 35 (translation, slightly modified, by R. G. Austin, *M. Tullii Ciceronis Pro M. Caelio Oratio³* [Oxford, 1960], 95). These charges Cicero turned back on the accusers, saying that if they were true they had all in-volved the woman who he claimed was behind the prosecution, Caelius' former lover, Clodia, a woman who gave herself to everyone, who welcomed the passions of every man to her house, her suburban estate, and her villa at Baiae.

29. Seneca *Epistulae Morales* 51. 1–4.

30. D'Arms 1970, 94–99. Nero's connections with Pompeii: Van Buren 1953. Further evidence of Nero's reciprocated fondness for Pompeii has emerged in the last twenty-five years: e.g., *AE* 1977. 217–218.

31. Delight in the sea at Baiae: Tacitus 15. 51. Poppaea: *CIL* X. 1906. Acte: *CIL* X. 903. Domitia: *Dio* 61. 17. 2; Tacitus 13. 21. Piso: Tacitus 15. 52. Cf. D'Arms 1970, 94–99.

32. Tacitus 15. 42, Suetonius 31. 3, Pliny 14. 68, Statius *Silvae* 4. 3. 7–8. On the remains, long overlooked, see Johannowsky 1990.

33. Suetonius 31. 3. The sketches are on glass flasks, presumably fancy souve-nirs, discussed by Ostrow 1979, 85–87, 127–130.

34. D'Arms 1970, 98, citing R. Meiggs, *Roman Ostia* (Oxford, 1960), 57–58; Johannowsky 1990, 8. Tacitus mentions slightly later a great wreck of the fleet on its way from Formiae to Misenum, in a storm which drove it onto the coast of Cumae: 15. 46. This is a notice tacked on to the end of the year 64. Tacitus is not bound to chronological order, and it could be that Nero's project was spurred by this disaster; at the least it will have helped. Julius Caesar likewise was said to have a plan to divert the Tiber southwards so as to have it join the sea near Terracina: Plutarch *Caesar* 59.

35. Pliny 14. 61. Indeed, Suetonius claims further (16. 1) that Nero intended to extend the city walls as far as Ostia and to dig a canal between Rome and the sea there. When the latter project was completed, he would thus have been able to travel all the way from Rome to Baiae on man-made waterways.

36. See the splendid analysis by T. Woodman, in Woodman 1992, 177–181, to which the following paragraph is indebted. It should be understood that Woodman's careful investigation is more concerned with Tacitus' presentation of reversal rather than the reversal itself, and the main point of his paper is that Tacitus' depiction of the banquet is so steeped in reminiscences of Alexandria as to portray Nero as thoroughly un-Roman, an Alexandrian monarch intent on turning Rome into an "alien capital."

37. Tacitus 15. 38. Dio mentions Pythagoras as Nero's husband at 62. 28. 3 and 63. 13. 2 (cf. 63. 22. 4, the speech of Vindex), each time because of Sporus. He must have discussed the wedding somewhere, but the text of Xiphilinus, our source for Dio here, moves without a break from the banquet (62. 15) to the Fire (62. 16). Pythagoras is otherwise, except for a passing reference in Martial (below), unknown.

38. Suetonius 29 (Gavorse translation, considerably modified).

39. Doryphorus was Nero's secretary in charge of petitions, *a libellis,* when he received a large cash gift from the young emperor (Dio 61. 5. 4, AD 54/59), and despite his power he was alleged to have been murdered for his opposition to the marriage with Poppaea (Tacitus 14. 65, AD 62). Cf. Bradley 1978, 164–165, et al.

40. Both Tacitus and Dio should have mentioned the scandal if they knew of it. To argue that there were two men with the same name would be an act of desperation. Either Suetonius has got the name wrong, or (more likely) his editors and readers have mistakenly capitalized the Greek word *doryphorus,* spear carrier.

41. Suetonius 28. 1: *super ingenuorum paedagogia et nuptarum concubinatus Vestali virgini Rubriae vim intulit.* The precise meaning of *paedagogia* ("training establishments for slave-boys," or, by extension, the boys themselves) is unclear, but the pederastic connotation is certain.

42. Suetonius *Augustus* 69, 71; *Caligula* 25; compare the astonishing list of the amours of Julius Caesar in Suetonius *Caesar* 50–52. The Rubria incident is mentioned only by Suetonius, and sounds like a standard anti-tyrant slander. As a vestal we can assume that she came from a senatorial family. A Rubrius Gallus, who must have been a close relative, was consul under Nero and led his forces against the rebels in 68; would Nero have entrusted his defense to a man whose family he had grossly insulted?

43. Combining Tacitus 13. 12, 13. 46; Suetonius 28. 1; Dio 61. 7. 1. *Contubernium* was a union where the partners could not be legally married because one was a slave. At 13. 46, Tacitus has Poppaea refer scornfully to Nero's "servile *contubernium*" with Acte, while Suetonius adjudges their union as full marriage in all but name.

44. Wealth: *PIR* C 1067. Dedication: Ruggeri 1994. Funeral: Suetonius 50.

45. Tacitus calls Nero an adulterer in both instances: 14. 60, 15. 68. On Poppaea, see Chapter 4 above.

46. Tacitus 15. 68–69; Suetonius 35. 1.

47. Dio 61. 9. 2–4; Tacitus 13. 25; Suetonius 26. 2.

48. E.g., Quintilian, *Institutes* 4. 2. 124 (C. Antonius); Tacitus *Histories* 1. 72 (Tigellinus), 3. 40; Pliny *Epistulae* 3. 14. 3; Suetonius *Domitian* 22. The standard treatment of concubines in Roman society is Treggiari 1981.

49. Suetonius 44. 1. Pseudo-Agrippina, a prostitute whom he "added to his concubines": Suetonius 28. 2, Dio 61. 11. 4. Pseudo-Poppaea: Dio 62. 28. 2. At 50, Suetonius calls Acte Nero's *concubina*.

50. Brilliantly and succinctly summarized by Wiseman 1985, 10–14: the words quoted are Wiseman's, from p. 11. On very similar lines, cf. Veyne 1985 and 1987, 204. On verbal aggression expressed in sexual terms, see Adams 1982, 124, 128, 133–134. A good history of Roman attitudes toward homosexual behavior is Macmullen 1982. To be used with caution is the collection of evidence by J. Boswell, *Christianity, Social Tolerance and Homosexuality: Gay People in Western Europe from the Beginning of the Christian Era to the Fourteenth Century* (Chicago, 1980), at 61–87: the basic assumption that gayness as such, or a perception of gayness, existed at Rome is simply unproven. Williams 1999, with full bibliography, is now standard; but see the important reservations in the review by B. W. Frier, at *BMCR* 11.05 (1999).

51. Dio 61. 9; Tacitus 13. 25; Suetonius 26, 28. The charge that Seneca was a lover of superannuated youths, and that he passed his taste on to Nero, is absurd, part of a scurrilous attack on the philosopher's character mounted at Dio 61. 10. 3.

52. Suetonius 35. 4. On the meaning of *conspurco,* see Adams 1982, 199.

53. The Latin in Tacitus 13. 17 is brutal, and difficult to render into English: *illusum isse pueritiae Britannici Neronem.* Agrippina and Britannicus: Tacitus 13. 14.

54. Again, see Wiseman 1985, 11–12, with examples.

55. Suetonius 29. *Conficere:* Adams 1982, 159, 196.

56. Tacitus 15. 49.

57. Juvenal 2. 117–126; Martial 12. 42.

58. Juvenal 2. 137–142; Martial 12. 42. 5–6; Suetonius 29; Dio 62. 28. 3a.

59. Juvenal 2. 65–148, at 83–126.

60. Colin 1955/56, especially 142–191. Colin was an exceptionally imaginative scholar whose work was more often stimulating than convincing. Verdière 1975, 20–21, accepted Colin's interpretation; Bradley 1978, 162, was sympathetic; Bessone 1978 discounted him, seeing pederasty as part of Nero's philhellenism; Koestermann 1968 and Kierdorf 1992 overlooked him, as did Williams 1999, and others. Juvenal calls the husband a *tubicen* indirectly and obscenely, at 2. 118: *cornicini, sive hic recto cantaverat aere.* For same-sex marriages, see the full and careful discussion in Williams 1999, 245–252 (summing up recent controversies), which nevertheless suffers—as Frier points out of the book in general (see note 50 above)—from "a chronic poverty of imagination"; as for such weddings, spe-

cifically, Frier wonders: "what did the participants think they were doing? Williams doesn't even conjecture."

As in so much else, Nero had a model in his uncle Gaius (Caligula): cf. Josephus *Jewish Antiquities* 19. 30, with Wiseman 1991 *ad loc.*: "For in the rites of a certain mystery-cult, which he had set up himself, Gaius used to put on women's clothes and invent wigs and other disguises for making himself look female."

61. Allen 1962, 104–107; Higgins 1985. Allen also suggested that the banquet of Tigellinus was Nero's own version of the rites of the Roman spring festival of Floralia, which was noted for its licentiousness, with naked courtesans, torch-lit theaters, and obscene gestures. Higgins approved of this, adding that roses were in evidence at the Floralia, as at the notoriously expensive banquet of Nero.

62. Higgins 1985 uses the word "parody" without explanation; Colin and Allen appear to take the matter seriously. Syrian Goddess: Suetonius 55.

63. Martial 11. 6.

64. In Martial 5. 83, 6. 39, 10. 42, 11. 81, 12. 43 *(Dindymi puellae)*, 12. 75; and cf. Didymus in 5. 41: sometimes clearly eunuchs. *Passer* as phallus: denied (unconvincingly) by Adams 1982, 32–33, with previous (favorable) bibliography; maintained by Kay 1985, 75–76.

65. Martial 4. 14, which is directly connected with 11. 6.

66. Dio 63. 13. 2; cf. Suetonius 29. Dio, who cannot bring himself to say what exactly Nero did, probably added the touch about boys and girls.

67. Habinek 1990, 58, n. 15 (in passing).

68. Tacitus 16. 19 (Church and Brodribb translation, modified).

69. Dio 63. 13. 3; Suetonius 51. Incensed at such profligacy, Dio ignores the setting. He seems to be discussing Nero's degenerate behavior in general, but a comparison with Suetonius shows that their common source discussed the breaking of the dress code in the context of the Greek tour, where such clothing would be natural, and the handkerchief was surely meant to protect the competitor's delicate throat. Nero took special care of his voice: Suetonius 20. 1; Dio 63. 26. 1–2; Pliny 19. 108. Cf. Seneca's indignation at the behavior of the notoriously effeminate Maecenas, who would not only walk around the city but even conduct official business in an unbelted tunic: *Epistulae* 114. 6 (a reference I owe to R. A. Kaster).

70. Suetonius 51 (Gavorse translation, substantially modified).

71. Martial's *Apophoreta,* a book of distichs describing gifts given on "the intoxicating days of Saturn," is a prime source. At 14. 1. 1–2 he begins with the two badges of Saturnalia: "The knight and the lordly senator rejoice in their *syntheses,* while the *pillea* which are now worn befit our Jupiter [the emperor Domitian]." The gift in 14. 141 is a *synthesis:* "While the toga is happy to rest for five days, this dress you can wear by right."

72. Dio 61. 5. 4 (Cary translation, modified). The sum has a symbolic sig-

nificance inappropriate for a freedman: since the time of Augustus it represented the minimum capital necessary to hold the rank of senator.

73. Plutarch *Antony* 4. 7–9.

74. Ibid., 4. 4–6.

75. See Zanker 1988, 45–46, 59–60, and more fully on Hercules and Antony, Ritter 1995, 70–85, and Huttner 1995. The use of the Hercules and Omphale story by Octavian's propagandists seems assured (Plutarch *Comp. Dem. Ant.* 3; Propertius 3. 11), the relevance of the Arretine bowl to real life less so: Ritter 1995, 81–82.

76. Plutarch 29. 4. Cf. Griffin 1985, 32–47, who is excellent on Antony's image and its strong attraction for Propertius. There is no good biography of Mark Antony. Highly recommended is C. B. R. Pelling's edition of *Plutarch, Life of Antony* (Cambridge, 1988). The articles of Perrin 1993 and Cizek 1993 on Nero and Antony deal with matters different from the present subject.

77. The suggestion here is that in imitating Hercules, Nero may have been imitating certain aspects conveyed by each of his ancestors: Augustus the world benefactor (see Chapter 5 above) and Antony the larger-than-life charismatic.

78. Appian *Civil Wars* 5. 76; Plutarch *Antony* 24, 33 (and a later visit at 57), with Pelling, *Plutarch, ad loc.* Plutarch's meaning in 33. 7 is obscured by wrestling jargon. Pelling offers as a translation: "probably 'grabbing the youths by their waists' (. . . less likely 'parting' them as umpire) 'he would twist their necks.'" The gymnasiarch in full dress can hardly be a competitor, but he must be in some way interfering, whether as official referee or not. I suspect that the action is explained by its Neronian imitation: "he practiced wrestling constantly, and all over Greece he had always viewed the gymnastic contests after the fashion of the judges, sitting on the ground in the stadium; and if any pairs of contestants withdrew too far from their positions, he would force them forward with his own hands" (Suetonius 53). That is, Antony was not parting the contestants but forcing them back together.

79. See Appian 5. 11; Dio 50. 5; and above all the brilliant sketch by Plutarch, at *Antony* 28–29.

80. Dio 50. 3. 5; Plutarch 58. 6.

81. Schumann 1930; Grimal 1971; Voisin 1987; Hemsoll 1990.

82. As described in Cicero *Philippics* 2. 63, in grotesque detail; whence Plutarch 9. 6.

83. Plutarch 29. 4.

84. Plutarch *Antony* 9.8; *Antony and Demetrius* 3. 3; *Antony* 26.

85. Disguise: Cicero *Philippics* 2. 77; Plutarch *Antony* 10. Prostitution and marriage: Cicero 2. 44–45, cf. 77 (not in Plutarch 2). Low company: Cicero 2. 57–58 (with Shackleton Bailey's translation, and cf. 62), 63, 67, 68; Plutarch 9 (the billeting is not in Cicero). For a most illuminating study of the concatenation—in Late Republican invective, if not in life—of passive homosexuality, transves-

tism, inebriation, late nights, dancing (often in the nude), perfume, and slavery, see Gonfroy 1978.

86. Menecrates, Spiculus, and Paneros: Suetonius 30. Vatinius: Tacitus 15. 34. Tigellinus: Scholia on Juvenal 1. 155, 158.

The *faenerator* Paneros ("Universal Love"; "Everyone's Lover"? "Potency"? cf. Pliny *Natural History* 37. 178), otherwise unknown, is intriguing. Suetonius calls him *Cercopithecus,* which translators routinely render as "monkey-faced," but there is more to it than that. *Cercops* and *cercopithecus* are indeed Greek words for a long-tailed monkey, but Festus tells us that the Greeks use *cercops* precisely of someone who wants to make a profit out of everything (Festus 49L). The island of Pithecusa, monkey-island (modern Ischia), off the Bay of Naples supposedly took its name from the Cercopes, a sinful people whom Jupiter turned into monkeys (Ovid *Metamorphoses* 14. 88ff.). According to another story, the trickster Cercopes brothers had annoyed Hercules, but they made him laugh so hard that he let them go. How any or all of this relates to Nero, I haven't the slightest idea, but Paneros must have amused him.

87. *Histories* 2. 71; cf. Suetonius 10. Compare Antony's progress through Italy, above: the Bacchanalian triumphal progress in Roman invective is a subject worth pursuing.

88. Turnus, the loser in what was essentially a civil war, is a startling role to choose, but there may be a logic to the choice. In effect, if we equate Nero with his ancestor Aeneas, Turnus should be seen as Vindex. That is to say, Nero meant to celebrate his victory by portraying the horrible and inevitable death of his enemy, just as four years earlier he had sung of the sorrows and death of Niobe, the arrogant victim of his own alter ego Apollo. The death of the loser would then emphasize the power and the glory of the victor.

89. Dancing Turnus: Suetonius 54. Turnus' speech: Suetonius 47. 2, from Vergil *Aeneid* 12. 646–649.

90. Seneca *Apocolocyntosis* 12. 2; cf. Petronius *Satyricon* 44. 3, Lucian *De Mercede Conductis* 16.

7. One House

1. Epigraphs: Tacitus 15. 36. 3, 37. 1; Suetonius 55.

2. The following account is in essence that of Tacitus at 15. 38–41, our fullest source, supplemented by other information, as noted. I have tried to remove Tacitus' rhetorical flourishes, his editorial comments, and his retailing of rumors.

3. The *monumenta Agrippae* in the Campus constituted a large complex of buildings erected or restored for public use by Nero's great-grandfather, including the Pantheon, the Baths of Agrippa, the porticus of Vipsania, and the great voting-enclosure of the Saepta Julia. Suetonius says simply that the people were driven by the disaster to take shelter in monuments and tombs: 38. 2.

4. It broke out *praediis Tigellini Aemilianis* (Tacitus 15. 41). What and where those were is unknown: see F. Coarelli, and E. Rodríguez Almeida, *LTUR* I, 18–20.

5. According to Tacitus, 15. 40–41. The evidence for the chronology is this: Tacitus reports that the fire started on 18 July (15. 41) and burned itself out "on the sixth day" (15. 40); Suetonius that the disaster raged "for six days and seven nights" (38. 2). Scholars therefore assume that it started on the night of 18/19 July, burned for the six days of 19, 20, 21, 22, 23, and 24 July, and burned itself out during the night of 24 July. Tacitus relates that it then broke out again (15. 40), but says nothing about how long it lasted, and Suetonius was apparently unaware of the second outbreak. However, the emperor Domitian later erected markers on the boundaries of the Neronian fire, three of which have survived (two *in situ*), all of them reporting that the city burned for nine days *Neronianis temporibus: CIL* VI. 30837, cf. *ILS* 4914. Therefore, the new flames apparently lasted three days— which three days is not clear, but the respite was brief, "before fear had been laid aside." The significance of these dates will emerge below.

6. Suetonius 38. 2 (Suetonius is clearly following the same source as Tacitus here); Dio 62. 18. 2. Our sources are frustratingly vague as to what burned and where. Tacitus names only five ancient buildings as examples, and while modern archaeological reports constantly mention evidence of the fire, no one has ever put the reports together. At the same time, there is no agreement as to precisely which regions were the ones Tacitus records as mostly ruined, quite destroyed, or untouched. Compare the analyses of Beaujeu 1964, 8–9, Palmer 1976, 52, and Griffin 1984, 129 (following H. Furneaux, *The Annals of Tacitus,* II [Oxford, 1907], 367): the three scholars agree on the assignment of eight of the Augustan regions to one or another of the three categories (X and XI destroyed, II, IV, XII, and XIII partly destroyed, V and XIV undamaged), but the other six are quite unsure—either wholly or partly destroyed (III, VIII), or partly destroyed or untouched (I, VI, VII, IX).

7. Tacitus 15. 43, 44; Suetonius 38. 3 (an obscure passage; cf. Bradley 1978 *ad loc.*); Dio 62. 18. 5.

8. Grain: Rickman 1980, 187–188, discussing the problems posed by Dio 62. 18. 5. Coinage: *RIC* 133–136.

9. Newbold 1974. The estimated number of homeless (ibid., 858) is admittedly speculative, based on presumptions about the regions devastated (see note 6 above), the number of apartment buildings lost, and the population of Rome (on which see the convenient summary of modern speculation by Hopkins 1978, 96–98); but it certainly indicates an order of magnitude: that is, perhaps a quarter or even a third of Rome's people were homeless.

10. Suetonius 38. 3. Echoed by Dio 62. 18. 5: he collected money from both individuals and communities, sometimes by force, sometimes as "voluntary" donations. Tacitus 15. 45. As far as temples in Greece and Asia are concerned,

Tacitus appears to be confusing money-raising with aesthetic pillaging (as indeed the very fact that they were Greek and Asian suggests: not that temples elsewhere were not rich, but that that is where the great art was to be found). Others unanimously suggest that Nero wanted the art for itself, not for its cash value: Pausanias 6. 25. 9, 10. 7. 1, 6. 26. 3; Pliny 19. 84, 34. 8; Dio of Prusa 31. 147–150.

11. All of this information is to be found in the three main accounts of the fire: Dio 62. 16; Suetonius 38; Tacitus 15. 38–40.

12. Pliny *NH* 17. 5: *lotoe . . . duraverunt . . . ad Neronis principis incendia . . . cultu virides iuvenesque, ni princeps ille adcelerasset etiam arborum mortem.* Townend 1960, 111 (followed by Bradley 1978, 231) regards the two references to the fire as later additions, but offers no argument: the only reason seems to be his notion of the value of Cluvius Rufus as a source, which was largely demolished by Wardle 1992.

13. *Octavia* 822ff. The value of Nero's alleged remarks about Priam (Dio 62. 16. 1) and about fire overwhelming the earth (Suetonius 38. 1) is severely diminished by the fact that both are also said to have been repeated "often" by the elderly Tiberius: Dio 58. 23. 4 (AD 33); cf. Suetonius *Tiberius* 62. 3 (the Priam remark, in another and more appropriate context). Nero *could* have been imitating Tiberius, but folklore or literary artifice seem more likely sources.

14. Eutropius 7. 14. 3. Cf. Jerome *Chron.* 183 H, et al. The case for absolving Nero is well summed up in Bradley 1978, 230–231, and see 226–235 on the general tendentiousness of Suetonius' narrative. A convenient summary and bibliography are given in Sablayrolles 1996, 788–793.

15. Yavetz 1975.

16. Note also that where Pliny (who was in Rome at the time) apparently calls the fire(s) *Neronis principis incendia* (*NH* 17. 5, on which see below), the boundary stones set up much later by Domitian (who was also in Rome in 64) refer neutrally to the city burning for nine days *Neronianis temporibus* (*ILS* 4914).

17. Accusations by the elite: First, the only eyewitnesses mentioned in the surviving accounts, the unnamed ex-consuls who found Nero's servants lurking on the properties with fire-starting materials: Suetonius 38. 1.

Second, the tribune of the praetorian guard, Subrius Flavus, on whom see below. He was a senior military officer and came of very good family. A typical praetorian tribune would have served many years in the army, rising to senior centurion, and then passing through tribuneships in the *vigiles* and the urban cohorts. A brother(?), Subrius Dexter, is also attested as praetorian tribune in 69 and as a procurator in 74, therefore of equestrian rank (Tacitus *Hist.* 1. 31. 2; *CIL* X. 8023); and the family entered the senate in the next generation: Syme IV (1988), 371–396.

Third, very likely, the brilliant young senatorial poet Lucan, although the matter is debated. Lucan had publicly fallen out with Nero and was banned from reciting his poetry and speaking in the law courts (Tacitus 15. 49. 3; Dio 62. 29. 4;

Vacca *Lucan*). The emperor's former friend developed into an outspoken tyrannicide and became virtually the standard-bearer of the Pisonian conspirators: *ad extremum paene signifer Pisonianae coniurationis extitit, multus in gloria tyrannicidarum palam praedicanda ac plenus minarum* (Suetonius *Lucan*). According to Suetonius, he harshly attacked both Nero and the emperor's most powerful friends in a slanderous poem, *famoso carmine*. The poem, not named, should be identified with his now lost *On the Burning of the City, De Incendio Urbis*, named by Vacca. In this work (in the words of Statius) Lucan described how "the unspeakable flames of the criminal tyrant roamed the heights of Remus"—this in a poetic list of Lucan's works addressed by the Muse Calliope to the infant Lucan, *Silvae* 2. 7, at 60–61 (*Dices culminibus Remi vagantis / infandos domini nocentis ignes*). If Statius is merely paraphrasing Lucan and not adding his own color, then Lucan must have blamed Nero for the fire.

The argument about the *De Incendio Urbis* was made fully by Ahl 1971, restated in Ahl 1976, 333–353. The debate pro and con is well summed up by H.-J. Van Dam, *P. Papinius Statius, Silvae Book II, A Commentary* (Leiden, 1984), 480–481, who decides against the identifications made above, and whose conclusion is accepted by Courtney 1993, 354. Readers may make up their own minds, but Ahl mounts a strong case that Vacca does *not* say that the *De Incendio Urbis* was in prose, and that Statius could perfectly well be referring to a poem. If it was indeed a prose work, then what was the apparently notorious *famosum carmen,* otherwise quite unidentifiable, attacking the emperor and his friends? There is no even remotely likely candidate other than the *Incendium* in the list of works we know to have survived Lucan.

On Petronius, see below.

18. Dio 62. 18. 3–4.

19. Tacitus 15. 50. 4, 44. 5.

20. Cf. Dio 57. 18. 4–5, with the comments of Potter 1990, 237 and 239.

21. Suetonius 39. 2. That is, Aeneas carried off his father from the ruins of Troy; Nero killed his mother. The pun in Latin on *tollere,* to remove, is hard to reproduce in English, but struck Romans as very clever; for other examples, see Courtney 1993, 479.

22. The sequence in Suetonius' thought is not chronological. He discusses the fire (64) in chapter 38, then other disasters in chapter 39, namely, a plague (?65), Boudicca's rebellion (60), and the disgraceful defeat in Armenia (62), then the various pasquinades, which the emperor suffered with remarkable equanimity. They are therefore *not* necessarily to be referred to the aftermath of the fire, and in fact only one of them, concerning the Golden House, is. The first epigram he mentions, naming Nero Orestes Alcmaeon, is in fact assigned by Dio (61. 16. 2) to the year 59.

23. Tacitus 15. 49–67; cf. Dio's limp account (in epitome) at 62. 24–25.

24. Tacitus 15. 67. 3. Note that the other accusations made by Subrius were all believed to be true.

25. It was said that he had considered assassinating the emperor as he ran around in the dark, unguarded, in his burning house: Tacitus 15. 50. 4.

26. Dio 62. 15.1; Tacitus 15. 33. Curiously, after his divorce and murder of Octavia and his marriage to Poppaea in mid-62, Nero recedes in the historical record. A few annalistic notices apart, his only appearance in 63 is connected with the birth and early death of his daughter Claudia.

27. The abandoned journey to the East is discussed at Suetonius 19. 1 and Tacitus 15. 36. Tacitus' account of Nero's explanation to the people is at 36. 3 and 37. 1.

28. On the *sacra*, see Dubourdieu 1989, 454–469.

29. Kinswoman: Augustus was a *cognatus* of Vesta, through his ancestor Aeneas, the son of Venus: Ovid *Fasti* 3. 426. Coins: *RIC* 61–62. Rebuilding of Atrium Vestae: Richardson 1992, 43.

30. Caedicius in 391: Livy 5. 32. 6–7. Cf. Cicero *De divinatione* 1. 101, which goes on to give a more elaborate version of the god's command—that the Romans should repair their walls and gates, because if they didn't Rome would be captured. Metellus in 241: the story is fascinatingly unraveled by Leuze 1905; Valerius Maximus 1. 4. 5 has the aborted journey; Pliny 7. 141 accepts the story as truth. In point of fact, as Leuze showed, Metellus was not blinded, and it was quite licit for a pontifex to see the *sacra*. Residence: *LTUR* II (1995), 165–166, *s.v. domus publica* (R. T. Scott).

Vestals in 14: Dio 54. 24. 2. I understand Dio's ἐτετύφλωτο to mean "was blinded [in the fire]" (not, as in the Loeb and Penguin versions, the awkward "had become blind"): the story has no point unless she was blinded in the fire; and if she were already blind Dio should have said simply "she was blind"; cf. Dubourdieu 1989, 503–504. Moreover, πρεσβεύουσα should mean not necessarily the eldest, but the first, that is, the Chief Vestal.

31. Cicero *Pro Scauro* 48, *quasi pignus nostrae salutis atque imperii;* repeated by Livy at 26. 27. 14, *conditum in penetrali [sc. Vestae] fatale pignus imperii Romani.* Cf. Servius *ad Aen.* 2. 166: *illic imperium fore ubi et Palladium.*

32. Cicero *Phil.* 11. 24: *id signum de caelo delapsum . . . quo salvo salvi sumus futuri.*

33. See Faraone 1992, 136–140 (Appendix 4, "The incarceration of dread goddesses"). That the Palladium caused blindness at Troy (ibid., 137) is, alas, not to be accepted. The sole source for this is Pseudo-Plutarch, *Parallela Graeca et Romana* 17 = *Mor.* 309F–310A), an absurd farrago of patently invented stories purporting to substantiate other, sometimes well-attested, stories: here, when the temple of Athena at Troy is burning, Ilus himself rushes to save the Palladium, is blinded, and regains his sight after placating the goddess ("so Derkyllos [un-

known outside of Pseudo-Plutarch] in the first book of his Foundations"), thus offering a precedent to "Antylus," the Roman nobleman whom crows force to return to Rome when he is leaving the city, and who saves the Palladium from fire, is blinded, and regains his sight after placating the goddess ("so Aristides of Miletus in his *Italica* [a work also otherwise unknown]").

34. So Koestermann 1968, 252; cf. H. Furneaux, *The Annals of Tacitus,* II, 2nd ed. (Oxford, 1907), 373; and others.

35. Three inscriptions for the altars (called by modern handbooks "Arae Incendii Neronis") have survived: *CIL* VI. 30837, cf. *ILS* 4914, with *LTUR* I (1993), 76–77 (E. Rodríguez-Almeida). The text common to all tells us that the altar below it was dedicated by Domitian "in accordance with a vow undertaken but long neglected and unfulfilled, in order to ward off fires, when the city burned for nine days in the times of Nero." This plainly means that the vow was made in 64, not later.

36. See Coarelli 1983, 161–178, now the *communis opinio:* the decisive text is Plutarch *Romulus* 27. 6. Curiously, Richardson 1992, *svv. Niger Lapis* and *Volcanal,* ignores Coarelli's arguments.

37. The Temple of Ceres, Liber, and Libera can be pinpointed by ancient references: *LTUR* II (1995), 260–261 (F. Coarelli). Moreover, while Libera was equated with Proserpina, the words of the Sibyl named *Proserpina,* not Libera: in Roman religion, getting the god's name right was of paramount importance.

38. Festus 126 L (Ceres); Macrobius *Saturnalia* 1. 16. 18 (Proserpina; Varro quoted).

39. Coarelli 1983, 199–226; clearly and forcefully restated by him in *LTUR* III (1996), 288–289.

40. Richardson 1992 accepts the identification of the "Volcanal" as the Ara Saturni (*Saturnus Ara,* cf. *Volcanal*), but refuses to allow the equation of the Umbilicus Romae with the *mundus.* In reviews of Coarelli's book, N. Purcell expresses doubts about the location of both *Ara Saturni* and *mundus* (*JRA* 2 [1989]: 162), while T. P. Wiseman accepts both (*JRS* 74 [1984]: 230). Only one *mundus: pace* Richardson 1992, 259–260, and others (cf. H. H. Scullard, *Festivals and Ceremonies of the Roman Republic* [Ithaca, 1981], 180–181), there is no hint in the ancient writers that there was more than one, and Plutarch (*Romulus* 11) says it was in the Comitium (regardless of how illogical the story may seem). If that is accepted, it must then be said on Coarelli's side that, if the "Volcanal" and the Umbilicus are not to be equated with the Altar of Saturn and the *mundus,* it is hard to see just where else they might be fitted into the Comitium.

41. Ceres' long-standing ties with the *populus Romanus:* B. S. Spaeth, *The Roman Goddess Ceres* (Austin, 1996), 81–102. Sacrifices to Vulcan by the people: Varro *De lingua latina* 6. 20. Addresses: Dionysius of Halicarnassus 7. 17, 11. 39.

42. G. Capdeville, *Volcanus. Recherches comparatistes sur les origines du culte de Vulcain* (Rome, 1995), 81–95.

43. The tremendously tangled tales about Manlius are fascinatingly unraveled, insofar as they can be, by Wiseman 1979 and Horsfall 1987 ("We should start from the assumption that there were no geese, that Manlius failed, and that the Capitol fell. Four years later, moreover, disgrace and execution. Beyond that, there is only speculation"). For Juno Moneta on the site of his house: Livy 7. 28. 4, cf. 6. 20. 13. For a previously existing temple: Plutarch *Camillus* 27. The archaeology is unsure: Richardson 1992, 215. Juno the Warner: e.g., Cicero *De divinatione* I. 101.

44. Tacitus 15. 41. 2. It has been calculated, for instance, that if the Senones burned the city in 390 BC (the traditional but not necessarily correct year), the 454-year interval would equal 418 years + 418 months + 418 days: Koestermann 1968, 245–246.

45. The best-known version of the stories that clustered around the Gallic invasion is that of Livy, at 5. 33–55, on which see the indispensable commentary by Ogilivie 1965, 699–752. The account in Plutarch's *Life of Camillus,* 14–32, is very close in both events and sequence. Similar stories appear, more briefly, in Dionysius of Halicarnassus, books 13 and 14. 1–3 (excerpts) and Diodorus Siculus 14. 113–117.

46. The proposed migration from Rome to Veii, though of very dubious historicity—Ogilvie 1965, 741–742, suggests an origin in the Social War, in the 90s BC—is a leitmotif heard before, through, and after the story of the Gallic invasion in our sources, and it is woven into the story of the Struggle of the Orders, the conflict over the extension of political rights between the patricians and the excluded plebeians. In the year after the capture of Veii, Livy claims, a patrician effort to settle 3,000 settlers on other territory was countered by a popular proposal that half of the population and half of the senate should move to the extremely beautiful city of Veii, a city which excelled Rome both in its site and in the magnificence of its private dwellings and its public buildings. The *optimates,* the best people (an anachronistic term from the late Republic), opposed the plan vehemently (traditionally in 395 BC). The struggle spilled over into the politics of subsequent years, the senatorial position being championed by Camillus himself, the conqueror of Veii. After the disaster of the Allia, the greater part of the Roman survivors fled to Veii rather than to their wives and children in Rome, and in Veii they plotted with the holdouts on the Capitol to bring Camillus back from exile. After the Roman victory under his dictatorship, the tribunes again agitated for the migration, and Camillus, "having saved the city once in war, without a doubt saved her again in peace, when he prohibited the people to migrate to Veii." Escorted by the entire senate, Camillus made a long and impassioned plea

to the people to stay and rebuild the city, and particularly the temples, of their ancestors; a fortuitous good omen persuaded everyone (see below); and the threat of Veii receded. In the following year (traditionally 389) a decree of the senate summoned back to their city those Romans who had remained to settle in Veii, on the threat of losing their citizenship. The great abandonment crisis was averted: Livy 5. 24. 5–13, 29. 1 – 30. 9, 38. 5, 9, 46, 49. 8 – 55. 2; 6. 4. 5; Plutarch gives more or less the same story.

47. Livy 5. 52. 2–3. On the central significance of place to Roman religion, see S. R. F. Price, "The Place of Religion: Rome in the Early Empire," *The Cambridge Ancient History,* 2nd ed., vol. X, *The Augustan Empire, 43 B.C.–A.D. 69* (Cambridge, 1996), 812–847.

48. Livy 5. 50. Also, the city of Caere, which had safeguarded the sacred objects and the priests of Rome at the time of crisis, thus ensuring the continuity of proper worship of the gods, was to receive a solemn treaty of guest-friendship with Rome; games, the Ludi Capitolini, were to be instituted to honor Jupiter Optimus Maximus for preserving his shrine on the Capitol intact; expiation was to be made to the nocturnal voice which had warned Marcus Caedicius of the Gallic onslaught, in the form of a shrine to be built on the spot in the Via Nova and dedicated to Aius Locutius, the Speaking Voice; and privileges were granted to the married women of Rome, the *matronae,* who had contributed their own gold to the demands of the Gauls, rather than have the treasuries of the gods looted (the nature of these privileges varied from author to author: see Ogilvie 1965, 741).

49. Ogilvie 1965 strips away much of the antiquarian accretion: see, e.g., pp. 750–751 on the palpably false tradition that Rome had been a rationally laid out city before the sack. For a clear and sober account of what really happened, see T. J. Cornell, "Rome and Latium to 390 B.C.," *CAH,* 2nd ed., vol. VII.2 (Cambridge, 1989), 243–308, esp. 302–308, "The Gallic Invasion." Diodorus without comment notes that the ransom was paid (14. 116. 7) and later recovered by the Caeritans in battle (117. 4; cf. Suetonius *Tiberius* 3. 2 for another version).

50. Livy 5. 49. 7, 7. 1. 9–10. Second founder: cf. Plutarch, *Camillus* 1. 31–32. Ogilvie 1965, 739, shows that the story of the second founder must go back at least to the second century BC, though of course it also had particular relevance to Augustus in the 20s, when Livy was writing, for the first emperor also posed as Father of his Country and Second Founder, and had considered taking the name Romulus. R. A. Kaster points out that at 7. 1. 10 Livy calls Camillus the *secundus* founder of Rome, whereas at 5. 49. 7 Camillus' soldiers call him the *alter* founder: both words mean "second," but "secundus" here implies a third, that is, Augustus.

51. Tacitus 15. 38. 1, 40. 2. Note, e.g., 41. 1, the list of temples destroyed, all antedating 390; or 43. 1, the contrast between the irregular old city built after the

Gallic fire with the regular new city. Dio 62. 17. 3; cf. Dio 62. 18. 2: this was the worst disaster to hit the city ever, except for the Gallic invasion. Suetonius 19. 1.

Petronius *Satyrica* 53. It has long been recognized that the gross but magnificent freedman Trimalchio in that work is in many ways a parody, sometimes of Nero, sometimes of those who would imitate Nero. Late in his nightmarish dinner party Trimalchio's accountant begins to read as if from the *acta urbis,* the city gazette, various events of 26 July which were of interest to his master, including "the fire that broke out in the *horti Pompeiani,* starting in the house of Nasta the bailiff." The parallel between this and the Fire of 64 breaking out anew on the *praedia Aemiliana* of the emperor's praetorian prefect Tigellinus is striking, taken in conjunction with the caricature of Nero and the city gazette. What renders it compelling is, first, the date of 26 July in the novel, which is the most likely date for the fire's breaking out again in Tigellinus' property in 64; and second, the arresting manner of its expression: *vii. kalendas Sextiles.* In 8 BC the month of Sextilis had been changed to August, in honor of the emperor Augustus, and the proper way to refer to the day would have been "on the seventh day before the kalends of August." The archaism is explicable only as it recalls the solemn archaism of 64, when (according to Tacitus) people reckoned by the kalends of Sextilis to recall the Gallic disaster. On all this, see the discussion of Baldwin 1976.

52. Livy 5. 55. 2–5.

53. Livy 6. 1. 3, 6, 5. 1–5 (meetings), 4. 4–5 *(nova urbs).* Cf. Diodorus 14. 116. 8–9; Plutarch *Camillus* 32. 3.

54. Tacitus 15. 38. 3. Dio too emphasizes the speed of the fire and the narrowness of the streets, at 62. 16. 4, while Tacitus has old-timers look back fondly on the protection from the sun afforded by the narrowness of the streets and the height of the buildings, at 15. 43. 5: now the broad ways give no shade.

55. Tacitus 15. 43. 1 (Church and Brodribb translation, modified).

56. Suetonius observes that Nero invented a new form for city buildings, and arranged for porticoes to be attached to houses and apartment houses at his own expense, so that fires might be fought from their roofs: 16. 1.

57. Gaius *Institutes* 1. 33: dated by Gaius only to Nero, but Griffin is surely right (1984, 130) in assigning the offer to the wake of the Great Fire.

58. Suetonius 31. 1–2; Tacitus 15. 42. 1 (Church and Brodribb translation, modified); Martial *De Spectaculis* 2.

59. Suetonius 31. 1: *Non in alia re tamen damnosior quam in aedificando domum a Palatio Esquilias usque fecit, quam primo transitoriam, mox incendio absumptam restitutamque auream nominavit.*

60. Tacitus 15. 39: *Eo in tempore Nero Antii agens non ante urbem regressus est quam domui eius, qua Palatium et Maecenatis hortos continuaverat, ignis propinquaret.*

61. Tacitus 43. 1; Martial *Spect.* 2. 4; Pliny 33.54, 36. 111; Suetonius 39. 2.

62. Ovid *Fasti* 6. 639–642; Herodian 4. 1. 2.

63. For the Bagni di Livia, in fact a nymphaeum, on the Palatine: *LTUR* II (1995), 199–202, *s.v. Domus Transitoria* (M. de Vos). (In fact, all but seven lines of this article are devoted to the nymphaeum.) Domus Tiberiana: Carandini 1990, 14–15. Carandini's formulation of domus-villa and villa-domus (that is, I presume, structures that combine elements of townhouse and country villa, with one or the other predominating), for which there is no ancient evidence, has been taken over by others: Krause 1995, 462–463, cf. *LTUR* II (1995), 189–197, *s.v. Domus Tiberiana* (C. Krause). On other structures attributed to the Domus Aurea, see Royo 1999, 311, and *LTUR* II (1995), 49, *s.v. Domus Aurea* (A. Cassatella). *LTUR,* the standard repertory of Roman topography, unfortunately includes an entry entitled *Domus Aurea: Complesso del Palatino: LTUR* II (1995), 63–64 (A. Cassatella).

64. La Rocca 1986, 32.

65. Van Essen 1954. Van Essen's deeply flawed study has been tremendously influential. His sketch plan of the Golden House is commonly reproduced, as in Ward-Perkins 1981, 60. Compare the elaborate map in *LTUR* II (1995), 397.

Warden 1981 sensibly reduced the area by half, from about 200 to about 100 acres, confining "The Golden House" to the slopes, not the summits, of the hills. Although nobody has paid this view much attention, it has the great advantage of making the area covered by the Oppian house and its grounds much more "transitional," not including but in a sense joining the hills (see below). It is still too large.

W. V. Harris, reviewing *LTUR* II, in *JRA* 10 (1997): 383–388, writes at 385: "I suspect that we may be in danger of exaggerating the amount of land which this admittedly huge complex occupied."

66. House under Venus and Rome (e.g., MacDonald 1982, 21–35): LTUR II (1993), *s.v. Domus Domitiana,* 92 (E. Papi). Cisterns of the Baths of Trajan: de Fine Licht 1990, 27. (Traces of remains beneath the cisterns are too scanty to attribute to the Golden House: ibid., 96–98.)

As it also happens, Martial seems to indicate that the portico of the Temple of the Divine Claudius on the Caelian was the boundary of the Golden House— *Claudia diffusas ubi porticus explicit umbras, / ultima pars aulae deficientis erat* (*De Spectaculis* 2. 9–10)—and Nero, who tore down the temple under construction (Vespasian completed the building), covered the hillside with a nymphaeum meant to be viewed from the house itself on the other side of the valley (Colini 1944, 154–156). Despite Van Essen and *LTUR* I (1993), 277–278, *s.v. Claudius, Divus, Templum* (C. Buzzetti), I can see no reason for assigning the area of the temple to the Golden House.

67. Forum Transitorium: see *LTUR* II (1993), *s.v. Forum Nervae,* 307–311 (H.

Bauer and C. Morselli), for the references. Note that Aurelius Victor also calls it (at 12. 2) "Forum Pervium," the Forum of Passage, or Thoroughfare.

68. See Griffin 1984, 138–141, discussing Van Essen 1954: an excellent summary of the problem, acknowledging discussion with N. Purcell. Largely ignored: but cf. now Darwall-Smith 1996, 37–38, who correctly concludes that the picture of the Golden House as Nero's private retreat is overdrawn, noting that it stood on arterial roads and contained public shrines, that the Macellum was too close to ensure privacy, and that Nero enjoyed giving large public banquets for which the House was a suitable setting: "Nero might see himself building a house where all the people of Rome could enjoy themselves with him." Similarly but independently: Champlin 1998 (from a conference held in 1995). Craze for popularity: Suetonius 53.

69. See Chapter 6 above for the evidence.

70. See Nielsen 1990, 45–47, with bibliography; cf. briefly F. Coarelli, *Roma,* new edition (Bari, 1995), 211. Not mentioned in *LTUR* V (1999), 66–67, *s.v. Thermae Titi/Titianae* (G. Caruso).

71. Baths of Nero in the Campus Martius: Ghini 1985, 1988; cf. *LTUR* V (1999), 60–62, *s.v. Thermae Neronianae/Alexandrinae* (G. Ghini).

72. See Panella 1990, 67–68, and especially her splendid book of 1996, 180–188; cf. *LTUR* II (1995), 51–55, *s.v. Domus Aurea: Area dello Stagnum* (C. Panella).

73. Thus portrayed, independently, by Zevi 1996, Champlin 1998.

74. In fact, much of Nero's construction after 64 did not tamper with private property, and if Vespasian returned one square foot to any previous owner we do not hear of it: see the excellent paper by Morford 1968, on "The Distortion of the Domus Aurea Tradition."

75. Other than the Domus Transitoria, the word seems in literature to be applied only to the Forum Transitorium: see references in *LTUR* II (1995), 308, *s.v.* Forum Nervae (H. Bauer and C. Morselli). Later epigraphy produces an otherwise unknown public location at Puteoli (*ILS* 5919, where the editor, H. Dessau, cites *Dig.* 43. 8. 2. 17: a small forum?), and a late fourth century Forum Transitorium at Lambaesis in Numidia (*CIL* VIII. 2722).

8. Triumph

1. Epigraph and quotation in text: Plutarch *Aemilius Paullus* 32–34. Cf. Josephus, *Jewish War* 7. 132–133, on the Jewish triumph of Vespasian and Titus, three years after Nero's death: "It is impossible to give a satisfactory account of the innumerable spectacles, so magnificent in every way one could think of, whether as works of art or varieties of wealth or rarities of nature; almost all the treasures that have ever come one at a time into the hands of fortune's favour-

ites—the priceless marvels of many different peoples—were brought together on that day, showing forth the greatness of the Roman Empire."

2. There is a rich modern bibliography on the triumph: Makin 1921; Coarelli 1968; Versnel 1970; Künzl 1988; Coarelli 1988, 363–414; Favro 1994; Halliday 1997. The following composite description rests on these, particularly on the details gathered in Versnel and Künzl.

3. Livy 37. 59. 3–5. Compare the booty mentioned in the triumphs of Aemilius Paullus and of Vespasian and Titus, n. 1 above.

4. The chariot of Augustus: Vermeule 1957, 244–245.

5. On the complicated relationship among the three parades and its origin, see Versnel 1970, 94–131.

6. Alföldi 1934 and Alföldi 1935 are fundamental here, especially 1934, 93–100, and 1935, 25–43 on triumphal costume, and 43–68 on military garb and military attributes in general; on the importance of Nero in the use of military garb, 1935, 5–9, recalling Laffranchi 1921. On Augustus' "manipulation of the triumphal theme," see Hickson 1991.

7. Tacitus 12. 1–4; Suetonius 7. 2.

8. Tacitus 13. 7–9.

9. Tacitus 13. 41 (Church and Brodribb translation, modified).

10. Tacitus 15. 18. The arch: Kleiner 1985; La Rocca 1992. For another celebration of Nero's victory over Parthia, nothing less than a huge inscription in bronze letters on the Parthenon in Athens, itself a monument to the defeat of Persia by Greece, see Carroll 1982.

11. Tacitus 15. 71–74; Suetonius 15. 2; Dio 62. 27. 4.

12. For the calculations, see Griffin 1984, 232 with n. 69.

13. Nerva: *ILS* 273 (Sentinum: Nerva came from Narnia). Epaphroditus: *ILS* 9505 (Rome) on which see Constans 1914, confirmed by Eck 1976. Posides: Suetonius *Claudius* 28. 1; cf. *Epitome de Caesaribus* 4. 7. Eck cites *CIL* VI. 3617 for another freedman similarly honored.

14. *IRT* 346 (Lepcis Magna). The interpretation followed is that of Eck 1976; cf. Maxfield 1981, 111. The centurionate of the knights was a purely civilian and occasional office held by highborn Roman youths: Y. Le Bohec, "Les centurions des chevaliers romains," *REA* 87 (1975): 108–124. It is not clear whether it is even connected with the honors on Asprenas' inscription, since they (as we know from Nerva's inscription, among others) could simply be inserted in the record without mention of the reason. For a different interpretation, see Mourgues 1988, 175, n. 85. Tacitus 15. 72.

15. Tacitus 15. 74. In treating it as a military affair, was Nero perhaps acknowledging that many of the conspirators were members of his own praetorian guard?

16. Tacitus 14. 13 (Church and Brodribb translation, considerably modified). Dio 61. 15. 1, 16. 1–4, 17. 1, cf. 18. 3: the inadequacies of the translation of this passage by E. Cary are discussed above, in Chapter 3.

17. Acts of the Arval Brothers: *CIL* VI. 2042. 24–32, now to be consulted in the indispensable edition of J. Scheid, *Commentarii fratrum arvalium qui supersunt* (Rome, 1998), 71, no. 28a–c. 25–30. The functions of Mars Ultor: Dio 55. 10. 2–5.

18. Tacitus 15. 28–29; Dio 62. 23. 1–4. What Dio means by "contrary to precedent" is not made explicit. He uses the same phrase in regard to Pompey's first triumph in 81 BC, when the young general was not yet a senator: 36. 25. 3.

19. Tacitus 15. 31; Pliny 30. 16; Dio 63. 1. 2 – 2. 4; 63. 6. 4–5 *(andrapodon)*. Pliny remarks on the burdens to the provinces of Tiridates' progress.

20. For the date, inferred from a postponement of sacrifices normally made at the time by the Arval Brothers, see Scheid 1990, 404–406. Rome emptied to meet Nero and Tiridates: Tacitus 16. 23–24 (unfortunately his narrative breaks off just before their entry into the city). The account presented here is an amalgam of the reports at Suetonius 13 and Dio 63. 3. 4 – 5. 3, which are clearly based on a common source.

21. Acts of the Arval Brothers: *CIL* VI. 2044 = Scheid, *Commentarii,* 79–85, no. 30; interpreted in Scheid 1990, 404–406. Janus coins: *RIC* I² 49–50, 58, 283–291, 300–311, 323–328, 337–342, 347–350, 353–355, 362, 366–367, 421, 468–472, 537–539. For a source problem about the closing of the temple, not too relevant here, see Townend 1980: the coins, issued after the settlement of 63, were probably premature in announcing Nero's closing of the doors of Janus, which did not happen until 66 (as Suetonius has it) and was probably not recognized by Vespasian. For the name Imperator, first attested in the Arval records mentioned above and on contemporary coins, see Griffin 1984, 233, with nn. 72 and 69.

22. A small bronze figure from northern Italy has been identified as the statue of a young Nero sitting in a (now lost) magistrate's chair and wearing a military cloak and breastplate with civilian (senatorial) shoes, to receive the submission of a barbarian. As such, it is presumed to reflect a lost triumphal monument. For the argument, see Sperti 1990.

23. There is no mention of any triumph in the extant narrative of Tacitus, which takes us right up to Tiridates' arrival at Rome: Tacitus surely would have remarked on it, if one had occurred. The epitomator is certainly confused, and Griffin 1984, 232–233 with n. 64, concludes that there is no reliable evidence for a triumph, but that is to ignore Pliny's remark at 30. 16. It should be noted that the epitomes of the events of 63 and 66 are by different hands.

24. Dio 63. 3. 2. For similar astonishing virtuosity in a Sasanian monarch, cf. R. Ettinghausen, "Bahram Gur's Hunting Feats, or the Problem of Identificat-

ion," *Iran* 17 (1979): 25–31. Tiridates as priest: Tacitus 15. 24, Pliny 30. 16–17. His wife's exchange of her veil for some sort of face-concealing helmet again looks like a compromise between two traditions.

25. Dio 63. 5. 2–3 (Cary translation, modified).

26. Lemosse 1960.

27. These figures are extremely rough, but they suggest an order of magnitude. On the one hand, calculation of total imperial expenditures must be an informed guess. After reviewing the elements of the imperial budget (three-fourths of which was consumed by the army), Duncan-Jones 1994, 33–46, estimates annual payments around the year 150 at a low figure of 832 millions and a high figure of 983. Goldsmith 1984, 268, n. 28 collects estimates by other scholars ranging from 600 millions through 825, to almost 1,000.

On the other hand, what exactly Nero spent on Tiridates, and how people knew, is unclear. Dio tells us that the public treasury paid 800,000 sesterces a day for the nine-month journey to Rome of the king and his entourage (63. 2. 2), and he claims that Nero gave gifts to Tiridates to the value of 200 millions (63. 6. 5). Suetonius reports, "though it may seem almost incredible," that the emperor spent 800,000 sesterces a day on Tiridates and gave him more than 100 million when he departed (30. 2). We seem to have a common source here, but what it said is uncertain: did the nine months, for instance, represent the entire journey of the prince from beginning to end, or only from the East to the gates of Rome, as Dio seems to imply?

Regardless, the nine months at 800,000 a day implies an expenditure of at least 200 millions on the trip, and possibly much more. Dio is thus suggesting a minimum total expenditure of 400+ millions, Suetonius 300+. Elsewhere, Tacitus tells us (*Historiae* 1. 20) that in the course of his reign Nero gave gifts to the value of 2.2 billion sesterces to individuals.

Whatever the actual sums expended, the financial burden of Nero's generosity must have ultimately been unbearable.

28. Pliny 30. 16–17, 14; Suetonius 34. 4 (Agrippina and the *magi*). Cumont 1933 is the standard interpretation of the initiation, disputed by Aiardi 1975–1976.

29. Augustus was the prime mover in restoring dignity to the theater: Suetonius *Augustus* 44, cf. the standard discussion of the Lex Iulia Theatralis in Rawson 1987. By "theater," I understand here amphitheater and circus as well, which were governed by similar regulations. On the appropriateness of the Forum to viewing gladiatorial combat, see Vitruvius 5. 1. 1–2.

30. Strabo 15. 3. 13. For the place of Mithra in ancient Zoroastrianism, and his association and identification with the sun, see Boyce and Grenet 1991, 300–304, 479–483; cf. Clauss 2000, 3–7.

It is important to realize that the Zoroastrian Mithra of ancient Iran is *not* the same as the famous Mithras who was invented, with his mysteries, at or near

Rome a generation after Nero's death: the god of Tiridates, known to Nero through his initiation, would mean little or nothing to the Roman in the street.

31. The following account is a synthesis of the reports of Suetonius at 25. 1–2 and Cassius Dio, 63. 20. 1 – 21. 1; these in turn clearly reflect a single common source, but there are sharp differences (on which, see below). Defeat of Diodorus: Dio 63. 8. 4. Return to Italy in the early fall?: Halfmann 1986, 175–176; and see Chapter 3 above.

32. Miller 2000, 417, poses the problem well (with bibliography): "Modern opinions differ on whether Nero intended to travesty the triumph as an institution, provocatively reordering artistic and military ideals in the Roman hierarchy of values, or was simply further extending the already loose application of triumphal honors to novel situations." It will be clear that a third possibility is preferred here.

33. Suetonius 25. 1: *sequentibus currum ovantium ritu plausoribus, Augustianos militesque se triumphi eius clamitantibus.* "Ovantium" here refers to a triumph, not an ovation. Miller 2000, 418, rightly emphasizes this histrionic self-identification by the Augustiani, but sees it as part of Neronian *imitatio Augusti* in the *triumphus in Palatio,* which not everyone will find convincing.

34. Routes: Dio 63. 20. 4 (Cary translation, modified); Suetonius 25. 2 (Gavorse translation, considerably modified). The route of the parade poses an insoluble problem. Dio's account moves from the tearing down of part of the wall and a gate to a description of the parade itself, then "after passing in this manner through the Circus and through the Forum in company with the soldiers and the knights and the senate, he ascended to the Capitol and from there to the Palatine." Suetonius likewise has the breaching of the wall and the description of the parade, but then writes, "having had the arch of the Circus Maximus taken down, he made his way through the Velabrum and the Forum to the Palatine and (the Temple of) Apollo." The two accounts, perhaps reflecting two sources, cannot be reconciled. Dio clearly has Nero go from Forum to Capitol to Palatine, Suetonius clearly has him go from Forum directly to Palatine. Could Dio have inadvertently introduced the Capitol? Could Suetonius have inadvertently omitted it? We do not know.

35. Robert 1938, 110–112. Other parallels between Nero's entry and that of a sacred victor may be seen in L. Robert, *Claros I: Decrets hellenistiques* (Paris, 1989), 21–22. I owe both references to an unpublished paper by J. Ma.

36. Livy 33. 33. 2; from Polybius 18. 46. 12. Cf. victory palms with *lemnisci* in Cicero *Pro Roscio Amerino* 100; laurel crown with *lemnisci* in Plutarch *Sulla* 27. 7. Servius quotes Varro as saying that crowns with *lemnisci* are particularly honorable (*Aen.* 5. 269), and he mentions that crowns won at games (which I presume is what his words *"coronae agonales"* mean) are *lemniscatae* (6. 772).

37. Suetonius 25. 1: *Reversus e Graecia Neapolim . . . Introit disiecta parte*

muri . . .; simili modo Antium, inde Albanum, inde Romam. Dio confirms the breaching of the wall of Rome, at 63. 20. 1.

38. Favorite residence: Griffin 1984, 163. Alban triumph: Kierdorf 1992, 193–194, cf. Miller 2000, 418.

39. Griffin 1984, 163. On the equation of *eiselasis* and *triumphus,* note especially Vitruvius 9. pr. 1, on the victors in sacred games: *Nobilibus athletis, qui Olympia, Isthmia, Nemea vicissent, Graecorum maiores ita magnos honores constituerunt, uti non modo in conventu stantes cum palma et corona ferant laudes, sed etiam, cum revertantur in suas civitates cum victoria, triumphantes quadrigis in moenia et in patrias invehantur e reque publica perpetua vita constitutis vectigalibus fruantur.* Compare Plutarch (admittedly writing after Nero) on eiselastic triumphs: *Marcellus* 8, 12; *Cato Minor* 31.

40. Suetonius and Dio differ disconcertingly in what they choose to recount. Dio (as ever, in epitome) has nothing about the preliminary entries into Naples, Antium, and "Albanum"; Suetonius ignores the chants of praise from "the entire population." Dio knows of only one triumphal garment, Suetonius of two. Dio has flowers, lights, and incense, where Suetonius has perfume, birds, ribbons, and sweets. Dio mentions only soldiers (presumably praetorian guards), knights, and the senate, whereas Suetonius names only the Augustiani. Dio gives the parade route as city gate–Circus–Forum–Capitol–Palatine, and afterwards back to the Circus for racing; Suetonius has city gate–Circus–Velabrum–Forum–Palatine, with the Temple of Palatine Apollo as Nero's goal: these are very different accounts. And both authors trail off into frustrating irrelevance: after reporting how Nero placed all of his racing crowns in the Circus and raced around them, Dio ends with the story of the man who offered him one million sesterces to play the lyre, and how Nero subsequently appeared on stage and in the circus (the fault here may be the epitomator's); Suetonius, after telling how Nero placed his crowns in his bedchambers, talks about statues representing him as a citharode, his extravagant concern for preserving his voice, and his appreciation of flattery. Again, two surviving authors seem to be following the lost accounts of two sources for a single event.

41. Suetonius 25. 2 (Gavorse translation, modified). Strictly speaking, *bellaria* include nuts and dried fruits as well as confectionary.

42. Nero: Suetonius 11. 2 (and Chapter 3 above). Domitian: Statius *Silvae* 1. 6, 9–20, 75–78. On such largesses, see Friedländer 1920–1923, II. 17. Curiously, here the situation is reversed: the people are showering their emperor with gifts. *Bellaria* were among the gifts normally showered on the people by a consul entering office: *HA Elagabalus* 8. 3.

43. The evidence is overwhelming and is confined, as far as I can see, to performances in theaters or theatrical settings: Sallust *Historiae* 2. 59; Lucretius 2. 416; Horace *Epistulae* 2. 1. 79; Propertius 4. 1. 16; Ovid *Ars Amatoria* 1. 104; Lucan

9. 809; Seneca *Epistulae* 90. 15; Pliny *NH* 21. 33; Martial 5. 25. 7–8, 9. 38. 5, 11. 8. 2; Fronto *De Eloquentia* 11 (140 vdH, marg. b); Apuleius *Metamorphoses* 10. 34. 2 (a pantomime in an amphitheater); *HA Hadrian* 19. 5.

Epilogue

1. Dio 79. 18. 1–3.

2. In English alone we have Miriam Griffin's standard biography of the emperor, and more recently Vassily Rudich's studies of the perils of dissidence in Neronian politics and literature, Shadi Bartsch's subtle investigation of the effects of the loss of freedom under the empire on action and language ("theatricality and doublespeak"), and the collection of essays edited by Jas Elsner and Jamie Masters on many different aspects of Nero's image ("reflections of Nero"); the latter, closest in conception to the present volume, differs from it in its greater variety and in having (as one reviewer of the collection observed) little interest in historical reality.

3. Inevitably reminiscent, in more ways than one, of Oscar Wilde: "I wish I was back in Paris, where I did such good work. However, society must be amazed, and my Neronian coiffeur amazed it." This from *The Letters of Oscar Wilde* (London, 1962), 147–148, May/June 1883, after having his hair curled in imitation of a bust of Nero in the Louvre.

4. Suetonius 55.

Acknowledgments

I am especially grateful for the warm welcome extended by two academic institutions during the long and fitful gestation of this book. The first was Christ Church Oxford, which honored me with election to the Fowler Hamilton Visiting Research Fellowship for 1989–1990. My thanks to the Dean and Students, and particularly to then Senior Censor Alan Bowman; my apologies that this is not the book I intended then to write; and my hopes that it is some small compensation for their hospitality. In the spring of 1994 I was honored to be Resident in Classics at the American Academy in Rome, and I had the subsequent pleasure of spending brief periods there in 1995, 1996, and 1999 as a Visiting Scholar. My thanks to the Directors and to all of their staff for providing some of the happiest memories of my life.

Parts of this book were presented to two graduate seminars at Princeton and profited greatly by discussion with the participants: in 1992, Katherine Eldred, Randy Ganiban, Noel Lenski, John Ma, Tina Najbjerg, and Ken Trethewey; and in 1998, Paolo Asso, Al Bertrand, Sean Corner, Chris Lee, Peter Turner, Liz Woeckner, and Jamie Woolard.

Tony Grafton, Caroline Llewellyn, Hugo Meyer, Richard Saller, Brent Shaw, and Henk Versnel all kindly read earlier versions of one or more chapters and provided wise counsel. I owe a special debt to Adrienne Mayor for her encouragement and her shrewd comments on Nero as a figure of folklore. At a crucial stage Bob Kaster read meticulously and greatly improved a complete draft of the work. Peg Fulton has supported the project for longer than I care to remember, and at the end was a model of encouragement and constructive criticism. Mary Ellen Geer has edited the book with unflagging tact and good judgment. I am particularly grateful to Peg Laird for preparing the maps and plans, and again to Liz Woeckner for logistical support beyond the call of duty. And I deeply appreciate the enthusiasm and the detailed comments of the readers for Harvard University Press, Tony Birley, Cynthia Damon, and Peter Wiseman.

To all of the above, my warmest thanks.

Princeton, New Jersey
May 2003

Illustration Credits

Title page: Graffito portrait of Nero, from P. Castrén and H. Lilius, *Graffiti del Palatino* II, *Domus Tiberiana* (Helsinki, 1970), 121, no. 3. Reproduced by kind permission of P. Castrén.

Page 33: Apotheosis of Nero, from the Bibliothèque Municipale de Nancy, France. Reproduced courtesy of the Bibliothèque Municipale de Nancy.

Page 87: Hiesinger (1975) Coin Type III, "Accession Type" = Bergmann-Zanker (1981) "Cagliari Type." Musei Capitolini, Rome, Inv. 418. Reproduced courtesy of Maria Teresa Natale.

Page 115: Hiesinger (1975) Coin Type IV = Bergmann-Zanker (1981) "Terme Museum Type." Museo Nazionale Romano delle Terme, Rome, Inv. 618. Reproduced courtesy of the Deutsches Archaeologisches Institut, Rome (neg. 62.536).

Page 148: Hiesinger (1975) Coin Type V = Bergmann-Zanker (1981) "Munich Type." Staatliche Antikensammlungen und Glyptothek, Munich, Inv. 321. Reproduced courtesy of the Staatliche Antikensammlungen und Glyptothek (neg. 2).

The maps on pp. 56, 67, 181, 189, and 204 were prepared by Margaret L. Laird.

Index

Page numbers in **bold** indicate map references.